Selected Writings
of
Gerald N. Lund

GOSPEL SCHOLARS SERIES

SELECTED WRITINGS OF GERALD N. LUND

DESERET BOOK COMPANY
SALT LAKE CITY, UTAH

Library of Congress Cataloging-in-Publication Data

Lund, Gerald N.
[Selections. 1999]
The selected writings of Gerald N. Lund.
p. cm. — (Gospel scholars series)
Includes bibliographical references.
ISBN 1-57345-549-0
1. Church of Jesus Christ of Latter-day Saints—Doctrines.
I. Title. II. Series.
BX8637.L792 1999
289.3'32—dc21 99-41730
CIP

Printed in the United States of America 72082-6474

10 9 8 7 6 5 4 3 2 1

Contents

Publisher's Preface

In recent decades, a number of exceptional Latter-day Saint scholars have expanded our understanding of many gospel subjects. In many cases, however, much of what they have written (or given as speeches) has been published for relatively small audiences, or it was published so long ago as to be unavailable or inaccessible to most readers; in some cases an article or paper has never been published at all. Now Deseret Book is pleased to bring together some of "the best of the best" in the Gospel Scholars Series.

Insights from the Scriptures

Chapter 1

Understanding Scriptural Symbols

What are we to do with all of the symbolic language in the Bible—the imagery, figurative expressions, parables, allegories, types, shadows, similes, and hyperbole? Sometimes this imagery is clear and powerful, but often it seems baffling and strange.

Approximately 27 percent of the 1,184 pages of the Old Testament is made up of prophetic writings, or what the people at the time of Christ called simply "the prophets." (See, for example, Luke 24:27, 44.) At almost any point in those writings, we are immediately confronted by symbolic language.

Sidney B. Sperry noted some years ago that this penchant for figurative language is partially due to the fact that the Bible is the product of Oriental or Eastern peoples—and Eastern peoples are much more prone to use imagery than are the Occidentals or Western cultures:

"We ofttimes read our Bible as though its peoples were English or American and interpret their sayings in terms of our own background and psychology. But the Bible is actually an Oriental book. It was written centuries ago by Oriental people and primarily for Oriental people. . . .

"It may be of interest to contrast the speech of modern and ancient Palestinians with our own. In thought and speech the Oriental is an artist; the Occidental, on the other hand, may be thought of as an architect. When speaking, the Oriental paints a scene whose total effect is true, but the details may be inaccurate, the Occidental tends to draw diagrams accurate in detail."[1]

While this difference provides some interesting challenges for the modern reader in our Western civilization, those challenges are not insurmountable, and when they are met, the returns can be productive and satisfying.

Since a thorough explanation of the use of symbolic imagery in the Old Testament, or even in "the prophets," would require a work far beyond the scope of this article, we shall only give a general introduction to the subject. This introduction, however, should serve to help decipher imagery wherever it is found in the scriptures.

The Prophet Joseph Smith said: "I make this broad declaration, that whenever God gives a vision of an image, or beast, or figure of any kind, He always holds Himself responsible to give a revelation or interpretation of the meaning thereof, otherwise we are not responsible or accountable for our belief in it. Don't be afraid of being damned for not knowing the meaning of a vision or figure, if God has not given a revelation or interpretation of the subject."[2]

There are occasional uses of figurative imagery, such as Ezekiel's "wheels" (see Ezek. 1:15–21), for which the Lord has not yet given us the interpretation. But for the most part, we do have the keys for understanding the symbolic imagery used by the Lord and his prophets.

Six guidelines can aid us as we deal with figurative language in the scriptures:

1. Do the scriptures give the interpretation of the symbol? Often the Lord reveals the keys to the imagery right in the scriptures. A classic example is the interpretation of Nebuchadnezzar's dream (see Dan. 2:19, 31–45). Another example is Isaiah. After using the imagery of a neglected and run-down vineyard, the Lord says, "For the vineyard of the Lord of hosts is the house of Israel, and the men of Judah his pleasant plant" (Isa. 5:7). There is no need for speculation or debate. The answer is clear.

In these two cases, the scriptural interpretations were given in context. More frequently, the interpretation is found elsewhere in scripture—sometimes even in a completely different work of scripture. For example, Daniel's use of the phrase "Ancient of days" (see Dan. 7:9, 22) refers to Adam, but we discover that through the Doctrine and Covenants (see, for example, D&C 27:11; 107:54).

2. Do the writings of modern prophets help us interpret the symbolic imagery? Sometimes the key to understanding a symbol may not be found directly in the scriptures, but prophets of the Restoration have helped clarify the meaning. A good example of this is found in one of Joseph Smith's sermons. While the Lord reveals through Daniel that the beasts he saw in Daniel 7 and 8 represent various kingdoms (see Dan. 8:20–21), the Prophet Joseph Smith helps us better understand why this imagery is used.

"You there see that the beasts are spoken of to represent the kingdoms of the world, the inhabitants whereof were beastly and abominable characters; they were murderers, corrupt, carnivorous, and brutal in their depositions."[3]

3. Use the study aids in the new editions of the scriptures. An invaluable source of help for English readers is found in the study aids of the LDS edition of the King James Version. Chapter headings, footnotes, cross-references, the Topical Guide, and the Bible Dictionary were prepared under the direction of the Scriptures Publication Committee (which consisted of several members of the Quorum of the Twelve). These provide consistent and important help in interpreting symbolic imagery.

For example, in the headings to Isaiah 13 and 14 we learn that Babylon is used as a type, or symbol, of the world. In footnote *b* to Jeremiah 23:5, we learn that "Branch" is a symbolic name for Jesus Christ. And note how a very puzzling reference to "palmerworms" and "cankerworms" is cleared up by footnote *a* to Joel 1:4.

4. Let the nature of the symbol teach you. While the Hebrews loved imagery and used it heavily, they did not choose their symbolism arbitrarily. They drew their imagery from the objects and events of everyday life and made spiritual parallels. This is a very important point, for often we can let the symbol itself teach us about its significance.

Again let us draw on some examples to illustrate. Jeremiah wrote the book of Lamentations when Judah fell captive to Babylon. In the closing chapter he laments, "The crown is fallen from our head: woe unto us, that we have sinned!" (Lam. 5:16). The imagery of the crown is clear. The crown is a symbol of the power to rule; therefore, Jeremiah's imagery tells us that Judah lost the governing power she once held. As another example, the Lord warns the northern kingdom of Israel that because of their wickedness he will "meet them as a bear that is bereaved of her whelps" (Hosea 13:8). The ferocity and terrifying destructive power of a mother bear separated from her cubs is clear and has great impact.

5. Listen to the inspiration and promptings of the Spirit. Elder Bruce R. McConkie noted that one of the reasons the Lord uses parables and other forms of symbolic imagery is that they can simultaneously *reveal* and *conceal* meaning, depending on the spiritual readiness of the hearer:

"Our Lord used *parables* on frequent occasions during his ministry to teach gospel truths. His purpose, however, in telling these short stories was *not* to present the truths of his gospel in plainness so that all his hearers would understand. Rather it was so to phrase and hide the doctrine involved that only the spiritually literate would understand it, while those whose understandings were darkened would remain in darkness. (Matt. 13:10–17; [JST] Matt. 21:34.)"[4]

As we search the scriptures, we have the right to pray for wisdom and inspiration to understand what is meant. We are also entitled to the help of the Spirit when interpreting the figurative language correctly. The Spirit is the great teacher.

6. Balance the interpretation of symbolism with other revelation and gospel knowledge. The final guideline, and one of the most important, is to fit the interpretation of any symbol into the overall scheme of gospel knowledge. No matter how clever, or how logical, or how ingenious our interpretation of a particular symbol may be, if it contradicts what is revealed in other places, we can assume it is wrong. One of the best illustrations of this principle is found in a puzzling passage in Daniel.

As he closes his book, Daniel says: "And from the time that the daily sacrifice shall be taken away, and the abomination that maketh desolate set up, there shall be a thousand two hundred and ninety days.

"Blessed is he that waiteth, and cometh to the thousand three hundred and five and thirty days" (Dan. 12:11–12).

What are these "days"? Are they literal days, or do they mean years? From what point of time are they marked? What future events were foretold in this passage?

Here is a case where the Lord has *not* yet given us the key for interpreting a passage. Yet time after time, in the past and in the present, people have sought to "crack the code." They use this passage to predict the date of the second coming of Christ or the events associated with it. The declaration of Christ himself is clear and unmistakable: "But of that day, and hour, *no one knoweth;* no, not the angels of God in heaven, but my Father only" (JS-M 1:40; italics added). This sets aside all attempts to date the Second Coming, no matter how clever or logical the interpretation of the Daniel passage may seem.

So it is with the interpretation of all scriptural symbols. They must harmonize with other doctrine and revelation or be rejected.

With these six guidelines in mind, let us examine some general categories of imagery used throughout many of the prophetic books of the Old Testament.

Symbolism Drawn from the Human Body

It is not surprising that almost every member and organ of the body is used figuratively in the scriptures. If we ask, "What function does this member of the body or organ serve for the whole person?" (guideline number 4), we gain a better understanding how that part of the body is used symbolically.

Since the *head* houses the thinking and governing organ and is also the topmost part of a person, it signifies such things as governing power (see Ezek. 16:12) or the relative importance of something (see Jer. 22:6). When the head is bowed (lowering it below its normal state), it connotes humility or shame (see Lam. 2:10). An uplifted head suggests the opposite (see Zech. 1:21). Anciently, to forcibly shave a man's head (to make him bald) was a deliberate humiliation, and thus baldness is often used as a symbol of God's judgment upon the people (see Isa. 15:2; Ezek. 7:18; Amos 8:10).

The *eyes* and *ears* are the primary organs of perceptions, so by extension they suggest perceiving God's will and doing it. To "give ear," for example (see Isa. 28:23), means to hearken or obey. On the other hand, ears that are "heavy" are symbolic of disobedient people (see Isa. 6:10). The phrase in Jeremiah 6:10, "their ear is uncircumcised," implies that there was nothing in the obedience of the people that justified their being known as the covenant people.

Since we breathe air through the *nose,* the nostrils were the symbol of life (see Isa. 2:22). And the tendency of the nostrils to flare out when angry or frightened helps us to understand such passages as 2 Samuel 22:9, 16 and Job 41:20.

The *mouth, lips,* and *tongue* are instrumental in eating and speaking. Proverbs 19:28 says, "the mouth of the wicked devoureth iniquity." And Isaiah's classic passage which says the "people draw near me with their mouth, and with their lips do honour me, but have removed their heart far from me" (Isa. 29:13) shows the power of this imagery (see also Isa. 59:3; Mal. 2:6).

Since things are hung around the *neck,* it is often associated with slavery or bondage. The "yoke" upon the neck (see Isa. 10:27; Jer. 27:2) and the "bands of thy neck" (Isa. 52:2) provide clear and powerful imagery of spiritual, and sometimes literal, bondage. On the other hand, when Isaiah says, "thy neck is an iron sinew" (Isa. 48:4), and when Jeremiah notes that the people "made their neck stiff, that they may not hear, nor receive instruction" (Jer. 17:23), the image is that of stubborn pride. The reason for this is linked to another function of the neck. It holds the head and turns it. Since the bowing of the head is a sign of humility, to be stiff-necked is the symbol of pride.

And so it is with the other parts and organs of the body. The *heart,* which is the organ of life, signifies the real, inward person. It is one of the most frequently used symbols of the body. In the Old Testament alone, references to the heart appear almost six hundred times, most of them signifying this concept of the inward man.

The *shoulders* bear burdens, and thus symbolize carrying or bearing (see Isa. 30:6; Ezek. 12:6). The *arm* is the symbol of strength and power (see Isa. 33:2; Jer. 21:5; Ezek. 30:21). This gives added meaning to the phrase "I will put not my trust in the arm of flesh" (2 Ne. 4:34; see also Jer. 17:5).

The *hand* is used almost as frequently in a figurative sense as is the heart. The hand is the instrument of doing and action. When Isaiah says "your hands are full of blood" (Isa. 1:15), he speaks of powerful condemnation. But when the Bible says of Ezekiel, "the hand of the Lord was there upon him" (Ezek. 1:3), Ezekiel is receiving a tender and moving commendation.

The *knees* are the symbols of submission, because when one kneels it brings his head much lower than the person before whom he kneels. Someday every knee will bow to God (see Isa. 45:23). Another derivation from the knees comes from the fact that when a man is frightened, his knees tend to tremble or feel weak. So at times the knees symbolize weakness or cowardice (see Isa. 35:3; Ezek. 7:17).

The *feet* serve as the instruments of mobility and stability. In the scriptures they may signify the idea of walking (i.e., living) either properly or wickedly (see Isa. 59:7). In the case of the great statue of Nebuchadnezzar's dream, they represent unstable kingdoms (see Dan. 2:41–43). To trample something underfoot (as in Isa. 26:6; Lam. 3:34) suggests subjugation, contempt, or conquest.

Note Isaiah's depiction of the house of Israel as a body full of sickness and disease when he said:

"Why should ye be stricken any more? ye will revolt more and more: the whole head is sick, and the whole heart faint.

"From the sole of the foot even unto the head there is no soundness in it; but wounds, and bruises, and putrifying sores: they have not been closed, neither bound up, neither mollified with ointment" (Isa. 1:5–6).

Imagery Drawn from Nature

Another common category of scriptural imagery consists of images and metaphors drawn from the world of nature. However, the meaning of these may not always be as readily evident as were those of the human body because many modern readers are not in the same daily, intimate contact with nature as were the peoples of Bible times. Where our life is highly mobile, fast-paced, and filled with technology, theirs was simple, uncomplicated, and relatively stable. In our modern age, the agrarian experience is foreign to most. Few have experienced the growing cycles of various crops, milked a cow, butchered an animal, or harvested grains. So we should not be surprised that we do not always grasp the significance of images drawn from agrarian life.

A classic example of this, and one of the most beautifully profound passages of Isaiah, is at first reading difficult to understand. After describing some of the judgments of God, Isaiah says:

"Give ye ear, and hear my voice; hearken, and hear my speech.

"Doth the plowman plow all day to sow? doth he open and break the clods of his ground?

"When he hath made plain the face thereof, doth he not cast abroad the fitches, and scatter the cummin, and cast in the principal wheat and the appointed barley and the rie in their place?

"For his God doth instruct him to discretion, and doth teach him.

"For the fitches are not threshed with a threshing instrument, neither is a cart wheel turned about upon the cummin; but the fitches are beaten out with a staff, and the cummin with a rod.

"Bread corn is bruised; because he will not ever be threshing it, nor break it with the wheel of his cart, nor bruise it with his horsemen.

"This also cometh forth from the Lord of hosts, which is wonderful in counsel, and excellent in working" (Isa. 28:23–29).

The footnote for verse 29 (remember guideline number 3!) gives us the first clue. It tells us that the reaping and threshing of the world (or, we might say, the judgments of God) will be properly done even as it is on a farm. The people of Isaiah's day were not confused by his language; they needed only to draw upon their everyday experience. Let us walk through the imagery to get a sense of the understanding they probably had.

Note the question in verse 24: "Does the plowman plow all day to sow?" A farmer plows only long enough to prepare the soil for planting. He doesn't plow a field over and over just for the sake of plowing it. When he has "made plain [or smooth] the face thereof" (v. 25), a process we call harrowing, he plants the crops. Anciently, the farmer walked in the field with a bag of seed and cast the seed across the ground in great sweeping arcs. Thus the phrase in verse 25, "he casts abroad."

Scholars believe "fitches" (v. 25) were the black poppy. Cummin (cumin) is still a common spice.

Isaiah here is likening Israel to God's field. When Israel has become hardened through apostasy and iniquity, they can no longer receive the seed of the gospel message. Thus, the Lord's chastisements and judgments serve as the plowing and harrowing processes. But like the wise farmer (see v. 26), God doesn't plow Israel with his judgments any more than is necessary to prepare them for growth and change. It is an act of love and wisdom, not vengeance.

In verses 27–28, the same idea is taught, but now the imagery changes from the time of planting to the time of the harvest. Any farmer knows different crops must be harvested in a different manner. Anciently, wheat was threshed by rolling or dragging heavy weights (such as a cart wheel) back and forth across the heads to separate the kernels from the husks. Sometimes a threshing sled was used.

But the seeds of the black poppy and cummin or cumin are not like the hard grains of wheat. Fitches and cummin were threshed by holding bunches of the stalks upside down, then striking them sharply with a stick so the seeds fell onto a cloth below (see v. 27). To put fitches or cummin under a cart wheel would turn the soft seeds to pulp.

So the imagery is the same as that in verses 24–25. God's judgments are like the various methods of threshing. If the spiritual state of the people is not too far gone, then a sharp rapping with a stick (or mild judgments) can bring them to productivity. In deeper stages of apostasy, however, more drastic methods may be required. An understanding of the symbolism used helps turn this passage from one of difficulty to one of power and beauty.

For another example of how an understanding of the imagery can add to our understanding of the message of the prophets, note Isaiah's description of Israel as "a cottage in a vineyard, as a lodge in a garden of cucumbers" (Isa. 1:8). Set in the midst of a series of scathing denunciations, this picture of Israel is a little puzzling. A cottage in a vineyard? That doesn't sound so bad. We tend to picture a quaint little English cottage with a thatched roof sitting in the midst of a green field of grapevines. Is this such a negative image? But this is an erroneous picture, because we are not familiar with what Isaiah depicts.

"When the vineyard and the cucumber crops were ready to harvest, small booths, or huts, were built in the fields so the owner or his servants could watch over the harvest and protect it from thieves or animals. These huts were generally crudely made and hastily erected. After the harvest, they were abandoned and quickly became dilapidated and forlorn relics of the harvest. Jerusalem was to be like that—once proud and useful, but now, through her own spiritual neglect, an empty and forlorn relic."[5]

There are a hundred other examples of such symbolism in the writings of the prophets. The most majestic tree of ancient Palestine was a type of cedar tree that towered a hundred feet or more. These were found only on the slopes of the mountain ranges of what was then and is still known as Lebanon. So the "cedars of Lebanon" (see Isa. 2:13) became a symbol of those who were proud and lifted up in their own sight.

Jeremiah challenged the people of his day, saying that if they were already troubled by the first of the Lord's judgments, how would they cope with the fury yet to come? Yet he couched it all in figurative language. "If thou hast run with the footmen, and they have wearied thee, then how canst thou contend with horses? and if in the land of peace, wherein thou trustedst, they wearied thee, then how wilt thou do in the swelling of Jordan?" (Jer. 12:5).

The annual flooding of the Jordan River, in the early summer just as the first of the grain harvest was beginning, drove the lions and other dangerous animals from the thick undergrowth that lined the banks. Because most of the people were in the fields for the harvest, these wild animals did great damage. Thus, Jeremiah's question, "Then how wilt thou do in the swelling of the Jordan?" is a powerful reminder that if Israel does not repent, much worse is yet to come.

Ezekiel's allegory of Israel as a vine tree—a grape plant (see Ezek. 15:1–8)—is yet another example of the power these ancient inspired writers found in the natural world around them. Ezekiel notes that the only value of the grapevine is the fruit it produces. Its wood is too twisted and gnarled to be used to make anything. So it is with Israel, the Lord warns. If it cannot produce good fruit, then the only alternative is to burn the vineyard.

From the plant and animal kingdoms, from the weather and the climate, from the daily life of farming and herding, from the geography that surrounded them, from political and historical settings, the prophets of ancient Israel constantly drew imagery and metaphors that would more powerfully convey their message. Through the prophet Hosea the Lord said, "I have also spoken by the prophets, and I have multiplied visions, and used similitudes, by the ministry of the prophets" (Hosea 12:10).

It is our privilege and blessing to learn to understand the similitudes and images, the symbols and metaphors designed by a wise and loving Father to more effectively teach his children. The imagery of the prophets was meant to be understood by the faithful and those who search His word with diligence. If we pay the necessary price, the writings that were so filled with life and power when first uttered by these inspired men can and will once again be filled with life and enter with great power into our minds and hearts.

Notes

From *Ensign,* October 1986, 22–27.

1. Sidney B. Sperry, "Hebrew Manners and Customs," *Ensign,* May 1972, 29, 30.
2. Joseph Smith, *Teachings of the Prophet Joseph Smith,* comp. Joseph Fielding Smith (Salt Lake City: Deseret Book Co., 1976), 291.
3. *Teachings of the Prophet Joseph Smith,* 289.
4. Bruce R. McConkie, *Mormon Doctrine,* 2d ed. (Salt Lake City: Bookcraft, 1966), 553.
5. *Old Testament: 1 Kings–Malachi: Religion 302 Student Manual* (Salt Lake City: The Church of Jesus Christ of Latter-day Saints, n.d.), 1371.

Chapter 2

"Types of Things to Come" (Mosiah 13:31)

Many in the world and even some in the Church think of the Old Testament as reflecting a pregospel culture centered around the Mosaic covenant which was given in place of the gospel laws. And it is true that the Israelites, when they rejected the higher law, were given a lesser law. But note what the Lord said about this law: "And the lesser priesthood continued, which priesthood holdeth the key of the ministering of angels and the *preparatory gospel; which gospel is the gospel of repentance and of baptism, and of the remission of sins, and the law of carnal commandments*" (D&C 84:26–27; italics added). They did not receive the *fulness* of the gospel, but they did receive a *preparatory* gospel, dealing with the basic principles of the gospel of Jesus Christ. As Paul taught the Galatian Saints, this was done so that they could be brought to Christ: "Wherefore the law was our schoolmaster to bring us unto Christ, that we might be justified by faith. But after that faith is come, we are no longer under a schoolmaster" (Gal. 3:24–25).

In short, the Old Testament is not pregospel but primary gospel; and we can expect that the Old Testament, especially in its types and symbols, will richly reflect that gospel, the gospel of preparation for faith in Christ. It can be a preparation of value to every person including those who have access to, though possibly not complete understanding of, the fulness of the gospel. Therefore, as Elder Bruce R. McConkie suggests, "It is wholesome and proper to look for similitudes of Christ everywhere and to use them repeatedly in keeping him and his laws uppermost in our minds."[1]

When is an act or object recorded in scripture to be taken literally and when should it be interpreted figuratively? Symbols can be taken too literally and their true meaning lost in a grotesque parody of reality. On the other hand, sometimes one can explain away the actual meaning of a passage by saying it is only figurative. The following guidelines may be helpful as one tries to decide how to interpret correctly the symbols used in the Old Testament:

1. Look beyond the symbol for its intended meaning.
2. Look for the interpretation of the symbol in the scriptures themselves.
3. Look for Christ in the symbols and imagery of the scriptures.
4. Let the nature of the object used as a symbol contribute to your understanding of its spiritual meaning.
5. Seek the reality behind the symbol.

One author used this interesting analogy:

"The most perfect representation of a steam-engine to a South-sea savage would be wholly and hopelessly unintelligible to him, simply because the reality, the outline of which was presented to him, was something hitherto unknown. But let the same drawing be [shown] to those who have seen the reality, such will have no difficulty in explaining the representation. And the greater the acquaintance with the reality, the greater will be the ability to explain the picture. The savage who had never seen the steam-engine would of course know nothing whatever about it. Those who had seen an engine but know nothing of its principles, though they might tell the general object of the drawing, could not explain the details.

"But the engineer, to whom every screw and bolt are familiar, to whom the use and the object of each part is thoroughly known, would not only point out where each of these was to be found in the picture, but would [show] what others might overlook, how in different engines these might be made to differ."[2]

The reality behind the Old Testament is Jesus Christ and his teachings of salvation. The better we understand him, the more clearly we will see the meaning of the symbols.

The preliminary exploration of Old Testament types and symbols which follows deals with three areas: ordinances, festivals, and historical events. Of course, space does not permit more than a sampling of the full range of symbols available in the Mosaic covenant.

Ordinances

Sacrifices and Offerings. Sacrifices and offerings represent the very center of the Mosaic law. Though they varied in the manner of offering, the requirements, the item offered, and the time of offering, all of the sacrifices and offerings had three general things in common: an offerer, the offering, and the priesthood. Adam was taught that the law of sacrifice was instituted as "a similitude of the sacrifice of the Only Begotten of the Father" (Moses 5:7). The similitude of Christ's sacrifice carries through all three aspects. One author explained the typology of all three aspects in this manner:

"What, then, is *the offering?* what *the priest?* what *the offerer?* Christ is the offering, Christ is the priest, Christ is the offerer. Such and so manifold are the relations in which Christ has stood for man and to man, that no one type or set of types can adequately represent the fulness of them. . . . As man under the law, our substitute, Christ stood for us towards God as offerer. . . . Thus His body was His offering: he willingly offered it; and then as priest He took the blood into the holiest. As *offerer,* we see Him *man under the law,* standing our substitute, for us to fulfil all righteousness. As *priest,* we have Him presented as the *mediator,* God's messenger between Himself and Israel. While as *the offering* He is seen *the innocent victim,* a sweet savour to God, yet bearing the sin and dying for it."[3]

Nephi taught that we are to follow the example of the Son of God (see 2 Ne. 31:10, 12–13, 16). Jesus asked, "What manner of men ought ye to be?" and then answered his own question by saying, "Even as I am" (3 Ne. 27:27). If Christ becomes our model for living, then in the three aspects of the law of the offerings, we too should be typified. In other words, just as all three objects and persons involved in the sacrifices were types of him, they should also serve as types of us. Thus, the offering becomes a type or symbol of our lives, our acts, our works, our being—our all—offered to God on the altar so that it becomes a sweet-smelling savor to him. The Saints are to become "kings and priests," or as Peter said, "a royal priesthood" (Rev. 1:6; 1 Pet. 2:9). Further, like Jesus they are to become the saviors of men by sharing the principles of his teachings and sacrifice with others (see D&C 103:9–10). In this manner they are typified by the priest. And the offerer also typifies us as well as Christ, for, like him, we must willingly yield ourselves to come into the proper relationship with God.[4]

Circumcision. Abraham was specifically commanded by the Lord to institute circumcision upon himself and all the males of his household as a token of the covenant made with God (see Gen. 17:9–14). In this passage in the Joseph Smith Translation of the Bible, we learn that circumcision was instituted as a token of the covenant; but the token was given because the people were in a state of apostasy, had lost sight of the true meaning of the ordinance of baptism, and were washing their children and sprinkling them with blood so that they would be free from sin.

Circumcision reminded the people that while children were born in the covenant they were not to be held accountable until they were eight years of age (see JST, Gen. 17:4–11).

Other scriptures provide additional clarification that it was not circumcision itself but what it stood for that gave it its greatest significance. In many places the Lord speaks of the true circumcision as being that of the heart or, in other words, loving God and being obedient to the Spirit. The "uncircumcised of heart" are the wicked, proud, and rebellious (see Deut. 10:16; 30:6; Jer. 4:4; Ezek. 44:7; Acts 7:51; Rom. 2:25–29; Col. 2:11). Though a person may have the token of circumcision in the flesh, unless he is righteous the covenant is invalidated and the circumcision becomes profitless. Thus, circumcision was only a sign or token of what needed to happen to the inward man. If the inward change had not taken place, then circumcision was virtually meaningless. Following the atonement of Christ, the token of circumcision was no longer required of God's covenant people since it was replaced by baptism, the symbol of Christ's own death and resurrection (see Jer. 9:25–26; Acts 15:22–29; 1 Cor. 7:19; Gal. 5:1–6; 6:12–15; Phil. 3:3–4).

The Abrahamic covenant makes frequent reference to one's seed, as for example, in Genesis 17:6–12. The organ of the male body that produces seed and helps bring about physical birth is the very part of the body that bears the token of the covenant. However, the organ of spiritual rebirth is the heart (see 3 Ne. 9:20). Thus, when a person was circumcised it signified that he, like a child, was born into the covenant but need not be baptized until he became accountable before the Lord. But spiritual circumcision, or the circumcision of the heart, must take place once one becomes accountable, or one is not considered as true Israel. As Paul said so aptly, "For he is not a Jew, which is one outwardly; neither is that circumcision, which is outward in the flesh: But he is a Jew, which is one inwardly; and circumcision is that of the heart, in the spirit, and not in the letter; whose praise is not of men, but of God" (Rom. 2:28–29).

Cleansing of the Leper. In Leviticus 14 we have a detailed description of the ritual that was to take place when a person's leprosy had been healed. Because of the nature of the ritual, many people have seen it as a primitive, superstitious, and abhorrent rite which makes the Israelites barely more than pagan. However, when we apply our guidelines for interpreting symbols, we find that the ritual is a beautiful representation of gospel truths. This case is worth examining in some detail in its twelve major aspects:

1. *The leper.* Leprosy in its various forms was a loathsome disease that involved decay and putrefaction of the living body; it required the sufferer to be

ostracized and cut off from any fellowship with the rest of the house of Israel. Because of these characteristics, leprosy was also an appropriate type or symbol of what happens to a man spiritually when he sins. Sin introduces decay and corruption into the spiritual realm as leprosy does into the physical. Also, a sinful person was cut off from fellowship with spiritual Israel and could not be part of the Lord's covenant people. So the leper himself provided a type or similitude of what King Benjamin called the "natural man" (see Mosiah 3:19).

2. *The priest.* The priest served as the official representative of the Lord, authorized to cleanse the leper and bring him back into full fellowship. As we have seen earlier, the priest was also a type of Christ.

3. *The birds.* The birds symbolized the candidate. Because of the two truths to be taught, two birds were required. The first bird was killed by the shedding of its blood, signifying that the leper (the natural man) had to give up his life. The second bird, after being bound together with other symbols, was released, signifying that the man had been freed from the bondage of sin.

4. *The cedar wood.* The cedar wood is still used today because of its ability to preserve surrounding objects from decay and corruption; its meaning is obvious.

5. *The scarlet wool.* The word *scarlet* (Lev. 14:4, note *a*) really meant a piece of wool or cloth dyed bright red, a reminder of blood, which is the symbol of life and also of atonement (see Lev. 17:11).

6. *The hyssop.* Though we are not sure exactly why, we do know that in Old Testament times the herb hyssop was associated with purification (see Ex. 12:22; Ps. 51:7; Heb. 9:19).

7. *The basin of water.* Notice that the blood of the bird was mixed with water. In Moses 6:59 we learn that blood and water are the symbols of birth, both physical and spiritual. Also, we know that the baptismal font, the place of spiritual rebirth, symbolizes the place where the natural man is put to death (see Rom. 6:1–6; D&C 128:12–13). Over the basin of water the first bird was killed, symbolizing the death of the natural man and the eventual rebirth of the spiritually innocent person. As noted, the release of the second bird symbolized the release of the man from the bondage of sin.

8. *The washing of the leper.* Both physically and spiritually, the washing was a symbol of cleansing.

9. *The shaving of the hair.* This act, including even the eyebrows, would make a person look very much like a newborn infant, who is typically virtually without hair. Thus, after going through the process of rebirth symbolically, the candidate graphically demonstrated on his own person that he was newly born spiritually.

10. *The sacrifice of the lamb.* The typology of the sacrifice of the lamb is clear, since the lamb offered had to be the firstborn male without spot or blemish. It symbolized the offering of the Son of God himself.

11. *The smearing of the blood on the parts of the body.* In Hebrew the word which is usually translated *atonement* literally means "to cover." Thus, when the priest touched something with the blood, his action suggested the sanctification of, or atonement made for, that thing. In this case we find the blood of the lamb sanctifying the instrument of hearing or obedience (the ear), the symbol of action (the hand), and the symbol of following or walking in the proper way (the foot). Thus, every aspect of the person's life was touched and affected by the atonement of Christ.

12. *The oil.* "The olive tree from the earliest times has been the emblem of peace and purity."[5] Olive oil may symbolize the Holy Ghost. To touch with oil thus suggests the effect of the Spirit on the same organs of living and acting that had previously been cleansed by the blood of Christ. Thus, every aspect of the candidate's life was purified and sanctified by both the Atonement and the Holy Ghost.

Feasts and Festivals

Special holidays and festivals were a common part of everyday life during biblical times. Moreover, unlike modern times, most of the feasts and festivals had religious significance and were an inseparable part of worship.

The Sabbath. Certainly the most frequent festival among the Hebrews was the weekly day of rest, instituted in similitude of what God had done during the creation of the earth when, we are told, the Lord "sanctified" the Sabbath and rested (Gen. 2:2–3).

In Exodus 31:13 the Lord revealed the basic key to understanding the significance of the Sabbath: "Verily my sabbaths ye shall keep: *for it is a sign* between me and you throughout your generations; *that ye may know that I am the Lord that doth sanctify you*" (italics added). In other words, the Sabbath is the day that man ceases his labors so that God can work his own work—the work of sanctification—on man. The requirement of a sabbatical year, that the land be left untilled, required man to exercise tremendous faith in God's ability to sustain his people both temporally and spiritually (see Lev. 25:1–7, 18–22). The promises for those who keep the Sabbath are beautifully outlined by Isaiah and in modern revelation (see Isa. 58:13–14; D&C 59:9–24).

The Feast of the Passover. Passover (which included the Feast of Unleavened

Bread) was one of the festivals which most clearly offered typologies of Christ and his atoning sacrifice (see "Actual Historical Events," below).

The Feast of Weeks. On the fiftieth day after Passover (a period of seven weeks of seven days, or a sabbath of weeks) a second major festival was held, though it lasted only one day. Christians are more familiar with this feast by its Greek title, Pentecost, which means "fiftieth." Elder McConkie explains in detail its important typology:

"It is not without significance that the Lord chose the Pentecost, which grew out of the final Passover, as the occasion to dramatize forever the fulfillment of all that was involved in the sacrificial fires of the past. Fire is a cleansing agent. Filth and disease die in its flames. The baptism of fire, which John promised that Christ would bring, means that when men receive the actual companionship of the Holy Spirit, evil and iniquity are burned out of their souls as though by fire. The sanctifying power of that member of the Godhead makes them clean. In similar imagery, all the fires on all the altars of the past, as they burned the flesh of animals, were signifying that spiritual purification would come by the Holy Ghost, whom the Father would send because of the Son. On that first Pentecost of the so-called Christian era such fires would have performed their purifying symbolism if the old order had still prevailed. How fitting it was instead for the Lord to choose that very day to send living fire from heaven, as it were, fire that would dwell in the hearts of men and replace forever all the fires on all the altars of the past. And so it was that 'when the day of Pentecost was fully come, they were all with one accord in one place. And suddenly there came a sound from heaven as of a rushing mighty wind, and it filled all the house where they were sitting. And there appeared unto them cloven tongues like as of fire, and it sat upon each of them. And they were all filled with the Holy Ghost' (Acts 2:1–4)."[6]

The Day of Atonement. The Day of Atonement, which took place each autumn, was the most sacred and solemn of all Israelite festivals. In it, the typology or symbolism of Christ's work for Israel fairly shines. A day of national fasting, it signified that the sins of Israel had been atoned for and that the nation and its people were restored to fellowship with God. The feast included the following major items as detailed in Leviticus 16:

1. The high priest had to go through meticulous preparation to be worthy to act as officiator for the rest of the house of Israel. He made sacrifices for himself and his house, as well as washing various objects in the tabernacle and purifying them through the sprinkling of sacrificial blood.

2. The high priest put off the official robes he normally wore and clothed

himself in simple, white linen garments, signifying "the righteousness of saints" (Rev. 19:8).

3. Two goats were chosen by lot. One was designated as the goat of the Lord, and one was designated as the scapegoat or, in Hebrew, the goat of *Azazel.* The goat of Jehovah was offered as a sin offering, and the high priest took its blood into the Holy of Holies of the tabernacle and sprinkled it on the lid of the ark of the covenant (called the "mercy seat"), thus making atonement for the sins of Israel.

4. The other goat, *Azazel,* was brought before the high priest, who laid his hands upon its head and symbolically transferred all of the sins of Israel to it. Then it was taken out into the wilderness and released where it would never be seen again. Commentators explain the significance of *Azazel* by saying that it represented "the devil himself, the head of the fallen angels, who was afterwards called Satan; for no subordinate evil spirit could have been placed in antithesis to Jehovah as *Azazel* is here, but only the ruler or head of the kingdom of demons."[7]

The apostle Paul in the book of Hebrews drew heavily on the typology of the Day of Atonement to teach the mission of Christ. In that epistle he pointed out that Christ is the great "High Priest" who, unlike the high priest of the Aaronic Priesthood, was holy and without spot and did not need to make atonement for his own sins before he could be worthy to officiate for Israel and enter the Holy of Holies (Heb. 3:1; 7:26–27). His perfect life was the ultimate fulfillment of the symbol of wearing white garments.

Furthermore, the true tabernacle (or temple, or house of the Lord) in which the priest officiated is in heaven, and the earthly tabernacle made by Moses was a "shadow" or type of the "heavenly" one (Heb. 8:2–5; 9:1–9).

Christ, as Lamb of Jehovah as well as High Priest, shed his own blood to enter the heavenly Holy of Holies where that blood ransomed from their sins those who would believe in him and obey his commandments (see Heb. 9:11–14; 24–28; 10:11–22; D&C 45:3–5).

The Feast of Tabernacles. The third of the national feasts requiring the attendance of all males was the Feast of Tabernacles (Hebrew *Sukkoth*), which took place five days after the Day of Atonement. It was a celebration of the completion of the harvest and was a time of great joy and thanksgiving. During the week of the festival, Israel was required to live in homemade tabernacles rather than in their homes, a reminder that they had dwelt in tents or tabernacles (the word *booth* is used in the King James Version) when the Lord brought them out of Egypt (see Lev. 23:42–43).

Elder McConkie points out that this will be the only Mosaic feast reinstituted in this gospel dispensation:

"In the full sense, it is the Feast of Jehovah, the one Mosaic celebration which, as part of the restitution of all things, shall be restored when Jehovah comes to reign personally upon the earth for a thousand years. Even now we perform one of its chief rituals in our solemn assemblies, the giving of the Hosanna Shout, and the worshipers of Jehovah shall yet be privileged to exult in other of its sacred rituals. . . . The fact that it celebrated the completion of the full harvest symbolizes the gospel reality that it is the mission of the house of Israel to gather all nations to Jehovah, a process that is now going forward, but will not be completed until that millennial day when 'the Lord shall be king over all the earth,' and shall reign personally thereon."[8]

Actual Historical Events

Nephi taught that "all things which have been given of God from the beginning of the world, unto man, are the typifying of [Christ]" (2 Ne. 11:4). One cannot read far into the Old Testament without discovering that Nephi's phrase, "all things," even includes actual historical events. We know that God raises up men for special purposes and uses nations to bring about his will. He calls Assyria "the rod of mine anger" (Isa. 10:5–7), Cyrus of Persia the "anointed" of the Lord (Isa. 45:1), and Nebuchadnezzar's kingdom a gift from "the God of heaven" (Dan. 2:37). But many people do not look beyond that kind of direct intervention in historical events to see that the Lord may also influence events in such a way that they take on symbolic significance. This does not, of course, suggest that the events did not happen as described. Rather, it means that in the reality of the events we also find the Lord's hand at work, giving history symbolical as well as historical significance.

The Testing of Abraham. Most people immediately see the symbolism of the divine Father offering his only Son in Abraham's test, but many miss the precision of detail which God used to show what he himself would have to do in the future with his own Son.

Abraham obviously was a type or similitude of the Father. Interestingly enough, his name, *Abram,* means "exalted father," and *Abraham* means "father of a great multitude" (see Gen. 17:5).

Isaac was a type of the Son of God (see Jacob 4:5). Note that, like Jesus, he was the product of a miraculous birth. Though not the literal son of God, like Jesus Isaac was conceived through the intervention of God. Paul called Isaac "his [Abraham's] only begotten son" when he referred to this event (Heb. 11:17).

Not only did the Lord ask Abraham to perform the act which would mirror his own future actions, but he also designated a specific place, Moriah—"upon one of the mountains which I will tell thee of" (Gen. 22:2). Mount Moriah today is one of the three major hills of Jerusalem. The traditional site where Abraham offered Isaac is the one occupied today by the Dome of the Rock, a beautiful Arab mosque. A few hundred yards to the north on that same hill system is another world-famous site known as Gordon's Calvary. Its Hebrew name was Golgotha. The specific location further strengthens the symbolism and echoes between the two sacrifices.

When they arrived at Moriah, the Genesis account says that Abraham "took the wood of the burnt offering, and laid it upon Isaac his son" (Gen. 22:6). The Joseph Smith Translation is even more specific: "laid it upon his back" (JST, Gen. 22:7). Some have seen here a similarity to Christ's carrying of the cross upon his shoulders on the way to the crucifixion.[9] Note also that both Christ and Isaac were "bound" (Gen. 22:9; Matt. 27:2).

One important aspect that is often overlooked is Isaac's voluntary submission to Abraham. The Old Testament does not give us enough detail to determine exactly how old Isaac was at the time of this event, but it is very likely that he was an adult, since, immediately following the account of the sacrifice on Mount Moriah, we are told that Sarah died at the age of 127 (see Gen. 23:1), which would have made Isaac 37 at the time of her death. Even if this journey to Moriah had happened several years before her death, Isaac would have been in his thirties. But the exact age is not really important. What is significant is that Abraham was well over a hundred years old and Isaac, almost certainly no child, could have put up a fierce resistance had he chosen to do so. Instead, he submitted willingly to his father, as did the Savior.

Once the intended sacrifice had been accepted, Abraham named the place *Jehovah-jireh,* which the King James Version translates as "in the mount of the Lord it shall be seen" (Gen. 22:14). Adam Clarke, citing other scholars, says the proper translation should be "on this mount the Lord shall be seen." Clarke then concludes: "From this it appears, that the sacrifice offered by Abraham was understood to be a *representative* one, and a tradition was kept up, that Jehovah should be seen in a sacrificial way on this mount. And this renders . . . more than probable . . . that Abraham offered Isaac on that *very mountain,* on which, in the fulness of time, Jesus suffered."[10]

Two other scholars, C. F. Keil and F. Delitzsch, note not only the significance of the site for the sacrifice of Jesus himself but also point out that it relates to the site of Solomon's temple: "The place of sacrifice points with peculiar clearness [to] Mount Moriah, upon which under the legal economy *all the typical sacrifices were offered to Jehovah; . . . that by this one true sacrifice the shadows of the typical sacrifices might be rendered both real and true."*[11]

The Exodus. In the events of Israel's deliverance from Egypt and its eventual return to the promised land, we see great and significant typology and many similitudes. This is true not only of the night of Passover but in subsequent events as well.

First, it should be noted that the very situation which led to the Exodus is a type of the children of God. Israel, the Lord's chosen people, was in bondage to an evil power. Note how Egypt, like Babylon, is used as a symbol of the world or spiritual wickedness (see Rev. 11:8). Also note how frequently sin is compared to bondage and how consistently Satan's power is acknowledged (see, for example, Rom. 6:12; 7:15; 2 Ne. 1:18; 2:29; 28:22–23; Alma 12:11; 34:35).

In spite of the great power demonstrated by Moses, again and again Pharaoh hardened his heart and refused to let Israel go. Finally, in the spring, the time when all nature seems to be coming to life again, the Lord revealed to Moses the final steps they must take to be delivered from bondage. This remarkable event, known as Passover, involved numerous items, all of which have typological significance, especially when one remembers that Israel's state of slavery was itself a type of our bondage to sin and Satan.

The Lord indicated that Israel's calendar was to begin its cycle from this event and was to be the beginning of the year (see Ex. 12:2). Symbolically speaking, the deliverance from the bondage of sin marks a new beginning, a new time, a new life, as it were.

A lamb, chosen on the tenth day of the month, was sacrificed in the evening of the fourteenth day (see Ex. 12:3–6). The lamb's typology is obvious. It had to be a male without any defects or blemishes. Each household in Israel was to take such a lamb, signifying that the coming deliverance from the angel of death applied to every household of the covenant.

Moses specified that each householder must place the blood on the door frame using the herb hyssop, a symbol of purification, as a brush or dauber (see Ex. 12:7). These instructions suggest two things: since the doorway to the home is the entry to be guarded if enemies are to be kept out, the blood not only kept out the angel of death (see Ex. 12:13), but also, the blood of the lamb on the lintels and sideposts would overshadow every entrance and exit of an individual—every thought, word, and action. Is this not related to the modern commandment that all of our ingoings and outgoings should be in the name of the Lord? (see D&C 109:17–18).

The family would then roast the entire lamb and consume it with unleavened bread and bitter herbs. Anything left of the lamb (the inedible parts, such as bones, feet, and so on) were to be burned with fire (see Ex. 12:10; also see Elder McConkie's statement in this chapter on the significance of fire). As the Lamb of God gave himself wholly to be sacrificed for the sins of the world, so must the *paschal* lamb (from *pesach,* the Hebrew word for passover) be wholly consumed. When food is eaten, it goes into the body and literally becomes part of us, sustaining life and giving us strength. So with the atoning sacrifice of the Savior; it must be partaken of and absorbed entirely so as to provide spiritual life and strength.

The Jews saw the bitter herbs as a reminder of the bitterness of their bondage in Egypt. The unleavened bread has its own significance. Leaven is a symbol of corruption because of its tendency to spoil. Christ warned the disciples about the leaven of the Pharisees and the Sadducees, defining it as the false teachings and the hypocrisy of these men (see Matt. 16:6–12; Mark 8:15; Luke 12:1). Following the actual Passover, the Israelites were commanded to observe the Feast of the Unleavened Bread, not only abstaining from any leaven for seven days, but also purging it out of their houses (see Ex. 12:18–19). Knowing that leaven is a type or symbol of corruption helps us see the beauty of this requirement. After deliverance from death and bondage by the blood of the Lamb, we are to purge all wickedness, pride, and hypocrisy from our lives. Paul also drew on the typology of leaven to teach about Christ (see 1 Cor. 5:7–8).

The feast was to be eaten hastily, with loins girded, shoes on the feet (which was contrary to normal custom), and staff in hand (see Ex. 12:11). The typology here is quite obvious: when the Lord delivers us from the bondage of sin there must be no tarrying, no delay.

At midnight the angel of death smote all the firstborn of the land but "passed over" the houses of the children of Israel marked by the blood of the lamb (see Ex. 12:29). Our deliverance from the angel of spiritual death comes only when we have partaken of the "flesh and blood" of the Lamb of God and have metaphorically placed his blood on the doorposts of our lives so that it overshadows all we do. We note also that Pharaoh (the type of Satan) absolutely refused to let Israel go free. The only thing which changed his mind was the death of the firstborn son (see Ex. 12:30–32).

The symbolic significance of the Passover night is clear and beautiful, but that did not end the Lord's teaching device. As noted above, he can influence history so that the events themselves take on the nature of a similitude and provide us with important symbols and types. Note the following events which became part of the Exodus experience.

At the command of the Lord, Moses stretched out his hand and the Red Sea parted, making a way for the Israelites to pass through the water and escape destruction (see Ex. 12:15–31). The only way any person can escape spiritual death and the bondage of sin is to demonstrate faith in Christ to the point of true repentance so that he can be "buried" in the waters of baptism and be born again by being drawn forth from those waters (see Rom. 6:1–6; John 3:3–5; Mosiah 27:24–25).

In the Exodus, the angel of God went before the Israelites in the form of a pillar of fire and smoke which overshadowed them by night and day (see Ex. 13:20–22; 14:19). Being baptized of water is not sufficient to save a person; he must also receive the Holy Ghost, whose influence and presence are symbolized, among other things, by fire and burning (see, for example, Acts 2:3–4; D&C 9:8–9). Receiving the Holy Ghost after baptism is likened unto being baptized by fire (see Matt. 3:11; 2 Ne. 31:17). As part of their deliverance from the slavery of Egypt, the Israelites were saved both by passing through the water and by being overshadowed by the fire (see 1 Cor. 10:1–4).

In the wilderness, the Israelites were sustained by the manna God sent forth, specifically called "bread from heaven" (Ex. 16:4). In the great "Bread of Life" sermon, Jesus pointedly taught that he was "the living bread which came down from heaven"; and John the Revelator promised certain faithful Saints that they could eat of "hidden manna" (John 6:51; Rev. 2:17).

In the wilderness, God provided Israel with his law and instructed Moses to build a tabernacle, or portable temple, so that the Lord could dwell in their midst (see Ex. 19–31). But rebellious Israel demanded that Aaron make them false gods to worship (see Ex. 32). For this and repeated rebellions, many Israelites were destroyed, a law of carnal commandments was given, and they were denied the full power of the priesthood (see D&C 84:24–27). Later, for further lack of faith, all adults but two were denied access to the promised land and made to wander in the wilderness for forty years (see Num. 14:30). Clearly, these events teach us that deliverance from the bondage of sin through baptism and receiving the Holy Ghost are not enough. We must maintain faith in the Lord and hearken to his commandments or lose the promised blessings. As Nephi taught, baptism is only the gate to the straight and narrow path, and we must "press forward with a steadfastness in Christ" if we are to achieve eternal life (2 Ne. 31:17–20).

In the wilderness of Zin, the Israelites ran out of water to drink and once again began to murmur to Moses. By command of the Lord, Moses and Aaron gathered the people before a rock, Moses smote it, water came forth, and Israel lived (see

Ex. 17:1–7). At the well in Samaria, Jesus told the woman of the "living water" he could give, which, if partaken of, would become "a well of water springing up into everlasting life" (John 4:14). In the closing parable of the Sermon on the Mount, Jesus likened his teachings to a rock. Moses and other Old Testament prophets called Jehovah the Rock of salvation (see, for example, Deut. 32:4, 15, 18; 2 Sam. 22:3, 47; Ps. 18:2, 31, 46). Thus we see that when Israel hungered they were fed the bread that came down from heaven and when they thirsted they received the waters of life from the Rock. Paul synthesized these events when he said, "Moreover, brethren, I would not that ye should be ignorant, how that all our fathers were under the cloud, and all passed through the sea; and *were all baptized* unto Moses *in the cloud and in the sea;* and did all eat the same spiritual meat; and did all drink the same spiritual drink; for they drank of that spiritual Rock that followed them: *and that Rock was Christ"* (1 Cor. 10:1–4; italics added).

While wandering in the wilderness, the Israelites were also afflicted with a plague of fiery serpents, and many died. The Lord told Moses to make a brass serpent and place it on a pole so that if a person were bitten he could look upon the brass serpent and he would live (see Num. 21:6–9). How can one miss the typology of that event? The covenant people, wandering in the wilderness (notice the similarity to Lehi's dream, 1 Ne. 8:4) because of rebellion were being bitten by serpents (a symbol for Satan) and were suffering death. To be saved, they looked to a figure lifted up on a pole and death was averted. Again, the evidence is clear that this event had more than mere historical coincidence (see John 3:14–15; 2 Ne. 25:25; Alma 33:19–21; Hel. 8:14–15).

Finally, the children of Israel crossed over Jordan and entered the promised land. Obviously, the ultimate promised land is the celestial kingdom, but one also enters a new land (or life) when he is born again through baptism (see Alma 37:45). With that in mind, notice the following interesting items associated with that event. The person who led Israel into the promised land was Joshua, whose Hebrew name is *Yehoshua* or *Yeshua.* When Greek became the dominant language of the Middle East, the name *Yehoshua* was transliterated into *Hee-ay-sous,* which in English became *Jesus.* But Jesus' Hebrew name was *Yehoshua* or *Joshua,* which interestingly enough means "God is help" or "Jehovah saves." Notice that twice in the New Testament the name Jesus is used when the speaker obviously means the Old Testament Joshua (see Acts 7:45; Heb. 4:8). So "Jesus" led Israel into the promised land.

Anyone who rebelled against the leadership of Joshua and refused to cross over Jordan was to "be put to death" (Josh. 1:18). Anyone who refuses to follow Jesus into the celestial kingdom will suffer some degree of spiritual death. That is, he will be separated from the presence of God.

Joshua called upon the people to "sanctify" themselves so they would be worthy to go into the promised land (Josh. 3:5). One must be sanctified, or cleansed from sin, in order to enter a new life with God.

The ark of the covenant, which symbolized the presence of Jehovah, went before the camp of Israel and led the way into the new land (see Josh. 3:11). Like the passing through the Red Sea, Israel again passed through the midst of the waters to enter the promised land (see Josh. 3:15–17). The Lord specifically connected the two events by asking that a memorial be built (see Josh. 4:20–24).

The crossing of Israel into the new land was done on the first day of Passover (see Josh. 4:19; Ex. 12:2–3), again invoking the typology of deliverance from bondage and death.

Once they entered into the promised land, Joshua was commanded to perform the ordinance of circumcision among the Israelites (see Josh. 5:2–7). While wandering in the wilderness, this token of the Abrahamic covenant had not been performed. Now that they had sanctified themselves and followed Jesus (seen in the types of Joshua and the ark of the covenant) into the promised land, they were once again the true covenant people and therefore the token was reinstituted.

Thus we see that while the Passover itself has great typological significance, in actuality the whole exodus from slavery to entry into the promised land provides a type or similitude of what must happen to each individual if he is to "[put] off the natural man and [become] a saint through the atonement of Christ the Lord" (Mosiah 3:19).

One does not go to a great museum like the Smithsonian in Washington, D.C., and fully explore its treasures in an hour or two. Similarly, one does not exhaust the typology of the Old Testament in so brief a presentation as this. A lifetime of exploration and pondering is required; the Lord revealed to what extent he has filled the treasure house when he said, "And behold, all things have their likeness, and all things are created and made to bear record of me, both things which are temporal, and things which are spiritual; things which are in the heavens above, and things which are on the earth, and things which are under the earth, both above and beneath: all things bear record of me" (Moses 6:63).

Notes

From *A Symposium on the Old Testament,* August 16, 17, and 18, 1979 (Salt Lake City: Corporation of the President of The Church of Jesus Christ of Latter-day Saints, 1979), 182–93.

1. Bruce R. McConkie, *The Promised Messiah: The First Coming of Christ* (Salt Lake City: Deseret Book Co., 1978), 453.

2. Andrew Jukes, *The Law of the Offerings,* reprint ed. (Grand Rapids, Mich.: Kregel Publications, 1976), 14–15.
3. Ibid., 44–45.
4. For a more detailed discussion of the typology of Old Testament sacrifices and ordinances, see Richard D. Draper, "Sacrifice and Offerings: An Ordinance Given by Jehovah to Reveal Himself as the Christ," *A Symposium on the Old Testament,* August 16, 17, 18, 1979 (Salt Lake City: Corporation of the President of The Church of Jesus Christ of Latter-day Saints, 1979), 71–78.
5. Joseph Fielding Smith, *Doctrines of Salvation,* comp. Bruce R. McConkie, 3 vols. (Salt Lake City: Bookcraft, 1954–56), 3:180; italics omitted.
6. McConkie, *Promised Messiah,* 431–32.
7. C. F. Keil and F. Delitzsch, *The Pentateuch: Three Volumes in One,* vol. 1 of *Commentary on the Old Testament in Ten Volumes,* 10 vols. (Grand Rapids, Mich.: William B. Eerdmans Publishing Co., 1973), 2 (The Third Book of Moses): 398.
8. McConkie, *Promised Messiah,* 432–33.
9. Adam Clarke, *The Holy Bible . . . with Commentary and Critical Notes,* 6 vols. (New York: N. Bangs and J. Emory, for the Methodist Episcopal Church, 1827–31), 1:134; John 19:17.
10. Clarke, *Holy Bible . . . with Commentary,* 1:146.
11. Keil and Delitzsch, *The Pentateuch: Three Volumes in One,* 1 (The First Book of Moses): 253; emphasis added.

Chapter 3

THE SPIRIT OF THE OLD TESTAMENT

Through the years I have discovered some interesting attitudes about the Old Testament. Several years ago I was home teaching a family I had just been assigned. The father was on the high council in our stake. As we made our first visit and were getting acquainted, we asked about him and his family, and he asked about me and my family. One of the questions he asked was what I did for a living. I told him I worked for the Church Educational System in the central office. He inquired further, asking specifically what I did. At that time, I was working for college curriculum, and we were writing the Old Testament student manual. I told him that. In utmost seriousness he said, "You know, you ought to leave the Old Testament alone. If God had meant for the Old Testament to be understood, he would have made it clearer when he wrote it."

I suspect there are many people who could sympathize with that feeling. I have heard others say, "I read the Old Testament once, but I have repented and will never do it again."

I have seen studies done on the number of Church members who have read the scriptures. They were so intriguing that some years ago I started to ask people in classes I taught—most of whom are active Latter-day Saint adults—how many of them had read the Old Testament from beginning to end, from Genesis 1 to Malachi 4. Even in that rather select group of active Latter-day Saints, only about 10 to 15 percent had read the entire Old Testament. Many people have read in it, and many know the stories, but I think it would be safe to say that it is the most neglected work of scripture. If that is true of active Latter-day Saints, imagine what that means for the total Church population. Figures would probably drop to around 5 percent of the members of the Church who could say they have read the entire Old Testament. And if one considers the world population, or even Christian nations like our own, the figures might drop to something like one in a thousand who could say they have read the Old Testament.

I suppose there are many reasons why this is the case. Here are a few possible reasons. First, it is the longest book of scripture. It is twice as long as the Book of Mormon, three times as long as the New Testament, five times as long as the Doctrine and Covenants, and forty-five times as long as the Pearl of Great Price. Second, it is further removed from us in both time and culture than the other scriptures. It is very different than what we are used to. Third, it is the most diverse in content. In the Book of Mormon, we find a historical story line along with doctrinal sermons. Basically, that is it. In the New Testament, we find the Gospels, the brief historical narrative in Acts, a collection of epistles, and that is it. In the Doctrine and Covenants, there is a collection of revelations.

But look at the Old Testament. In its pages we find history, doctrine, prophecy, sermons, letters, lengthy genealogies, census records, real estate plot descriptions, legal codes, architectural blueprints (in verbal form, of course), detailed instructions for priesthood ordinances, outlines for holiday—or holy day—observance. There are songs, poetry, and even a funeral dirge in the book of Lamentations. There is one entire book of proverbs and maxims. There are even instructions for making detailed medical diagnoses. All of this provides a challenge. As teachers we would probably admit it is hard to motivate a ninth-grader, or even an eighteen-year-old, enough to get him interested in how to diagnose and recognize the symptoms of leprosy.

I think another reason the Old Testament is the neglected work of scripture is that it is full of troublesome and troubling questions. Let me just list some quickly:

Is God a loving father or a harsh, punitive deity who demands blood sacrifice of his followers and capital punishment for infractions of the law?

Why did the Lord command Moses and Joshua to kill all the Canaanites, including women and children?

How could Jacob receive a valid patriarchal blessing when he used deceitful means to get it?

Why would the Lord strike a man dead for touching the ark of the covenant when all he was trying to do was stop it from toppling over?

And on and on. The Old Testament is also full of passages that seem out of sorts with the gospel. When we start reading passages about smearing blood on the ear and on the thumb and on the right big toe, we may be troubled. Or try to explain to women in this day of feminism why a woman after pregnancy was unclean for forty days if she had a male child, but if she had a female child, she was unclean for seventy days.

It is little wonder, then, that people feel intimidated and overwhelmed by the Old Testament and often shy away from it.

In order to appreciate the Old Testament we need to consider the spirit of the Old Testament. I was really intrigued about how we use the word *spirit.* We say, "It was a spirited discussion." "We need more school spirit." "She has a sweet spirit," and "He is really out of spirits today."

In a book called *The Synonym Finder,* there are some interesting synonyms for spirit. Here are just a few: animating principle, life, consciousness, soul, mind, intellect, reason, understanding, intelligence, heart, motivating force, dominant character, essence, core, meaning, underlying message, gist, tenor, purpose, and intention.[1]

To intelligently assess the spirit of the Old Testament I asked myself these additional questions: What is the "animating principle" of the Old Testament? Should I focus on what is the "soul" and "heart" of the Old Testament, or should I try to define the "essence" or "core" of the Old Testament?

I finally came to an answer by analogy, and the analogy is Disneyland. What if we asked that same question of Disneyland? What is the spirit (essence, core, heart) of the Disneyland experience? Obviously there would be many possible answers. One person might say it is fun. Another might say it is entertainment. It is a learning experience. It is a fantasy experience. I finally concluded that the best possible way to define the spirit of Disneyland would be to actually take a person there and let him experience it and come up with his own conclusion.

Further suppose that in this analogy we had to tour Disneyland in an hour and a half, with the brevity of our Disneyland tour roughly the same as the limitations of one small chapter in a book. If that were my challenge, I would pick out a few highlights that would give a good sampling of the Disneyland experience. If we use that analogy in trying to come to sense the spirit of the Old Testament, then the task becomes the same.

I will pick two or three samplings from the Old Testament that provide a good representative experience and let you decide for yourself just what it means to talk about the spirit of the Old Testament. Some people might choose other samples, but I am the guide now, and so I get to choose. Later someone might take you back to the Old Testament and say, "No, *this* is the spirit." That would be fine, for it may be different to each of us.

The three items I have chosen as my sampling of what constitutes the essence or spirit of the Old Testament are the following:

The Old Testament is scripture.

The law of Moses captures the essence of the Old Testament.

The Old Testament is a voice from the past with a message for the present.

The Old Testament Is Scripture

Let us work through a scripture chain—a series of scriptures linked together by topic. Remember that everything we read has reference to what we call Old Testament scripture. It probably applies to all scripture as well, but the person speaking had the Old Testament in mind.

In 1 Nephi 19:22–23, Nephi, speaking of Laman and Lemuel (as tough a fifth-period class as is found anywhere), said:

"It came to pass that I did read many things to them, which were engraven upon the plates of brass, that they might know concerning the doings of the Lord in other lands, among people of old.

"And I did read many things unto them which were written in the books of Moses [what we today call the Pentateuch]; but that I might more fully persuade them to believe in the Lord their Redeemer I did read unto them that which was written by the prophet Isaiah."

Then comes a statement we use all the time when we talk about scripture. It includes two comments about the value of the Old Testament. Nephi said, "For I did liken all scriptures unto us, that it might be for our profit and learning" (1 Ne. 19:23).

In 2 Timothy 3:15, note what Paul had to say about the Old Testament. Paul was speaking to Timothy, who was evidently a bishop at that time. He told Timothy, "From a child thou hast known the holy scriptures." Since the New Testament had not yet been compiled, Paul must have been referring to scriptures that are part of the Old Testament. He told Timothy that these scriptures "are able to make thee wise unto salvation through faith which is in Christ Jesus" (v. 15). This is a marvelous statement about the Old Testament. The Old Testament is able to make us wise enough to achieve salvation.

Paul then continued:

"All scripture is given by inspiration of God, and is profitable for doctrine, for reproof, for correction, for instruction in righteousness:

"That the man of God may be perfect" (vv. 16–17).

These phrases contain a marvelous testimony about the value of the Old Testament.

One of the scriptures in this chain that has impressed me the most is in Luke 24. It impresses upon my mind the power of the Old Testament, that it is scripture in every sense of the word. In chapter 24, starting in verse 13, we read of two disciples who were walking on the Sabbath day of the Resurrection on the road to Emmaus. (Elder Bruce R. McConkie believes one disciple may have been Luke himself.[2]) They were talking about the events that had taken place in the previous three days. They were joined by a man they did not recognize, and he asked them what they were discussing. When they told him about the events of the previous few days—the arrest, the trial and crucifixion, and finally the electrifying news of an empty tomb—he chastised them a little. In verses 25–26 we read:

"O fools, and slow of heart to believe all that the prophets have spoken:

"Ought not Christ to have suffered these things, and to enter into his glory?"

And then to prove his point, where did he go? "*And beginning at Moses and all the prophets,* he expounded unto them in all the scriptures the things concerning himself" (v. 27; emphasis added). Oh, how I would have loved to have been there that day, just walking along behind, to see what references he used from the Old Testament as he taught them. But the important thing is that he did not have to reveal new scripture. It was there in what we now call the Old Testament.

Our next reference is also in Luke 24. The Savior had appeared in the upper room and eaten the piece of fish and honeycomb. "And he said unto them, These are the words which I spake unto you, while I was yet with you, that all things must be fulfilled, *which were written in the law of Moses, and in the prophets, and in the psalms,* concerning me" (v. 44; emphasis added). The Savior did not seem to feel the Old Testament was insufficient scripture. It bore witness of the things he wanted to bear witness of.

I suppose the ultimate scriptural statement that the Old Testament is scripture is found in 1 Nephi chapters 3 and 4. When I taught the Book of Mormon, I used to ask my students why Lehi sent his sons back for the plates of brass. Usually they would respond that the plates were important. Then I would ask how important they were. The bottom line is that the Old Testament was important enough to kill for. Nephi was told that "it is better that one man should perish than that a nation should dwindle and perish in unbelief" (1 Ne. 4:13). The Old Testament had the power to save an entire nation. That is a testimony of marvelous proportions. As I thought about that, I realized the first essence of the spirit of the Old Testament is simply that *it is scripture.*

The scriptures have a threefold purpose. After some careful thought, it occurred to me that the scriptures seem to have a threefold mission or purpose. Their purpose is to bring us to Christ through showing us what God is really like, what man is really like, and how man can be reconciled to God and become like him. If we apply that purpose to the Old Testament, again we see clearly that the Old Testament fully qualifies as scripture.

Let us review the three purposes one at a time. The first purpose of the scriptures is to show us what God is really like. The nature of God is defined as clearly and sharply, if not more so, in the Old Testament as in any other scripture.

I spent three years at Pepperdine University taking New Testament classes. Pepperdine University is run by the Church of Christ, and I took classes from the best of their ministers and the best of their teachers. It was a positive and beneficial experience. But after two years of studying the finest in Bible scholarship and many of the writings of Christianity's finest theologians, I came to an important conclusion that the entire Christian world is in serious theological trouble. One of the primary reasons, I am convinced, is that it has largely forgotten the God of the Old Testament and looks only to the God of the New Testament. We know, of course, that they are one and the same God. The Jehovah of the Old Testament is the Jesus of the New Testament.

The placing of both perspectives side by side adds a whole different dimension, especially on the nature of God. The same God who said to turn the other cheek and love your enemies (see Matt. 5:39, 44) also told Israel to utterly destroy the Canaanites (see Deut. 7:2).

The same God who said, "Judge not, that ye be not judged" (Matt. 7:1) also said that a wicked and rebellious son should be taken by his parents to the elders to be stoned (see Deut. 21:18–21).

The same God who warned that "an evil and adulterous generation seeks after a sign" (Matt. 12:39) also told Moses and Elijah to use tremendous signs as evidence of their power from God (see Ex. 4:30; 1 Kgs. 18:36–39).

When the two disciples, James and John, the sons of thunder, came back from a Samaritan village, the Samaritans would not give them a place for the Savior to stay. They were angry and asked the Lord if they should call down fire and destroy the whole village. The Savior's response was in the form of a rebuke: "The Son of man is not come to destroy men's lives, but to save them" (Luke 9:56). But it was the premortal Savior who sent down fire and totally destroyed Sodom and Gomorrah (see Gen. 19:28; 3 Ne. 9:3–12).

I do not believe that these examples from the Old Testament and the New

Testament are contradictions. I believe every one of them is explainable. It certainly balances our idea of what God is really like and what his nature really is. If we neglect that Old Testament perspective, our concept of God may be perilously lacking.

We said the second function of the scriptures is to show the nature of man. Again the Old Testament provides a critical dimension. I cannot think of a greater commentary on the nature of man than you find in the placement of three kings side by side. The Lord controlled the order of birth, I am sure, and placed Saul, David, and Solomon one after another to teach us some important lessons. Let us note some paired scriptures on those three kings. This is what makes the Bible such great literature. The writer never says he has something he wants to show us, he just teaches by what he writes and in the way he places things together.

In 1 Samuel 9:2 we read, "And he had a son, whose name was Saul, a choice young man, and a goodly; and there was not among the children of Israel a goodlier person than he."

Now let us read in 1 Samuel 15:17 after Saul has disobeyed the Lord. Note Samuel's description of Saul now: "When thou wast little in thine own sight, wast thou not made the head of the tribes of Israel?"

And then in verse 28, Samuel says, "The Lord hath rent the kingdom of Israel from thee this day, and hath given it to a neighbour of thine, *that is better than thou*" (emphasis added).

A few years before, Saul was the goodliest person: now there was an even better one, namely David. Yet again note the description of this goodliest person, David, a few years later. In 2 Samuel 12:9–10, we read:

"Wherefore hast thou [David] despised the commandment of the Lord, . . . thou hast killed Uriah the Hittite. . . .

"Now therefore the sword shall never depart from thine house; because thou hast despised me."

It is almost an identical comparison to the life of Saul.

Now let us go over a little further to 1 Kings 3:3. Note the description of Solomon: "And Solomon loved the Lord." Verse 5 states, "In Gibeon the Lord appeared to Solomon in a dream." Imagine that the Savior comes to Solomon in a dream. In 1 Kings 9:2 the Lord appeared to Solomon a second time. Imagine a man of such righteousness that he sees God twice. Yet just two chapters later, we read:

"But king Solomon loved many strange women. . . .

"Solomon clave unto these in love. . . .

"For it came to pass, when Solomon was old, that his wives turned away his heart after other gods: and his heart was not perfect with the Lord" (2 Kgs. 11:1–2, 4).

What a dramatic lesson. If we miss that lesson on human nature, we are not reading the Old Testament very carefully.

As another example of the Old Testament's insights into human nature, take the lesson of Uzzah and the ark of the covenant (see 2 Sam. 6:1–7). I do not know of any other scripture that teaches this principle in quite the same way. You know that what happens is that the ark comes back and starts to totter, and Uzzah reaches up to touch it. Let me quote some statements—one from the institute Old Testament student manual, one from a book by C. F. Keil and F. Delitzsch, who are famous scholars, and one from President John Taylor—to show you the insight of human nature that you get from this one single event.

"However well-meaning his intentions, Uzzah approached casually what could only be approached under the strictest conditions. [The high priest could only go into the Holy of Holies once a year, and then only after a lengthy ritual of cleansing and purification.] He had not faith in God's power. He assumed that the ark was in danger, forgetting that it was the physical symbol of the God *who has all power.* Uzzah tried to use his power to prevent it from being hurt. What man can presume to save God and his kingdom through his own efforts?"[3]

"Uzzah was therefore a type of all who with good intentions, humanly speaking, yet with unsanctified minds, interfere in the affairs of the kingdom of God, from the notion that they are in danger, and with the hope of saving them."[4]

President John Taylor said: "Do not think you are wise and that you can manage and manipulate the priesthood, for you cannot do it. God must manage, regulate, dictate, and stand at the head, and every man in his place. The ark of God does not need steadying, especially by incompetent men without revelation and without knowledge of the kingdom of God and its laws."[5]

So, one of the great insights into human nature comes from this Old Testament story of Uzzah and the ark. However, we do not learn about human nature from the Old Testament only through bad examples. In fact, some of the finest examples of people who have overcome the natural man are found in the Old Testament.

Joseph is one who comes immediately to mind. When Pharaoh raised him up to be vice-regent, second only to Pharaoh himself in power, consider what thoughts Potiphar's wife must have had that day. She was the one who sent Joseph to prison. How she must have trembled in her chambers, waiting for the ax of retribution to fall, and yet it never did.

Think about Abraham. There are many lessons we could learn from him, not least of which is that we can have great wealth and still be faithful to God. From Elijah we learn that even in the midst of great righteousness there can be loneliness and frustration (see 1 Kgs. 19:10).

From Moses there are other lessons, too. In the LDS Bible Dictionary there is this statement about Moses: "Moses, stirred with indignation at the suffering of his brethren, 'refused to be called the son of Pharaoh's daughter' (Heb. 11:24), *one of the noblest acts of self-sacrifice known to history*" (s.v. "Egypt"). I have walked the halls of those mighty Egyptian temples and palaces. Moses willingly gave that up to walk the sands of Sinai. That is a contrast.

And so we see that in the Old Testament, there are great insights into the nature of God and the nature of man. There are also insights into the reconciliation process between man and God.

Psalm 111:2 states, "The works of the Lord are great, sought out of all them that have pleasure therein." Think about that for a moment. One of the works of the Lord is the work we call the Old Testament. And in that work is all of the grandness and perfection we have come to expect in all the Lord's works.

Here is what Andrew Jukes said about scripture as the Lord's work:

"Man's work, if we are continually poring over it, will soon weary us—a little attention will in time make us masters of it. God's work, the more we examine and look into it, will only attract us the more. The more it is studied, the more it opens out, at every step unfolding fresh and endless objects. . . .

" . . . Merely to look upon His work in nature, shews, indeed, that the hand that made it is divine. The first glance, cursory as it may be, gives a satisfying impression, an impression of perfectness. . . . But in each part of that scene, so cursorily glanced at, every minutest portion will bear the strictest inspection. . . .

"And God's Word, in all these particulars, is like God's work. . . .

"The microscope may be used here as well as in the physical world."[6]

I love that statement.

There are some tough questions in the Old Testament, troubling questions. I wish I had answers for all of them. Often when these problems occur people tend to assume that there is something wrong with the scriptures or even with God, who revealed them. In fact, it was that kind of thinking that led to the whole "death of God" philosophy. Scholars read the Old Testament and said, "We don't like this god. The problem must be with our concept of him. Let's get rid of it." So they put the blame on God and rejected the scriptural account. That is the story of much of modern biblical scholarship: it seeks to show that the biblical record is terribly flawed.

There is an alternative assumption. When I find something I do not understand in the scriptures, perhaps there is something wrong with my understanding of the scriptures. So it is with the Old Testament. If I take out the microscope, the calipers, the tape measure, and the ruler and get down and really take a close look, I find the marks of God's perfection, and it is a marvelous testimony.

So, my first answer to the question of "What is the spirit of the Old Testament?" is simply that *it is scripture.*

The Law of Moses Captures the Essence of the Old Testament

My second answer to the question on the spirit of the Old Testament is that the law of Moses captures the essence of the Old Testament. If *spirit* really means "animating principle" or "dominant factor," then the law of Moses would certainly qualify for being a large part of the spirit of the Old Testament.

There are five aspects of the law of Moses that I would like to discuss briefly. They are: (1) The law of Moses required the spirit of prophecy. (2) The law of Moses was part of the gospel. (3) The law of Moses was a case law approach to law. (4) The law of Moses was a law of daily performances and ordinances. (5) The law of Moses was full of types, shadows, and similitudes designed to teach us of Christ and lead men to him. Let us look at these characteristics one at a time.

The law of Moses required the spirit of prophecy. A scripture in the Book of Mormon is one of the best commentaries on the Old Testament we have anywhere. In Alma 25, Mormon pauses in his narrative of the historical record to comment on the law of Moses. This is significant because Mormon lived in the time when the law of Moses had been fulfilled. He had a vision of the law that the early writers might not have fully had. Speaking about the Anti-Nephi-Lehies, the people of Ammon who were converted in that great missionary work, he said:

"Yea, and they did keep the law of Moses; for it was expedient that they should keep the law of Moses. . . .

"But notwithstanding the law of Moses, they did look forward to the coming of Christ, considering that the law of Moses was a type of his coming, and believing that they must keep those outward performances" (v. 15).

Now note what follows: "Now they did not suppose that salvation came by the law of Moses; but the law of Moses did serve to strengthen their faith in Christ; and thus they did retain a hope through faith, unto eternal salvation, *relying upon the spirit of prophecy*" (v. 16; emphasis added).

Mormon indicates that the spirit of prophecy is what made the law of Moses operative in their lives, so they came to Christ. In Revelation 19:10, we find a definition of the spirit of prophecy. It is "the testimony of Jesus." In light of what we said earlier, the whole problem with contemporary biblical scholarship rests right there. Those scholars do not have the spirit of prophecy. They do not have a testimony of Jesus Christ in the full sense of the word. This is a vital key to our understanding of the law of Moses. First and foremost, we must have the spirit of prophecy if we ever hope to understand the law of Moses.

The law of Moses was part of the gospel. A common misconception, even among some members of the Church, is that the gospel was taken away from ancient Israel after the golden calf incident. Instead, the law of Moses was put in its place. In Galatians 3:8 and in the Joseph Smith Translation, Galatians 3:19, the Apostle Paul makes it clear that Abraham had the gospel long before Moses. And then, through their spiritual immaturity, the house of Israel received the law of Moses. But the law of Moses did not replace the gospel. Paul says it was added to it. That is an important difference.

In Doctrine and Covenants 84:26 the law of Moses is called a "preparatory gospel." It is part of the gospel. It is in harmony with the gospel. Much of the world has a tendency to forget that, but throughout the law of Moses we find numerous gospel principles. They are not couched in quite the same way as we find them in the New Testament, but they are there. Let us note some examples.

In Leviticus 19:9–10 we read:

"And when ye reap the harvest of your land, thou shalt not wholly reap the corners of thy field, neither shalt thou gather the gleanings of thy harvest.

"And thou shalt not glean thy vineyard, neither shalt thou gather every grape of thy vineyard; thou shalt leave them for the poor and stranger."

I suggest this as one alternative to the Department of Health, Education, and Welfare. A way for ancient Israel to show their love for their fellowman and to care for the poor was to not totally strip their fields in the harvest.

In Leviticus 19:14, note the lesson on how to treat the handicapped: "Thou shalt not curse the deaf, nor put a stumblingblock before the blind." Consider the spirit of that. Look at what is happening today to the rights of the handicapped. We are finally moving to take away some of the stumbling blocks for the deaf and the blind. But this counsel is over three thousand years old.

Still in Leviticus is another lesson: "Thou shalt not go up and down as a talebearer" (Lev. 19:16). Or we could cite the passage the Lord himself cited: "Thou shalt love thy neighbour as thyself" (Lev. 19:18).

As another example, let us go to Deuteronomy 20. I find this interesting, having spent some time in the military. Typically, life in the military in most countries is coarse, often crude, and filled with men of foul mouths and low morals. In the law of Moses, even life in the military is not overlooked by the Lord.

"When thou goest out to battle against thine enemies, and seest horses, and chariots [and tanks and machine guns], and a people more than thou, be not afraid of them: for the Lord thy God is with thee, which brought thee up out of the land of Egypt.

"And it shall be, when ye are come nigh unto the battle, that the priest shall approach and speak unto the people" (vv. 1–2).

That is interesting. Not the general, not the president, not the king, but the priest—the religious leader, the chaplain, if you will—shall approach the people and say, "Fear not, and do not tremble, neither be ye terrified because of them" (Deut. 20:3). In verse 5 we read, "And the officers shall speak unto the people, saying, What man is there that hath built a new house, and hath not dedicated it? let him go and return to his house, lest he die in the battle, and another man dedicate it."

Continuing on in verse 6 we read, "And what man is he that hath planted a vineyard, and hath not yet eaten of it? let him also go and return unto his house, lest he die in the battle, and another man eat of it." In verse 7 we read, "And what man is there that hath betrothed a wife, and hath not taken her? let him go and return unto his house, lest he die in battle."

When I read this verse, I think of an experience I had in 1983. We entered Israel with our Lands of the Scriptures workshop the day after Israel invaded Lebanon. While we were staying in the hotel in Accho, we witnessed a wedding. The groom was in his military uniform, and the rabbi came in his military uniform. These were their wrinkled and faded fatigues, not dress uniforms.

I said something to our guide to the effect that it was surprising that they did not dress up a little more formally for the wedding. Somewhat to my chagrin, he said that these men had been released for twenty-four hours to come from the battlefront—the rabbi to perform the wedding and the bridegroom to be married. Both would return to the front lines the next morning. Think of the anguish of that bride, to send the man she loves to battle before she has even spent one full day with him. Under the law of Moses, such a thing would not have happened. How does that relate to the Savior's admonition, "All things whatsoever ye would that men should do to you, do ye even so to them"? (Matt. 7:12).

As another example of the Golden Rule in practice, note that the law required that when a person built a new house, he was to put a battlement around the roof (see Deut. 22:8). Why? Because in those times the roof was a living place, like a patio, and someone might accidentally slip and fall off. Would we like our children falling off our neighbor's roof? Of course not. So, based on the Golden Rule, what do we do? Exactly what we would wish our neighbor would do: build a guardrail so our children will not fall off the roof.

Now, as I said, the gospel principles are not taught in quite the same way, but I find the law of Moses absolutely steeped in gospel principles. This brings us to a third point.

The law of Moses was a case law approach to law. For this insight, I have to give credit to a man named Rousas John Rushdoony, a Christian minister who has great insights into Old Testament writings. In his book, *The Institutes of Biblical Law,* he explains what he means by a case law approach to law.[7] We should be familiar with it because we practice case law in the United States and many other western countries as well.

If someone were to mention *Miranda v. Arizona,* most people would know what is referred to. This was the famous case where the Supreme Court ruled that a person must know his civil rights at the time of his arrest, or else his conviction may be overturned. When we see on television or in the movies a policeman reading a person his rights, it is because this single case has established the entire scope of the law in this area. Other examples of modern case law milestones would be *Roe v. Wade,* which established a woman's right to abortion, and *Brown v. Board of Education of Topeka, Kan.,* which established the law on the question of civil rights. These pivotal cases outline the parameters of law.

Now let us see how this case law approach works in the law of Moses. When I was teaching institute in California, I once knew a person, not a member of the Church, who said, "You find me one place in the scriptures where abortion is forbidden." I did not know what to say. I looked under *A* in the index, but it was not there. Do you know why? Because it does not have to be. In Exodus 21:22–24 we read:

"If men strive, and hurt a woman with child, so that her fruit depart from her, and yet no mischief follow [if two men erupt in a fight and a pregnant woman standing by is accidentally hit and caused to miscarry, and she does not die]: he shall be surely punished, according as the woman's husband will lay upon him. . . .

"And if any mischief follow, then thou shalt give life for life.

"Eye for eye, tooth for tooth."

This is an excellent example of case law. If the law punishes a man who *accidentally* caused a woman to miscarry, that automatically establishes that *willful* termination of pregnancy is forbidden. That simple case clearly sets forth how the Lord feels about protecting the unborn child.

The law of Moses was a law of daily performances and ordinances. Abinadi said that the law of Moses was "a very strict law" of daily performances and ordinances (Mosiah 13:29; see also vv. 30–31). This is a key concept. We must contrast that idea with the sweeping statements of principles that the Savior made when he said such things as "Whatsoever ye would that men should do to you, do ye even so to them" (Matt. 7:12), and "A new commandment I give unto you, That ye love one another; as I have loved you" (John 13:34).

That is one difference between the Old Testament and the New Testament. The Old Testament tells us what to do. We build battlements on our roofs. When we go to war, we send new bridegrooms home. We do not place stumbling blocks in front of the blind. The law outlines what to do on a daily basis. And from those daily performances and ordinances we draw gospel principles.

When Christ came, he changed that approach. Instead of specific, day-to-day requirements, he taught sweeping gospel principles that we have to decide how to apply on a day-to-day basis. When he says "A new commandment I give unto you" (John 13:34), the challenge is to love everyone. But what does that mean in day-to-day life? It is easy to "love everyone," but the challenge is to love George, Sally, the neighbor who turns his dogs loose every night at eleven o'clock, and the boss who is obnoxious and oppressive. That is where the challenge comes—in the daily application of the principle. But in the law of Moses, it was just the opposite. The daily performances were outlined, and from those the principles were taught.

Now, if I were to ask you as teachers which is the better way to teach, how would you answer? Do you give daily performances and let your students draw out the principles, or do you give them the principles and let them draw out the daily performances? Which is better? I think we would have to agree that the answer is *both methods.* There are some who are taught better with daily performances. Children are a good example of this. But when they become more spiritually mature, the other approach is better. This is why the Lord said it is not necessary that he command us in all things (see D&C 58:26–28). Or, as the Prophet Joseph Smith suggested, we should give the principles and let the people govern themselves.

The Law of Moses was full of types, shadows, and similitudes designed to teach us of Christ and lead men to him. Speaking of the Jews, Nephi wrote that they did "turn their hearts aside, rejecting signs and wonders" (1 Ne. 19:13). The great tragedy of ancient Judaism was that they had all the scriptures, all the signs and tokens, all the symbols, all of the outward forms that pointed to the Savior, yet they missed what it was all meant to represent.

Christ is the center of the Old Testament, and there is no question about that. We see him at every turn. We see it in even the tiniest detail. And the law of Moses was in the forefront of that. Paul taught that the law was the "schoolmaster to bring us unto Christ" (Gal. 3:24). And, Nephi, Abinadi, and Amulek all taught that the law of Moses was given to point the way to Christ (see 2 Ne. 11:4; Mosiah 13:31; Alma 34:14).

In the Old Testament, and more especially in the law of Moses, we have many types and symbols of the Savior. We have historical types or symbols. For example, the man Adam, as he is often called, represents all of us in our journey in mortality and then back to God. Noah is a great symbol of rebirth and baptism (see 1 Pet. 3:20–21). There are so many types and symbols of Christ in the law of Moses. There are types in the Exodus and the great night of the Passover. There are types in the wanderings in the wilderness, in the baptism of the Red Sea, and in the pillar of fire (see 1 Cor. 10:1–2). The manna and the water from the rock are likewise types or symbols of the Savior (see vv. 3–4). There are symbols, types, and similitudes in the tabernacle, in the clothing of the priests, and in the feasts and festivals. Everywhere one looks, everything bears witness of the Savior in the law of Moses.

So, our second point in what constitutes the spirit of the Old Testament has to do with the law of Moses. We can truly say that the law of Moses in and of itself captures the essence of the Old Testament.

A Voice from the Past with a Message for the Present

The third sample I would like to use to suggest what constitutes the spirit of the Old Testament is that the Old Testament is a voice from the past with a message for the present. Every major Book of Mormon writer told us that they were writing not for their generation but for some future generation—in essence, for us in the latter days. I have not found any place in the Old Testament where the writers specifically say that, but I think it is just as true of the Old Testament as it is of the Book of Mormon. It is in verity a book for our day.

For example, I started some time ago to make a list of what I call Whole Sermons in Single Questions. I have started highlighting some questions that are asked by various people in the Old Testament from which we could draw a whole talk or sermon. Let us list a few of these quickly.

God to Adam shortly after the Fall: "Where art thou?" (Gen. 3:9). Surely the Lord was not asking because he did not know where Adam was. And we ought to ask ourselves the same question. Where are we in our relationship to God?

Cain to the Lord: "Am I my brother's keeper?" (Gen. 4:9).

Joseph to Potiphar's wife: "How then can I do this great wickedness, and sin against God?" (Gen. 39:9).

Samuel to Saul: "Hath the Lord as great delight in burnt offerings and sacrifices, as in obeying the voice of the Lord?" (1 Sam. 15:22).

David to his brother, Eliab, on the hills overlooking the valley of Elah and the encampment of the Philistines (remember that Eliab had chided David for being foolish and told him to go home because he was a young boy and should not be on the battlefield): "Is there not a cause?" (1 Sam. 17:29).

Wicked Ahab to Elijah: "Art thou he that troubleth Israel?" (1 Kgs. 18:17). Elijah replied, "I have not troubled Israel; but thou, and thy father's house, in that ye have forsaken the commandments of the Lord" (v. 18).

Elijah to the Israelites on Mount Carmel, where Israel had gathered to watch Elijah's confrontation with the priests of Baal: "How long halt ye between two opinions?" (1 Kgs. 18:21).

The servant of Elisha to Elisha when the Syrian army surrounded their village: "Alas, my master! how shall we do?" (2 Kgs. 6:15). Sometimes when we find ourselves in desperate straits and want to cry out, "Alas, Lord, how shall we do?" how wonderful it would be if we could remember Elisha's response. He opened the eyes of the young man so he could see that "the mountain was full of horses and chariots of fire round about Elisha" (v. 17).

Mordecai to Esther, who knew that if she went into the king without permission, she could be killed: "Who knoweth whether thou art come to the kingdom for such a time as this?" (Esther 4:14). That is a great question to ask your young people. Who knows but what they have come to this time and this place for some grand purpose.

The Lord to all of Israel: "Can two walk together, except they be agreed?" (Amos 3:3). That is a question that could be asked of every married couple, of priesthood quorums, or of corporate executives.

Job to his wife: "What? shall we receive good at the hand of God, and shall we not receive evil?" (Job 2:10).

Malachi to all Israel: "Will a man rob God?" (Mal. 3:8).

And finally, perhaps one of the greatest of all questions, Micah to the house of

Israel: "What doth the Lord require of thee, but to do justly, and to love mercy, and to walk humbly with thy God?" (Micah 6:8).

Here is another example of how the Old Testament serves as a message for today. In 1976 we celebrated the bicentennial anniversary of the adoption of the U.S. Declaration of Independence. President Ezra Taft Benson, President J. Reuben Clark, Jr., and others have warned us about the dangers of losing some of the freedoms we possess. Here is a very pointed message for today. Let us read Deuteronomy 4:7–9 and look at it in terms of the Constitution and the freedoms we hold dear:

"For what nation is there so great, who hath God so nigh unto them, as the Lord our God is in all things that we call upon him for?

"And what nation is there so great, that hath statutes and judgments so righteous as all this law, which I set before you this day?" (vv. 7–8).

Now comes the warning: "Only take heed to thyself, and keep thy soul diligently, lest thou forget the things which thine eyes have seen, and lest they depart from thy heart all the days of thy life: but teach them thy sons, and thy sons' sons" (v. 9). What a great message for today.

Here is another message. In lands such as the United States and Canada, where we have riches beyond the wildest dreams of any emperor of ancient times, where we have the most beautiful fabrics, an abundance of food, transportation, and communication that much of the world's population will never see, here is another message for today from the past:

"For the Lord thy God bringeth thee into a good land, a land of brooks of water, of fountains and depths that spring out of valleys and hills;

"A land of wheat, and barley, and vines, and fig trees. . . .

"A land wherein thou shalt eat bread without scarceness, thou shalt not lack any thing in it: a land whose stones are iron, and out of whose hills thou mayest dig brass" (Deut. 8:7–8).

Again, note the sobering warning:

"When thou hast eaten and art full, then thou shalt bless the Lord thy God for the good land which he hath given thee.

"Beware that thou forget not the Lord thy God, in not keeping his commandments, and his judgments, and his statutes, which I command thee this day:

"Lest when thou hast eaten and art full, and hast built goodly houses, and dwelt therein; . . .

"Then thine heart be lifted up, and thou forget the Lord thy God, which brought thee forth out of the land of Egypt" (Deut. 8:10–12, 14).

In days and times of great turmoil and deception, of wickedness in high places, once again the voice from the past offers a message for the present:

"Neither shall he [the ruler] multiply wives to himself, that his heart turn not away: neither shall he greatly multiply to himself silver and gold.

"And it shall be, when he sitteth upon the throne of his kingdom, that he shall write him a copy of this law in a book out of that which is before the priests the Levites:

"And it shall be with him, and he shall read therein all the days of his life: that he may learn to fear the Lord his God, to keep all the words of this law and these statutes, to do them:

"That his heart be not lifted up above his brethren, and that he turn not aside from the commandment, to the right hand, or to the left: to the end that he may prolong his days in his kingdom, he, and his children, in the midst of Israel" (Deut. 17:17–20).

Read that in the halls of Congress or in the palaces of the world, and see what kind of reception it would generate.

I think of a day of bulimia and anorexia, when the world is trumpeting that to be happy we must be lean and tan and lovely, and I think of 1 Samuel 16:7 where the Lord says, "Look not on his countenance, . . . for the Lord seeth not as man seeth; for man looketh on the outward appearance, but the Lord looketh on the heart." The Lord does not care what we look like. He does not care if we are tall, dark, and handsome or short, plump, and bald. What he cares about is what is in our hearts. In our world today, the second greatest cause of death among teenagers is suicide, and we are obsessed with dieting and weight loss and the "in" brand names of clothing. If that scripture is not a message from the past for today, I do not know of any other.

Summary and Conclusion

What is the spirit of the Old Testament? What is its essence? What are its overriding principles? First, it is scripture. Second, it is the law of Moses. Third, it is a voice from the past with a message for the present.

If I were ever cast into prison or stranded on a desert island and given nothing but the Old Testament, I bear solemn witness that from it I could learn what I need to know about God. I could learn what I need to know about man. I could learn what I need to know about how to reconcile myself and come unto Christ. And I could do all this by just studying the Old Testament. When all is said and done, that is the spirit of the Old Testament.

Notes

From *Old Testament Symposium Speeches* (Salt Lake City: The Church of Jesus Christ of Latter-day Saints, 1987), 34–41.

1. See Jerome Irving Rodale, *The Synonym Finder* (Emmaus, Pa.: Rodale Press, 1978), s.v. "spirit."
2. See Bruce R. McConkie, *Doctrinal New Testament Commentary,* 3 vols. (Salt Lake City: Bookcraft, 1965–73), 1:850.
3. *Old Testament: Genesis–2 Samuel,* Religion 301 student manual (Salt Lake City: The Church of Jesus Christ of Latter-day Saints, n.d.), 292.
4. C. F. Keil and F. Delitzsch, *Joshua, Judges, Ruth, 1 & 2 Samuel,* vol. 2 of *Commentary on the Old Testament,* 10 vols., reprint ed. (Grand Rapids, Mich.: William B. Eerdmans Publishing Co., 1980), 33.
5. John Taylor, *The Gospel Kingdom,* sel. G. Homer Durham (Salt Lake City: Bookcraft, 1964), 166.
6. Andrew Jukes, *The Law of the Offerings* (Grand Rapids, Mich.: Kregel Publications, 1976), 9–12.
7. See Rousas John Rushdoony, *The Institutes of Biblical Law* (n.p.: Presbyterian and Reformed Publishing Co., 1973), 11.

Chapter 4

EZEKIEL: PROPHET OF JUDGMENT, PROPHET OF PROMISE

As I looked over the assignment to cover the entire book of Ezekiel in a fifty-minute lecture, it occurred to me that the job is somewhat analogous to trying to guide a tour to a large national park in one hour. If I were a guide and had to do that for you, I'd really come down to one of two options. One way to do it would be to go inside the park and in that hour's time, driving as fast as we could, try to see as many things as possible, by necessity choosing only the highlights. Then our time would be gone. We would just have to say, "When you come back be sure and see this or that." But there is another option for the guide who really desires to be helpful. We could open up a map of the park and spend the hour orienting you to the layout of the park and its significant features, pointing out what to look for and how to enjoy it when you get more time to go back.

The same problems are encountered in trying to cover Ezekiel in a brief discussion. We can choose three or four special areas, focus on them in some detail, and tell you that the rest are also interesting. Or we can give an overview, orienting you to the layout of the book, so that when you return to it with more time, you can find your own way about.

Obviously, if that is really what we are limited to, both options have their frustrations and their drawbacks. But I choose the second option. We are going to discuss the book of Ezekiel using the "map" approach. I accept the inherent frustrations in that approach with the hope that when you come back to Ezekiel on your own, you will be better oriented, will know what to look for, and will therefore have a more meaningful experience.

As I look at the book of Ezekiel, I find four points of orientation that help us chart our course. They are all interdependent and interwoven, but they still can be seen as four ways to view Ezekiel: (1) Ezekiel the man, (2) Ezekiel the captive, (3) Ezekiel the answerer, and (4) Ezekiel the writer.

Ezekiel the Man

Considering the length of his book, we know surprisingly little about Ezekiel the man. His name means "God strengthens,"[1] or, as one scholar translated it, "God will prevail" or "whom God has strengthened."[2] This name is significant and appropriate.

We know from his own record that he was the son of Buzi (unfortunately we don't know who Buzi was), and that he was a priest (Ezek. 1:3). Almost certainly he was carried away captive into Babylon in the second group of captives taken by Nebuchadnezzar (see 2 Kgs. 24:10–16). Some scholars have speculated that he may have served in the temple in Jerusalem before he was taken captive into Babylon, because in the later chapters it is obvious that he is intimately familiar with the temple rituals and other things that took place there. But he himself makes no mention of it, so that is merely speculation.

Josephus says that Ezekiel was carried away when he was young, implying that he may have been a young man or even a boy.[3] That he was a boy doesn't seem likely, however, for several reasons. First, it was in the fifth year of his exile that he was called to be a prophet (Ezek. 1:2). Second, in chapter 4, verse 14, Ezekiel spoke of his youth as though it was long past. Third, in the ninth year of his captivity, Ezekiel's wife died (Ezek. 24:16–18), which again would seem to imply that he was a little older man. Finally, Ezekiel 1:1 contains an interesting phrase to consider: "Now it came to pass in the *thirtieth* year, in the fourth month, in the fifth day of the month . . ." (emphasis added). Though Ezekiel doesn't say the thirtieth year of what, some scholars have assumed that maybe it was the thirtieth year of his own life. If that were the case, he would have been about twenty-five when he was taken into captivity. However, if it refers to the thirtieth year of his captivity, we cannot say for sure how old he was. (See similar dating references in Ezek. 29:17; 31:1.)

In two or three places in Ezekiel, we learn that while he was in exile the elders of the Jews came to his home to counsel with him (for example, see Ezek. 8:1; 14:1; 20:1). Most often they rejected his counsel, but it is interesting that he functioned as a prophet in a very personal, face-to-face setting. It was for this reason that one scholar referred to him as a "pastor as well as prophet."[4]

We know from Ezekiel's own record that he lived among the exiles in Tel Abib (Ezek. 1:1, 3; 3:15), which seems to have been a colony of the Jewish exiles on the river Chebar, probably a small tributary of the Euphrates a little east of the city of Babylon itself. He spent his life among the captives, and the record indicates that he ministered for at least twenty-two years after his call as a prophet. Some questionable traditions indicate that he died a martyr at the hands of one of the Jewish leaders offended by his prophecies.[5] Beyond that we know virtually nothing more about Ezekiel the man.

However, the Book of Mormon provides one additional interesting insight. In 1 Nephi 1:4, Nephi writes, "For it came to pass in the commencement of the first year of the reign of Zedekiah, king of Judah, (my father Lehi, having dwelt at Jerusalem in all his days); and *in that same year there came many prophets,* prophesying unto the people that they must repent, or the great city Jerusalem must be destroyed" (emphasis added). Ezekiel was contemporary with Lehi and could easily have been one of those prophets. We know the names of four of the prophets of that day—Lehi, Ezekiel, Jeremiah, and Daniel. Lehi's call was to lead a colony out of Jerusalem to a promised land. Jeremiah's call was to stay and bear witness of the destruction of Jerusalem. Daniel was called into exile, but he went into the royal courts and there was allowed to get a picture of the grand world view of history. Ezekiel was called to go among the captives and explain to them why this terrible tragedy had happened.

Ezekiel the Captive

When I talk about Ezekiel the captive, I refer to the historical setting in which he lived and wrote. And to do that, I first need to talk about some historical and prophetic antecedents that are relevant to his time. Then we also need to explain the historical setting in which Ezekiel was found.

Probably the most important historical and prophetic antecedent dates back to Moses and his warnings to the people of Israel as they entered the promised land. Leviticus 26 and Deuteronomy 28 are whole chapters warning the people that once they entered the land of promise they would incur a solemn obligation. As long as they were faithful, righteous, and committed to the covenant, Moses promised them blessings. The land would be blessed, their enemies would be set aside, and so on (see Lev. 26:1–13; Deut. 28:1–14). But then Moses began a series of grim warnings of things to come if they broke that covenant (see Lev. 26:14–39; Deut. 28:15–68). In both chapters Moses warned that the conditions would be such that cannibalism would result (see Lev. 26:29; Deut. 28:53, 57). That prophecy was fulfilled not once but several times (see 2 Kgs. 6:29; Lam. 4:9–10).[6]

The second historical precedent was the echoing of Moses' warning by virtually every prophet after Moses. Joshua, Elijah, Elisha, Isaiah, Amos, Hosea, Micah—everywhere we look, the prophets are found reminding Israel of the basic choice: either be faithful and reap blessings or be unfaithful and reap curses and punishments. The third historical prophetic antecedent occurred approximately one hundred years before Ezekiel's time when the Northern Kingdom was taken captive by Assyria. It was destroyed, annihilated—it ceased to exist. The people were taken north into Assyria, scattered and assimilated, and lost to history. At the time when the Northern Kingdom fell, the southern border of the kingdom of Assyria was five miles north of Jerusalem. Judah escaped the fate of the Northern Kingdom only by divine intervention because King Hezekiah heeded the counsel of the prophet Isaiah (see 2 Kgs. 18–19; Isa. 36–37). Sennacherib laid siege to Jerusalem. Isaiah told Hezekiah not to worry, that not a single arrow would be fired against the city. And that night, in the quaint translation of the King James Version, 185,000 people woke up dead (see 2 Kgs. 19:35) and so Judah was delivered.

That event should have been such a graphic demonstration of the principle of spiritual survival—turn to God and live or face destruction—that Judah would have repented. But less than a century later, we find Judah back in the same state of wickedness facing a similar threat of destruction at the hands of Babylon. That is what we mean by the historical/prophetic antecedents of Ezekiel's time. He knew the warnings, he knew the doctrine, he knew the inevitable certainties if Judah did not repent.

Now let us look at the historical setting of Ezekiel's own day. In 612 B.C., Babylon began to seriously challenge the might of Assyria. Assyria was in a state of serious decay, so Babylonia moved north, and in 612 B.C. Nineveh fell. Basically that signaled the end of the Assyrian Empire. In 609 B.C. Egypt, preferring a weak Assyria to a strong Babylonia, made an alliance with Assyria. When the final battle between those two empires began, Egypt moved north to side with Assyria. It was at that time, though the scriptural record doesn't say why, that the righteous King Josiah of Judah tried to stop Pharaoh Necho at Megiddo. As nearly as we can tell, it was like a fly trying to stop a bull. Necho swatted the fly and moved on, leaving Josiah dead and Judah mourning (see 2 Kgs. 23:29–30; 2 Chron. 35:20–24). Though Assyria was destroyed, the battle between Egypt and Babylon ended more or less in a draw. Pharaoh Necho made Judah a vassal state, appointed King Jehoiakim as his puppet king, and made Judah pay tribute (see 2 Kgs. 23:31–35).

But Babylon was not through with Egypt. In 605 B.C., in what is called one of the significant battles of history, Egypt challenged Babylon in the battle of Carchemish. This time Babylon crushed Egypt and drove her all the way down into the plains of Philistia, which bordered Judah on the west. While he was there, King Nebuchadnezzar, having decided that he would teach this state of Judah who their new master was, besieged Jerusalem. Jerusalem was no match for his power and therefore capitulated easily. Nebuchadnezzar withdrew, taking a small group of captives back with him to Babylon. This was the first of three times captives were taken. Daniel was almost certainly taken to Babylon in this first group.

Even though Jehoiakim was now a vassal king to Babylon, for some reason not fully explained in the scriptures he still gave his allegiance to Egypt. Both Jeremiah and Ezekiel warned that Egypt was weak and not to be trusted (see Jer. 44:29–30; 46:1–2; Ezek. 17:15; 29:3, 19). Surprisingly, Egypt and Babylon clashed again in 601 B.C., but fought to a standstill this time. So Nebuchadnezzar withdrew back to Babylon. Ignoring the prophetic warnings, Jehoiakim decided that Babylon wasn't nearly as strong as Nebuchadnezzar had claimed, and he openly switched his allegiance to Egypt and stopped paying tribute to Babylon.

About 598 B.C. (traditional dating), Nebuchadnezzar decided to teach Judah a lesson. He laid siege to Jerusalem, killed King Jehoiakim, threw his body off the walls, and took three thousand captives.[7] Jehoiachin was appointed as the successor king.

In 2 Kings 24 we read the final outcome of this event. The passage beginning in verse 14 is particularly noteworthy in our study of Ezekiel: "And he carried away all Jerusalem, and all the princes, and all the mighty men of valour, even ten thousand captives, and all the craftsmen and smiths: none remained, save the poorest sort of the people of the land.

"And he carried away Jehoiachin to Babylon, and the king's mother, and the king's wives, and his officers, and the mighty of the land, those carried he into captivity from Jerusalem to Babylon.

"And all the men of might, even seven thousand, and craftsmen and smiths a thousand," and so on, and so on.

So Nebuchadnezzar virtually took the entire upper and middle classes of Jerusalem captive. Ezekiel, being a priest, was certainly included. Even though Ezekiel was now in Babylon, the events in Jerusalem still affected him and his work and are therefore of interest to us.

During the next ten years, Zedekiah, who was appointed to replace Jehoiachin as the ruler in Jerusalem, did not learn a thing from the previous tragedy, nor did Judah. In Jerusalem, false prophets began to abound, predicting that Babylon would be overthrown and the captives returned. While both Jeremiah and Ezekiel strongly denounced these men (see Jer. 28, 29; Ezek. 13), their presence added to the general confusion abounding in Jerusalem.

Then a second interesting event happened. Two prophets, Jeremiah and Ezekiel, reportedly uttered "contradictory" prophecies. Because these two prophecies seemed to directly contradict each other, Zedekiah rationalized that the two true prophets couldn't be trusted and went on listening to the false prophets. Let's examine the "contradictory" prophecies.

Jeremiah 34:2–3 says: "Thus saith the Lord, the God of Israel; Go and speak to Zedekiah king of Judah, and tell him, Thus saith the Lord; Behold, I will give this city into the hand of the king of Babylon, and he shall burn it with fire:

"And thou [Zedekiah] shalt not escape out of his hand, but shalt surely be taken, and delivered into his hand; [and then notice this phrase] *and thine eyes shall behold the eyes of the king of Babylon,* and he shall speak with thee mouth to mouth, and thou shalt go to Babylon" (emphasis added). That is Jeremiah's prophecy.

But in Ezekiel 12:13, Ezekiel said of Zedekiah, "My net also will I spread upon him, and he shall be taken in my snare: and I will bring him to Babylon to the land of the Chaldeans; *yet shall he not see it,* though he shall die there" (emphasis added).

It is obvious why the king thought the two prophets contradicted each other. Jeremiah said Zedekiah would look into the eyes of the king of Babylon, while Ezekiel said he would be taken into the land of the Chaldeans but would not see it, even though he would die there.

But of course they did not contradict each other. The fulfillment is an interesting one. When Nebuchadnezzar came a third time and conquered Jerusalem in 587 B.C., his generals captured all of the nobles, including Zedekiah and his sons (except Mulek, who escaped), and brought them north to the encampment of their king. Nebuchadnezzar came face to face with his prisoners (so they looked into his eyes) and killed the sons of Zedekiah as Zedekiah watched. Then he put out Zedekiah's eyes, blinding him, and carried him away captive into Babylon. Thus both predictions were fulfilled: Zedekiah looked into the eyes of the Babylonian king, yet he never saw the land of Babylon, where he was carried captive and later died.

But whatever the cause, Zedekiah and Judah did not repent. Again they revolted against Babylon, and so in 589 B.C. Nebuchadnezzar returned. This time he said, in effect, "We'll provide a lesson that everyone will listen to. Let us show the world what happens to those who rebel against Babylon." He left Jerusalem leveled and in ruins, and Judah was no more.

That is the historical setting in which Ezekiel lived and prophesied. Without an understanding of those circumstances, the meaning of Ezekiel's writings will largely remain obscure.[8]

Ezekiel the Answerer

In the face of Nebuchadnezzar's successes in Palestine and the eventual fall of Judah, four important questions naturally arose in the minds of the people:

1. *Is Jerusalem really going to be destroyed?* In those last ten years of the reign of Zedekiah, that question was asked again and again. This was partly because the false prophets were confusing the people and partly because the Jews couldn't believe "God's people" would ever fall.

2. *If God is really God, and we are really his chosen people, why is he allowing this to happen?*

3. *If we are being destroyed for being like the other nations* (which Ezekiel and other prophets had said many times), *then why aren't those nations destroyed?*

4. *What will this tragedy mean for the covenant?* What will happen to all of the promises God has made about Israel's eventual triumph and salvation?

Now, those are some profound questions, and Ezekiel answered each one of them. And in fact, it is in understanding those questions and seeing how Ezekiel sought to answer them that we gain the greatest insights into his book. As much of his work is aimed at answering those questions, let's take them one at a time.

1. *Is Jerusalem really going to be destroyed?* Ezekiel gives an unqualified, resounding, thundering yes! It is the major theme of chapters 4, 5, 6, 7, 8, 9, 11, 12, 15, 19, 21, 22, and 24. They all say Jerusalem has had it. That is a pretty hard answer to miss. Ezekiel himself went through several typological or symbolic actions to dramatize the coming disaster. For example, in chapter 4 he took a tile and drew a picture of Jerusalem on it. Then he put an iron pan against it. In that same chapter, by command of the Lord, he had to lie on his side for so many days, symbolizing the captivity, and then he was told to cook his bread with cow dung to symbolize that the people in Judah would eat defiled bread in coming times. In chapter 5 Ezekiel cut his hair and divided it into thirds, burning some and scattering

some, again symbolizing what the people would suffer. In chapter 12 he moved his whole household, showing that the house of Judah was going to be moved out of their dwelling place in Jerusalem.

In chapter 24 we read that Ezekiel's wife died on the very day Nebuchadnezzar besieged Jerusalem (see vv. 1–2). Here was given the ultimate symbol or type of Jerusalem's coming destruction. Beginning in verse 15, note what the Lord told him:

"Also the word of the Lord came unto me, saying,

"Son of man, behold, I take away from thee the desire of thine eyes [that is a Hebrew euphemism for *wife*] with a stroke: *yet neither shalt thou mourn nor weep, neither shall thy tears run down.*

"Forbear to cry, make no mourning for the dead, bind the tire of thine head upon thee, and put on thy shoes upon thy feet, and cover not thy lips, and eat not the bread of men.

"So I spake unto the people in the morning: and at even my wife died; and I did in the morning [within twelve hours of his wife's death!] as I was commanded" (emphasis added).

Isn't that something? The Lord said in essence that the death of Ezekiel's wife would serve as a type and symbol of Jerusalem's destruction. When the people saw his wife die and saw that Ezekiel did not mourn, they asked why. In verse 22 the answer was given: "Ye shall do as I have done: ye shall not cover your lips, nor eat the bread of men." And then in verse 24 the Lord explained: "Thus Ezekiel is unto you a sign: according to all that he hath done shall ye do." Jerusalem was the bride of Jehovah, but there could be no mourning, for her tragedy was just and fully deserved.

So in answer to the people's first question, "Will Jerusalem really be destroyed?" Ezekiel gives a clear and unmistakable answer—yes.

2. *If God is really God, and we are really his chosen people, why is he allowing this to happen?* To this second question, once again Ezekiel answers that God is God and Israel is the covenant people. But they have rejected the covenant through wickedness; therefore, the Lord allows these things to happen. Note how clearly Ezekiel responds to this second question:

Ezekiel 5:8: It is the Lord specifically who executes these judgments.

Ezekiel 7:4: The Lord not only refuses to have pity but specifically states, "I will recompense thy ways upon thee."

Ezekiel 7:19: Riches and wealth are "the stumblingblock of their iniquity."

Ezekiel 8: This entire chapter is devoted to a vision of the wickedness of Judah, including rampant idolatry which had even found its way into the temple (see vv. 3–10). The Lord concludes by saying, "*Therefore* [because of this wickedness] will I also deal in fury" (v. 18; emphasis added).

Ezekiel 16: This chapter contains a scathing denunciation of Israel. The chosen people are described as an illegitimate child; the Lord not only took her in (vv. 3–9) but adorned her like a bride (vv. 10–14) and married her himself. Instead of being faithful to her marriage to Jehovah, Israel played the part of the harlot (v. 15), whoring after false gods. Indeed, the Lord said, she was worse than a harlot, for such a woman is unfaithful because her lovers give her money and gifts. In her spiritual adultery, Israel actually gave gifts to her lovers—the false gods (vv. 26–34). Then in that same chapter, in equally vivid imagery (see vv. 44–59), the Lord compared Judah to her spiritual sisters, Samaria (i.e., the northern kingdom of Israel, now lost and destroyed) and Sodom (the epitome of spiritual corruption).

And so Ezekiel's answer to the second question thunders out again and again. Judah and Jerusalem will reap the whirlwind they have sown in wickedness for generations. In chapter 33, Ezekiel gives one of the most profound and clear expositions of why judgments come upon a people. Clearly, Ezekiel explains, God takes no pleasure in sending these judgments, but the people leave him no choice. Note especially the language of verses 10–11.

3. The third question raised by the tragedy of Judah has to do with the surrounding nations. The Lord often noted that the Jews were no different than their neighbors. Because they had committed whoredoms with Egypt, Assyria, and the Chaldeans, they were facing destruction. That is understandable, but the spinoff question is, *Why doesn't God destroy the other nations too?* Ezekiel answers this question in two ways. The first answer is based on the principle taught in Doctrine and Covenants 82:3, that "unto whom much is given much is required; and he who sins against the greater light receives the greater condemnation." Note how Ezekiel repeatedly reminded the people that they were the Lord's chosen, that they had the law and the covenant. They were not like the Gentiles in light and knowledge, but they had lowered themselves to maintain the same standards of behavior. (The following references are only a brief sampling of many where Ezekiel teaches this principle: Ezekiel 3:4–7; 5:5–7; 8:17–18; 9:9; 13:2–10; 16:6–9, 15; 20:5.) So his first answer to the third question is simply: You have greater light than they; therefore, more is required of you.

His second answer is also clear and simple: Whoever said that the other nations are exempt from the wrath of the Lord? Chapters 25 to 32 and chapter 35 describe the judgments that would come or had already come upon Ammon, Moab, Edom,

Philistia, Tyre, Sidon, Egypt, Assyria, and Babylon. While these nations were sometimes used by the Lord as the rods for punishing Israel, Ezekiel's prophecies show that they were not exempt from his judgments either.

4. The fourth question that arises out of the tragedy of these times is this: If Jerusalem is destroyed, if the temple is lost, if we are scattered among the Gentiles, *what does this mean for the covenant?* Are we totally rejected by God? Are the promises and prophecies now set aside?

In his answer to the first three questions Ezekiel is a "prophet of judgment," but his answers to this final question make him a "prophet of promise." A careful study of his writings shows that even the most harsh and caustic predictions and judgments were counterbalanced by an immediate addendum of hope. For example, after making dire and specific predictions of Jerusalem's destruction through famine, pestilence, war, and cannibalism (see Ezek. 5:5–17), after predicting that Israel will be smitten with such devastation that the bones of the people will lie unburied at the altars of their false gods (see Ezek. 6:4–5), the Lord tells Ezekiel: "Yet will I leave a remnant. . . . And they that escape of you shall remember me among the nations. . . . And they shall know that I am the Lord" (Ezek. 6:8–10).

Chapters 7 through 11 give an unremitting, uncompromising picture of Judah's wickedness and the consequent fury of the Lord—desolation, war, pestilence, destruction, widespread slaughter, and the carrying away of the survivors into captivity. But then again, once the Lord has poured out a picture of grim and stark despair he immediately, with two simple words, changes the tone. "*Although* I have cast them far off . . . *yet* will I be to them as a . . . sanctuary" (Ezek. 11:16). Then follows a specific prophecy of Israel's restoration—a prophecy of great hope and tremendous promise:

"Therefore say, Thus saith the Lord God; I will even gather you from the people, and assemble you out of the countries where ye have been scattered, and I will give you the land of Israel.

"And they shall come thither, and they shall take away all the detestable things thereof and all the abominations thereof from thence.

"And I will give them one heart, and I will put a new spirit within you; and I will take the stony heart out of their flesh, and will give them an heart of flesh:

"That they may walk in my statutes, and keep mine ordinances, and do them: and they shall be my people, and I will be their God" (Ezek. 11:17–20).

This pattern of judgment and hope is repeated over and over. Earlier in this chapter, mention was made of the scathing denunciation of Judah in chapter 16, where the covenant people are compared to a harlot and to the cities of Sodom and

Samaria. The words almost smoke even after twenty-six centuries. And yet when the denunciation was finished, there followed a promise of the restoration of the everlasting covenant, beginning with the hope-laden word "nevertheless" (Ezek. 16:60–63).

Additionally, we find in Ezekiel's writings some of the grandest and most promising prophecies of Israel's future restoration and acceptance by the Lord:

1. Israel will return to the covenant and experience an eventual conversion to the gospel (Ezek. 6:8–10; 11:17–20; 16:60–63; 17:22–24; 20:33–44; 33:11–16; 36:25–28; 37:1–14).

2. Israel will again have true prophets, loving pastors, and even the Messiah, the new David, to rule over them and teach them (Ezek. 34:16–25; 37:24–28).

3. The land of Israel will be blessed and become fruitful, productive, and inhabited again (Ezek. 33–35; 47:1–11).

4. Latter-day scripture will be joined with the writings of Judah (Ezek. 37:15–20).

5. Joseph and Judah will become one nation again, united under the gospel covenant (Ezek. 37:21–25).

6. The temple will be rebuilt in Jerusalem (Ezek. 37:26–28; see also chapters 40–47).

7. The nations of the world will gather against Israel, but will be defeated through the help of the Lord, bringing in an era of peace and triumph for them (Ezek. 38–39).

8. Israel will receive the land of promise as their permanent inheritance (Ezek. 47–48).

What a message of hope and inspiration! And note how directly each of those prophecies serves to answer these questions. Has the Lord forgotten Israel? Is the covenant no longer valid? Are the chosen people to be destroyed? Is the promised land lost forever? Thus we can truly call Ezekiel the prophet of judgment and promise.

Ezekiel the Writer

Our final area of examination is to look at the organization of Ezekiel's book. The text gives no clue to who collected and organized his writings into the book we now find in the Old Testament. It may have been Ezekiel himself, but whoever did it seems to have understood the four basic questions and Ezekiel's answers to them. Note the following structure:

- Chapters 1–3: God is God; he is real and has all power. He has called me, Ezekiel, as his prophet.
- Chapters 4–24: Because of idolatry, wickedness, and rejection of the covenant, Jerusalem is going to be destroyed and Israel scattered.
- Chapters 25–32: The surrounding nations are likewise going to reap the judgments of God because of their wickedness.
- Chapters 33–48: But God will still fulfill the covenants he made with the ancient patriarchs. Israel will not be totally destroyed. In the future they will be restored to their lands, converted to the true covenant, have righteous prophets, rebuild their temple, and accept the Messiah as their ruler.

Summary and Conclusion

There you have it—a quick "map tour" around Ezekiel. I admit that we have had to ignore much that is of great interest, much that is of great worth. And while this approach has been somewhat frustrating and incomplete, at least I hope you will return at your own leisure to read the book of Ezekiel and to study him in depth, using this introduction to help you find greater satisfaction and fruitfulness.

Notes

From Monte S. Nyman, ed., *Isaiah and the Prophets: Inspired Voices from the Old Testament,* vol. 10 in the Religious Studies Monograph Series (Provo: Religious Studies Center, Brigham Young University, 1984), 75–88.

1. J. D. Douglas, ed., *The New Bible Dictionary* (Grand Rapids, Mich.: Wm. B. Eerdmans Publishing Co., 1962), 406.
2. Samuel Fallows, *The Popular and Critical Bible Encyclopedia,* 3 vols. (Chicago: Howard-Severance Co., 1911), 1:639.
3. Flavius Josephus, *Antiquities of the Jews,* in *Josephus: Complete Works,* trans. William Whiston (Grand Rapids, Mich.: Kregel Publications, 1960), 10.6.3.
4. James Hastings, ed., *Dictionary of the Bible* (New York: Charles Scribner's Sons, 1909), 251.
5. Ibid.; see also Fallows, *Bible Encyclopedia,* 1:639.
6. See also Josephus, *Wars of the Jews,* in *Complete Works,* 6.4.4.
7. Josephus, *Antiquities of the Jews,* 10.6.3.
8. For excellent summaries of this period of history see Harry Thomas Frank, *Discovering the Biblical World* (New York: Harper and Row, 1975), 124–30; Michael Avi-Yonah, ed., *A History of the Holy Land* (Jerusalem: Jerusalem Publishing House, 1969), 90–97; *Great People of the Bible and How They Lived* (Pleasantville, N.Y.: Reader's Digest, 1974), 230–45.

Chapter 5

"Things Which Must Surely Come to Pass"

"One of the Plainest Books . . . Ever Written"

The original Greek title for the book known to us in English as the book of Revelation is *Apocalypsis.* The word is formed from the preposition *apo,* which has the basic meaning of separation, and the verb *kalypto,* which means "to cover, cover up" or "to hide, veil, i.e. to hinder the knowledge of a thing."[1] Thus, *apocalypsis* means "to remove or take away the covering, to unveil so as to make seen," and this definition explains the book's English title, which is based on the verb *reveal.* Scholars and students of the New Testament have noted the seeming irony of that title. Many find this unique work of scripture anything but a revealing of that which is hidden or an uncovering of the unknown. Indeed, they say it is one of the most veiled and difficult of all the scriptural books. It is a book that can be simultaneously fascinating and frustrating, intriguing and irritating, exciting and exasperating. Someone even explained its difficulty by suggesting that the book was written in code so that John could safely smuggle it past his Roman guards on the prison island of Patmos. Some Latter-day Saints have concluded that Nephi's prophecy that certain "plain and precious things" of the Bible would be lost (1 Ne. 13:28–29) is especially true in the case of the book of Revelation. They think *all* the plain and precious things have been removed.

Though such explanations may make us feel good about our inability to understand John's writings, they do not agree with the conclusion of the Prophet Joseph

Smith, who said, "The book of Revelation is one of the plainest books God ever caused to be written."[2] Elder Bruce R. McConkie said, "Most of the book—and it is no problem to count the verses so included—is clear and plain and should be understood by the Lord's people." Further, he said that the Lord "has not withheld the book of Revelation, because it is not beyond our capacity to comprehend."[3]

Even the most complex and baffling thing is simple to those who fully understand it. This is true also of the book of Revelation, and it explains why the Prophet found it to be one of the plainest books God ever caused to be written. He understood the doctrine and the things that John saw and therefore found it to be a plain and easily understood book. While many things would probably add to our understanding of Revelation, we can begin by using these three keys: (1) pay the price required, (2) learn the divine esoteric language, and (3) learn the organizational structure of the book.

The Apocalypse was written primarily for Saints of latter days. It reveals or uncovers the events of our own day and the near future. Therefore, it is of great value for us to put forth the effort necessary to make it a book of revealing, a book of revelation.

Paying the Price Required

It is obvious to even the beginning student of the scriptures that some portions of the scriptures are easier to understand than others. For example, the story of the sons of Mosiah and their mission to the Lamanites is exciting, fast moving, and easily understood. Isaiah, Revelation, and other portions of the scriptures are just the opposite, and most people have difficulty understanding them. Recognizing the greater difficulty of the book of Revelation, Elder Bruce R. McConkie said, "The language and imagery is so chosen as to appeal to the *maturing gospel scholar,* to those who already love the Lord and have some knowledge of his goodness and grace."[4] Clearly, we could not expect to sit down and read Revelation through once or twice and fully comprehend it. We must pay a price in diligent study, careful pondering, and spiritual development if the Apocalypse is to be a plain book. It was meant to be understood, but the Lord has apparently couched it in such a way that this understanding can be won only through personal effort. Three specific kinds of effort prove to be especially helpful in the case of the book of Revelation.

1. *We must develop a sensitivity to spiritual promptings as they relate to the study of the Revelation of John.* When all is said and done, the book of Revelation can be understood only by revelation. "In this connection, however," Elder

McConkie explained, "we must always remember that prophecy, visions, and revelations come by the power of the Holy Ghost and can only be understood in their fullness and perfection by the power of that same Spirit."[5] Often, as we study in the book, we find that the Spirit will gently confirm a particular interpretation of a passage or perhaps convey a quiet sense of uneasiness that suggests the interpretation is not correct. Following those subtle but very important promptings is one of the most important keys to understanding Revelation. And, of course, this sensitivity comes only when a price is paid in personal worthiness and by gaining experience in listening to the promptings of the Holy Ghost.

2. *We must have a broad knowledge of the gospel and the standard works.* On a flight from Salt Lake City, as the plane came over the San Bernardino Mountains and descended for its final approach into Los Angeles, we could see a grand vista spread out below us. Desert winds had polished away the smog, and the visibility was remarkable. The vast metropolis of southern California lay sprawled out below in crystal clarity. A young couple excitedly commented on the panorama before their eyes. "Oh, look!" one would cry, "that must be an airport." And then a moment later, "Look at that big stadium coming up there," or "That must be a freeway interchange down there. Look at all those cars." A man in the seat in front of the couple looked down at exactly the same scene, but he saw much more. As the couple spoke, the man thought, *Yes, that's Norton Air Force Base, and the big stadium is the Rose Bowl. The interchange is where the Santa Monica, San Bernardino, Hollywood, Pomona, and Santa Ana freeways meet.* He could not only identify particular freeways, parks, schools, and other landmarks, he could even look down and say to himself, *There is Jim Jones's home, and Karl Fisher's, and there's the 7-Eleven store that opened up last month.*

What made the difference in what these three people saw? Not what was there or even the clarity of the scene. It was their knowledge or lack of knowledge of the area. The man had lived in Los Angeles for several years. He had driven the streets, visited the houses, passed the parks, shopped in the stores. The young couple were visiting Los Angeles for the first time.

This analogy illustrates the importance of having a broad gospel knowledge if we are to understand Revelation. The Lord had John write the book for knowledgeable, spiritually aware Saints. Often, key concepts are not explained because John assumes his readers have a knowledge of the subject covered. He does not take time to say, as it were, "The big stadium is the Rose Bowl where some very important football games are played," and so on. He assumes that his readers are native to the area and that he need only mention the landmarks for them to know exactly what he refers to.

The area that John covers is the gospel and the scriptures, and the assumption is that his readers are natives of that area. The Lord has seen fit to reveal knowledge in a special way, as he himself says: "Here a little, and there a little" (D&C 128:21). One concept is planted here and another there, and thus the scriptures form a great latticework of interwoven, interdependent concepts. The more familiar we are with that latticework and those concepts, the more quickly we will understand and recognize them when John uses them. And though John had only former-day scriptures, the power of inspiration is such that he uses many concepts and ideas that are found only in latter-day scripture. That is one reason why only the Latter-day Saints can understand Revelation. Many keys to the knowledge John assumes his readers have are not found in the Bible.

Note, however, that we are not saying that Latter-day Saints *will* understand Revelation, only that they *can,* if they will gain a broad knowledge of the gospel and the language of the four standard works. Only then will they recognize the concepts, images, and doctrines revealed to John.

3. *We must diligently study the book of Revelation itself, probing, pondering, and searching for understanding.* The third price that must be paid in order to gain an understanding of Revelation is in the book itself. Our society is churning out so much information so fast that it is a valuable asset to be able to read, and read quickly. When this habit is carried over to the scriptures, however, it becomes detrimental. The primary purpose of reading scriptures is not to see how fast we can *cover* them but to see how much we can *absorb* of what is in them. This is true of all scripture, but it is especially true of Revelation. We must firmly grab ourselves by the mental collar again and again and pull ourselves back, asking the questions, Why does the Lord say that? What is the Lord trying to teach me with that image? Why does the Lord use that symbol? What does this convey? Why is that important? How am I to interpret this?

In many cases the very act of stopping, pondering, and probing for meaning will bring additional insights and important understanding. But often a further price of study must be paid through searching other scriptures for knowledge and insight (in other words, increasing our general knowledge of the gospel). More will be said later about how the scriptures can increase our understanding of Revelation, so let it suffice here to say only that time and time again the answer to the why or what or how of a specific verse can be clearly and easily answered from the scriptures themselves. Sometimes, however, the interpretation of a symbol or the explanation of a certain phrase is found not in the scriptures but in an understanding of the history and culture of John's time. We must realize that John wrote in a particular setting and that his readers were part of that same setting. He did not intend his writings to be obscure or incomprehensible to his readers. He wrote in their language. He was part of the same cultural background and heritage as they were, and they were familiar with special idioms or events that he used.

Every language and culture develops idioms—special phrases and ways of expression that are unique and yet easily understood within the culture. For example, one night a television talk-show guest referred to "the peanut farmer from Georgia." There were probably very few of the thousands watching who didn't know exactly what was meant by that phrase. But let's suppose that a thousand years from now, some enterprising archaeologist, excavating in the ruins of New York City, discovers a videotape of this show and replays it. Will he not, upon hearing the phrase "peanut farmer from Georgia," be puzzled and miss the significance of the phrase?

That is the situation we face in the case of the Apocalypse. Many of the phrases were clearly understood by the Saints of John's day, but we are far removed from those times, those situations, and that language. We must, through a study of nonscriptural sources, bridge that cultural gap and seek for the original, intended meaning. For example, in Revelation 13:16 John says, "And he [the beast] causeth all, both small and great, rich and poor, free and bond, to receive a mark in their right hand, or in their foreheads." Numerous interpretations of that passage have been given by various commentators, ranging all the way from saying it is a specific mark placed on the body of a person to wildly spiritualistic interpretations; however, knowledge of an ancient custom and a secondary practice derived from this custom sheds light on what John may have been trying to convey.

In the Roman empire there were vast numbers of slaves. Often a slave would run away from his master, go to a large city such as Rome, and try to disappear into the population. Since nothing about a human being marks him naturally as either a slave or free man, such runaways could pass as free persons as long as no one could personally identify them. To protect against that practice, slave owners would often brand their slaves with marks to identify them, just as modern stockmen permanently mark their animals for identification. To make this brand impossible to hide under clothing, most slaves were marked either on the palm of the right hand or on the forehead directly above the eyes. Therefore, it would have been common in John's time to see a person walking down the street with a mark on his right hand or on his forehead and to instantly identify him as a slave.

Out of that practice grew a secondary custom. Worshipers of various gods in the Roman pantheon, to symbolize the fact that they were totally dedicated to their god—in other words, that they were slaves or servants of their god—would also mark themselves on the right hand or the forehead. In this case they would mark themselves with a symbol of their god. Thus, a person might be seen walking down the street with a thunderbolt on his forehead, which symbolized that he was totally devoted to—that is, a slave to—Jupiter. A person marked with a trident said symbolically, "I am a servant of Poseidon, the god of the sea," and so on. John's readers, familiar with that concept and its significance, would not have puzzled over what he meant. To say that a person had the mark of the beast suggested that he was a slave of, or totally subservient to, the beast. Note that John uses the same imagery in a positive sense, indicating that there are those who are sealed in their foreheads with the mark of God (see Rev. 7:3). This use clearly signifies that these are people who belong to God; they are God's servants. Thus, while it is true that only Latter-day Saints have the additional keys necessary to correctly interpret Revelation, a careful study of non-LDS sources can bring many valuable cultural, linguistic, and historical insights that can greatly enhance our understanding of John's vision.

An understanding of Revelation can be won by those willing to pay the price and put forth the required efforts in terms of study, pondering, and personal preparation. But if we expect to master the book at any lesser cost, we will likely be disappointed.

Learn the Divine Esoteric Language

Esoteric language is words and phrases that have special meaning or significance only to an initiated "in group." The story is told that during the Six-Day War of 1967, the Syrian government broadcast a warning to the Druze, an Arabic people living in northern Galilee, that Israeli troops were slaughtering this people. When thousands of the Druze began to flee to Syria, the Israeli army went on the radio and announced that the reports were false. Almost as one, the Druze returned to their homes. When asked by a reporter how they knew that the Israelis were telling the truth and that this was not just some propaganda trick, the people replied that Druze never lie. They said that when the Israelis put a Druze on the radio and he denied the Syrian reports, they knew it was true. "But," the reporter persisted, "how could you be sure it was really a Druze on the radio? It could have been an Israeli trick." One Druze shook his head. "The Druze religion is secret, known only to our own people. When the man on the radio used words and phrases that have special meaning only to a Druze, we knew he was Druze." This is a dramatic instance of the use of esoteric language.

The Lord told his disciples that he taught in parables so that those who are spiritually sensitive might receive the message of his teachings, but the message would be missed by those who "seeing see not; and hearing they hear not" (Matt. 13:13). Elder McConkie said of the Lord's use of parables: "His purpose . . . was *not* to present the truths of his gospel in plainness so that all his hearers would understand. Rather it was so to phrase and hide the doctrine involved that only the spiritually literate would understand."[6] In other words, the Lord used a form of spiritual esoteric language to simultaneously *reveal* and *conceal* the meaning, depending on his listeners' gospel readiness.

This is a concept that has tremendous implications for a study of Revelation, for this is a book filled with esoteric language. Virtually every verse has words, phrases, symbols, numbers, and other verbal devices *that were designed to be understood* but *only by spiritually mature and sensitive Saints.*

As mentioned earlier, some Latter-day Saints have suggested that an explanation for the obscure nature of the book is that it was mutilated by apostate religionists who took out the "plain and precious things," as Nephi foresaw. But I am firmly convinced that just the opposite is true. Because these persons had no spiritual discernment, they missed the true significance of the divine esoteric language and left it relatively intact. This seems to be supported by the fact that Joseph Smith made fewer substantive changes in Revelation than he did in other parts of the New Testament (see chapter 6 of this volume for a fuller treatment).

This, of course, provides the modern reader with the challenges of learning the significance behind the spiritually loaded terminology and imagery. Three things seem to be especially helpful in interpreting the esoteric language of Revelation: the scriptures, the writings of the modern prophets, and the nature of the symbols themselves.

1. *Do the scriptures themselves give the key to the esoteric language?* Joseph Smith said, "I make this broad declaration, that whenever God gives a vision of an image, or beast, or a figure of any kind, He always holds Himself responsible to give a revelation or interpretation of the meaning thereof, otherwise we are not responsible or accountable for our belief in it. Don't be afraid of being damned for not knowing the meaning of a vision or figure, if God has not given a revelation or interpretation of the subject."[7] In hundreds of cases, we have no excuse for not understanding the divine imagery revealed to John, for the Lord has clearly

specified how the symbols are to be interpreted. Sometimes the key is given in the same context as the symbol itself; other times he explains its significance later on in the vision; or in many cases, the key is given somewhere else in the standard works.

Examples of passages whose interpretation is given in context:

- The "seven golden candlesticks" (Rev. 1:12) are "the seven churches" (Rev. 1:20).
- The "golden vials full of odours [incense]" (Rev. 5:8) are "prayers of saints" (Rev. 5:8).
- The "dragon" (Rev. 12:3) is "that old serpent, called the Devil, and Satan" (Rev. 12:9).
- The "fine linen, clean and white" (Rev. 19:8) is "the righteousness of saints" (Rev. 19:8).

Examples of passages whose interpretation is given elsewhere in Revelation:

- The "morning star" (Rev. 2:28) is Jesus Christ (see Rev. 22:16).
- The "seven heads [of the beast]" (Rev. 13:1) are "seven mountains, on which the woman sitteth" (Rev. 17:9).
- The "many waters" upon which the whore sits (Rev. 17:1) are "peoples, and multitudes, and nations, and tongues" (Rev. 17:15).

Examples of passages whose interpretation is given elsewhere in scripture:

- The "rod of iron" by which the nations are broken into pieces (Rev. 2:27) is "the word of God" or the gospel (1 Ne. 11:25).
- "Michael" (Rev. 12:7) is "Adam" (D&C 107:54).
- "Babylon" (Rev. 14:8; 16:19; etc.) is a symbol of the world and spiritual "wickedness" (D&C 133:14).
- The "white stone . . . [with] a new name" (Rev. 2:17) is a "Urim and Thummim" given to those who go to the celestial kingdom (D&C 130:10–11).

2. *Do the prophets give the key to the esoteric language?* We believe that what is written or spoken by the prophets under the inspiration of the Holy Ghost constitutes scripture (see D&C 68:2–5). In some cases prophets of the last dispensation have given us further clues for interpreting the divine esoteric language of Revelation. Though technically it could be classed as canonized scripture and placed in the first category, one of the most important prophetic writings is the Joseph Smith Translation of the Bible. His corrections and additions to Revelation

become important sources of interpretation. In addition he gave other clues in his sermons and writings, some of which dealt directly with John's visions. Other prophets and apostles have also provided us with significant interpretations that help us better translate the esoteric imagery.

The following are examples of interpretations given in the Joseph Smith Translation or other writings of Joseph Smith:

- The seven "angels of the seven churches" (Rev. 1:20) become the "servants," or leaders, of the seven churches (JST, Rev. 1:20).
- The "Lamb . . . having seven horns and seven eyes" (Rev. 5:6) becomes the "Lamb . . . having twelve horns and twelve eyes," perfecting the symbolism to identify Jesus and the twelve Apostles (JST, Rev. 5:6).
- The "woman" and the "man child" (Rev. 12:1–5) are clearly identified as the "church of God" and "the kingdom of our God and his Christ" (JST, Rev. 12:7).
- The "beast(s)" seen by prophets (Rev. 13:1–5) are representations of "the degenerate kingdoms of the wicked world."[8]

Examples of interpretations given by other apostles and prophets:

- The "angel [flying] in the midst of heaven" (Rev. 14:6) represents the angels of the Restoration, including Moroni, Peter, James, and John.[9]
- The time when "every island fled away" (Rev. 16:20) refers to the time when the continents will be rejoined into one land.[10]
- The binding of Satan (Rev. 20:2–3) will be accomplished through the righteousness of the Saints.[11]

3. *Does the nature of the symbol give insights into its significance?* The peoples of the ancient Middle East loved imagery and figurative language and used them constantly. They saw spiritual parallels in the natural characteristics of things that were around them every day. Animals, objects, events, and actions were observed and then used to express or teach figurative truths. In other words, the choice of symbols was not arbitrary or capricious; it was the nature of the item used that led to its use as a symbol. Therefore, if we take time to examine the symbols and ponder why the ancients chose them to represent symbolic truths, we often find important insights into their meaning. For example, trumpets were used anciently to sound an alarm, signal for battle, or announce the arrival of royalty. The sounding of trumpets, therefore, symbolized heralding or announcing something highly significant. This knowledge helps explain why the seven angels sound trumpets as each new judgment of the seventh seal is shown forth (see Rev. 8 and 9).

The candlestick is not a *source* of light but a *holder* of the light. Since the Church of Jesus Christ is not the actual source of truth but merely holds up Jesus Christ—the true light of the world—for all to see, the candlestick provides a beautiful representation of the church (Rev. 1:12–13, 20; cf. 3 Ne. 18:24).

Another example is the imagery of keys (see Rev. 9:1; 20:1). Anciently, locks were hand-carved out of wood or hand-forged out of metal and were large, bulky, and very expensive. They were used only to protect valuable treasures or stores and were rarely owned by the common people. The keys for such locks were also necessarily large and were typically worn around the neck on a chain. Because of what they guarded, the keys were given only to highly trusted or respected individuals. Therefore, anciently, if one saw a man on the street wearing a key or keys, one could rightly assume that he was a man of power and authority. In this manner keys came to be a symbol not only of control over something but also of invested power and authority.

Again and again we find that taking time to ponder the natural characteristics of the item chosen as a symbol becomes an important key for understanding the imagery. We should constantly ask, What is it about this thing that would have caused it to be used symbolically? Often we can answer this question from our own experience, but sometimes further research is necessary to see what the item was or how it was used anciently. Here again we see how non-LDS sources may be of value to us; and, more important, we see that a price must be paid in personal thought, study, and effort.

There are, perhaps, other ways for interpreting the divine esoteric language of Revelation, but these three—the scriptures, the prophets, and an examination of the symbol itself—are very helpful in understanding what was signified when John received the revelation. In some places in Revelation, none of these three sources provide the keys to understanding the language, and we must pass them over for now. But those passages are relatively few in number. For the most part, the Lord has made it possible to learn the key to what he says. It is an understanding of this esoteric language that then makes the book "one of the plainest books God ever caused to be written."[12]

Learn the Organizational Structure of the Book

One important question to be answered before we can understand any work of scripture has to do with its basic structure: how it was organized and the purposes for which it was written. The Book of Mormon follows a basically historical structure with pauses in the narrative to emphasize selected sermons; however, the chronological flow of the narrative is broken in several places. For example, Words of Mormon, written about A.D. 385, is inserted between writings completed more than five hundred years earlier. And Moroni, who wrote around A.D. 400, inserted into the record the book of Ether, which begins at the time of the Tower of Babel, about 2200 B.C. There are also numerous digressions and flashbacks in the basic historical story line. But if we understand that Mormon was writing an abridgment of many records and that his purpose was to bear witness of Jesus Christ for those living in the latter days, these seeming anachronisms become perfectly logical and do not violate the basically chronological development of the book.

The New Testament, on the other hand, has a completely different organizational structure. There is no grand unifying chronological development. It is a series of short works and letters collected into one book, and it would be foolish to look for a narrative flow such as we find in the Book of Mormon.

Thus, knowing the organizational structure of a work becomes very important if we wish to better understand its contents. This is especially true of Revelation. Understanding how it is laid out becomes critical not only to understanding the book as a whole but also for interpreting specific imagery and symbolic language. Three concepts related to the organizational structure are particularly helpful to remember as we examine how Revelation is organized: (1) John's vision revealed the history and destiny of the earth in chronological order; (2) the major emphasis of the vision is on only a small portion of that chronological line; (3) the chronological narrative is interrupted periodically with "teaching interludes." Before examining each of these concepts, let us first note that we will be talking only about the actual vision given to John. The introductory material (chapter 1), the letters to the seven churches of Asia (chapters 2 and 3), and the concluding summary (chapter 22, verses 8 through 21) will not be discussed here. We will examine only what John saw when he saw that "a door was opened in heaven" and he was told to "come up hither" (Rev. 4:1). This vision comprises the majority of the book (chapters 4 through 22) and is the heart of the Apocalypse.

1. *The vision given to John revealed the history and destiny of the earth in chronological order.* Throughout the centuries one of the most hotly debated questions about Revelation has had to do with the question of where it fits into history; that is, was what John saw related to his own time (which for us makes it history), or did it depict only future events (which are now becoming current or near future for us), or was it a combination of both? Some scholars even suggest that the vision was to be interpreted spiritually and has no correspondence to actual events in

either history or prophecy. Impressive evidence and persuasive arguments are marshaled for each point of view. But as we have already noted, the only way to understand Revelation is through revelation, and again we see why only the Latter-day Saints have the key for understanding this work.

In March 1832 Joseph Smith received a revelation (D&C 77) in which fifteen questions about the book of Revelation were asked and answered. Though some people would like to have seen more than fifteen questions asked, upon careful study we find that these fifteen do provide the key to understanding Revelation.

The word *key* is a good one. The Apocalypse is like a huge house whose doors are locked and whose windows are shuttered. We can peek in through a crack here and there and glimpse what is inside, but most of it remains hidden from our view. Section 77, however, gives us the key to the house. It does not tell us everything we would like to know about John's vision, but it provides a means whereby we can open the door, go inside the house, and begin to explore what is there.

The single most important clue for interpreting Revelation was given in this revelation received by the Prophet. The first thing John saw in heaven was a glorious being on a throne (Rev. 4:2–3) surrounded by various beings, all giving praise to him. The figure on the throne represented Elohim because he reigns supreme in heaven. In his right hand was a book (probably a scroll, since that was the common form of books of the day) that was sealed with seven seals (Rev. 5:1). An angel asked who was worthy to open the book, but no person in heaven or on earth or under the earth was worthy. Sensing the significance of this, John began to weep (Rev. 5:2–4). Then he was shown that there was no cause to weep because there was one person who could open the book—the Lamb of God (Jehovah, or Jesus Christ). When the Lamb took the book and prepared to open the seals, all heaven burst forth in a great hymn of praise (see Rev. 5:5–14).

Understanding what is symbolized by the book in the right hand of God becomes critical to understanding the book of Revelation, because the remainder of the vision is what John sees as the Lamb opens the seals one at a time. Section 77 explains what the book symbolizes. We are told that it symbolizes the history of the earth, which was to last for seven thousand years (D&C 77:6), and that each seal represents one of the thousand-year periods (D&C 77:7). The book is shown in God's hand because it is under his control and management. Only the Lamb of God is worthy to open it because only through the atonement of Jesus Christ does the history and destiny of the world unfold.

If each seal represents one thousand years of the earth's history, then we can assume, since the seals are opened in order, one at a time, that Revelation is a chronological outline of the history of the earth.

Because John describes in figurative and highly symbolic language what he sees as each seal is opened, it is difficult for us to instantly recognize this chronology. But knowing what the structure is—that it is basically a chronological unfolding of the history of the earth—helps us tremendously in interpreting the symbols and understanding the book. Without this key to the organizational structure, a key given in D&C 77, we can stray far afield in interpreting the book. For example, one Christian commentator was misled by not knowing how the book is structured. Speaking of the locusts seen as part of the opening of the seventh seal, John wrote, "And it was commanded them that they should not hurt the grass of the earth, neither any green thing, neither any tree; but only those men which have not the seal of God in their foreheads" (Rev. 9:4). This commentator gives the following fascinating explanation of John's imagery. Speaking of the time when the armies of Mohammed swept out of Arabia and across most of the known world, he says:

"I have a copy of the military command given to this great cavalry army by Abu-bekr, their commander, in A.D. 632, when they were on the verge of entering upon their invasions of Syria. He dispatched a circular letter to the Arabian tribes which reads as follows: 'When you fight the battles of the Lord, acquit yourselves like men, without turning your backs; but let not your victory be stained with blood of the women or children. *Destroy no palm trees, nor burn any fields of corn. Cut down no fruit-trees,* nor do any mischief to cattle, only such as you kill to eat.' . . .

"The prophecy [of John] did not say that the more humane injunctions here would be scrupulously obeyed, but the prophecy did say that it was so commanded them. What a wonderful fulfillment of prophecy this is—a command given to the advancing hosts, recorded in Scripture nearly 600 years before it was given by the military commander!"[13]

This is a brilliant and plausible explanation except for one serious problem. Revelation 9 takes place in the seventh seal or last thousand years (D&C 77:13), while the Moslem invasions described took place in the fifth thousand years!

Most Bible scholars assume that the person on a white horse seen when the first seal was opened (Rev. 6:2) symbolized Jesus Christ—again a reasonable and appealing explanation if we do not understand the chronology revealed in the vision. Knowing that the first seal represents the first thousand years (approximately 4000 to 3000 B.C.) and using John's imagery, we come to a different conclusion.

White. This symbol indicates righteousness, purity, sanctification.

Horse. In the ancient Middle East the horse was not used as a domesticated work animal, but was seen only at times of warfare and conquering armies. Therefore, throughout the Bible the horse is a symbol of war, conquest, and military power.[14]

Bow. In ancient warfare a man with a bow and arrow had one of the most effective weapons; it extended his power to strike far beyond his own person, silently and swiftly and with deadly accuracy. Therefore, the bow is a symbol of effectiveness in warfare.

Crown. Anciently royalty or people with ruling power wore crowns; therefore, the crown is a symbol of political position and power.

Conquest. This is not so much a symbol as it is a piece of information telling us that this person was successful in conquering.

We conclude that Enoch and his ministry best fit the known facts and the imagery. He lived in the first thousand years; he was a man of great righteousness (whiteness); he established a city called Zion, which eventually was translated (the crown of gold); and he led the people of God to battle (the horse) with great power (the bow). (See Moses 7:13–15.)[15]

While there is not space to examine fully the imagery of each seal and give its interpretation, a close examination of John's vision shows that the chronology is followed through from the times of Adam to the end of the world.

2. *The major emphasis of John's vision is only a small part of the chronology.* Though we have established that the structural outline of Revelation is chronological, it would be a grave error to conclude that John's purpose was simply to give an overview of the history and destiny of the world. The Prophet Joseph Smith said: "The things which John saw had no allusion to the scenes of the days of Adam, Enoch, Abraham or Jesus, only so far as is plainly represented by John, and clearly set forth by him. John saw that only which was lying in futurity and which was shortly to come to pass."[16] And twice in Revelation we are told that the emphasis was to be a future one (Rev. 1:1; 4:1).

So, while the flow of Revelation is organized around a chronological outline, we are not suggesting that every part of the chronology receives equal emphasis. A brief examination of the number of verses used to describe what is seen in each seal quickly shows where the major emphasis was to be. The first four seals are covered in two verses each (Rev. 6:1–8). Remembering that each seal covers a thousand years of history, we can safely conclude that John could do no more than highlight or emphasize one aspect of that period of history. Even in the fifth seal, the seal in which John himself lived, only three verses are used to describe what is seen when the seal is opened. So we can safely say that the Lord was not going to emphasize

The Visions of John—
A Chronology of the Earth's History

1st Seal	Enoch and Zion
2nd Seal	Wickedness and the Flood
3rd Seal	Famine and Israel
4th Seal	Age of the Empires
5th Seal	Age of Martyrdom
6th Seal	Restoration of the Church
	Natural Calamites
	Half-Hour of Silence
	Trumpets Announce Judgments
7th Seal	Babylon Is Destroyed
	Christ Comes in Glory
	Satan Is Bound
	Righteous Join Christ
	Millennium of Peace
	Satan Loosed for a Season
	Last Great Battle
	Final Judgment
	Earth Celestialized

even John's own time to John. Only when we come to the sixth seal does the detail start to expand. This seal (Rev. 6:12–17; 7:1–8) takes fourteen verses, a discussion that is seven times greater than each of the first four seals but still represents only a tiny part of the vision.

It is the seventh seal and the events thereof that comprise the vast majority of John's vision. We might expect that the Millennium, with its thousand years of peace, harmony, and righteousness would be a major emphasis of John's vision, but such is not the case. Even if we include the binding of Satan in preparation for the Millennium and the calling forth of the righteous to join Christ at the beginning

The Vision of John—Where Is the Emphasis?

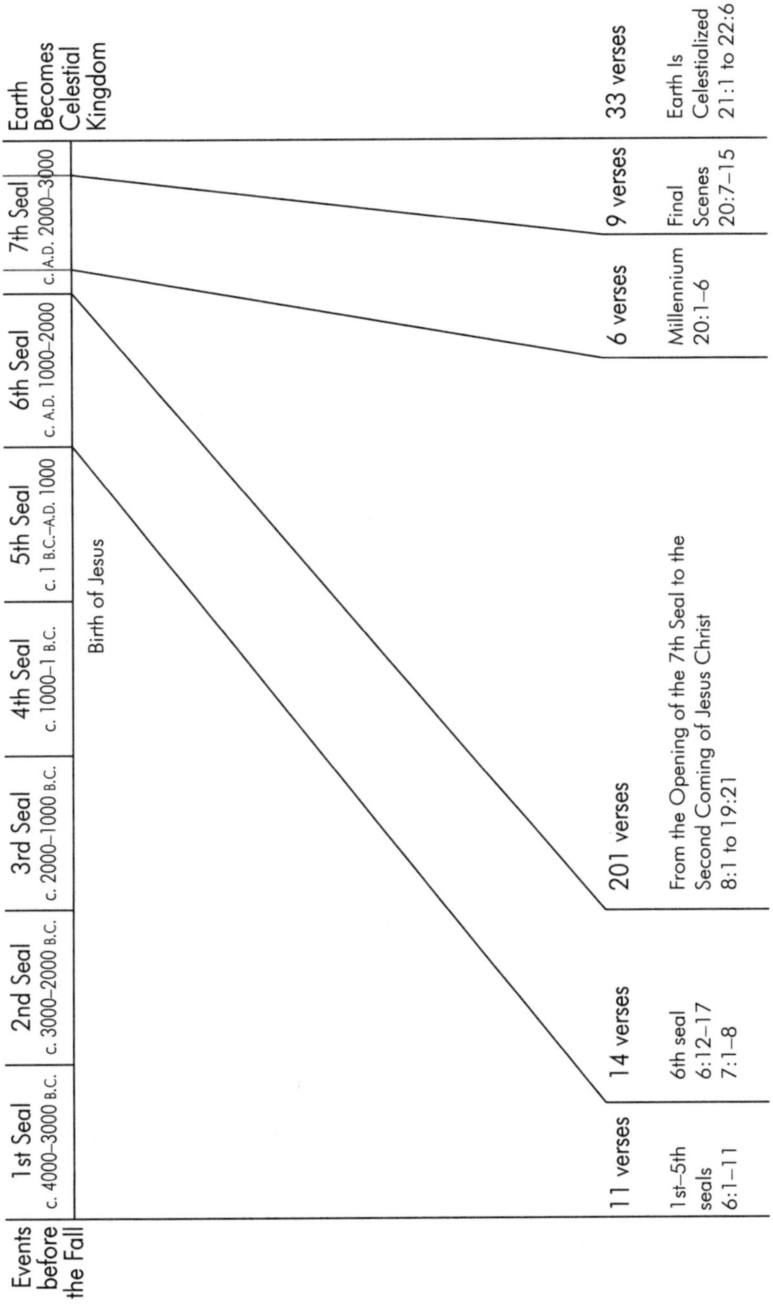

of the Millennium, only six verses describe the Millennium itself (Rev. 20:1–6). The final winding-up scenes of the earth's history, including the last great battle (Rev. 20:7–10), the final judgment (Rev. 20:11–15), and the celestialization of the earth (Rev. 21:1–27; 22:1–6), while given in some detail, comprise a total of only forty-two verses—still a small percentage of the total. Clearly John's major emphasis is on that tiny part of history that begins at the opening of the seventh seal and ends up with the second coming of Christ. Here again is dramatic evidence that Revelation is primarily a book for the Latter-day Saints. Though John had the stewardship for writing it (1 Ne. 14:18–28), most of it obviously deals with the times in which we are now living or will soon enter. It provides a vivid, detailed description of what Saints can expect in preparation for the second coming of Christ.

3. *The chronological narrative of the vision is interrupted periodically with "teaching interludes."* We have stated emphatically that the basic organizational structure of the Apocalypse is a chronological one. Immediately objections can be raised to that statement on the basis of the content. For example, in Revelation 12:7–9 we are given a brief description of the war in heaven, which took place before the world was even created. Yet chapter 12 is placed in that portion of the vision which is part of the seventh seal, or the last thousand years of the earth's history. For another example, Revelation 14:6–7 speaks of another angel flying through heaven with the everlasting gospel. This is a well-known reference to the restoration of the gospel in the last day. Since this took place in the early 1800s, this event would be part of the sixth seal, yet we find it in the midst of that part of the vision when the seventh seal is opened.

How do we explain these contradictions, these anachronisms in the chronological flow? As noted earlier, once we understand the purposes and organization of the Book of Mormon, the anachronisms of that book become clear and logical. So it is with the vision given to John.

Consider this analogy to help explain why there are pauses or digressions in the chronological flow of Revelation. A master teacher moves through a presentation in an organized and logical fashion. He has a clear idea of the concepts he wants to teach. Occasionally, however, he pauses in the logical flow in order to lay the foundations for concepts important to the overall development of his theme. To one who does not see the overall unity of his thematic development, such digressions may seem illogical and off the point. But in fact, they are necessary to the better understanding of the concepts to follow. We could refer to such digressions as teaching interludes.

This analogy helps us not only to explain the supposed anachronisms in the chronological flow of Revelation, but also to better understand what is happening and why. Like a master teacher, the Lord occasionally pauses in the development of the vision as it is being given to John and shows him other things that will support, explain, or expand his knowledge so that he (and his readers) can better appreciate the overall impact of what he is seeing.

The idea of teaching interludes can most easily be seen in Revelation 10, the so-called "little book" chapter. It is inserted in the midst of the vivid imagery John is using to describe the vast army of Armageddon (see Rev. 9:1–21), the last great battle in Jerusalem, and the two prophets who prophesy there (see Rev. 11:1–3). The "little book" chapter at first seems totally out of place and not part of the chronological flow. A mighty angel appears, gives John a small book, and requests that he eat it. When John does so, he finds it as "sweet as honey" in his mouth, but it makes his "belly bitter" (Rev. 10:1–11).

Through latter-day revelation we are given the interpretation of the little book, which helps us understand why this chapter is inserted where it is. In the fifteen questions found in Doctrine and Covenants 77, we find that the Prophet asked the significance of the little book that John ate. He was told that "it was a mission, and an ordinance, for him [John] to gather the tribes of Israel" (D&C 77:14; 7:3). In other words, in the midst of the vision of the last days, it is as if the Lord pauses and says to John, "Since you will live during these times, you may wish to know what you'll be doing. Here is your mission and calling."

There are five such interludes in the vision given to John. I believe that the teaching interlude concept explains the so-called anachronisms of Revelation. For example, the reference to the war in heaven (Rev. 12:7–11) comes in the midst of the kingdoms interlude and explains that Satan's opposition to the kingdom of God really began before the creation of the world. And the reference to the angels of the restoration (Rev. 14:6–7) shows that it is through the restoration in the latter days that Christ's kingdom will triumph over Satan's.

Summary and Conclusion

Joseph Smith said, "The book of Revelation is one of the plainest books God ever caused to be written" (*Teachings,* p. 290). When we come to see the structure and outline of the book and understand the divine esoteric language by paying the required price in diligent study and prayer, we will be able to nod our heads in agreement with the Prophet. Joseph did not suggest that it was one of the *easiest*

THE BOOK OF REVELATION

THE SEVEN SEALS
(The Seven 1,000-Year "Days" of the Earth's Temporal Existence*)

ETERNITIES PAST

Premortal Existence — Creation

FALL OF ADAM

1	2	3	4
Adam's ministry begins	City of Enoch translated	Abraham's ministry	Israel divided into two kingdoms
Wickedness begins to spread	Noah's ministry	Isaac, Jacob, and twelve tribes of Israel	Isaiah's ministry
Repentance taught by prophets	The Great Flood—mankind begins again	Joseph; Israel's bondage in Egypt	Ten tribes conquered and lost
Adam gathers and blesses his children	Tower of Babel	Moses' ministry	Prophets rejected
Adam dies	Jaredites come to Promised Land	Conquest of land of Canaan	Judah taken captive
Enoch's ministry		Israelites begin to have kings	Period of apostasy

Joseph Smith said: "The things which John saw had no allusion to the scenes of the days of Adam, Enoch, Abraham or Jesus, only so far as is plainly represented by John. . . . John saw that only which was lying in futurity and which was shortly to come to pass" (*Teachings,* p. 289). That such is the case is evident when we see that the first five seals are dealt with in 11 verses (only 3% of the total verses) while 281 verses (70%) deal with the events of the sixth and seventh seals and the final glory of the earth.

The Kingdom of God—

John summarizes the highlights of the first five seals	Great calamities to be shown during the 6th seal	Destruction is held back while righteous are sealed—gospel's restoration	Seven trumpets announce coming judgments	Two witnesses in Jerusalem during great war there	7th trumpet sounds—voices in heaven announce triumph of kingdom
(6:1–11)	(6:12–17)	(7:1–8)	(8:1–13; 9:1–21)	(11:1–13)	(11:13–19)

John sees those saved in God's kingdom

Just prior to the sounding of the seven trumpets of judgment, John is shown the multitude of those who have achieved salvation praising God and the Lamb in the celestial kingdom (7:9–17).

The "little book" interlude

Between the sounding of the sixth trumpet and the vision of the two witnesses in Jerusalem, an angel delivers a book to John and commands him to eat it. We know from latter-day revelation that this symbolized a special mission given to John to participate in the gathering of Israel (D&C 77:14). Thus John is shown his part in the great events of the future which he sees in vision (10:1–11).

An explanation of the kingdom of God and its opposition from Satan's kingdom

The voices in heaven announced the coming triumph of the kingdom of God. This kingdom and its great satanic counterpart are now discussed in some detail.

I. THE CHURCH & KINGDOM OF GOD

A. The Church (the ecclesiastical aspect of the kingdom) brings forth the kingdom where Christ reigns as king (the political aspect of the kingdom).

B. The Church and kingdom of God are opposed by the great dragon (Satan).

C. This opposition actually began in the premortal existence and caused war in heaven.

D. The church of John's time would not bring forth the kingdom but would be driven into the wilderness (apostasy) by the dragon (12:1–17).

*These "days" should not in any way be confused with the major gospel dispensations. Such dispensations have not been initiated at regular intervals but have been subject to the wisdom of God and the willingness of man to believe the prophets.

Our Day: The Saturday Evening of Time

The Earth's Sabbath

5	6	7
John the Baptist's ministry	Renaissance and Reformation	Final destruction of the wicked
Christ's ministry	Industrial Revolution	Christ comes to reign as King of kings
Church established	Joseph Smith's ministry	Earth receives paradisiacal glory
Atoning sacrifice made	Church becomes world church	Satan bound
Gospel taken to the Gentiles	Saints prepare for Christ	Millennial era of peace, love
Great Apostasy and the Dark Ages	Great calamities worldwide	Earth celestialized at close of Millennium
	Zion fully established	

FALL OF ADAM

ETERNITIES FUTURE

Probationary Period Ended

Degrees of Glory Realized

While the events of the future ages were revealed around the basic chronological framework of the seven seals, it does not seem to have been the Lord's purpose to arrange every aspect of the revelation in a strict order of their occurence. Like a master teacher who digresses from his presentation to further clarify or expand what he teaches, even so the Lord interrupts the order of the presentation to give greater insight, further truths, deeper knowledge of the marvelous future destiny of his kingdom. These "teaching interludes" are shown on the chart below.

Its Triumphant Destiny

Vials of judgment poured out on the world—wicked still do not repent	Voice announces in heaven the final triumph of Christ's kingdom	Christ comes as King of kings—final destruction of the wicked	Satan is bound	The righteous are redeemed, and the Millennium begins	Satan loosed at end of Millennium; his final conquest and banishment	The great and last judgment	A new heaven and new earth—the world is celestialized
(15:5–8; 16:1–21)	(19:1–10)	(19:11–21)	(20:1–2)	(20:3–6)	(20:7–10)	(20:11–15)	(21:1–27; 22:1–5)

II. THE CHURCH & KINGDOM OF SATAN

A. John sees the beast from the sea and is shown that Satan has power over earthly kingdoms (the political aspects of his kingdom).
B. John sees the beast from the earth exercising great evil through religious power (the ecclesiastical aspects of his kingdom).
C. The followers of the beast are sealed in their foreheads to mark their allegiance (13:1–18).

III. THE FINAL OUTCOME

A. John sees the Lamb on Mount Zion with those who have been sealed in their foreheads by God (the 144,000).
B. John sees the angelic restoration of the gospel, which signals the fall of Satan's dominions.
C. The Son of Man is seen in heaven with the sickle and winepress. The great harvest (judgment) of the wicked is to begin (14:1–20).

The destruction of Satan's kingdom

After the seven vials of judgment have been poured out, an angel explains the symbolism of the great whore and the beast. He is then shown the great overthrow of the whore (the symbolic representation of Satan's kingdom and the counterpart of the true church—the bride of Christ). The world laments in great sorrow the fall of Satan's empire (17:1–18; 18:1–24).

John sees those saved in God's kingdom

Just prior to the pouring out of the vials of judgment, John is shown the multitude of those who overcame the beast praising God and the Lamb in the celestial kingdom (15:1–4).

books to understand, only one of the *plainest.* And since it reveals our time and the fast-approaching future, it is of critical importance that it become plain to us.

Notes

From "The Book of Revelation: Three Keys for Making It a Book of Revelation," in *A Symposium on the New Testament* (Salt Lake City: The Church of Jesus Christ of Latter-day Saints, 1984), 114–21.

1. Carl Ludwig Wilibald Grimm, *A Greek-English-Lexicon of the New Testament,* trans. and rev. Joseph Henry Thayer (Grand Rapids, Mich.: Baker Book House, 1977), 57, 323. This reference is commonly known as *Thayer's Greek-English Lexicon of the New Testament.*
2. Joseph Smith, *Teachings of the Prophet Joseph Smith,* comp. Joseph Fielding Smith (Salt Lake City: Deseret Book, 1976), 290.
3. Bruce R. McConkie, "Understanding the Book of Revelation," *Ensign,* September 1975, 87.
4. Ibid., 89; emphasis added.
5. Ibid., 86.
6. Bruce R. McConkie, *Mormon Doctrine,* 2d ed. (Salt Lake City: Bookcraft, 1966), 553.
7. Smith, *Teachings of the Prophet Joseph Smith,* 291.
8. Ibid., 289.
9. James E. Talmage, *Articles of Faith,* 3d ed. (Salt Lake City: The Church of Jesus Christ of Latter-day Saints, 1916), 308; Bruce R. McConkie, *Doctrinal New Testament Commentary,* 3 vols. (Salt Lake City: Bookcraft, 1965–73), 3:527–29.
10. Joseph Fielding Smith, *Church History and Modern Revelation* (Salt Lake City: The Council of the Twelve Apostles of The Church of Jesus Christ of Latter-day Saints, 1953), 1:264; see also D&C 133:23.
11. Eldred G. Smith, in Conference Report, April 1970, 142; see also 1 Ne. 22:26.
12. Smith, *Teachings of the Prophet Joseph Smith,* 290.
13. H. M. S. Richards, Jr., *What Is in Your Future?* (Los Angeles: Voice of Prophecy, 1972), 23–24; emphasis added.
14. Samuel Bishop Fallows, *The Popular and Critical Bible Encyclopedia* (Chicago: The Howard-Severence Co., 1904), s.v. "horse"; James Hastings, *Dictionary of the Bible* (New York: Scribner, 1963), s.v. "horse."
15. See also McConkie, *Doctrinal New Testament Commentary,* 3:476–78.
16. Smith, *Teachings of the Prophet Joseph Smith,* 289.

Chapter 6

Insights from the Joseph Smith Translation into the Book of Revelation

As noted in the previous chapter, the book of Revelation is one of the most intriguing and controversial books in the biblical library. Most scholars agree that it is one of the most difficult books in either the Old or New Testaments.[1] Typically, modern readers, including Latter-day Saints, find its imagery strange, its prophecies filled with bizarre and baffling imagery, its message unclear. Not surprisingly, therefore, it is largely left alone and unread.

As mentioned before, the title of the book in Greek is *Apocalypsis,* from which we get its other common name, the Apocalypse. *Apocalypsis* is formed from two Greek words—*apo,* a preposition meaning separated or removed from, and *kalypto,* a verb meaning to cover, hide or conceal.[2] *Apocalypsis* literally means to remove or to take away the covering or veil.[3] Hence its title in English, the book of Revelation (or the uncovering or unveiling).

Some would say that without question that title is one of the most ironic or misleading titles in the whole of scripture. There is no book, they say, that is more veiled or unrevealing than this one.

One of the Plainest Books

Even some Latter-day Saints find it difficult to believe that the book reveals or uncovers much truth. But the Prophet Joseph Smith, in a sermon delivered in 1843, stated that "the book of Revelation is one of the plainest books God ever caused to be written."[4] And his work on the new translation of the Bible bears that out. If the book is obscure and mystifying because of a great loss of original material, the Prophet did not see fit to restore the lost material. While admittedly this is an argument from silence, it is interesting to compare his work on Revelation with his work on some other books thought to be more plain and clearly understood.

For example, the Gospel of Matthew is not generally considered to be a mysterious or difficult book. Yet in his work on that book, the Prophet made changes in 618 of the 1,071 verses in Matthew, or 58 percent of the total. In addition to the changes, he added the equivalent of 51 verses of totally new material, which is an expansion of another 5 percent of the total text.[5] Compare these changes with the book of Revelation, where he added only three new verses (JST Rev. 1:7; 2:27; 12:7) and made changes in only 90 of the 394 verses, or 23 percent of the total.[6] In the book of Genesis, as another comparison, the Prophet changed about half the verses and added the equivalent of about 250 new verses, literally pages and pages of new material.[7] Yet the book of Revelation gets only three new verses and relatively few other changes.

Some might think those figures could be the result of the fact that the Prophet worked through the Bible sequentially. Since the book of Revelation is last, it received the least amount of work and therefore reflects the smallest number of changes. Again the evidence does not substantiate this.

As Robert J. Matthews notes, while the Prophet did not generally indicate which portion of the scriptures he was working on at various times, nor how long he spent on any one book, we do have some solid evidence that "in the work of revision the Prophet was moving back and forth in the New Testament rather than working continuously through the Bible in a consecutive order."[8] We find this entry in the Prophet's history: "Upon my return from Amherst conference, I resumed the translation of the Scriptures. . . . Accordingly, on the 16th of February, 1832, while translating St. John's Gospel, myself and Elder Rigdon saw the following vision."[9] Then followed section 76. On 1 March 1832 we find this entry: "About the first of March, in connection with the translation of the Scriptures, I received the following explanation of the Revelation of St. John."[10] Section 77 follows. As Matthews concludes, "It is unlikely that the work would have progressed consecutively in the short span of two weeks from Chapter 5 of John to the Book of Revelation. A more plausible conclusion suggests that the brethren were not following the New Testament consecutively."[11]

The Book of Revelation: Meant to Be Understood

We are left with the clear conclusion that John's Revelation was meant to be understood when it was first written, and was meant to be understood today. The

Prophet said it was one of the plainest of books, and so it should be. Elder Bruce R. McConkie in response to the question, "Are we expected to understand the book of Revelation?" answered:

"Certainly. Why else did the Lord reveal it? The common notion that it deals with beasts and plagues and mysterious symbolisms that cannot be understood is just not true. It is so far overstated that it gives an entirely erroneous feeling about this portion of revealed truth. *Most of the book*—and it is no problem to count the verses so included—*is clear and plain and should be understood* by the Lord's people. . . .

". . . He [the Lord] has withheld the sealed portion of the Book of Mormon from us because it is beyond our present ability to comprehend. We have not made that spiritual progression which qualifies us to understand its doctrines. But he has not withheld the book of Revelation, because it is not beyond our capacity to comprehend; if we apply ourselves with full purpose of heart, we can catch the vision of what the ancient Revelator recorded."[12]

The World's Confusion

All of this is not meant to imply that the book of Revelation is simple or easily understood. In the quote above, where he talked about it being understandable, Elder McConkie added the qualifying phrase, "If we apply ourselves with full purpose of heart." He went on in the same article to say, "The language and imagery [of the book of Revelation] is so chosen as to *appeal to the maturing gospel scholar, to those who already love the Lord and have some knowledge of his goodness and grace.*"[13]

An understanding of the book comes only when a price is paid in study, pondering and general gospel knowledge. But that alone is not enough. Bible scholars pay the price in terms of time and effort. They study the culture and background. They pore over the original Greek, looking for every nuance and clue. They know the emperors and the historical milieu in which John wrote. They know all of that, and yet there is still no consensus as to what is truly revealed by John.

To illustrate the confusion and babble of interpretive voices, let us just take one example of the world's attempt to explain a highly symbolical passage found in chapter 9 of Revelation. Under the sounding of the fifth trumpet, John saw a "star fall from heaven" and open the "bottomless pit" (Rev. 9:1–2). Out of the pit came a vast cloud of locusts which John says were commanded "that they should not hurt the grass of the earth, neither any green thing, neither any tree; but only those men which have not the seal of God in their foreheads. And to them it was given that they should not kill them, but that they should be tormented five months" (Rev. 9:3–5).

Note just a sampling of the scholars' attempts to explain what John saw. Adam Clarke, in the first half of the nineteenth century, wrote:

"*Locusts]* Vast hordes of military troops: the description which follows certainly agrees better with the *Saracens* than with any other people or nation, but may also apply to the Romans.

"*As the scorpions of the earth have power]* Namely, to hurt men by *stinging* them. Scorpions may signify *archers;* and hence the description has been applied to *Cestius Gallus,* the Roman general, who had many *archers* in his army. . . .

"*That they should be tormented five months]* Some take these months *literally,* and apply them to the conduct of the Zealots. . . . Others consider the *months* as being *prophetical* months, each *day* being reckoned for a *year;* therefore this period must amount to one hundred and fifty years."[14]

Dummelow, another nineteenth-century scholar, did not believe they were men at all. He says, "from the smoke issue *evil spirits with the appearance of locusts.* They are not to hurt green things, for they are not really locusts."[15] Merrill C. Tenney cites Mauro, who concludes that since trees are used elsewhere as symbols for human greatness or people of eminence (e.g., see Jer. 7:20; Ezek. 31:3), the "grass of the earth" (Rev. 9:4) would be the masses of common people.[16] Clearly nervous about that interpretation, Tenney finally only ventures that the locusts "are really an invasion from another world of malicious embodied spirits whose mission is destruction."[17]

One of the more creative attempts to explain the symbolism is by H. M. S. Richards, Jr., who equates Mohammed, founder of the Islamic faith, to the star that fell from heaven, and the bottomless pit to "the waste of the Arabian desert."[18] He then goes on to explain the symbolism of the locusts:

"I have a copy here of the military command given to this great cavalry army by Abu-bekr, their commander, in A.D. 632, when they were on the verge of entering upon their invasions of Syria. He dispatched a circular letter to the Arabian tribes which reads as follows: 'When you fight the battles of the Lord . . . *destroy no palm-trees, nor burn any fields of corn. Cut down no fruit-trees.*'"[19]

These are the acknowledged experts in the New Testament, and yet they still cannot come to a consensus of opinion. But, one asks, doesn't this very confusion disprove your statement that the book of Revelation was meant to be understood? No. What we are saying is that to the world it is a confusing book and that study alone is not enough to open its mysteries to our view.

THE INSTRUMENTALITY OF JOSEPH SMITH

It was Peter who said that "no prophecy of the scriptures is given of any private will of man. For the prophecy came not in old time by the will of man. But *holy men of God* spake as they were moved by the Holy Ghost" (JST 2 Pet. 1:20–21; emphasis added).

It is through the instrumentality of a prophet, the Prophet Joseph Smith, that the correct interpretation of John's vision is to be had. Without it, it is indeed a book covered by a veil, hidden from our view. But with what the Prophet has revealed it becomes understandable. It fulfills and justifies its title as a book of revelation.

The Prophet gave us access to the mysteries of Revelation through four major means:

1. Latter-day scripture.
2. Non-scriptural sermons and writings.
3. Doctrine and Covenants 77.
4. Joseph Smith Translation revisions of the text of Revelation.

Since the focus of this chapter is the contributions of the JST to our understanding of the book of Revelation, we shall skip over the first two quickly, giving only an example or two of each.

One example of a contribution from latter-day scripture is found in Doctrine and Covenants 130:7–11. There the Prophet explained the meaning of two important symbols used by John, namely the sea of glass before the throne of God (see Rev. 4:6) and the white stone given to the faithful (see Rev. 2:17). Another is found in Moses 4:1–4 and Doctrine and Covenants 76:25–30, which give more information about the war in heaven, which John barely mentions (see Rev. 12:7).

One example of the Prophet's contribution through his nonscriptural sermons or writings is where he said that John "saw the same things concerning the last days, which Enoch saw."[20] That is a significant clue to help us as we interpret Revelation. Another example is a lengthy sermon given in Nauvoo on 8 April 1843.[21] The whole sermon is an exposition of John's revelation. In a few instances, the Prophet verbally corrected passages in the New Testament, but for one reason or another those changes never made it into the Joseph Smith Translation.[22] Two such changes involved verses in the book of Revelation.[23]

Section 77: The Key to Understanding Revelation

The third area of contribution in which the Prophet Joseph added to our understanding of the book of Revelation is section 77 of the Doctrine and Covenants.

In his journal, the Prophet noted, "About the first of March, in connection with the translation of the Scriptures, I received the following on the Revelation of St. John:"[24] Section 77 was then given.

Though not actually part of the JST text, section 77 was given as part of the translation process and therefore must be considered as part of the Joseph Smith Translation contributions. And though not part of the actual text, section 77 certainly ranks as one of the most important, if not the most important, contributions of the Prophet in aiding our interpretation of the book of Revelation.

Section 77 contains fifteen questions and answers about the text of the book of Revelation, though the Prophet gives no indication whether the questions were his or were part of the revelation. Fifteen questions seems at first to be a woefully inadequate amount when one considers the number of questions raised as the text is read. Nevertheless, a careful study of section 77 shows that these fifteen questions do indeed provide the key so we can enter into the "house" of Revelation and begin to explore. Smith and Sjodahl, expanding upon the analogy of the key, say:

"But this Revelation [section 77] is not a complete interpretation of the book. It is a *key.* A key is a very small part of the house. It unlocks the door through which an entrance may be gained, but after the key has been turned, the searcher for treasure must find it for himself. . . . From the key thus given, from the Old Testament prophecies, and from history, ecclesiastical and political, it should be possible to interpret the rest. As Champollion, by the key furnished in the brief text on the Rosetta stone, was able to open the secrets of Egyptian hieroglyphics, so the Bible student should be able to read the Apocalypse with a better understanding of it, by the aid of this key."[25]

The key lies in the fifteen questions asked and answered in the section.

The Textual Changes

The final contribution of the Prophet to our understanding of the Apocalypse is in the actual work he did on the text of Revelation as part of his inspired translation of the Bible. As was noted earlier, he deleted from, added to, or changed a total of ninety verses. Obviously, not every one of those changes is of equal significance. The committee that worked on the LDS edition of the King James Version included changes for only forty-seven of the ninety verses, or just slightly better than half of the total changes. Taking that as some indication of the number of significant changes, we could say that the Prophet significantly altered only 12 percent of the total verses. Twelve percent is not a staggering proportion, but that percentage does not convey the importance of the contribution made by the Prophet's work on the text of the Apocalypse. Much in the same way as section 77, the verses so changed often become a key to opening our understanding to a passage or even sometimes to a whole concept taught by John.

Now that we have briefly discussed the four areas of contribution made by the Prophet, we shall begin an analysis of the Revelation of John to see how the Prophet has opened this book to our understanding. Since our focus in this chapter is primarily on the contribution of the JST to our understanding of Revelation, we shall focus on the contributions of section 77 and the actual textual changes of the JST, though where appropriate we may note contributions from latter-day scripture or the Prophet's other writings. Space allows discussion of only the most significant of the contributions from all four areas.

The Vision Opens: Chapter 1

John says it was on Patmos, on a Sunday, that he received the grand and glorious visions recorded in Revelation (vv. 9–10). Chapter 1 provides the prologue to all that follows, and interestingly enough the Prophet made more changes in this opening chapter than in any other chapter except chapter 12. From those changes we learn the following:

1. The Revelation is of John. It is his testimony and witness that is being recorded (see JST Rev. 1:1, 2, 4, 5). This in no way lessens the fact that the source of the vision and inspiration is divine, but the KJV suggests that the revelation is from God to Jesus Christ (see v. 1). The JST clearly identifies it as being given to John, a servant of God, *from* Jesus Christ. Why is this significant? It is another example of how the Savior views his prophets and apostles. They are his servants and he honors them for their faithfulness.

2. The KJV indicates that the revelation was given because "the time is at hand" (v. 3). The JST clarifies what time is meant when it says, "for the time of the coming of the Lord draweth nigh" (JST v. 3).

3. In several places in the opening chapters, reference is made to "seven Spirits" (Rev. 1:4; 3:1; 4:5) and seven angels or "angels of the seven churches," each of which is then identified with a particular group of Saints (see Rev. 1:20; 2:1, 8, 12, 18; 3:1). As is, this makes it sound as though the seven spirits and the seven angels are different things. But the Prophet changed or explained all references to the seven spirits and the seven angels to show that the seven spirits and the seven angels both refer to the leaders of the seven churches (see JST for all of the above verses). John, who at this time is the leader of the Church, is writing to seven

branches of the Church in Asia. The JST makes it clear that he specifically addresses the leaders (the bishops or branch presidents, as it were) of each of these branches.

4. Also the JST makes it clear that the seven spirits (now servants) are the receivers, not the source, of the vision (see JST Rev. 1:4).

5. Finally, the Prophet added to the concept of Christ's second coming that he would come clothed in "the glory of his Father" and be accompanied by "ten thousand of his saints" (JST Rev. 1:7). Perhaps here is a good time to note that in Greek the largest named number was ten thousand, which is the word "myriad."[26] Often it is used symbolically to express uncountable numbers.

The Seven Letters: Chapters 2 and 3

Immediately following the opening vision, the Savior, through the angel representing him, dictated seven letters to the seven churches of Asia. Though often neglected in favor of the prophetic visions, these seven letters are choice, individualized pieces of personal revelation. The Prophet made very few changes, the most significant of which include:

1. As noted above, throughout these letters the Prophet changed the wording to make it clear that each letter was addressed to the presiding authority of each church.

2. The bed into which the false prophetess and those who followed after her was to be cast is actually "hell" (see JST Rev. 2:22).

3. Those who are faithful in Thyatira are promised that they will be given power over nations and will rule them with a rod of iron, smashing them to pieces like clay pots (Rev. 2:26–27). This seems contradictory in the KJV. Faithful Saints are promised the power to smash the nations to pieces. This symbolism is strongly suggestive of tyranny. The imagery of Nephi's vision shows that the iron rod is a symbol of the word of God (see 1 Ne. 15:23–24), which helps somewhat, but in the JST, the Prophet dropped the imagery of smashed pottery and turned it instead into the idea of a potter shaping and molding vessels. He said that those who were faithful in keeping the commandments would rule the nations "with the word of God; and they shall be in his hands as the vessels of clay in the hands of a potter; and he shall govern them by faith, with equity and justice" (JST Rev. 2:26–27). This is a very different imagery from that of the KJV.

The Vision of Heaven: Chapter 4

Once the seven letters are finished, John is invited to come into the heavens so that he can see things which will be "hereafter" (Rev. 4:1). Thus opens the great prophetic vision for which the Apocalypse is famous. John first describes—or rather, attempts to describe—the majesty and magnitude of the celestial kingdom where God dwells. In a way it is an impossible task—trying to use the finite to describe the infinite. Almost instantly the reader is confronted with a baffling array of symbols, figures, and images, some of which, on the surface at least, border on the bizarre.

And here it is that Joseph Smith's work becomes significant, becoming the key to our understanding. While the Prophet made a few textual changes in these chapters, which we will note, the major contribution comes from section 77 of the Doctrine and Covenants. As was mentioned, fifteen questions are asked in that section about the book of Revelation. Seven of the fifteen are questions relating to chapters 4 and 5. From the Prophet's work we learn the following:

1. The earth in its celestialized future state will become like a massive Urim and Thummim to its inhabitants (see D&C 77:1; 130:7–9).

2. Animals from our own world and from other worlds are celestialized and dwell in the presence of God (see D&C 77:2–3; see also the Prophet's discourse on the meaning of the beasts[27]).

3. The rather bizarre imagery of beasts covered with eyes and wings is actually symbolical of their celestial nature (see D&C 77:4).

4. The seven leaders of the churches as well as twenty-four elders from the seven churches were going to dwell in the presence of God (see JST Rev. 4:5; D&C 77:5). In times of intense persecution and martyrdom, this would have served as a great encouragement to the faithful to stay true to their commitments.

The Sealed Book and the Seven Seals: Chapter 5

It doesn't take a lot of study of the book of Revelation to come to the conclusion that the imagery of chapter 5 is pivotal to the whole structure of the book. John saw in the right hand of the Father a book (most likely a scroll) which was sealed with seven seals (see Rev. 5:1). He also saw that no one in heaven or earth was able or worthy to open the book, except for the Savior (vv. 2–14). Since the rest of the vision describes what John sees as each of the seven seals is opened by the Lamb, an understanding of the sealed book is critical to our whole understanding of the book of Revelation.

And here it is that the Prophet Joseph Smith made his greatest contribution to our ability to unveil the veiled, to reveal the revelation. He answered two significant questions: What is the meaning of the book and what is the meaning of the seals? Certainly more than any other single thing, his answers to those questions (see D&C 77:6–7) become *the key* to gaining access to the "house" of Revelation. From what was revealed in those two verses we then can derive the following:

1. The book in the right hand of the Father represents the history and destiny of the world. It is in his right hand to suggest he controls everything in and about our world. No one except the Savior was worthy to open the book because the atoning sacrifice was what made the whole of world history possible and meaningful.

2. The seven seals represent the seven thousand-year periods which the earth will have during its temporal existence. This not only provides us one of the most specific clues we have as to the closeness of the Second Coming, but it also shows that the book of Revelation is basically structured chronologically, unfolding the earth's history from the time of Adam until the earth is celestialized.

3. Studying that chronological structure carefully, we can see that John's Revelation focuses most heavily on that short period of time between when the last period of a thousand years begins and when Christ comes. Note the amount of time spent on each of the seven seals. The first five (Rev. 6:1–11) are covered briefly, merely highlighting the thing of greatest import to the covenant people that happened in that time frame. The sixth seal, the one in which we currently live, is expanded considerably (Rev. 6:12–7:17) but still takes only a few verses of the total. Knowing that the Millennium is the major event of the seventh seal, we might expect John to dwell at great length on that. But the opening of the seventh seal begins in the first verse of chapter 8. The Second Coming and the Millennium are not seen until chapters 19 and 20. Thus, clearly, the majority of the revelation focuses on that period "after the opening of the seventh seal, before the coming of Christ" (D&C 77:13).

4. This understanding of the time frame aids us greatly in interpreting the symbols used by John. For example, a man on a white horse is seen in Revelation 6:2. That same imagery is used of the Savior in 19:11. Therefore, one might think both places refer to the Master, and this is indeed a common interpretation of the scholars.[28] But knowing that the first seal represents the first thousand years of the earth's history (approximately 4000 to 3000 B.C.) makes that interpretation no longer tenable. That single piece of information helps us look for someone or something in

that period of time that meets all of the symbolic conditions. With that we conclude it is not Christ but Enoch that is represented.[29] And there are other examples of how this key to the chronology becomes a key to the correct interpretation of the symbolism.

Similarly, the rather ingenious interpretation mentioned above—the locusts not hurting grass and trees being interpreted as the Arab general's order to his troops to leave vegetation alone—can now be rejected, since the events described occurred midway in the fifth seal, and John sees the locusts appear after the opening of the seventh seal.

The Opening of the Seals: Chapters 6 to 11

Again, more through what we learn from section 77 than through actual textual changes, the Prophet greatly adds to our understanding of what John saw as the various seals were opened. Nothing is said about the first five seals, either through section 77 or through JST changes. But when we get to the opening of the sixth and seventh seals—those of our own time, as it were—we are helped immensely and learn the following:

1. The "angel from the east" is Elias (D&C 77:9). This at first may not seem helpful, but we know that the concept of Elias is as a forerunner, and that here it refers to the restoration of the gospel in the last days.[30] Applying that interpretation to John's vision makes perfect sense. Before the angels of destruction are loosed, the servants of God will be sealed and thus saved from destruction, through the restoration of the gospel, with its priesthood and ordinances. Commenting on these very verses, the Prophet later explained that the sealing "signifies sealing the blessing upon their heads, meaning the everlasting covenant, thereby making their calling and election sure. When a seal is put upon the father and mother, it secures their posterity, so that they cannot be lost, but will be saved by virtue of the covenant of their father and mother."[31]

2. The Prophet clearly indicates that the twelve thousand sealed from each of the twelve tribes is not just a symbolic representation of the forces of righteousness, as some scholars maintain. They are a great missionary force of the sixth seal (see D&C 77:10). Joseph Smith shows us that they are ordained high priests chosen from among every nation to carry forth the gospel and bring as many as will come to the true Church (see D&C 77:11). In another revelation the Prophet indicated that these 144,000 would also stand on Mt. Zion with the Savior (see D&C 133:18 and compare with Rev. 14:1–5).

The Prophet also said, shortly before his death, "I attended prayer-meeting with the quorum in the assembly room, and made some remarks respecting the hundred and forty-four thousand mentioned by John the Revelator, showing that the selection of persons to form that number had already commenced."[32] This statement would seem to indicate that this great body of missionaries may be composed of mortals and immortals together.

3. Though the Prophet did not give us specific help in interpreting the various images mentioned under the sounding of the seven trumpets that begin in chapter 8, two things he revealed are of great help as we study this section of Revelation. First, he revealed that the trumpets represent the judgments of God which will prepare the world and cleanse it for the millennial reign of Christ (see D&C 77:12). Second, he clearly specifies that these trumpets (or judgments) happen in the seventh seal (see D&C 77:12–13). Since the evidence suggests we have not yet entered that last period of a thousand years, this prophecy is yet future to us. In fact, once the judgments happen it may be that the imagery used by John in this section will become much more clear. It also tells us that any attempt to tie these judgments with past historical events is not justified.

4. In chapter 10, there is a brief pause in the description of the judgments in which John is given a little book to eat. This seems puzzling at first, but again the information revealed through the Prophet Joseph Smith helps us with the interpretation. He explains that the book is symbolic of the mission of John himself during these great events, which mission is to help gather the tribes of Israel (see D&C 77:14). We know from scripture that John is privileged to continue his ministry on the earth until the Savior returns (see John 21:22–23; D&C 7). It is almost as though the Lord says to John in chapter 10, "Since you will still be living at the time all these things I have shown you are transpiring, would you like to see what you will be doing?" At a conference of the Church in June 1831, the Prophet confirmed that the "little book mission" was being fulfilled when he said that "John the Revelator was then among the ten tribes of Israel who had been led away by Shalmaneser, king of Assyria, to prepare them for their return from their long dispersion."[33]

6. Finally, we learn from the Prophet's revelations that the "two witnesses" seen by John as playing a pivotal role in the great battle of Armageddon were two prophets raised up to the Jewish nation (not necessarily Jewish themselves, as some have maintained) in the last days, who would work among the Jewish people in their homeland (see D&C 77:15). Elder Bruce R. McConkie said that these two prophets would be "followers of that humble man, Joseph Smith. . . . No doubt they

will be members of the Council of the Twelve or of the First Presidency of the Church."[34]

The Church and Kingdom of God

After the sounding of the seven trumpets of judgment, John heard "great voices in heaven, saying, The kingdoms of this world are become the kingdoms of our Lord, and of his Christ" (Rev. 11:15). Then, much as a teacher pauses in the course of his lecture to explain an important point, the Lord pauses in his vision of the judgments to explain some significant things about these kingdoms he has just mentioned.

Chapter 12, where this explanation begins, was altered more by the Prophet in his revision of the book of Revelation than any other chapter. He changed most of the verses, rearranged the order of them, and added one new verse—the only place where a significant amount of new material is added in all of Revelation (see JST Rev. 12:7).

While there is much we could study in these changes, space permits us to focus only on the most important insight derived from those changes. Chapter 12 contains three great figures or signs "in the likeness of things on the earth" (JST Rev. 12:1)—a woman who is pregnant, a man child to whom she gives birth, and a great red dragon. The dragon is clearly identified as Satan (see JST v. 8). Most commentators agree that the woman represents the Church of Jesus Christ, a fact which Joseph Smith definitely confirmed (see JST v. 7). But it is the man child that has caused commentators the most difficulty. We are told in both the KJV and the JST that the man child is to rule all nations with the rod of iron and that he will be caught up to the throne of God (see v. 5; JST v. 3). Nearly identical imagery is used in Revelation 19:15, and so most scholars assume the man child is none other than the Savior.

But in chapter 12, if that is the correct interpretation, there is a problem with the imagery. The woman is pregnant with, or in other words gives birth to, the man child. But if the woman is the Church and the man child the Savior, this is contrary to what we know to be true. The Church does not bring forth Christ. Just the opposite is true.

Others have suggested, since it is specified the child is male, that the baby represents the priesthood. But again we have the same problem. The Church does not give birth to the priesthood, but just the opposite.

One simple phrase added by the Prophet in this chapter brings the whole matter into perfect clearness. In fact, it becomes a key to our understanding of this whole section on the kingdoms of the world and of Christ. He changed verse 8 in the KJV to read, "And the dragon prevailed not against Michael, neither the child, nor the woman *which was the Church of God,* who had been delivered of her pains, and *brought forth the kingdom of our God and his Christ"* (JST Rev. 12:7; emphasis added).

Sometimes in the Church we use the phrase "the kingdom of God" to refer to the Church itself, but technically it has a more specific meaning. Elder Joseph Fielding Smith said:

"After Christ comes, all the peoples of the earth will be subject to him, but there will be multitudes of people on the face of the earth who will not be members of the Church; yet all will have to be obedient to the laws of the kingdom of God, for it will have dominion upon the whole face of the earth. These people will be subject to the *political government,* even though they are not members of *the ecclesiastical kingdom which is the Church.*

"This government which embraces all the peoples of the earth, both in and out of the Church, is also sometimes spoken of as the kingdom of God, because the people are subject to the kingdom of God which Christ will set up."[35]

Now the imagery is consistent and logical. Eventually there will be a political kingdom led by Jesus Christ which will rule all nations with the word of God. That political kingdom will grow out of, and is made possible by (that is, is given birth by) the church of Jesus Christ. And since the creation of the political kingdom of Christ signals the end to the kingdoms of the world, it is little wonder that Satan seeks to destroy the man child. During the meridian of time, the Church was not able to bring forth that political kingdom, but itself was taken into the wilderness, or went into apostasy (see JST Rev. 12:14; D&C 86:3). The man child, or the political kingdom, was thus taken to heaven to await the day of the Restoration.

Such a clear and reasonable explanation of this chapter is made possible only through the JST and the instrumentality of the Prophet Joseph Smith.

Conclusion and Summary

In Nephi's grand and glorious vision, he was privileged to see from his own time down through the stream of history to the end of the world. He was allowed to write most of the things he saw, including some things fulfilled in our own generation (e.g., see 1 Ne. 14:12). But at the point where he began to see things still future to us, he was told that he could write no more of them, even though he would be allowed to see them. He was told that he could not write them because it was a stewardship that belonged to another (see 1 Ne. 14:20–21, 25). It belonged to one of the apostles of the Lamb, and, said Nephi, "I . . . heard and bear record, that the name of the apostle of the Lamb was John" (1 Ne. 14:27).

The fulfillment of that stewardship is found in what we call the Apocalypse, or the book of Revelation. It was written for our time and primarily about our time. It is a book of eminent importance to Latter-day Saints.

And it is through the instrumentality of the Prophet Joseph Smith, and especially his work on the new translation of the scriptures, that the book of Revelation has become just that for us. It is a book that stands revealed, as the Prophet said, as "one of the plainest books God ever caused to be written."[36]

Notes

From Monte S. Nyman and Robert L. Millet, eds., *The Joseph Smith Translation: The Restoration of Plain and Precious Things,* volume 12 in the Religious Studies Monograph Series (Provo, Utah: Religious Studies Center, Brigham Young University/Salt Lake City: Bookcraft, 1985), 251–70.

1. Canon Leon Morris, *The Revelation of St. John* (Grand Rapids, Mich.: Wm. B. Eerdmans Publishing Co., 1969), 15.
2. Joseph Henry Thayer, trans., *Greek English Lexicon of the New Testament* (Grand Rapids, Mich.: Zondervan, 1962), s.v. "apo" and "kalypto."
3. Ibid., s.v. "apokalypsis."
4. Joseph Smith, *Teachings of the Prophet Joseph Smith,* comp. Joseph Fielding Smith (Salt Lake City: Deseret Book Co., 1976), 290.
5. Joseph Smith, *Joseph Smith's "New Translation" of the Bible* (Independence, Mo.: Herald Publishing House, 1970), 236–317.
6. Ibid., 513–23.
7. Ibid., 27–116.
8. Robert J. Matthews, *Joseph Smith's Revision of the Bible* (Provo: Brigham Young University Press, 1969), 10.
9. Joseph Smith, *History of The Church of Jesus Christ of Latter-day Saints,* 7 vols. (Salt Lake City: The Church of Jesus Christ of Latter-day Saints, 1946), 1:245.
10. Ibid., 1:253.
11. Matthews, *Joseph Smith's Revision of the Bible,* 10. For additional evidence see his whole discussion, 8–13.
12. Bruce R. McConkie, "Understanding the Book of Revelation," *Ensign,* September 1975, 87; emphasis added.
13. Ibid., 89; emphasis added.
14. Adam Clarke, *The Holy Bible . . . with Commentary and Critical Notes,* 6 vols. (Nashville, Tenn.: Abingdon Press, n.d.), 6:1001; emphasis added.
15. J. R. Dummelow, *A Commentary on the Holy Bible* (New York: Macmillan Publishing Co., 1936), 1080; emphasis added.
16. Merrill C. Tenney, *Interpreting Revelation* (Grand Rapids, Mich.: Wm. B. Eerdmans Publishing Co., 1957), 75.
17. Ibid.
18. H. M. S. Richards, Jr., *What Is in Your Future?* (Los Angeles: Voice of Prophecy, 1972), 23.

19. Ibid., 23–24; emphasis added.
20. Smith, *Teachings of the Prophet Joseph Smith,* 84.
21. Ibid., 287–94.
22. Robert J. Matthews, *"A Plainer Translation": Joseph Smith's Translation of the Bible, A History and Commentary* (Provo: Brigham Young University Press, 1975), 210–12.
23. Ibid.
24. Smith, *History of the Church,* 1:253.
25. Hyrum M. Smith and Janne M. Sjodahl, *Doctrine and Covenants Commentary,* rev. ed. (Salt Lake City: Deseret Book Co., 1951), 478.
26. Thayer, *Greek English Lexicon of the New Testament,* s.v. "myrios."
27. Smith, *Teachings of the Prophet Joseph Smith,* 287–94.
28. See for example, Dummelow, *Commentary,* 1078; R. C. H. Lenski, *The Interpretation of St. John's Revelation* (Minneapolis: Augsburg Publishing House, 1963), 221–22.
29. Bruce R. McConkie, *Doctrinal New Testament Commentary,* 3 vols. (Salt Lake City: Bookcraft, 1966–73), 3:476–77.
30. Ibid., 3:491–92.
31. Smith, *Teachings of the Prophet Joseph Smith,* 321.
32. Smith, *History of the Church,* 6:196.
33. Ibid., 1:176, note.
34. McConkie, *Doctrinal New Testament Commentary,* 3:509.
35. Joseph Fielding Smith, *Doctrines of Salvation,* 3 vols. (Salt Lake City: Bookcraft, 1954–56), 1:229; emphasis added.
36. Smith, *Teachings of the Prophet Joseph Smith,* 290.

Chapter 7

The Book of Mormon—Keystone of a Happy Marriage

The topic of marriage seems to have nothing to do with the Book of Mormon. Somebody recently said to me, "You know, there's not a single scripture in the Book of Mormon about marriage." And I said, "You're right." Not *specifically* about marriage, that is.

I had an interesting experience some years ago. I'd spoken at a Know Your Religion seminar in southern California, and Sunday morning when I got back on the plane, I found I was sitting next to Brent Barlow, a professor at Brigham Young University who has studied the LDS family and has written a great deal about family relationships, including a column for the *Deseret News* and several books. Brent and I have been friends for quite a while. He was coming back from having spoken at another program, and as we visited he said he was going to work on the Book of Mormon as a handbook for marriage. At that, I guess I looked a little perplexed, so he opened his briefcase and said, "Get out your Book of Mormon. I'm going to show you something." And he had me turn to the introduction, which is right behind the title page. He read me something we have all known, heard, and read.

In the introduction is a paragraph that we read together: "Concerning this record the Prophet Joseph said, 'I told the brethren that the Book of Mormon was the most correct of any book on earth and the keystone of our religion and a man would get nearer to God by abiding by its precepts than by any other book.'"

Brent reminded me of President Ezra Taft Benson's plea that we recommit ourselves to the Book of Mormon and make it a new covenant in the Church. Then he said, "I decided that if I was really going take that seriously, it would apply to the Book of Mormon and marriage." I saw him a short time later, mentioned the project, and asked him how it was going.

"You would not believe it," he said. "I'm reading the Book of Mormon with a whole new set of eyes." That was such an intriguing comment to me that I started reading the Book of Mormon with the same goal in mind—and I had an incredible experience.

I went through every page of the Book of Mormon, looking at the things I had marked over the years and seeing which ones apply to marriage. I ended up with five single-spaced handwritten pages. I think there is a reason for that long list of applicable scriptures, even in a book of scripture that doesn't seem to talk specifically about marriage. If you think about it, the gospel itself is a blueprint for a happy marriage.

Let me share with you three statements by presidents of the Church that support this idea. John Taylor said: "It is impossible to produce a true and correct union without the spirit of the Living God, and that spirit can only be imparted through the ordinances of the gospel."[1]

President David O. McKay: "I regard it as an incontrovertible fact that in no marriage circle can true peace, love, purity, chastity and happiness be found in which is not present the spirit of Christ."[2]

And Joseph Fielding Smith: "If a man and his wife are earnestly and faithfully observing all the ordinances and principles of the gospel there could not arise any cause for divorce."[3]

That's an interesting chain of reasoning. The Book of Mormon contains the fulness of the gospel. The gospel is the blueprint for a happy marriage, and therefore the Book of Mormon, which contains the gospel, is a handbook for happy marriage. And if I understand our theology correctly, it doesn't matter where we are now; if we're going to be gods, if we're going to achieve exaltation, some day we're going to have to build an eternal relationship with a person of the opposite sex.

Some rare couples discourage us by saying things like, "In thirty-two years of marriage, my wife and I have never once quarreled." I want you to know I consider my marriage with my wife, Lynn, to be a remarkable marriage and a very happy one, but we have had our problems. All of us who are married would have to admit that we have some problems or adjustments in our marriages. It is a rare marriage where there are not some remaining pockets of discord, areas of conflict, places where you have challenges to work through, things that could be improved.

"It Was Not Good That the Man Should Be Alone"

I'm really struck with a statement in the book of Moses: "And I the Lord, God, formed man from the dust of the ground" (Moses 3:7). In verse 7 we read that "he was "the first flesh." Then we read in verse 18: "And I, the Lord God, said unto mine Only Begotten, that it was not good that the man should be alone." I have a testimony of that. It is not good for man to be alone. So, the Lord says, "I will make an help meet for him [Adam]" (v. 18). Then what happens next? The creation of Eve, right? No, not immediately. "And out of the ground I, the Lord God, formed every beast of the field, and every fowl of the air; and commanded that they should come unto Adam, to see what he would call them" (v. 19). In Hebrew in the Genesis account, the word when he names the animals implies much more than simply naming them. It's a verb that implies that he watched them, studied their characteristics, and then gave them a name that fit. He didn't just go out on the veranda and watch out on the plains and say, "Oh, yeah, a zebra, yeah, I like that, zebra. Hippopotamus, oh, I love the ring of hippopotamus." I don't think he did that. I say that because how long would it take to study the animals and name them all. A while, right? Weeks, at least. Possibly months, maybe even years. So then comes this interesting thing that I'd never really noticed before, in verse 20: "And Adam gave names to all cattle, and to the fowl of the air, and to every beast of the field; but as for Adam, *there was not found an help meet for him*" (emphasis added).

That's an interesting sequence of events: the Lord says it's not good for man to be alone. He suggests, "Let's make him an helpmeet." He asks Adam to go out and name the animals. When he's through with the task, Adam says, "I didn't find any helpmeet out there."

"And I, the Lord God, caused a deep sleep to fall upon Adam; and he slept, and I took one of his ribs and closed up the flesh . . . ; And the rib which I, the Lord God, had taken from man, made I a woman, and brought her unto the man" (vv. 21–22).

Adam then said, "This I know now is bone of my bones, and flesh of my flesh; she shall be called Woman." What is he doing? He's naming the last of God's creations, the crowning creation, and what does he call her? Woman, "because she was taken out of man" (v. 23). In Hebrew, the meaning is "female man." Adam seems to be saying, "It's a female me, literally."

"Therefore," continues the scriptural account, with Adam speaking, "shall a man leave his father and his mother, and shall cleave unto his wife" (v. 24). I think that verb *cleave* is a very interesting one. Compare it with a meat cleaver, which separates the meat. I wonder if it has anything to do with the symbolism of the rib. We know the account of Eve's being made from a rib is probably not a literal description of how it was done. But Adam has been separated from part of himself, and only when that cleavage is overcome does he become whole again. "Therefore shall a man leave his father and his mother, and shall cleave unto his wife; and they shall be one flesh."

Now, that provides some interesting challenges. I really believe that this challenge to become one flesh is one of the great laboratories of godhood. In marriage we really learn something about what it means to be a god.

Differences between Men and Women

There's more to that challenge than simply the intensity of the relationship. I think it would not come as a tremendous revelation if I told you that men and women are different, but the differences are more profound than we usually think, in so many ways. It only *begins* with the physical differences.

We really do see things differently. Men tend to be task oriented. Women tend to be people oriented. I once read an interesting study in which a psychologist reported on a series of tests he had done on the brain patterns of men and women. He took a group of men and women, hooked them up to the electroencephalogram, and then gave them a complex task like working on a Rubik's Cube or something else that took real concentration and watched their brain wave patterns. He discovered that men (and this varied depending on the man) tended to use either the left brain or the right brain, whereas a woman tended to use both sides of her brain simultaneously. And then he said something like this, as I remember: "In my opinion that explains why women tend to be so much more perceptive to the subtle cues that typically go on in a relationship."

I've seen that in my own marriage. We'll go to a party and come home and my wife, Lynn, will say, "That's sure too bad George and Sally are having problems."

I'll answer, "George and Sally are having problems? How do you know that?"

"Well, didn't you watch them?"

"Yeah, I watched them. What?"

"Well, you could just tell."

I couldn't tell. We tend to see things differently. We tend to perceive things differently.

I grew up in a family of boys. I have only one sister, and she's five years younger than me. Shopping was a whole new experience for me. I can still remember the first time I went through a mall with my wife. We were headed for a movie and she said, "Oh, let's go in there." So we went into a department store, but she didn't seem to be interested in buying anything. She just moved from place to place. Finally I said, "Honey, what is it you need?" "Well, I don't need anything. I just want to look." My idea of shopping is that you know exactly what you want, approximately what you are willing to pay for it, and where to go to get it. You get in. You get out. And you're done. "Just looking" baffled me.

We tend to perceive relationships differently. Here's an interesting experiment. Some time when you're visiting friends for dinner, and they serve you pork chops, take the man aside and say, "Thanks, we really appreciate it. That was a great dinner. Where did you get those pork chops?" And the most common answer the man will give you is, "I don't know. Albertson's, Safeway." Then take the woman aside and say, "That was a great dinner. Oh, by the way, where did you get those pork chops?" A common response is, "Why? Was there something the matter with them?" That's an interesting difference.

If a man's birthday comes along and his wife forgets it, which is really unusual, almost unthinkable—as far as the man is concerned, the wife has forgotten his birthday. But if a man forgets his wife's birthday, as far as she's concerned, he has forgotten *her.* Another important difference.

I read the other day of a couple who set as their wedding date the 23rd of February. The man said, "Oh, that's a great idea. That's the day after Washington's birthday. I'll never forget our anniversary because it's the day after Washington's birthday." And the woman said, "You know, I'll never forget Washington's birthday because it's the day before our anniversary." Two different ways of looking at things.

Some time ago, my wife shared with me an article she had read on communication in marriage, which illustrates this principle. The article was about Nan Kline, a clinical psychologist. The lead paragraph of the article asks, "How does a clinical psychologist describe the way men and women communicate? 'Same language, different planets.'"

"If you are getting married and you think you are marrying your best friend," Nan Kline says, "you're wrong. You're actually marrying someone from an alien culture." And that's because, as she says, "men and women communicate differently." Then she illustrates: "Let's go back to childhood and notice the patterns. Little girls, for example, have best friends. The basis of that deep, deep friendship is communication, especially the sharing of secrets." And then she says something very significant: "For girls, the process of communication is important, more so than the content."

"Female play groups tend to be difficult to join," says Kline, who has done research on the subject. But she adds, "Once you're in, you're in. You are equal to the other girls. Adult women also typically suppress any notion that anyone in the group is better than anyone else. They tend to diminish competition, and their communication often to a man seems to have nonsignificant content." Why? Because it's not the content of the communication that matters.

"Little boys, on the other hand, don't spend much time whispering. They are out on the playground doing stuff. . . . Researchers have found that boys' play groups are easy to join, but once you are in . . . , you earn a place by competition." Therefore, the conversation and communication patterns are these: "Boys swap stories. Their stories are all about prowess. . . . They don't communicate to be closer to each other. They communicate to compete, to withstand challenges and define their identity."

And then she said—and this is why I found the article to be so interesting—"A woman [who understands only the way women communicate] feels the relationship is deteriorating when her husband doesn't share his innermost thoughts. She . . . is being rejected." And the man, when he senses that, is baffled because those are not his feelings at all.[4]

Now let me describe something that has happened in the home of most married couples. The newspaper comes and you sit down together to read the paper. Generally the wife is through it very quickly, unless she's spending time on the advertisements. But typically the man moves through more slowly, reading the editorials and going through the sports page and so on.

When the wife is finished, she watches him for a minute and says something, and he mutters, "Um, hm." Then she'll say, "Honey, I want to talk to you."

"Okay." Then he waits. When nothing happens, what does he do? He starts reading the paper again.

"Honey, I want to talk to you. Now, put down the paper. I don't want you reading the paper while I'm talking. Just talk to me."

So he says, "Okay." He folds up the paper and puts it away. "What do you want to talk about?"

"Well, I don't know. I just want to talk."

He's task oriented, so he pursues his own line of reasoning: "What have you got on your mind? Let's talk about it and then I can get back to reading the paper." But what is she after?

A man often sees communication as communication. A woman hopes to get communion out of communication. That difference presents some interesting challenges. So how do you deal with those challenges? I submit that if the gospel is a blueprint to a happy marriage, the Book of Mormon contains the fulness of the gospel, so it will contain the principles that teach you how to have a happy marriage.

There are hundreds of examples, but we're going to discuss only a few.

Free to Choose

Here's a simple one: The concept that you are free to choose. There are many places where this is taught in the Book of Mormon, but we'll discuss 2 Nephi, chapter 2, where Father Lehi is speaking to his son Jacob. He speaks about the Messiah coming and bears testimony that he will redeem the children of men; then comes this statement: "And because that they are redeemed from the fall they have become free forever, knowing good from evil; to act for themselves and not to be acted upon" (2 Ne. 2:26).

What has that got to do with marriage? In marriage, each of us, because we have been redeemed from the fall of Adam, have become free forever. We are first of all given the knowledge of good and evil. How many of us have ever done something in our marriages that we knew was a little destructive, and we knew it was wrong at the very moment we were doing it? Probably every one of us. We know good from evil, and we are free to act for ourselves and not to be acted upon. Let me give you some examples of this principle.

I was a sociology major in both my bachelor's and master's programs; one of the reasons I studied sociology is that I wanted to better understand people. I remember one professor who talked about the causes of behavior. They call it the "simple SR theory": namely, a given stimulus will trigger a response. Let me give you an actual example that applies to marriage. I'm going to use a lot of examples from various marriages, and to protect the guilty I'm going to name them all George and Sally.

George and Sally are newlyweds. One day George gets up and goes to work. Sally is picking up clutter around the house when all of a sudden she remembers that today is their third-month anniversary. It has been three months to the very day that they were married. Sally becomes so excited about that significant day that she decides she is going to do something really special. She goes through the house and gives it a thorough cleaning, even though it's already in pretty good shape. She then decides that they need a candlelight dinner. So she rushes out to the store and buys the candles. She gets out the silver and her best china, buys fresh flowers, and then proceeds to cook a marvelous dinner. By the time she's through with the roast and potatoes and gravy and vegetables, she's got pans stacked up in the sink, gravy oozing down the burners and over the front of the stove. (She's still learning.) But by five o'clock she is so excited she just quietly shuts the door to the kitchen, goes to the front room, sits down, and waits for George.

She hears the car drive up, but as George gets out he notices something in the backyard, so he goes directly around back to fix it—and then comes through the back door. Suddenly we hear, "Sally, what in the world have you been doing? Look at this mess. I can't believe this!" Okay, now that's the stimulus.

Would you like to predict the response? My college professor said that actually the SR model of behavior is too simple. We've learned that it's really more than simply stimulus-response. It would be more accurate to say that stimulus creates feelings, and feelings then trigger a response.

We can predict what Sally's feelings are going to be. Hurt, rejected, angry. She may run into the bedroom to cry, and George will say, "What did I do? What did I do?" At first when our class discussed that, I thought, "Mm, that makes sense. That's a really good model."

Then one day I was in a religion class and a professor opened my eyes with a new concept. He said, "There is a different model. You have to add one more thing. In the gospel, you have to add agency. There is a stimulus, but you are free to choose how you will respond to that stimulus. You are free to act and not to be acted upon. The stimulus does not force you into a particular response. That is your choice and your freedom."

Suppose I could go into the bedroom where Sally is crying and just whisper in her ear: "Sally, let me tell you something. Did you remember that today George went up for that promotion he has been after for the last six months? Did you remember that? He worked on it all month long. He lost it. One of the guys in the meeting even snickered when he made the presentation." Would that change Sally's feelings at all? It would. Why? We haven't changed the situation where she is feeling hurt. But she would respond differently, we hope, because she chooses to feel a different way.

You are free to choose. A wife is free to choose whether to be angry or hurt or patient when her husband says something dumb (and he will). You're free to choose whether to retaliate when you are wronged (and you will be) or whether to forgive. You're free to choose whether to put your spouse's happiness as a number-one priority or whether to put other things first. You have choices every day of your marriage, and the Book of Mormon says you are free to choose whether to act or to be acted upon. This is a solid keystone to a happy marriage. It is a way to become one.

Follow the Prophets

Here is a second example of how the Book of Mormon can guide us in marriage. I would like to create a scripture chain to set up this second principle, starting with 1 Nephi 22:2: "And I, Nephi, said unto them: Behold they were manifest unto the prophet by the voice of the Spirit; for by the Spirit are all things made known unto the prophets, which shall come upon the children of men according to the flesh."

What are married couples trying to become? One flesh. How do you learn how to deal in things of the flesh? You listen to the prophets. That's an important insight.

The second scripture in the chain comes from 3 Nephi 10. As I went through and started picking out principles that would apply to marriage, I was amazed to see where they came from. Here's one in the midst of the description of the destruction that preceded the coming of the Savior. The voice has catalogued all that's happened, and the people are mourning and weeping, and then in verse 12 it says, "And it was the more righteous part of the people who were saved."

Have you ever thought about what that means? These people had experienced a selective earthquake, a selective lightning storm, and a selective windstorm, all of which took only the more wicked part of the people. And what is it that determined their righteousness or wickedness? "And it was they who received the prophets and stoned them not" (v. 12). It is apparent that the Lord feels strongly about how people respond to his prophets.

Another scripture for our chain is found in Mosiah 8, which talks of the Ammon who went in search of the colony that disappeared. Ammon found King Limhi, whose people had discovered twenty-four gold plates that they were anxious to get translated. So Limhi asked Ammon if he could do the translation, and Ammon answered, "No, but King Mosiah can. He's a seer." Then in verse 15, we read, "The king said that a seer is greater than a prophet." And Ammon said, "A seer is a revelator and a prophet also; and a gift which is greater can no man have, except he possesses the power of God."

The next two verses give us a valuable truth about marriage: "But a seer can know of things which are past, and also of things which are to come, and by them shall all things be revealed, or, rather, shall secret things be made manifest, and hidden things shall come to light, and things which are not known shall be made known by them, and also things shall be made known by them which otherwise could not be known.

"Thus God has provided a means that man, through faith, might work mighty miracles; therefore he becometh a great benefit to his fellow beings" (Mosiah 8:17–18).

For example, why does the prophet say to young people, "Don't date until you're sixteen"? What does he "see" that we may not? I heard of a mother who said, "If my daughter is not going steady by the time she's fourteen—how will she ever get a date for the school dances?" I could just weep, because I know a bishop is very likely to see that girl down the road, as she comes to him to confess serious transgressions. If she's going steady at fourteen, there will usually be problems later. Why? Because youth are not yet mature enough to understand the powers of sexual attraction and how easily young couples can get into moral trouble. But the prophet understands. The prophet can see things that other people cannot see, and he has counseled the youth not to date until the age of sixteen. If a prophet and seer can foresee how to help our youth avoid moral tragedy, can he not also see things that will help husbands and wives build stronger marriages?

Now let's add to our scripture chain the final one, from Helaman 13. Samuel the Lamanite, a prophet, has come to teach the people and is not well received. In verses 26 and 27 of Helaman 13, he notes how differently true prophets (who testify of the people's iniquity) and false prophets (who say the people are doing wonderfully) are treated. The true prophets get killed. The false prophets get rich. In verse 29 he laments: "O ye wicked and ye perverse generation; ye hardened and ye stiffnecked people, how long will ye suppose that the Lord will suffer you?" And then he asks, "Yea, how long will ye suffer yourselves to be led by foolish and blind guides?" Samuel is contrasting a seer, one who sees, with one who is blind. How often we listen to those that are blind!

Again, we might ask, "What has that got to do with marriage?" President Ezra Taft Benson, in the October 1987 general priesthood session, said, "In latter-day revelation the Lord . . . said, 'Thou shalt love thy wife with all thy heart, and shall cleave unto her and none else' (D&C 42:22). To my knowledge there is only one other thing in all of scripture that we are told to love with all of our hearts, and that is God himself. Think what that means!

"This kind of love can be shown for your wives in so many ways. First and foremost, nothing except God Himself takes priority over your wife in your life—not work, not recreation, not hobbies. Your wife is your precious, eternal helpmate—your companion."[5] A prophet and seer is saying, in effect, "Brethren, here are your top priorities. You'd better pay attention."

We frequently see evidence of the problem of misplaced priorities. Let me show you a typical pattern in marriage that's related to failing to put your spouse as the number-one priority.

George and Sally are these two separate, totally independent individual entities. One day they meet. Their eyes catch each other. They start to date, and they are drawn toward each other by a powerful attraction. They start surrendering their personal wants in order to please each other. The craziest kinds of things happen. George actually buys flowers for Sally. I don't think he even knew what flowers were before he met her. Finally they say, "Let's get married," and they supposedly become one—legally, emotionally, spiritually, economically.

Then a troubling thing happens. The problem is described by a Christian minister, Rousas John Rushdoony. Speaking of Adam, he notes that Adam's calling was to work. "Go out, dress the garden, Adam. Keep it. Conquer and subdue the earth and so on," the Lord said to him. Rushdoony then states, "Because of the centrality of work to a man, one of the chronic problems of men is their tendency to make work a *substitute religion.* Instead of deriving the meaning of life from God and his law-order, men often derive their private world of meaning from their work. The consequence is a disorientation of life, family, and order."[6]

George gets hired by a new corporation or he starts a new business or whatever he happens to do. The first thing his boss says is, "Now, George, where are your priorities?" And I'm telling you the typical boss isn't anxious to hear this answer from his employees: "No success can compensate for failure in the home." What he wants to hear is "Boss, you know this company comes first."

So George starts up the corporate ladder or he's in his own business, and he says, "I've got to put in the time. You know, I'm the only one." So he's working Saturdays and sometimes Sundays, and Sally starts to miss the relationship they've built. She starts to feel the separation again. So often she will say, "Honey, spend some time with me." But he's too busy and so she tries again, but the defenses start to come up, and the scar tissue starts to form, and sometimes the couple ends up with what I call an emotional divorce.

As the years go on, some face the midlife crisis. A man realizes that he's not going to do everything he thought he was going to do. So then what does the man start to long for? A warm, nurturing, caring relationship. But he can't find it with Sally because there's too much pain now. What does he do instead? He turns to this sweet, young secretary or the lady down the hall or whoever it happens to be, and she provides him all the things that Sally wanted to give him in the first place but he didn't have time to accept.

What a tragic commentary about the price of not putting your spouse first. A prophet has given us wise counsel on the matter, and yet some of us just don't apply it to our marriage.

I've been addressing mainly the men in their marriage relationships. But these principles also apply to women.

Elder Boyd K. Packer has said, "My young [sisters], you have had some very choice, intimate, cherished times with your mother talking over things that are sacred and personal. Now all of these moments belong to your husband, and only rarely and on superficial things would you have to run back to Mother—maybe for an occasional recipe or a remedy, but on all of the sacred and deep and important problems, you belong to one another and you solve them between the two of you."[7]

I'm shocked to hear what women share with each other sometimes about their marriages. When I was in a restaurant not long ago, five women came in who didn't know I knew them, but I knew they were all Latter-day Saints. I believe they were all friends and not relatives. They began to talk loudly enough that it was impossible *not* to hear them. I couldn't believe what one woman was telling her friends about her marriage relationship—the emotional problems, sexual problems, on and on. When she finished, one of the ladies next to her said, "Hey, divorce that jerk." And I watched her face and it seemed she was thinking, *Yeah, yeah, maybe I'd better.* All too often a woman tends to go outside of the marriage to share and to feel that communion with others. The prophets say to be careful of that. It's something to watch for.

Follow the prophets. Are you going to listen to seers or are you going to listen to blind guides? One of the blindest of guides is the media. You look at what the media is telling women today, for example, about what it takes to be happy, and it's no wonder that so many women struggle with feelings of inadequacy. But it's a lie.

Follow the Holy Ghost

Let's go to another principle: having the Holy Ghost in your relationship. Paul, in Galatians, talks about the fruits of the Spirit (see Gal. 5:22–23). Wouldn't you like those fruits in your marriage? Happiness, joy, peace, long suffering, gentleness. Those are the fruits of the Spirit.

Again, we can turn to the Book of Mormon to learn about the Spirit. Here is one very famous example: Nephi, Laman, Lemuel, and Sam were sent from the wilderness back to Jerusalem to get the brass plates. They failed and then failed again. Laman and Lemuel grew highly frustrated. But Nephi said, "We are going do what the Lord said." He went back into the city, "and I was led by the Spirit, not knowing beforehand the things which I should do" (1 Ne. 4:6).

How does this apply to a marriage? Remember the quotation from John Taylor that we read earlier: "It is impossible to produce a true and correct union without the spirit of the living God."[8] That is the key. There is no way you can possibly do all that has to be done, and do it right, without the help of the Spirit.

I really believe that in a marriage we can receive constant promptings from the Holy Ghost. I think sometimes the Holy Ghost says things like this:

- "Ask her how it was today for her. Ask her how her day was."
- "Tell her she looks attractive in that dress."
- "Don't respond to that comment even though it hurt."
- "Don't withdraw, don't retreat into that shell of silence; tell her what you're thinking. Tell her what you're feeling when she says that."
- "You shouldn't be sharing that with others."
- "Tell her you love her."

Unfortunately, though, too often we brush those feelings aside and don't act on them.

Think about marriage as it relates to the plan of salvation. Most of Christianity believes that being saved means that we get to go back and live with Heavenly Father. And we believe that too, but we say we not only want to be *with* him, but we also want to be *like* him. That is the whole purpose of the gospel. That is the role of the Holy Ghost—to make us like God. Have you ever thought that the more godlike you are, the easier it is to love you? It's when we act in non-godlike ways that people get hurt and angry and frustrated.

A young co-worker once said to me, "You know, I'm getting wiser in my old age." He was thirty years old. He and his wife had four little children, including twin boys, with the oldest being six years old. He said, "Sometimes I come home and Sally is so strung out, she's just ready to explode." He continued, "When I used to come home and see her like that, I'd put my arms around her and say, 'Honey, I love you. Just relax. Don't get so uptight. It's all right.'"

I said, "Oh, how did she respond to that?"

He smiled ruefully, "Oh, she'd blow up. She'd say, 'Don't tell me to relax, and don't tell me it's all right!'"

Then this wise young man taught me the lesson. He went on, "Now I'm a little wiser. Now if I see that Sally's uptight when I come home, I do one of two things. I either get her out of the house or I get the kids out of the house. Then later, when the kids are in bed and all is quiet, I put my arms around her and say, 'Honey, I love you.' And she says, 'I know.'"

There's a man who understands that the Spirit can make him more like God, and the more we are like God, the easier it is for our spouse to love us. The easier it is to become one flesh. When a man and a woman are both striving to be godlike, with the promptings of the Spirit, think what it does for their marriage.

If you want another interesting scripture chain, go through the scriptures and find out what it is that brings the Spirit. As you do, you'll feel pricks of guilt as you see those things you do in your marriage that are contrary to the Spirit. Study unrighteous dominion. Study pride. Study contention. Study all the things that grieve the Spirit and thereby lessen the power in our marriages.

George Q. Cannon said, "How many of you . . . are seeking for these gifts that God has promised to bestow? How many of you, when you bow before your Heavenly Father in your family circle or in your secret places contend for these gifts to be bestowed upon you? How many of you ask the Father, in the name of Jesus, to manifest Himself to you through these powers and these gifts? Or do you go along day by day like a door turning on its hinges, without having any feeling on the subject, without exercising any faith whatever . . . ? If any of us are imperfect, it is our duty to pray for the gift that will make us perfect. Have I imperfections? I am full of them. What is my duty? To pray for God to give me the gifts that will correct these imperfections. If I am an angry man, it is my duty to pray for charity, which suffereth long and is kind. Am I an envious man? It is my duty to seek for charity, which envieth not."[9]

Nephi taught essentially the same thing when he said, "Angels speak by the power of the Holy Ghost; wherefore, they speak the words of Christ. Wherefore, I said unto you, feast upon the words of Christ; for behold, the words of Christ will tell you all things what you should do" (2 Ne. 32:3). When you are in conflict with your spouse, if you have the Holy Ghost you'll speak the words of Christ. You can look to Christ and ask, "What will I do or say if I look to Him as my model?"

I had an interesting experience with that very thing with one of my children. Our son was about twelve years old. It was nine o'clock Sunday morning and we were almost late for church, so I yelled, "Come on, we're leaving." He came into the room wearing tennis shoes and Bermuda shorts and no shirt. I said, "What are you doing?"

"I'm not going to church today. I don't want to."

My initial reaction was, *Oh, yeah? Don't want to—what does that have to do with anything?* Instead I just said, "Come on, now, get dressed. We're late."

Then he said, "I'm not going and you can't make me."

I remember thinking, *I can't make you? We'll see about that.* But at that moment, I thought, *How would Christ deal with a teenage boy who is saying, "No, I'm not going to church"?* With that simple question, a thought popped into my mind, and I said, "Son, I don't know why you're telling me that. It's not my meeting. Why don't you go down to your bedroom and tell the Lord why you're not going to sacrament meeting. It's his meeting. He's your Father. Go tell him, and we'll see you when we come home."

I didn't make it to the door before he said, "All right, all right, I'm coming." That's what the Spirit can do, and that's how it works.

Marriage and the Gift of Charity

Let's go to one last way in which the Book of Mormon guides us in our marriages. I wish we had time to look at faith, hope, and charity, the three great Christian characteristics of discipleship. But let us look at the last of those because it's so important to becoming one. In teaching his son, Moroni, Mormon speaks of faith and hope, and then says, "If we have these we must needs have charity, for if he have not charity, he is nothing." Another way to put it is this: "And the marriage must needs have charity, for if it have not charity it is nothing. Wherefore, it must have charity." Then Mormon listed the qualities of charity: "Charity suffereth long, and is kind, and envieth not, and is not puffed up, seeketh not her own, is not easily provoked," and so on. Finally he says a second time, "Wherefore, my beloved brethren, if ye have not charity, ye are nothing" (Moro. 7:44–46).

Those are exactly the same qualities that the apostle Paul gives in 1 Corinthians 13. Some years ago when I was working on some New Testament studies, I ran across a modern version of the New Testament called the Phillips Translation. I am very dissatisfied with most such versions, but the Phillips Translation was done by a faithful Christian man who has tried to keep to the spirit of the original and the beauty of the poetry, while at the same time trying to make the message more understandable to the modern reader. Here is how he translated 1 Corinthians 13:4–8, Paul's description of charity:

"This love of which I speak is slow to lose patience—it looks for a way of being constructive. It is not possessive: it is neither anxious to impress nor does it cherish inflated ideas of its own importance.

"Love has good manners and does not pursue selfish advantage. It is not touchy. It does not keep account of evil or gloat over the wickedness of other people. On the contrary, it is glad with all good men when truth prevails.

"Love knows no limit to its endurance, no end to its trust, no fading of its hope; it can outlast anything. It is, in fact, the one thing that still stands when all else has fallen."[10]

Let's look at each of those qualities:

Love is slow to lose patience. We are so quick to be impatient. One of the things we learn very quickly is all the vulnerable spots in our spouses. Within the first year we learn all of the weaknesses, we learn where the jugular is. One of Satan's great promptings is to go for the jugular when you've been hurt. Strike back at the place where you know it will do the most damage. We have to fight that misguided impulse. We have to fight our irritation and our impatience. Love is slow to lose patience, or as Paul and Moroni said, "It suffereth long."

Love looks for a way to be constructive. We use the word *edification* all the time in the Church. Edification is closely related to the word *edifice.* Both words come from the same Latin root, *aedes,* which is the Latin word for a temple. That gives me a whole new insight into edification. What you do when you edify is to build a spiritual structure, a spiritual temple, in the life of someone you love. Sometimes you build brick by brick, and sometimes you throw up a whole wall together. But that's what love is. It is constructive. It is edifying. It is not destructive.

Let me give you an example. I see this sort of thing all the time in good marriages. Lynn and I had some good friends years ago, and I'm ashamed to admit I was a little critical of the wife. She had eight children and still weighed only 118 pounds. After every child, she went onto a crash starvation diet. She tried every fad diet ever invented. I worried about her health; and I just kept saying, *This is foolish. She doesn't need to be so worried about keeping her weight down.* I don't think the Lord is going to have a set of bathroom scales at the Judgment. I find it very hard to picture the Lord saying, "Well, I've reviewed your case, and you're celestial in every way, but you're twenty pounds overweight and so I can't let you in." Yet to hear some people talk about weight, you'd think it was that significant.

One night we were going out to dinner with these friends, and when we arrived she wasn't quite ready. We waited in the living room, visiting with her husband. Then she came down the hall from the bedroom. Remember, she weighs only 118 pounds after eight children. Her husband looked up at her and said, "Oh, honey, you really look heavy in that dress." And I thought, *Now I understand why she is so sensitive about her weight.* That's hardly what you would call constructive. That's destructive.

Love has good manners. We used to go to the temple with other couples when we lived in California, and then we would go to dinner afterward. One night we were at a restaurant, and the waiter brought us our salads without asking us what dressing we'd like. They just brought the house dressing, which was vinegar and oil. Well, olives, vinegar and oil, and dirty bath water are not high on my list of edible foods, so, I said, "Vinegar and oil doesn't do a thing for me. Would anybody like my salad?"

George, who was sitting next to me, said, "Oh, I love vinegar and oil. I'll have your salad."

Then Sally said, loud enough for the whole restaurant to hear, "As fat as you are, you're going to have a second salad?" You could see her comment hit him right in the face. Surprise. He didn't take my salad.

But on the way home I got to thinking about that. George was not the heaviest person at the table. Alan was. (That's not his real name, either.) I thought to myself, *Suppose Alan had said to me, "Oh, yeah, Jerry, I love vinegar and oil. I'll take your salad."* Do you think Sally would have said to Alan, "As fat as you are, you're going to have a second salad?" She may have thought it, but she would never have said it to him. With George, though, it was open season. Love has good manners, and it seemed to me that good manners were forgotten that night.

Love is not anxious to impress nor does it cherish inflated ideas of its own importance. Do you remember Corianton's problem on his mission? Alma's youngest son fell into immorality. But what got him into the problem? Alma said, "You went about boasting in your own strength." Love does not, as Moroni said it, vaunt itself. It does not hold a cherished idea of its own importance. Love does not pursue selfish advantage. How often we see this violated. A spouse is not a servant. A spouse is not a helper. A spouse is not an assistant. A spouse is a partner.

We were good friends with a man who mortgaged his home and put everything into a new business venture. He had high expectations for it. Three months later everything crashed. He lost it all. Some time after that Sally was in our home and I could tell she was extremely upset. Afterwards I asked my wife what was going on. She said, "Sally's going crazy. She says she has no idea where they stand. She goes to George and says, 'Honey, the kids need shoes. Can I write a check or can't I?' And he'll say, 'Honey, don't worry about it. Money is my problem. Don't worry about it.' Sally said, 'I don't know whether to buy food. I don't know what to do about anything.'"

A few days later I happened to be with George privately and I said, "How's it going, George?"

"Oh," he said, "I don't know if we're going to be able to keep the house. I don't know what I'm going do."

I said, "Have you ever talked to Sally about this?"

"No," he said, "I don't want to worry her." I thought to myself, *It's lucky that Sally's not your business partner or you'd have a lawsuit on your hands.* Can you imagine saying to your business partner, "Don't worry about the money. Let me handle it." I know that in this case George's intentions were good. He didn't want to worry his wife. But that is a selfish decision and suggests he doesn't trust her enough to share financial things with her. He felt his judgment was more important, more trustworthy.

Here is another example of seeking selfish advantage. One night George and Sally (a different set) were in our home. They had just had a new baby, and somehow the conversation turned to diaper changing. It was obvious George was not wild about that activity. My wife, who has strong feelings about that, jumped on that one, and she said, "Oh, you don't change diapers?"

"Well, yeah," George admitted, "I do a few."

She said, "A few?"

"Yeah," he said, "I don't mind changing a wet one now and then, but oh, those messy ones. I can't stand that."

Curious, I jumped in. I said, "Oh, really, why not?"

"Oh," he said, "I can't stand the smell."

I couldn't resist. I said, "You know, you're really fortunate to have a wife who loves it."

George apparently considered his discomfort more important than Sally's discomfort. He can't stand the smell of messy diapers, but he assumes—I guess he assumes—that she loves it. In other words, his first priority was himself.

Love is not touchy. Have you ever brushed by somebody who is badly sunburned? Have you ever touched a fully inflated balloon with a pin? Sometimes people are like that. The tiniest little thing, and pow!—they just explode. You are free to choose not to be touchy. Think how that would bless a marriage.

Love does not keep account of evil or gloat over wickedness. How many times do we have a fight with our spouse and bring up all the unrelated things he or she has done? It is like we carefully watch for things we can hang on to to bring up when tension rises, and we think, *Oh, that's a good one. I'm going to save that for the next time.* And so we keep a running tally of the bad things our spouse does so we can use it as ammunition later. But the scriptures say that love does not keep account of evil. Instead—

Love is glad when truth prevails. We rejoice in our hearts when something good happens, when the truth prevails. Sometimes that truth proves us wrong. But we're still glad if we truly have charity. How wonderful that can be in marriage.

I love the way Phillips concludes this section of his translation: There is "no limit to its endurance, no end to its trust, no fading of its hope."[11] What would happen if every time we did something wrong God went into a pout or struck back in anger? What if he became furious when people did their own thing? Some day your husband is going to get fat and bald and old and sick, maybe even having Alzheimer's, and some day your wife is not going to be as wonderfully slender and maybe not quite as energetic and all the things that you wish. What does that matter? Love knows no limit to its endurance, no end to its trust, no fading of its hope.

When I think of the endurance of love, I think of one of my favorite stories. This story was told by Elder Robert D. Hales a few years ago. It's about a poet named Thomas Moore. Thomas Moore came home from a business trip after being gone for several weeks and found his wife locked in her bedroom. She was a beautiful woman with a wonderfully white, smooth complexion. But while he was gone she had contracted smallpox, which had terribly scarred her face. She had locked herself in the room, pulled all the shutters down, and was sitting there in the dark. He pleaded with her to let him in. She refused. She said, "Thomas, don't press me on this one, please, just go away and leave me alone."

Here is how Elder Hales tells the story: "Moore did go. He went downstairs and spent the rest of the night in prayerful writing. He'd never written a song before, but that night he wrote not only words but he composed the music. As daylight broke Moore returned to his wife's darkened room. 'Are you awake?' he said. 'Yes, but please do not come in.' 'I'll sing to you then,' he said. Then Thomas Moore sang to his wife the song that still lives today. You know it. 'Believe me, if all those endearing young charms / Which I gaze on so fondly today, / Were to change by tomorrow, and fleet in my arms, / Like fairy gifts fading away, / Thou wouldst still be adored, as this moment thou art, / Let thy loveliness fade as it will, / And around the dear ruin each wish of my heart / Would entwine itself verdantly still.'"

Then Brother Hales said, "The song ended. As his voice faded, Moore heard his bride arise. She crossed the room to the window, reached up and slowly drew the shutters and let him in."[12]

Love knows no end to its endurance, no end of its hope, no fading of its trust. It is the thing which brings us to oneness.

"Do Not Procrastinate the Day of Your Repentance"

I would like to close with a prayer that comes out of Alma. Consider it in terms of the eternal marriage you are trying to build. In Alma 13:27 we read: "And now, my brethren, I wish from the inmost part of my heart, yea, with great anxiety even unto pain, that ye would hearken unto my words, and cast off your sins, and not procrastinate the day of your repentance."

Do you have problems in your marriage? Stop procrastinating. Get them out. Cleanse the inner vessel.

The prayer continues: "Humble yourselves before the Lord, and call on his holy name, and watch and pray continually, that ye may not be tempted above that which ye can bear, and thus be led by the Holy Spirit, becoming humble, meek, submissive, patient, full of love and all long-suffering;

"Having faith on the Lord; having a hope that ye shall receive eternal life [which includes being one flesh]; having the love of God always in your hearts, that ye may be lifted up at the last day and enter into his rest.

"And may the Lord grant unto you repentance, that ye may not bring down his wrath upon you [or your marriage], that ye may not be bound down by the chains of hell, that ye may not suffer [the death of a good marriage]" (Alma 13:28–30).

I leave that with you as the testimony that the Book of Mormon is a key to becoming *one.* It is a keystone to a happy marriage.

Notes

From an address given at a Church Educational System symposium on the Book of Mormon, Salt Lake City, Utah, 15–17 August 1990.

1. John Taylor, in *Journal of Discourses,* 26 vols. (London: Latter-day Saints' Book Depot, 1854–86), 18:137.
2. David O. McKay, in Conference Report, April 1952, 87.
3. Joseph Fielding Smith, "The Divine Family," *Improvement Era,* June 1965, 495.
4. Susan Lyman-Whitney, "Men and women communicate as if on different planets," *Deseret News,* 4 February 1980, 8G.
5. Ezra Taft Benson, in Conference Report, October 1987, 61.
6. Rousas John Rushdoony, *The Institutes of Biblical Law* (n.p.: The Presbyterian and Reformed Publishing Co., 1973), 346.
7. Boyd K. Packer, "Family Togetherness—the Core of the Church," Education Week devotional address, Brigham Young University, Provo, Utah, 13 June 1963, 3.
8. John Taylor, in *Journal of Discourses,* 18:137.
9. George Q. Cannon, as quoted in *The Doctrine and Covenants Student Manual* (Salt Lake City: The Church of Jesus Christ of Latter-day Saints, 1981), 101–2.
10. Phillips Modern English Translation, as cited in *The New Testament in Four Versions* (Washington, D.C.: Christianity Today, Inc., 1965), 533.
11. Ibid.
12. Robert D. Hales, "We Can't Do It Alone," *New Era,* January 1977, 37.

Chapter 8

An Anti-Christ in the Book of Mormon—The Face May Be Strange, but the Voice Is Familiar

Korihor and the Word of God—A "Foil" in the Book of Mormon

At what is very near the exact center of the Book of Mormon, we have what appears to be an anomaly in terms of scripture content. In several places the major writers of the Book of Mormon tell us that they are interested only in sharing the spiritual history of their peoples. They clearly state that their focus is on Christ and on the spiritual things of history. (For example, see 2 Ne. 5:32 where Nephi says he is only going to engrave those things which are pleasing to God.) Yet in the thirtieth chapter of Alma, we have a whole chapter on the doings of an anti-Christ, including a detailed summary of the false doctrine that he taught. Why would Mormon take time to do that? Do we really need a summary of the teachings of evil men? What is it about Korihor that was so compelling to Mormon that he felt justified to give it four pages of textual treatment? The purpose of this chapter is to explore those questions and assess the significance of the Korihor material.

One of the first things to note is that in this portion of the Book of Mormon, Korihor is a good example of a scriptural "foil." One of Webster's definitions of a foil is something that is used "to enhance by contrast." For example, a jeweler places diamonds on black velvet to provide a contrasting backdrop, or foil, for the gems. There are numerous places in the standard works where the scriptural writers use that same technique, placing two contrasting principles or examples side by side to show even more clearly what they were trying to teach.

For example, it is interesting that the parable of the good Samaritan, one of the most powerful lessons on Christian service found in any of the standard works (see Luke 10:25–37), is followed immediately by the story of Mary and Martha (see Luke 10:38–42), which teaches another very different lesson about service. This is what we mean by "scriptural foils."

Perhaps scriptural foils provide one answer to the question, Why would Mormon take time and space to tell us of a person who taught false and evil doctrine? The Korihor story is an obvious foil in one sense and a subtle but perhaps even more significant foil in another sense. The obvious one is that we find a story of an "evil missionary," a man who seeks to preach false doctrine and proselytize people to his way of thinking, sandwiched right in between the account of the sons of Mosiah and their mission to the Lamanites, and Alma's great mission to the Zoramites. Is that an accidental thing, this "missionary foil" that we find here?

But there is something more subtle than this. There is an interesting conceptual chain related to the "power of the word" that flows through this section of the Book of Mormon. As the account of the mission of the sons of Mosiah begins, Alma testifies that through personal preparation, including scripture study, fasting, and prayer, these brethren were able to teach the word "with power and authority of God" (Alma 17:3). Then, in the very next verse, Mormon notes that they had great success in bringing the Lamanites to the gospel because of "the power of their words" (Alma 17:4). The next ten chapters show just how true that statement is.

But as we come to the end of their fourteen-year mission, what do we find again? In Alma 26, Ammon begins to review their tremendous successes. And what does he credit for this incredible conversion story? "The power of *[God's] word* which is in us" (Alma 26:13; emphasis added).

Chapters 27 and 28 finish out the account of their mission, telling us how the Lamanites were settled among the Nephites and so on. But chapter 29 breaks off the historical narrative. At that point, Mormon chooses to insert a prayer of Alma's. And what does he pray for? Note his words: "O that I were an angel, and could have the wish of mine heart, that I might go forth and speak with the trump of God, with a voice to shake the earth, and cry repentance unto every people!" (Alma 29:1). In other words, Alma's prayer is that he might have even greater power to preach the word than he has hitherto had.

This is what precedes the Korihor account. For a moment now, let's skip Alma 30 and Korihor and see what immediately follows. In chapter 31, Alma learns that the Zoramites are in a state of apostasy—a situation that has grave political overtones because of their proximity to the Lamanites. So Alma decides to begin his own mission to an apostate people. Mormon is careful to note why Alma chooses this avenue of response: "And now, as *the preaching of the word* had a great tendency to lead the people to do that which was just—yea, it had had *more powerful effect upon the minds of the people than the sword, or anything else,* which had happened unto them—therefore Alma thought it was expedient that they should try the virtue of the word of God" (Alma 31:5; emphasis added).

Alma's mission, however, is not the only thing to follow the story of Korihor. In chapter 32, when Alma begins to teach the Zoramite poor how to find God, he uses a powerful analogy of a seed. Often in the Church, we refer to Alma 32 as being a great chapter on faith. This is not incorrect; but the seed Alma refers to is not faith, it is *the word of God* (see Alma 32:28). After talking about the power of the word in Chapter 31, Alma teaches the Zoramites how to take the word and bring it to the point where it has great power in our lives.

Thus we see in one place after another in this section of the Book of Mormon, beginning in Alma 17 and going through Alma 33, there is reference after reference to the *power of the word.* And what is placed right in the middle of this chain? Korihor! And therein lies the more subtle scriptural foil. Korihor himself is an example of the "power of the word," only this time it is a negative example. Just as Ammon and his brothers and Alma lead many into the Church by preaching the word to the people, Korihor leads many people away from the Church by his *preaching his own word.*

In light of that foil, let us now examine what Korihor taught and see if we can determine why Mormon would devote space on the plates to describe the doctrine of this anti-Christ.

The Korihor Philosophy—A New Face and Old Voice

If we could take a moment to talk in philosophical terms, there are three branches of philosophy which have a great deal to do with what a person believes, how they approach life, and what constitutes their value system: metaphysics, axiology, and epistemology.

Metaphysics is the branch of philosophy that deals with the nature of reality. It tries to answer the question "What is real?" *Meta* is a Greek prefix meaning "after" or "beyond," so metaphysics means, literally, "beyond physics." In other words, metaphysics asks whether there is something more than (or beyond) the physical world that we see around us. Is there some reality higher than the natural world—literally, a *supernatural reality?*

The second branch of philosophy that has much to do with our discussion is axiology. *Axi* comes from the Greek root which means "worth" or "value." Axiology is the study of ethics and values. It wrestles with such questions as "What is good?" and "What is right and wrong?"

The third branch of philosophy is epistemology. *Epistem* is a root meaning "knowledge." (An *epistle,* which comes from the same root, is a message—or knowledge—sent by writing.) Epistemology is the study of *how* we know what is real or what is true. Since epistemology is central to our discussion on Korihor, a brief review of some of the major epistemological systems will serve to illustrate better what is meant by the term.

Authoritarianism is the system wherein truth is derived from those viewed as authorities or experts in an area. The recent crisis in the Middle East has illustrated how often we turn to experts for truth and information. We have seen on television a wide range of experts on war, military logistics, Islam, politics, government, etc.

Rationalism is an epistemological system wherein truth is derived through logical processes such as deduction, induction, and so on. In rationalism we ask, "Does this make sense? Is it logical?"

Pragmatism is a system in which truth is determined by whether or not something works. For example, the business world is very pragmatically oriented, constantly focusing on whether a new product or marketing strategy actually produces the projected results. If it does, it is true; if it doesn't, it is rejected.

Empiricism is the gaining of knowledge through observation or experience. The scientific method, wherein one conducts an experiment and observes the results, is based heavily on the empirical method. Empirical evidence is often what people mean when they talk about hard or measurable evidence.

If one were to ask which of the above epistemological systems Latter-day Saints subscribe to, we would probably agree that we accept all of them as valid means of gaining knowledge or truth. However, in our theology, there is yet one more system, and this takes priority over the others.

Revelation is the finding of truth through communication of God's mind and will to man. In Latter-day Saint theology, revelation comes via the Spirit or through direct manifestations (such as visions) to man.

There are other epistemological systems, or ways of knowing truth, but these are the main ones and will serve our purpose here. These three branches of

KORIHOR'S PHILOSOPHICAL FOUNDATIONS

Epistemology: "How do you know things?" Empiricism and Rationalism (Alma 30:12–15)

You cannot know what you cannot see.	You cannot know the future (if you can't see it).	Prophecies (of future) can't be true (no revelation).	You can't know of Christ (or his atonement and redemption).

Metaphysics: "What is real?" Humanism and Naturalism (Alma 30:17–18)

People fare by their own management.	Success depends on one's strength and genius.	There is nothing beyond this life.	Human beings are the supreme reality in a natural world.

Axiology: "What is good? What is right?" Relativism, No Absolutes (Alma 30:17)

No God, no revelation; human beings are the supreme reality.	No divine set of laws, no ultimate right or wrong.	Whatever people do is not a crime.	Morals, values come only from human experience.

philosophy—metaphysics, axiology, and epistemology—have a profound effect upon how people view life, what they value, and how they act in various situations.

This proves to be true in the case of Korihor as well. A careful reading of Korihor's "doctrine" reveals three linchpins, or pivotal points, of his entire philosophy. Chart 1 illustrates how these three fundamental points target the very areas we have described above. To put it more simply, Korihor defines how people come to know truth (epistemology), he talks about what constitutes reality (metaphysics), and defines what is good and what is evil (axiology).

Looking at Korihor's teachings carefully, we see that he starts with an epistemology based on strong empiricism. He states it very simply: "Ye cannot know of

TWO COROLLARY ISSUES

How do you explain people who have faith?
You have been propagandized by:
1. The foolish traditions of your fathers (religious upbringing)
2. Religious leaders whose true motives are gain and power

Which has resulted in psychological problems:
1. Frenzied minds
2. Mental derangement

So what does all this mean in practical terms?
You are not bound down to any imposed set of religious or traditional values.

You can live as you please without fear of eternal consequences.

things which ye do not see [or we would say, *experience*]" (Alma 30:15). His metaphysics openly rejects any kind of supernatural explanation of reality. In Korihor's doctrine, there is no other dimension of reality beyond the physical world—no God, no angels, no Spirit that brings revelation. From his metaphysics comes the natural conclusion that "when a man was dead, that was the end thereof" (Alma 30:18). From Korihor's epistemology (the denial of revelation) and his metaphysics (there is only the natural world, and man is the supreme reality in it), flows his axiology (the only good or bad is that which is decided by man himself). This is often the case. In other words, how we answer the questions "How do we know what is true?" and "What constitutes reality?" often determines how we perceive what is good and bad, right and wrong.

This gets at the crux of the matter and explains why Satan would take such an interest in philosophy. Out of Korihor's basic philosophy now flow two important corollaries. When Korihor was arrested and taken before the high priest, he boldly challenged the position of the religious leaders (see Alma 30:23–28). Giddonah challenged Korihor to explain why, if what Korihor said was true, the people gained so much joy from their religion.

Korihor's first corollary answers that very neatly. Chart 2 diagrams his answer. There are two reasons people believe in these false ideas. The first is that they have been indoctrinated by their parents (the "foolish traditions" of their fathers) or that they have been deceived by false religious leaders who seek personal gain or power.

This indoctrination leads to psychological abnormalities, a "frenzied mind" or "derangement" (see Alma 30:16).

Out of the first corollary flows a second. This is the final, practical conclusion of Korihor's philosophy. He states that there are no ultimate values set by religion or tradition that put us in jeopardy of some eternal punishment. Therefore, we can live as we please without fear of eternal consequences.

This is the heart of the matter. This is what it is all about. I don't believe for a moment Satan cares about philosophy as a mental game or academic exercise, only where it can take us. Now that can be most productive in terms of Satan's ultimate purposes. And Mormon clearly identifies that end result of deceiving philosophy: "And thus he did preach unto them, leading away the hearts of many, *causing them to lift up their heads in their wickedness,* yea, leading away many women, and also men, to commit whoredoms" (Alma 30:18, emphasis added).

What a victory, from Satan's point of view. This is not just wickedness, it is wickedness in which people take pride. They lift up their heads in it. And why shouldn't they? Korihor has provided the ultimate rationalization—there is no God; there is no ultimate right and wrong; man is the supreme being. All the guilt and shame people feel (psychological hang-ups) are simply the result of the foolish teachings of their parents or the designs of evil religious leaders.

The Age of Information but Not the Age of Truth

In recent years, numerous people have begun to note that society is going through a massive wave of change. It has been called by various titles—the technological revolution, the information age, the info/tech age. Alvin Toffler calls it the Third Wave. According to Toffler, the history of the world shows three great waves of change that have influenced the way we and all world societies live. The first massive wave of change was when man moved from hunting and gathering to an agricultural society. The second wave was when the world moved from an agricultural society to an industrial society. Now we are in the third wave, a wave that will take us from the industrial society to a new age based on technology and information.[1]

John Naisbitt, in a best-seller some years ago called *Megatrends: Ten New Directions Transforming Our Lives,* outlined ten of the great changes society would face in the last part of the twentieth century. One of those "megatrends" is the change to an "information" age. Naisbitt says: "In 1956, for the first time in American history, white-collar workers in technical, managerial, and clerical positions outnumbered blue-collar workers. Industrial America was giving way to a new society, where, for the first time in history, most of us worked with information rather than producing goods."[2]

Later he says that we have for the first time an economy based on a key resource that is not only renewable but self-generating. Running out of it is not a problem, but *drowning* in it is. For example:

- Between 6,000 and 7,000 scientific articles are written each day.
- Scientific and technical information now increases 13 percent per year, which means it doubles every 5.5 years.[3]

He had already noted: "Farmer, laborer, clerk—that is a brief history of the United States. . . . In fact today there are more people employed full-time in our universities than in agriculture."[4]

An interesting sidelight to note is that even some of our more popular games reflect this change to an information society. "Trivial Pursuit" and its numerous spinoffs are all based on the mastery of information. And the most popular television game show *Jeopardy* has the contestants vie to see who has the most information at their fingertips (or perhaps "mind-tips").

But even though we may live in the age of information, this does not necessarily mean we are living in the age of truth. Not all information is of the same value. Naisbitt, for example, suggests that "we are drowning in information but starved for knowledge." For example, he notes that scientists now say that "it takes less time to do an experiment than to find out whether or not it has already been done."[5]

With this age of information has come an accompanying age of secularism. Rejection of traditional religious values is commonplace. In a talk given some years ago, Elder Neal A. Maxwell described the difference between an eternal and a secular outlook:

"For the purpose of this brief discussion, eternalism is defined as that view of man and the universe which not only acknowledges, but exults in, the existence of a Heavenly Father, his Son Jesus Christ, and the Holy Ghost, who have authored and implemented a redeeming plan for mankind. Secularism is herein defined as that view of man and the universe which is essentially irreligious with regard to the existence of God and cosmic purpose for man, but which is not necessarily irreverent with regard to man and his worth."[6]

We are not only drowning in a sea of information, we are also drowning in a sea of secularism. In many ways we have reached the same point Ezekiel described around 600 B.C., a condition, incidentally, which led to the destruction of the Jewish nation. Ezekiel said, "Her priests have violated my law, and have profaned mine holy things: they have *put no difference between the holy and profane, neither have they shewed difference between the unclean and the clean*" (Ezek. 22:26; emphasis added).

Our educational institutions, our media, and our entertainment are all permeated with philosophies that are similar to those taught by Korihor. For example, note the following excerpts from "Humanist Manifesto II," a document stating the beliefs of those who call themselves humanists. I shall take the liberty to insert a few quotations from Korihor at appropriate places:

"We believe . . . that *traditional* dogmatic or authoritarian religions that place revelation, God, ritual, or creed above human needs and experience do a disservice to the human species. . . . *Traditional* religions often offer *solace* to humans, but, as often, they *inhibit* humans from helping themselves or experiencing their full potentialities. . . . Too often *traditional* faiths encourage dependence rather than independence."

["They are foolish traditions of your fathers. . . . It is the effect of a frenzied mind; and this derangement . . . comes because of the traditions of your fathers" (Alma 30:14, 16).]

"We can discover no divine purpose or providence for the human species. . . . *No deity will save us;* we must save ourselves. Promises of immortal salvation or fear of eternal damnation are both illusory and harmful. They distract humans from present concerns, from self-actualization, and from rectifying social injustices."

["There should be no Christ. . . . When a man was dead, that was the end thereof" (Alma 30:12, 18).]

"Science affirms that the human species is an emergence from natural evolutionary forces. As far as we know, *the total personality is a function of the biological organism transacting in a social and cultural context.*"

["Every man fared in this life according to the management of the creature; therefore every man prospered according to his genius, and that every man conquered according to his strength" (Alma 30:17).]

"We affirm that moral values derive their source from human experience. Ethics is *autonomous and situational,* needing no theological or ideological sanction. Ethics stem from human need and interest."[7]

["Whatsoever a man did was no crime" (Alma 30:17).]

This manifesto was signed by 113 individuals when it was published. Signers include such notables as Isaac Asimov, a famous science fiction writer; B. F. Skinner, an influential psychologist from Harvard University; Andrei Sakharov, a famous Russian scientist and dissident; and James Prescott, who at the time was the director of the National Institution for Child Help and Human Development. Of the total, more than 50 were college professors, some 10 were authors, and 11 were listed as ministers. In other words, more than half of the endorsers were people who are in positions of influence in the teaching of others. Not surprisingly, then, these secular philosophies permeate much of our society today.

The final statement quoted reveals the humanist view of ethics, declaring them to be "situational" and derived from "human experiences." Again, we find some interesting parallels to Korihor in modern society.

There is a whole body of ethical thought today known as "situation ethics," which states that there are no absolutes by which we determine what is right or wrong. Rather, the situation determines what is good or bad. Joseph Fletcher has given situational ethics its most articulate airing. Dr. Fletcher claims to be a Christian ethicist. In fact, he was a former dean of St. Paul's Cathedral in Cincinnati, and at the time he wrote his book, *Situation Ethics,* he was a professor of social ethics at the Episcopal Theology School in Cambridge, Massachusetts. Dr. Fletcher argues that love is the highest good and that what determines whether something is right or wrong is simply whether or not it is the "loving thing" to do. Here are some excerpts from his book *Situation Ethics: True or False?*

"Love is the highest good and the first-order value, the primary consideration to which in every act . . . we should be prepared to sidetrack or subordinate other valued considerations of right and wrong. . . . Whether we ought to follow a moral principle or not *would always depend upon the situation.* . . . In some situations unmarried love could be infinitely more moral than married unlove. Lying could be more Christian than telling the truth. . . . Stealing could be better than respecting private property. . . . *No action is good or right of itself.* It depends on whether it hurts or helps. . . . There are no normative moral principles whatsoever *which are intrinsically valid or universally obliging.* We may not absolutize the norms of human conduct."[8]

In the book itself he says, "If we are, as I would want to reason, obliged in conscience sometimes to tell white lies, as we often call them, then in conscience we might be obliged sometimes to engage in white thefts and white fornications and white killings and white breakings of promises and the like."[9]

Mormon noted that the end result of Korihor's philosophy was a breakdown of morality among the people. The end result of situation ethics leads to much the same result. In Dr. Fletcher's earlier book, *Situation Ethics: The New Morality,* he reasoned away any moral standard as we know it in terms of sexual morality:

"What sex probably needs more than anything is a good airing. . . . People are learning that we can have sex without love, and love without sex; that baby-making can be (and often ought to be) separated from lovemaking. It is, indeed, for re-creation as well as for pro-creation. But *if people do not believe it is wrong to have sex relations outside marriage, it isn't,* unless they hurt themselves, their partners, or others. . . . All situationists would agree with Mrs. Patrick Campbell's remark that they can do what they want 'as long as they don't do it in the street and frighten the horses.'"[10]

Remember, this teaching comes from a man who calls himself a Christian ethicist. In a debate with another Christian minister, Fletcher shared some of his feelings toward Christ. When the other minister cited a New Testament statement made by the Savior to support the point he was making, Fletcher labeled Jesus as "a simple Jewish peasant" and said that he didn't look to Jesus for philosophical sophistication.[11]

It is not hard to see why Satan would rejoice in such philosophy. Mormon said Korihor taught the people to "lift up their heads in their wickedness" (Alma 30:18). Fletcher's philosophy provides a similar rationalization. As long as it is the "loving thing" to do, it is not sin.

Elder Neal A. Maxwell described the eventual results for a society that accepts ethics that are not based on absolute, God-given truths:

"Relativism involves the denial of the existence of absolute truths and, therefore, of an absolute truthgiver, God. Relativism has sometimes been a small, satanic sea breeze, but now the winds of relativism have reached gale proportions. Over a period of several decades relativism has eroded ethics, public and personal, has worn down the will of many, has contributed to a slackening sense of duty, civic and personal. The old mountains of individual morality have been worn down. This erosion has left mankind in a sand-dune society, in a desert of disbelief where there are no landmarks, and no north, no east, no west, and no south! There is only the dust of despair."[12]

When we look at teachings that permeate our day, we begin to sense why Mormon felt it important to include Korihor's philosophies in the Book of Mormon. President Ezra Taft Benson specifically said this was one of the values of the Book of Mormon for our day:

"The Book of Mormon exposes the enemies of Christ. *It confounds false doctrines* and lays down contention (see 1 Nephi 3:12). It fortifies the humble followers of Christ against the evil designs, strategies, and *doctrines of the devil* in our day. *The type of apostates in the Book of Mormon are similar to the type we have today*. God, with His infinite foreknowledge, so molded the Book of Mormon that we might see the error and know how to combat false educational, political, religious, and philosophical concepts of our time."[13]

A Prophet's Answer to the Philosophies of Satan

We have now examined the teachings of Korihor in some detail, and we also have seen how they parallel some of the common teachings of our day. If Mormon had included nothing but those teachings, they would have been of great value to us. But he did more than that. He also included Alma's answer to Korihor. It is an interesting contrast not only to Korihor's teachings but also to his whole situational philosophic approach.

The first thing to note is that Alma does not get into a philosophical debate with Korihor. He does not talk about metaphysics or axiology or epistemology. He does not allow himself to get pulled onto the ground that Korihor tries to define as the area of debate. There is a great lesson in that. Alma teaches that we should combat false philosophies with revelation and doctrine, not with academic debate.

This is not to imply that Alma dodges the issues; in fact, he confronts Korihor's criticism directly by proving that it is contradictory. Firstly, Alma points out that Korihor knows that the Church leaders do not receive anything for their labors in the Church except the joy they receive for teaching truth (see Alma 30:35). Yet Korihor has claimed that the leaders "glut" themselves upon the labors of the people (Alma 30:27). Alma then concludes that since what Korihor knows to be true and what he says to be true clearly oppose one another, Korihor deliberately twists the truth.

In his second answer, Alma is absolutely brilliant. Let's follow that one for a moment to see what he is suggesting. Korihor has stated that people can believe only that which they can see, or that which they can prove to be true. Then he categorically states that he believes there is no God. Alma points out that he is trapped in his own epistemology, saying, "And now what evidence have ye that there is no God, or that Christ cometh not? I say unto you that ye have none, save it be your own word only" (Alma 30:40). If Korihor really were consistent (in believing only that which he can experience), then he cannot believe there is no God, because he cannot prove there is no God.

Let's see if we can illustrate the force of this argument. Suppose that a person decided he wanted to prove once and for all there is no God. Since the scriptures claim that God dwells in the heavens, the first task the person would have is to

ALMA'S ANSWER (ALMA 30:32–45)

You know:	But you say:	Therefore:	Final conclusion:
We don't profit from our service in the Church.	We glut ourselves on the labor of the people.	You deliberately twist the truth.	You are possessed of a lying spirit.
You cannot prove there is no God.	You believe only what can be proved.	You are not consistent with yourself.	
You believe there is a God.*	You cannot believe in him.	You are lying to yourself and to us.	
There are many signs that prove God lives.	You won't believe unless you see a sign.	You won't accept truth when it is given to you.	

*Note Korihor's confirmation of this in Alma 30:52.

examine every cubic inch of the heavens (the universe), to see if there was no God. But even that impossible task creates a new set of problems. First of all, it would have to be an examination in the fullest sense of the word. Human beings *see* only visible light, which is a tiny portion of the electromagnetic spectrum. If by *see* we mean only what the eye can register, God would be totally missed if he exists at another frequency of the light spectrum. In other words, suppose God were at the ultraviolet or infrared frequencies. This person looking for God would miss him completely.

But examining every inch of the universe across the fulness of the electromagnetic spectrum still wouldn't provide irrefutable proof. Suppose the person marked out the universe in a grid and began to search it systematically, square by square, from A to Z, and didn't find God in any of the squares. Could that person then say there was no God? No! What if God was in square L when the searcher started in square A, but by the time that person reached square L, God had moved back to square B or C?

Let's put it simply. Korihor says he will only believe what can be seen or proven. Yet he says he believes there is no God. To prove there is no God, a person would have to perceive (in the fullest sense of the word) every cubic inch of the entire universe simultaneously! In other words, *one would have to be a god in order to prove there is no God.* And yet Korihor blithely denies any belief in God's existence. In other words, Korihor is acting as much on faith (not righteous faith, but at least belief based on evidence that cannot be seen), as are those who believe there is a God. No wonder Alma accuses Korihor of having a "lying spirit" (Alma 30:42).

There is one more thing on Chart 3 that ought to be noted. After pointing out that there is much evidence that God does exist, Alma asks Korihor if he believes these things are true. Without waiting for an answer, he flatly states, "Behold, I know that thou believest" (Alma 30:42). Is this just a prophet's attempt to confound an argumentative person? Hardly. A few verses later, after having called down the sign upon himself, Korihor confirms Alma's statement, saying, "I *always* knew that there was a God" (Alma 30:52; emphasis added). So again, Alma shows that Korihor's real problem is that he is a liar.

The Word of God and Its Power

Let's return back to the scriptural foil that we began with. We showed that through this portion of the book of Alma there is a focus on the power of the word. It starts in the account of Ammon and his brothers and continues through Alma's mission to the Zoramites. Right in the middle of that chain, we see Korihor, a compelling, negative example of the power of the word. This serves as a foil that contrasts the power of God's word and truth with the power of Satan's word and untruth.

As we close our discussion of Korihor, we note two great ironies that also seem to be part of that scriptural foil as well. When Korihor demanded to have a sign before he would believe, Alma warned him of consequences of this action. But the anti-Christ still demanded proof. Of all the things the Lord could have chosen to convince Korihor of his power, what did he choose to do? Korihor is struck dumb (see Alma 30:49–50). In other words, *Korihor's power to persuade others by the word was taken from him.*

When Alma refused to lift the curse from him, Korihor left the land of Zarahemla and went over among the Zoramites. There he was "run upon and trodden down, even until he was dead" (Alma 30:59). Here is the second great irony. The Zoramites were a group of apostates who had left the Nephite religion and started their own church. In chapter 31, we are given an account of their teachings in some detail. Note the following phrases from that chapter which describe the doctrines of the Zoramites. Mormon tells us they had "fallen into great errors" (v. 9); they rejected the traditions of their Nephite brethren as being "handed down to them by the childishness of their fathers" (v. 16); they did not want to be "led away after the foolish traditions of our brethren, which doth bind them down to a belief in Christ" (v. 17); and they refused "to believe in things to come, which they knew nothing about" (v. 22).

Familiar echoes? Indeed they are. The Zoramites are a reflection of some of Korihor's primary teachings. In other words, the Zoramites represent the end result of Korihor's philosophy. This is where his doctrine leads people. What an irony that Korihor should come to his end by the hands of the very people who practiced what he preached.

Elder Maxwell, citing C. S. Lewis, pointed out that this is typical of those who try to reject God as part of their philosophy:

"C. S. Lewis wrote well when he asserted: 'What Satan put into the heads of our remote ancestors was the idea that they . . . could . . . invent some sort of happiness for themselves outside God, apart from God. And out of that hopeless attempt has come nearly all that we call human history—money, poverty, ambition, war, prostitution, classes, empires, slavery—the long terrible story of man trying to find something other than God which will make him happy. . . .

"'That is the key to history. Terrific energy is expended—civilizations are built up—excellent institutions devised; but each time something goes wrong. Some fatal flaw always brings the selfish and cruel people to the top and it all slides back into misery and ruin. In fact, the machine conks. It seems to start up all right and runs a few years, and then it breaks down. They are trying to run it on the wrong juice. That is what Satan has done to us humans.'"[14]

Might this not be the very thing that caused Mormon, working under the inspiration of God, to include in the Book of Mormon an account of this anti-Christ and his teachings? It is for our benefit. It helps us see false teachings for what they are and the end result of them. This is partly what is meant by the "power of the word." This is part of the power of the Book of Mormon. President Benson made this clear:

"It is not just that the Book of Mormon bears testimony of Christ, though it indeed does that too. But there is something more. There is a power in the book which will begin to flow into your lives the moment you begin a serious study of the book. You will find greater power to resist temptation. You will find the power to avoid deception. You will find the power to stay on the strait and narrow path. The scriptures are called 'the words of life' (see D&C 84:85), and nowhere is that more true than it is of the Book of Mormon. When you begin to hunger and thirst after those words, you will find life in greater and greater abundance. These promises—increased love and harmony in the home, greater respect between parent and child, increased spirituality and righteousness—these are not idle promises, but exactly what the Prophet Joseph Smith meant when he said the Book of Mormon will help us draw nearer to God."[15]

Korihor tried to teach people that there is happiness and joy to be found outside of God and the gospel. The Book of Mormon clearly shows that this is not true. It reminds us of the power of God's word, the power to change our lives, the power to bring us peace and joy and the answers to those issues in life that trouble us. As we learn this lesson from Korihor, we again are reminded of the promise of President Ezra Taft Benson, the living Prophet:

"I bless you with increased discernment to judge between Christ and anti-Christ. I bless you with increased power to do good and resist evil. I bless you with increased understanding of the Book of Mormon. I promise you that from this moment forward, if we will daily sup from its pages and abide by its precepts, God will pour out upon each child of Zion and the Church a blessing hitherto unknown."[16]

Notes

From Monte S. Nyman and Charles D. Tate Jr., eds., *The Book of Mormon: Alma, The Testimony of The Word,* Sixth Annual Book of Mormon Symposium (Provo, Utah: Religious Studies Center, Brigham Young University/Salt Lake City: Bookcraft, 1992), 107–28.

1. See Alvin Toffler, *The Third Wave* (New York: William Morrow & Co., 1980).
2. John Naisbitt, *Megatrends: Ten New Directions Transforming Our Lives* (New York: Warner Books, 1982), 12.
3. Ibid., 24; emphasis added.
4. Ibid., 14.
5. Ibid., 24.
6. Neal A. Maxwell, "Eternalism vs. Secularism," *Ensign,* October 1974, 69.
7. "Humanist Manifesto II," *The Humanist* 33, no. 5 (September/October 1973): 5–6; emphasis in original.
8. Joseph Fletcher and John Warwick Montgomery, *Situation Ethics: True or False?* (Minneapolis: Dimension Books, 1972), back cover; emphasis added.
9. Ibid., 15.
10. Joseph Fletcher, *Situation Ethics: The New Morality* (Philadelphia: Westminister Press, 1969), 140; emphasis added.
11. Fletcher and Montgomery, *Situation Ethics: True or False?,* 55.
12. Neal A. Maxwell, "Some Thoughts on the Gospel and the Behavioral Sciences," *Ensign,* July 1976, 74.
13. Ezra Taft Benson, *The Teachings of Ezra Taft Benson* (Salt Lake City: Bookcraft, 1988), 56; emphasis added.
14. C. S. Lewis, *Mere Christianity* (New York: Macmillan Publishing Co., 1958), 39; as cited in Maxwell, "Eternalism vs. Secularism," 71.
15. Benson, *The Teachings of Ezra Taft Benson,* 54.
16. Ibid., 65.

Jesus Christ and His Atonement

Chapter 9

"The Birth of Jesus Christ Was on This Wise" (Matthew 1:18)

"*And in the sixth month the angel Gabriel was sent from God unto a city of Galilee, named Nazareth*" (Luke 1:26).

The rabbis of ancient Israel had a saying: "Judea is wheat, Galilee straw, and beyond Jordan, only chaff."[1] The urbane and worldly wise Jerusalemites, privileged to dwell in the Holy City, looked down on all others with condescension; but they especially viewed the Galileans as crude, unlearned, and earthy peasants. For the most part the people of Galilee were men of the soil and of the sea. This kept them in touch with basic values; and in spite of the feelings of the Judeans, they were known for being hard-working and warm-hearted, and for showing unrestrained hospitality and uncompromising honesty.

As for Nazareth itself, like many other villages of Judea and Galilee, it sat amid steep, tree-covered hillsides so as not to utilize precious agricultural land. For a village now so famous to us, it seems to have been of singular insignificance then. It is not even mentioned in the Old Testament or in the extensive writings of the ancient historian Josephus. Nathanael expressed what must have been a common feeling even among the Galileans when he said, "Can there any good thing come out of Nazareth?" (John 1:46). Evidently, the suggestion that the Messiah had come from such a civic backwater was unthinkable.

But that is not to say that this home village of Mary and Joseph, and later the Master himself, was a drab and dull setting. One writer describes it as follows: "You cannot see from Nazareth the surrounding country, for Nazareth lies in a basin; but the moment you climb to the edge of the basin . . . what a view you have.

Esdraelon lies before you, with its twenty battlefields. . . . There is Naboth's vineyard and the place of Jehu's revenge upon Jezebel; there Shunem and the house of Elisha; the Carmel and the place of Elijah's sacrifice. To the east the valley of Jordan, . . . to the west the radiance of the Great Sea. . . . You can see thirty miles in three directions."[2]

This was the setting in which our story begins.

Engagement of Joseph and Mary

" . . . To a virgin espoused to a man whose name was Joseph, of the house of David" (Luke 1:27).

As we begin reading their story, we learn immediately that Joseph and Mary are "espoused" (Matt. 1:18). Espousal among the Hebrews was significantly more binding than are our engagements today. The couple entered into it by written agreement and considered it the formal beginning of the marriage itself. While the couple might not actually live together for as much as a year after the betrothal—a time designed to allow the bride to prepare her dowry—the espousal was as legally binding as the formal marriage.

The scriptural text gives no hint of the age of either Mary or Joseph, but from existing sources we can make some educated guesses. We know that puberty began somewhat earlier in the Middle East than is common in Western countries today. Therefore, marriage at earlier ages than we are accustomed to was the general rule. Speaking of men, one rabbi described the stages of development as follows: At five he began study of Torah; at ten, study of the Mishnah (the oral laws); at fifteen, the study of Talmud (the extensive commentaries on the scriptures). *At eighteen,* he married; at twenty, he pursued a trade or business.[3] For a girl, probably the most common age of marriage was fifteen or sixteen. Sometimes it was later, sometimes earlier, but it is likely that Mary was around sixteen and Joseph, her espoused husband, only two or three years older than that.

Nazareth was a small village. Joseph and Mary must have known each other well. How fascinating it would be to know the circumstances that brought them to the point of betrothal. Much is made of the fact that in those days families arranged marriages through a matchmaker. No doubt that was true, but that does not mean that the individuals involved had no voice in the matter. We know from contemporary sources that, once the arrangements were made, the consent of the couple was required. The man had a direct say in the choice of his bride, and the woman could refuse the marital arrangements if not to her satisfaction.[4] So what was it that drew these two together?

We know Mary must have been of unusual loveliness. Nephi saw her in vision six hundred years before her birth and described her as "exceedingly fair" and "most beautiful and fair" (1 Ne. 11:13, 15). But did Joseph see only the outward beauty, or did he sense the same qualities that caused Gabriel to declare that this woman was "highly favoured" of the Lord? (Luke 1:28). No wonder Joseph loved her! Imagine finding a woman of such remarkable grace and beauty in a small village in the mountains of the Galilee.

And what of Joseph? What was it about this man that caused Mary to give her consent to the marriage arrangements? Only a few scriptural verses tell us about Joseph. He was a carpenter, that we know (see Matt. 13:55). And because fathers commonly taught their sons their own trade, Joseph was likely reared in a carpenter's shop at his father's knees. His hands would have been rough and callused. He was a man of labor, a man who created things through his own craftsmanship.

Matthew also describes him as a "just man" (Matt. 1:19). It is a simple phrase, yet it speaks volumes, for those same words are used to describe men such as Noah, Job, Nephi, and Jacob. Was it purely by accident that such a man was in Nazareth waiting to be Mary's partner in this most significant of dramas? Surely God the Father had seen in Joseph a man worthy to raise His Son and help prepare him for his mortal ministry. While it would not be Joseph's privilege to actually father the "Firstborn," it would be his labor that would provide for Jesus' needs, his voice that would encourage the child's first steps, his hands that would guide the boy's fingers across the sacred scrolls of the Torah in those first Hebrew lessons. Joseph was also the one who would put a mallet and chisel and plane in those smaller hands so that one day this boy from Nazareth would also be known as "the carpenter" (Mark 6:3). No wonder Mary loved him!

The Name Mary

"And the virgin's name was Mary" (Luke 1:27).

One of the most common feminine names in the New Testament is Mary—*Miryam* (Miriam) in Hebrew. One Bible concordance identifies at least seven different Marys in the New Testament, so it is not surprising to find a virgin of that name in the village of Nazareth.[5] But perhaps there is more to it than that. Among Book of Mormon prophets, even a hundred years before the birth of the Savior, the actual name of the woman who was to mother the Messiah was known: It was to be Mary (see Mosiah 3:8; Alma 7:10). If that was so among Book of Mormon prophets, is it not possible that the name was also known among Old Testament prophets as well, and therefore among the people of the Holy Land?

We know from existing records that the people at the time of Christ's birth generally believed that the birth of the long-awaited Messiah was imminent. What mother would not hope that her daughter might be the promised vessel for such an honor? Such maternal optimism might explain the frequency with which daughters were named Mary. But for whatever reason, Mary's mother fulfilled prophetic promises when she named her child, no doubt little dreaming that her daughter indeed would be the one to do so.

Gabriel's Salutation

"And the angel came in unto her, and said, Hail, thou that art highly favoured, the Lord is with thee: blessed art thou among women. And when she saw him, she was troubled at his saying, and cast in her mind what manner of salutation this should be. And the angel said unto her, Fear not, Mary: for thou hast found favour with God. And, behold, thou shalt conceive in thy womb, and bring forth a son, and shalt call his name Jesus" (Luke 1:28–31).

It was early July in Galilee.[6] The heat, even at night, can be stifling and oppressive. Luke indicates that Mary and Joseph were likely of poor families.[7] If that be the case, the house of Mary's family would have been small, no more than one or two rooms curtained off for sleeping and privacy at night.

We are not told whether it was day or night, or whether she was alone in the house; surely she must have felt a sudden clutch of fear when she looked up and saw a personage standing there before her. All of us have had someone come up behind us or appear in a doorway unexpectedly and startle us. We give an involuntary cry of surprise and feel the quick burst of adrenaline that leaves the heart pounding, the palms sweaty, and the mouth dry. So it is not difficult to imagine the shock of having not just a man appear suddenly in your room, but a being of transcendent radiance and glory.

But the shock of Gabriel's sudden appearance could not have been any greater than the stunning impact of his words. First there was the "impossible" announcement that she was about to conceive. Her response is so spontaneous, so logical. It adds even further to the power and simplicity with which Luke tells us of this night. One can almost picture her blurting it out, in spite of the glory of the being standing before her: "How shall this be, seeing I know not a man?" (Luke 1:34).

But that was only the first of the stunning pronouncements. The Messiah had been foretold for four millennia. Now to realize that the long centuries of waiting had come to an end, that the Messiah was about to be born, and that she—Mary of Nazareth—was to be the mother! Add to that the declaration that, for the first and only time in the history of the world, this was to be a virgin birth, and the revelation was even more staggering. This simple, pure woman from a little-known city in Galilee was to carry in her womb the divine offspring of the great Elohim himself. Her son would be the Son of God!

Only when we consider the magnitude of those statements do we begin to appreciate how marvelous is Mary's answer. There were no questioning looks, no stammering demands of "Why me?" There were no murmurs of doubt. There was no disputation, no hesitation, no wondering. She simply said, in glorious and touching simplicity: "Behold the handmaid of the Lord; be it unto me according to thy word" (Luke 1:38).

Mary's Pregnancy

"Now the birth of Jesus Christ was on this wise: When as his mother Mary was espoused to Joseph, before they came together, she was found with child of the Holy Ghost" (Matt. 1:18).

At the command of Gabriel, Mary left Nazareth to visit her cousin Elizabeth, wife of Zacharias the priest, living in Judea. Elizabeth was six months pregnant with a miracle of her own, and Mary abode with her kinswoman about three months until the time came for Elizabeth to deliver.

Consider for a moment what coming back to Nazareth at that point must have meant for Mary. She suddenly, unexpectedly departed from her home for an extended stay far to the south. After she returned, the fact of her pregnancy would have become increasingly obvious. It is not a secret that can be hidden for long.

This was not a society like our own where immorality is not only tolerated but often openly flaunted. Modesty and virtue were deeply ingrained into the fiber of the nation and were especially strong in the small towns and villages of Israel. Imagine the effect on that tiny village when Mary returned and the first of the village women began to notice the change in her.

Anyone who has ever lived in the tightly knit, closely bonded society of a small town or village can predict with some accuracy what happened next. At first there would have been only questioning looks and quick shakings of the heads. Surely such could not be so. Not Mary. Perhaps she was just putting on a little weight.

Then more and more voices would have questioned, not openly, of course, but in whispers, at the well each day as they came together for water, or while doing the laundry on the banks of a stream.

Was Mary allowed to tell others of her visit from Gabriel? Matthew's comment, "she was *found* with child," would imply not (v. 18; emphasis added). But even if she were allowed to tell, would such a wildly fantastic claim have quelled the rumors? A virgin birth? Mother of the Messiah? A child fathered by God himself? Either she was mad or took them for absolute fools to imagine they would believe such a story. To the villagers, her departure from the village "with haste" took on new and ominous significance (see Luke 1:39). And poor Joseph—a victim of such "infidelity." What would he do now?

Joseph Takes Mary to Wife

"Then Joseph her husband, being a just man, and not willing to make her a public example, was minded to put her away privily. But while he thought on these things, behold, the angel of the Lord appeared unto him in a dream, saying, Joseph, thou son of David, fear not to take unto thee Mary thy wife: for that which is conceived in her is of the Holy Ghost. . . . Then Joseph being raised from sleep did as the angel of the Lord had bidden him, and took unto him his wife" (Matt. 1:19–20, 24).

Neither Luke nor Matthew gives us much detail, but we can read the pain and embarrassment between the lines. Here was a good man, faithful in every respect. What pain must have filled his soul to learn that his betrothed was with child! Surely not Mary, not his lovely and chaste Mary. We can only guess at the agony of spirit he must have experienced at the confirmation of her "unfaithfulness."

How many men would let the bitterness and anger of such betrayal fester and boil over into a blind desire for revenge that can cause people to strike out, seeking to hurt as deeply as they themselves are hurt? By Mosaic law, adultery was punishable by death (see, for example, John 8:5; Lev. 20:10). Joseph could have taken Mary to the elders of the village and demanded justice. But, despite the pain he must have felt, despite the personal humiliation, he would not put his beloved Mary through the shame and danger of a public trial. He would simply dissolve the marriage contract quietly.

But then again, in one blinding instant of revelation, all was explained and put right. In response to Gabriel's incredible announcement, Mary had simply said, "Behold the handmaid of the Lord." Now Joseph heard the same stunning pronouncement. We gain a glimpse of the greatness of the man from his response. Matthew says it in one phrase: "Then Joseph *being raised from sleep* . . . took unto him his wife" (Matt. 1:24; emphasis added). The verse suggests that little time elapsed between the announcement and the marriage, perhaps even occurring entirely before dawn.

As with Mary, Joseph accepted without question the fantastic nature of the declaration. There was no vacillation. Surely he knew his fellow villagers well enough to know that a hasty marriage would only fuel the rumors. All he would accomplish by such an action would be to bring the onus of doubt and shame upon himself. But the angel had spoken. His doubts were resolved. His Mary had been proven faithful. And so he arose from his bed and took her to be his wife.

The Town Called Bethlehem

"And it came to pass in those days, that there went out a decree from Caesar Augustus, that all the world should be taxed. . . . And all went to be taxed, every one into his own city. And Joseph also went up from Galilee, out of the city of Nazareth, unto Judaea, unto the city of David, which is called Bethlehem; (because he was of the house and lineage of David:) to be taxed with Mary his espoused wife, being great with child" (Luke 2:1, 3–5).

Bethlehem. The city of David. Ancient homeland of Israel's greatest king. In Hebrew it is called *Beth Lechem.* Literally, *Beth Lechem* means "The House of Bread."[8] How perfect that he who was to take the throne of David and become Israel's ultimate king should come to earth in the city of his illustrious ancestor! How fitting that he who would be known as the Bread of Life should enter mortality in the tiny village called "The House of Bread" (see John 6:35).

Though his birth is celebrated in December, latter-day revelation explains that it actually occurred in the spring (see D&C 20:1).[9] The time would have been late March or early April when Joseph moved southward with Mary at his side, heavy with the living treasure in her womb. Spring is a time of glorious beauty in Israel. The "latter rains" water the parched soil, and in gratitude the earth responds with an explosion of grass and wildflowers. New life springs from the old with the wildest abundance. What better season to welcome him who would be called the "Prince of Life"? (see Acts 3:15).

Search for Lodgings

"And so it was, that, while they were there, the days were accomplished that she should be delivered. And she brought forth her firstborn son, and wrapped him in swaddling clothes, and laid him in a manger; because there was no room for them in the inn" (Luke 2:6–7).

No room in the inn. If, as we believe, it was April and not December, then it was very likely Passover season in Jerusalem. This could explain the reason Joseph took Mary on the rigorous, sixty-mile journey to Judea when she was in the final month of her pregnancy. The Roman "taxing" mentioned by Luke was more accurately a census or enrollment. Each family head had to register and give an accounting of their property so that taxes could be levied. But while there was considerable flexibility in timing allowed to meet this requirement, if it was Passover season, that would allow them to meet two responsibilities. The Mosaic law required that every adult male bring his sacrifices before the Lord (i.e., to the temple) each year at Passover (see Ex. 23:14–19). So by choosing this time of year, Joseph could fulfill both requirements.

Today we can hardly conceive of the magnitude of this most important of all Jewish festivals. From all over the empire, Jews returned to their homeland at Passover. Though determining exactly how large Jerusalem was during this period is difficult, a fairly accurate guess would place the population between one and two hundred thousand. Josephus tells us that during Passover "innumerable multitudes came thither [to Jerusalem] out of the country."[10] In another place, he was even more specific. Because the Paschal lamb had to be totally consumed by the family in the ritual meal, tradition stated that no fewer than ten and no more than twenty could gather for each lamb sacrificed (see Ex. 12:10). Josephus tells us that during one Passover of his time (about A.D. 70), 256,500 lambs were sacrificed.[11] Even using the more conservative figure of ten participants at each ritual meal, that still means the population of Jerusalem at Passover had swollen by more than 1,000 percent to the staggering number of nearly three million people.

The throngs must have been incredible, the facilities throughout the city taxed beyond belief. And with Bethlehem only six miles south of Jerusalem, no wonder there was no room at the inn. Luke probably could have said with equal accuracy, "There was no room anywhere."

Often in the art and literature surrounding the Christmas story, the unknown, unnamed innkeeper of the scriptural account is viewed as selfish and uncaring, an insensitive oaf unmoved by the plight of a woman heavy with child. This may make for interesting art and literature, but it is not justified by the scriptural record. In the first place, the "inns" of the Middle East were not quaint and homey little buildings with thatched roofs and latticed windows from which warm lamplight beckoned the weary traveler. The inns of the Holy Land were typically large, fortress-like buildings, built around a spacious open square. Called *khans* or *caravanserai,* they provided stopping places for the caravans of the ancient world.

Just as modern hotels and motels must provide parking for automobiles, so did *caravanserai* have to provide a place where the donkeys, camels, and other animals could be safely cared for. Inside the *khan,* which was usually of two-story construction, all the "rooms" faced the courtyard. They were typically arched, open antechambers facing out onto the square. Here the traveler could build a small fire or sleep within clear view of his animals and goods. "In these hostelries, bazaars and markets were held, animals killed and meat sold, also wine and cider; so that they were a much more public place of resort than might at first be imagined."[12]

Even if there had been room at the inn, a *caravanserai* was hardly the ideal place for a woman in labor. Perhaps the innkeeper, moved with compassion at Mary's plight and knowing of her need and desire for privacy, offered them his stable. Perhaps Joseph found the place on his own. The scriptures do not say. But one thing is very probable, and this contradicts another popular misconception. The birth likely did not take place in a wooden shed with pitched roof as is so commonly depicted in nativity scenes around the world.

In Bethlehem today stands the Church of the Nativity. Beneath the church is a large grotto or cave. In southern Judea, including the area around Bethlehem, limestone caves are common. Such caves provided natural shelter for the flocks and herds of ancient Israel. They were warm, safe from inclement weather, and could easily be blocked to keep the animals safe for the night. The tradition that this grotto was the stable of Luke's account is very old and accepted by many scholars. President Harold B. Lee, then of the Council of the Twelve, visited this grotto in 1958 and confirmed that in his mind it was "a hallowed spot, . . . a sacred place."[13]

So there in the sheltered warmth of the cave, beneath the limestone hills of Bethlehem, he who was to become the Good Shepherd—not of the sheep that grazed the hills of Israel, but of the human flock—was born and cradled in a manger.

That seems almost beyond our comprehension. Here was Jesus—a member of the Godhead, the Firstborn of the Father, the Creator, Jehovah of the Old Testament—now leaving his divine and holy station; divesting himself of all that glory and majesty and entering the body of a tiny infant; helpless, completely dependent on his mother and earthly father. That he should not come to the finest of earthly palaces and be swaddled in purple and showered with jewels but should come to a lowly stable is astonishing. Little wonder that the angel should say to Nephi, "Behold the condescension of God!" (1 Ne. 11:26).

Announcement to the Shepherds

"And there were in the same country shepherds abiding in the field, keeping watch over their flock by night. And, lo, the angel of the Lord came upon them, and the glory of the Lord shone round about them: and they were sore afraid. And the angel said unto them, Fear not: for, behold, I bring you good tidings of great joy, which shall be to all people. For unto you is born this day in the city of David a Saviour, which is Christ the Lord. And this shall be a sign unto you; Ye shall find the babe wrapped in swaddling clothes, lying in a manger" (Luke 2:8–12).

One of these verses is frequently misquoted: "Keeping watch over their *flocks* by night." But the verse does not say *flocks,* plural, but *flock,* singular. One scholar explained the significance: "There was near Bethlehem, on the road to Jerusalem, a tower known as *Migdal Eder,* or *the watchtower of the flock.* Here was the station where shepherds watched the flocks destined for sacrifice in the temple. . . . It was a settled conviction among the Jews that the Messiah was to be born in Bethlehem, and equally that he was to be revealed from Migdal Eder. The beautiful significance of the revelation of the infant Christ to shepherds watching the flocks destined for sacrifice needs no comment."[14] The flock mentioned in the scripture, then, apparently was the one used for temple sacrifices, and the shepherds thus had responsibility for the most important flock in the region.

Sometimes in translation the power of the original language is considerably lessened. While the words, in English, of the angel to the shepherds are beautiful and significant, we miss much of the electrifying impact the original words must have had on those men of Judea. Let us just examine two or three of the phrases as we assume they were given in Aramaic to the shepherds that night.

"In the city of David." We have already seen that the Jews expected Bethlehem to be the birthplace of the Messiah. This in part stemmed directly from the prophet Micah, who centuries before had specified the place (see Micah 5:2).

"Is born a Savior." The word that meant "Savior" was *Yeshua.* In the Greek New Testament that name was transliterated into *Hee-ay-sous,* or, in English, "Jesus." When the angel announced to Joseph that Mary would bear a son, note

what he said: "Thou shalt call his name Jesus [*Yeshua*]: for he shall *save* his people from their sins" (Matt. 1:21; emphasis added).

"Which is Christ." Our English word *Christ* is derived directly from the Greek, *Christos*. It means "the anointed one."[15] *Christos* was a direct translation of the Hebrew word, *Messhiach,* which meant exactly the same thing—the anointed one. *Messhiach* is of course transliterated into English as "Messiah."

"The Lord." The simple title, "Lord," is perhaps the most significant of all, yet we totally miss its importance in the translation. In the Old Testament the name of God was written with four Hebrew consonants: YHVH. Because they did not write vowels, there has been some debate as to its proper pronunciation. Modern scholars often write it as *YAHVEH,* but the King James translators wrote it as *JEHOVAH.*

The Jews of ancient times, however, viewed the name as being so sacred that it should not be pronounced out loud. Whenever they found it written, they would substitute the Hebrew word *Adonai,* meaning the Lord. The translators who produced the King James Version of the Old Testament honored that tradition of the Jews, and where they found the name YHVH, they wrote in (with very few exceptions) "the Lord." However, *adonai* can also be used as a title of respect for men, such as in the phrase, "My lord, the king." To distinguish between the two uses, the translators wrote *Lord* in small capital letters if it represented the name of deity, and regular upper and lower case letters if used normally (see, for example, 2 Sam. 15:21, where both uses are found in the same verse). The declaration of the angel to the shepherds obviously used *Lord* or *Adonai* in reference to deity; literally it could be translated *Jehovah.*

Now we begin to sense the impact of the angel's words upon these shepherds. In essence, here is his pronouncement: "Unto you is born this day in the city prophesied to be the birthplace of the Messiah, *Yeshua* [or Jesus], the Savior, who is the Anointed One (the Messiah), and who is also Jehovah, the God of your fathers."

"And they came with haste, and found Mary, and Joseph, and the babe lying in a manger. And when they had seen it, they made known abroad the saying which was told them concerning this child. And all they that heard it wondered at those things which were told them by the shepherds. But Mary kept all these things, and pondered them in her heart" (Luke 2:16–19).

Notes

From "Reflections on the Christmas Story," in *A Celebration of Christmas* (Salt Lake City: Deseret Book Co., 1988).

1. Alfred Edersheim, *Sketches of Jewish Social Life in the Days of Christ* (Grand Rapids, Mich.: Wm. B. Eerdmans Publishing Co., 1979), 70.

2. *Smith's Historical Geography,* as cited in Merrill F. Unger, ed., *Unger's Bible Dictionary,* 3d ed. (Chicago: Moody Press, 1966), 779.
3. See Edersheim, *Sketches of Jewish Social Life,* 105.
4. Ibid., 143–44.
5. See Robert Young, *Analytical Concordance to the Bible* (Grand Rapids, Mich.: Wm. B. Eerdmans, 1972), 647.
6. From D&C 20:1 we learn that the birth date of the Savior was April 6. See also James E. Talmage, *Jesus the Christ,* Classics in Mormon Literature Edition (Salt Lake City: Deseret Book Co., 1982), 96–98 (102–4 earlier editions). Counting nine months backwards puts the time somewhere around July.
7. In Luke 2:24, we are told that Mary and Joseph offered as the required sacrifice for their firstborn son two turtledoves or pigeons. In Leviticus 12:6–8, where the requirement is given, we are told that the sacrifice should be a lamb, but if the family "be not able" (that is, they are financially unable to afford a lamb), they may instead offer the turtle-doves or pigeons.
8. See Unger, *Unger's Bible Dictionary,* 40.
9. See D&C 20:1; see also note 6 above.
10. Flavius Josephus, *The Antiquities of the Jews,* in *Josephus: Complete Works,* trans. William Whiston (Grand Rapids, Mich.: Kregel Publications, 1960), 17.9.3.
11. See Josephus, *Wars of the Jews,* in *Complete Works,* 7.9.3.
12. Unger, *Unger's Bible Dictionary,* 527.
13. Harold B. Lee, "I Walked Today Where Jesus Walked," *BYU Speeches of the Year,* 10 December 1958, 5.
14. M. R. Vincent, *Word Studies in the New Testament* (MacDill AFB, Florida: MacDonald Publishing Company, n.d.), 142.
15. See Unger, *Unger's Bible Dictionary,* 195.

Chapter 10

"His Name Shall Be Called . . ." (Isaiah 9:6)

Wherefore, *thou shalt do all that thou doest in the name of the Son,* and thou shalt repent and call upon God in the name of the Son forevermore" (Moses 5:8; emphasis added). So spoke the angel to Adam at the beginning of the world's history. And thus spoke the Lord through the Prophet Joseph Smith in our dispensation: "And again, I say unto you, *all things must be done in the name of Christ"* (D&C 46:31; emphasis added).

From the *foundation* of the world to the present day, our Lord and Savior Jesus Christ has been the central figure in the plan of the Father to bring to pass the immortality and eternal life of man.

He it was who stepped forward in the Great Council in heaven and offered his life as ransom for all (see Moses 4:1–2). He it was who, under the direction of the Father, created worlds without number (see Moses 1:32–33).

He it was who directed men as Jehovah, God of the Old Testament, for the first four thousand years of this world's history (see, for example, Abr. 2:6–8).

He it was who put aside his godly glory, thinking it not unseemly to take upon himself the frail and corruptible body of mortality (see Philip. 2:6–8).

He it was who sweat blood for us in a garden of olive trees; who endured mockery and cruel jibes; who stood with others' spittle running down his face; who endured the lacerating pain of a Roman scourging and the unspeakable horror of death by crucifixion—all that he might save us from the results of our foolishness and rebellion (see Luke 22:44; Mark 14:65; 15:29–32; 1 Ne. 19:9).

He it is who will overthrow Babylon and cause the kingdoms of the world to become the kingdoms of our God and his Christ (see Rev. 11:15). He it is who will come again in such resplendent glory that the mountains will flow down at his presence and the sun will hide its face in shame (see D&C 133:44, 49).

It is little wonder then that Nephi proclaimed, "We talk of Christ, we rejoice in Christ, we preach of Christ, we prophesy of Christ, and we write according to our prophecies, that our children may know to what source they may look for a remission of their sins" (2 Ne. 25:26).

If one were to count all the times the various names and titles of Jesus are used in scripture—Lord, Savior, Redeemer, Messiah, God, the Lamb, Jesus, Alpha and Omega, the Son of Man, Christ, Master, and dozens more—the total would approach some twenty-five thousand usages in the four standard works. That averages about *ten uses per page of scripture!* Surely that says something about the central role he plays in our lives and in the destiny of all mankind.

Moses Converses with Jehovah

After Israel had been captive in Egypt for four hundred years, Jehovah called to Moses out of the burning bush and commanded him to deliver the children of Israel. Moses asked an intriguing question of the Lord: "When I come unto the children of Israel, and shall say unto them, The God of your fathers hath sent me unto you; and they shall say to me, What is his name? what shall I say unto them?" (Ex. 3:13).

Perhaps after such long exposure to the idolatry and ways of the Egyptians, and after encountering the dozens of foreign gods of the cultures Egypt traded with, the memory of the true God and his name had become dim. Whatever the reason, when Moses mentioned the name of God, the Israelites would know that Moses did not represent one of the many gods they had heard of. In fact, the name of God would become a memorial to all generations that followed: "God said unto Moses, I AM THAT I AM: and he said, Thus shalt thou say unto the children of Israel, I AM hath sent me unto you. . . . The Lord God of your fathers, the God of Abraham, the God of Isaac, and the God of Jacob, hath sent me unto you: this is my name for ever, and this is my memorial unto all generations" (Ex. 3:14–15).

The Bible, indeed, is consistent in using the names of God to identify God to the people and to bring him and some aspect of his godhood to remembrance. In his marvelous prophecy of the future Messiah, Isaiah was not content to just declare that he would be born, but he also told us what his name would be: "His name shall be called Wonderful, Counsellor, The mighty God, the everlasting Father, The Prince of Peace." (Isa. 9:6.) By these names, we would recognize the Messiah and know his greatness. Following are some of the names by which we should know Jesus Christ. Each reminds us of a facet of the godhood Jesus possesses.

Symbolic Titles Associated with the Events of the Savior's Birth

He was known as the *Prince of Life* (Acts 3:15) and the source of all life (D&C 88:13); in fact, he was born in the spring (D&C 20:1), when all life is renewed.

He was called the *New David* (Jer. 23:5–6) and the *Root of David* (Rev. 5:5). He was born in Bethlehem, which was the city of David (Luke 2:4).

He who is the *Lion of the Tribe of Judah* (Rev. 5:5) was born in Judea (Luke 2:4), ancestral homeland of the tribe of Judah.

He who is the *Bread of Life* (John 6:48) was born in the city of Bethlehem (Luke 2:4), which in Hebrew means "the house of bread."

He who is the *Lamb of God* (John 1:29) was born during Passover season (D&C 20:1) when the Paschal lambs were being offered (Ex. 12:3–6). The Lamb of God (John 1:29) was born in a stable (Luke 2:7).

He who is the *Good Shepherd* (John 10:14) had his birth first announced to shepherds in the fields (Luke 2:8).

He who took upon himself the form of *a Servant* (Philip. 2:7) was born into the humblest of circumstances (Luke 2:7).

At the birth of him who is the *Light of the World* (John 8:12), darkness was banished as a sign of his birth (3 Ne. 1:15, 19).

At the birth of the *Bright and Morning Star* (Rev. 22:16), a new star appeared as a sign of his birth (Matt. 2:2, 9; 3 Ne. 1:21).

At the birth of the *Savior* (Acts 13:23), those who were facing death because they believed on his name were saved (3 Ne. 1:4–18).

He who is called the *King of Kings* (Rev. 19:16) and the *Governor that shall rule Israel* (Matt. 2:6) was greeted by visiting magi and given gifts as though he were a king (Matt. 2:11).

Additional Scriptural Titles of Jesus

1. The Lord (1 Ne. 1:1)
2. The Lord of Hosts (2 Ne. 8:15)
3. The Lamb (John 1:29)
4. The Light (John 1:7, 8)

5. The Anointed One (Acts 4:27)
6. The Prophet (Deut. 18:15)
7. The Advocate (D&C 45:3–5)
8. The Governor (Matt. 2:6)
9. The King (Matt. 27:42)
10. The King of Glory (Ps. 24:7–8)
11. The Great Creator (2 Ne. 9:5–6)
12. God with Us (Matt. 1:23)
13. The Comforter (John 14:16)
14. The Word (John 1:14)
15. The Rock (Deut. 32:4; 1 Cor. 10:1–4)
16. The Good Shepherd (John 10:11, 14)
17. The True Vine (John 15:1–5)
18. The Lion of Judah (Rev. 5:5)
19. The Door (John 10:7, 9)
20. The Root of David (Rev. 5:5)
21. Only Begotten (Moses 1:6, 21)
22. The Son of God (Heb. 10:29)
23. The Way (John 14:6)
24. The Chief Cornerstone (Eph. 2:20)
25. The Stone of Stumbling (1 Pet. 2:8)
26. The Stumblingblock (1 Cor. 1:23)
27. The Messenger of the Covenant (Mal. 3:1)
28. The Mediator (D&C 107:19)
29. I Am (John 8:58)
30. The Great I Am (D&C 39:1)
31. The Life (John 14:6)
32. He Who Treads the Winepress (D&C 133:50)
33. A Consuming Fire (Heb. 12:29)
34. The Amen (Rev. 3:14)
35. The Living Bread (John 6:51)
36. The High Priest (Heb. 3:1)
37. The Bright and Morning Star (Rev. 22:16)
38. The Bridegroom (D&C 33:17)
39. The Prince of Life (Acts 3:15)
40. The Judge (Gen. 18:25; Acts 10:42)
41. The Deliverer (Rom. 11:26)
42. The Power (1 Cor. 1:24)

43. The Redeemer (D&C 8:1)
44. The Savior (1 Ne. 10:4)
45. Our Passover (1 Cor. 5:7)
46. The Head of Every Man (1 Cor. 11:3)
47. The Captain (Heb. 2:10)
48. Our Peace (Eph. 2:14)
49. The Foundation (1 Cor. 3:11)
50. The Author of Our Faith (Heb. 12:2)
51. Alpha and Omega (D&C 19:1)
52. The Beginning (D&C 35:1)
53. The End (D&C 35:1)
54. The Faithful Witness (Rev. 1:5)
55. The Resurrection (John 11:25)
56. The Truth (John 14:6)
57. The Seed of Abraham (Gal. 3:16)
58. The Physician (Luke 5:31)
59. The Mother Hen (Matt. 23:37)
60. Our Propitiation (Mercy Seat) (Rom. 3:25)
61. The Potter (Jer. 18:6)
62. The Rock of Offense (Rom. 9:33)
63. The Mighty One of Israel (1 Ne. 22:12)
64. The Holy One of Israel (2 Ne. 9:12)

For more than thirty years, I have had the opportunity to serve in the Church Educational System of The Church of Jesus Christ of Latter-day Saints. As seminary teacher, institute instructor and director, curriculum writer, and administrator, I have been privileged to spend much of my adult life reading, studying, teaching, and writing about the life and mission of the Savior of the world. It has been a labor accompanied by a never-ending and ever-growing sense of awe at the majesty and perfections of the Son of Man. I understand now with much greater clarity the Master's statement when he said, "My yoke is easy, and my burden is light" (Matt. 11:30).

My own testimony is, as King Benjamin said it so well twenty-one hundred years ago, "there shall be no other name given nor any other way nor means whereby salvation can come unto the children of men, *only in and through the name of Christ,* the Lord Omnnipotent" (Mosiah 3:17; emphasis added).

Note

From Gerald N. Lund, *Jesus Christ, Key to the Plan of Salvation* (Salt Lake City: Bookcraft, 1991), 1–3, 76–80.

Chapter 11

"Among His Own Kin, and in His Own House" (Mark 6:4)

Even a quick reading of the Gospels and Acts shows that the New Testament writers did not intend to give a comprehensive picture of the personal life or family of Jesus. Their purpose was to portray Jesus as the Christ and to convey the significance of that fact to the world. This intent partially explains why we have almost no information about the early years of Jesus and why references to his family life are scanty and usually incidental to the main narrative. Still, one naturally wonders about Jesus' family, who they were and what they did.

Brothers and Sisters of Jesus

We do know that Jesus had four brothers and more than one sister. The people of Nazareth objected to the divine calling of Jesus on the grounds that he was someone who had grown up in their midst. "Is not this the carpenter's son?" they asked in astonishment. "Is not his mother called Mary? and his brethren, James, and Joses, and Simon, and Judas? And his sisters, are they not all with us?" (Matt. 13:55–56). This last verse and its parallel passage in Mark 6:3 contain the only references to the sisters of Jesus in the New Testament, and nothing is known of their involvement with the church or their attitude toward the Savior.

The brothers of Jesus—or more correctly, the half-brothers of Jesus—receive more mention, however. John relates an interesting event concerning the brethren of Jesus by telling us that they did not fully accept him as the Messiah while he was laboring among them: "Now the Jews' feast of tabernacles was at hand. His brethren therefore said unto him [their brother, Jesus], Depart hence, and go into Judaea, that thy disciples also may see the works that thou doest. For there is no man that doeth any thing in secret, and he himself seeketh to be known openly. If thou do these things, shew thyself to the world. For neither did his brethren believe in him" (John 7:2–5).

The brothers knew something of Jesus' work and miracles and of his following, but they were doubtful themselves, or at least wished him to be more open about his mission. They did not believe in him, which may refer to the claims he made about being the Messiah and the Son of God. In fact, when the people of Nazareth rejected the Savior, he exclaimed, "A prophet is not without honour, but in his own country, and among his own kin, and in his own house" (Mark 6:4). But evidently the brothers were converted shortly thereafter, for Luke records that immediately after Christ's ascension into heaven, the church met in "prayer and supplication, with the women, and Mary the mother of Jesus, and with his brethren" (Acts 1:14). Also, Paul includes James in his list of those who had seen the resurrected Lord (see 1 Cor. 15:7).

James

More is known about James than any of the other brothers of Jesus. He is mentioned several times in Acts and in the Epistles as playing a prominent role in church leadership. For instance, when Peter is imprisoned in Jerusalem and an angel frees him, Peter tells the first group he meets, "Go shew these things unto James, and to the brethren" (Acts 12:17). James also takes a leading role in the great Jerusalem Council, which debated the issue of circumcision for Gentiles (see Acts 15). James was the one who suggested that a letter be drafted outlining the official church position on this matter (see Acts 15:13–21). Some have erroneously assumed that this James was James, the son of Zebedee, who served in the presidency of the early church with Peter and John. That James, however, was killed by Herod in a wave of persecution against the church (see Acts 12:1–2). This occurred about A.D. 44, just before Peter's imprisonment and five or six years before the Jerusalem Council.

In his letter to the Galatian Saints, Paul refers to James, the Lord's brother, as an apostle (see Gal. 1:19) and classes him, Peter, and John as "pillars" of the church (see Gal. 2:9). Some have conjectured from the latter comment of Paul that James, the brother of the Lord, not only became an apostle but even filled the vacancy in the leadership of the Twelve caused by the martyrdom of James, the son of

Zebedee. The fact that James declared the official policy of the church at the Jerusalem Council and that Paul reported to him after one mission (see Acts 21:17–19) would lend added support to that supposition. Of course, based on what we know, it remains conjecture.

James, the brother of Jesus, was also the one who wrote the epistle of James. Not only does this short letter contain some of the great teachings of gospel doctrine, but in it Joseph Smith found the words (see James 1:5–6) that sent him to the Sacred Grove in the spring of 1820. Note in that epistle that James does not refer to himself as the brother of the Lord but as his servant: "James, a servant of God and of the Lord Jesus Christ" (James 1:1).

Ancient tradition, preserved for us by Eusebius, a Christian historian who lived about A.D. 300, states that James became bishop of the church at Jerusalem and was called James the Just, respected by Jews and Christians as being the most just man alive. It is said that he prayed so often and so long for the people that his knees became as hard as camel knees.[1]

Josephus, a Jewish historian and general who lived during the lifetime of James, mentioned James's death. Ananus, a chief priest who was a Sadducee (the Sadducees violently opposed the resurrection), "assembled the sanhedrim of the judges, and brought before them the brother of Jesus, who was called Christ, whose name was James, and some others, . . . and when he had formed an accusation against them as breakers of the law, he delivered them to be stoned." Ananus soon lost his position as high priest because of this incident.[2]

Jude and Simon

The writer of the Epistle of Jude refers to himself this way: "Jude, the servant of Jesus Christ, and the brother of James" (Jude 1:1). Most scholars assume that the name James refers to the Lord's brother, identifying the writer as the Judas who is another of the Lord's brothers. Though Jude does not call himself an apostle, the fact that his letter has been recognized and accepted from very early times as authoritative suggests that he too may have been an apostle.

Nothing more is recorded of Simon and Joses in the New Testament. Interestingly, another Simon, or Symeon, is mentioned by Eusebius. This Simon, according to tradition, was the son of Clopas, Joseph's brother, and Mary, whom Matthew called "the other Mary" (Matt. 28:1) and who was one of the women at the cross and one of the first to see the resurrected Christ (see Matt. 27:55–56; 28:1–10; Mark 15:40). This Simon was thus Jesus' cousin. He succeeded James the

Lord's brother as bishop of the church in Jerusalem and was finally crucified in the Roman persecutions under the emperor Trajan.[3] The Bible scholars F. N. Peloubet and William Smith say that many have identified this Symeon with Simon the Lord's brother, though this argument is full of difficulties.[4]

Joseph

We know quite a bit about Joseph, Jesus' stepfather, during the early years of his marriage. Matthew tells us that he was of the lineage of King David, that he was a just and considerate man, that in a dream an angel told him who Jesus would be, that he was obedient, and that he gave Jesus his name, which means *savior* (see Matt. 1). We know that he took Mary to Bethlehem, where Jesus was born (see Luke 2:4–6). Less than two years later, Joseph took his family into Egypt to escape Herod, after being warned in a dream. In Egypt, a dream again told him when to return, and another dream told him to go to Galilee (see Matt. 2:13–15, 19–22). Four dreams from God! Joseph must have been an exceptionally visionary and spiritually sensitive man.

Joseph and Mary also attended the Passover in Jerusalem faithfully every year (see Luke 2:41). One incident at the Passover, when Jesus was twelve (see Luke 2:42–49), suggests how well Joseph taught the scriptures to his children. Jewish tradition laid the primary emphasis for the education of children, which emphasized study of the Torah, on the father, though the mother could also teach her children the scriptures.[5] So when Jesus was "in the temple, sitting in the midst of the doctors, both hearing them, and asking them questions," and "all that heard him were astonished at his understanding and answers" (vv. 46–47), his ability positively reflected on Joseph's (and also Mary's) understanding of the scriptures and the teaching Jesus had received. Joseph's knowledge that Jesus was Emmanuel (see Matt. 1:23) had undoubtedly lent urgency to Joseph's teaching.

Though the record is silent concerning the later life of Joseph, most scholars assume that he died sometime during the eighteen years between the family's visit to Jerusalem when Jesus was twelve and the beginning of Christ's formal ministry. If Joseph had been alive, he would likely have been mentioned as being at the marriage celebration in Cana (see John 2:1–11) and almost certainly Jesus would not have given John the charge to care for his mother (see John 19:25–27).

MARY

Aside from the reference to Mary meeting with the church shortly after the ascension of her Son (see Acts 1:14), we have no record of her after the events of the crucifixion. Ancient traditions, which are not always reliable, tell us that Mary associated with the church in Jerusalem for many years, and finally accompanied John to Ephesus, where she eventually died.

But Mary's contribution to the church and to the work of Jesus Christ may be more lasting than most people realize. As mentioned earlier, she contributed to the training of her son Jesus. Her knowledge of the scriptures was thorough, as indicated by her spontaneous words of rejoicing when she met Elizabeth, words that echo numerous passages in the Old Testament (see Luke 1:46–55).

Furthermore, Luke frankly admits that he is writing his gospel from material he had gathered from eyewitnesses of Christ's life (see Luke 1:1–4). Many Bible scholars believe that Luke gathered these materials for his gospel while Paul was imprisoned in Caesarea for two years, before Paul was sent to Rome for trial before the emperor (see Acts 24:26–7). Caesarea was only about fifty miles northwest of Jerusalem. If Mary was still in Jerusalem, what better source of information concerning the life of the Master could there be than his mother?

Some unique characteristics of Luke's gospel support the possibility that Mary was one of Luke's sources. First, only in Luke is there a detailed record of the story of the birth of Christ. Matthew records the visits of the angel Gabriel and of the later visit of the wise men, but we turn to Luke to read of the manger and the shepherds, the crowded inn and the swaddling clothes. Only in Luke do we find an account of Gabriel's words to the young Mary (see Luke 1:26–38) and of Mary's visit to Elisabeth (see Luke 1:39–56). Luke's gospel is the only one that relates the nativity (see Luke 2:1–20), the circumcision of Jesus and the inspired declarations of Anna and Simeon in the temple (see Luke 2:21–38), and the teaching of the young Jesus in the temple at the age of twelve. And interestingly enough, Luke, who exhibits some of the most polished and refined Greek in the New Testament, uses a rough Greek filled with Hebraic style in the chapters that tell us of the infancy and childhood of Jesus. So markedly different is it from the rest of his work that it almost seems as if Luke were translating, a concept that would support the idea that Mary supplied the material.

The information about the family of Jesus that has survived the erasing effects of time is sketchy and incomplete. Yet the evidence we do have suggests strongly that the family of the Savior played active and prominent roles in the early development and history of the church of Jesus Christ.

Notes

From "I Have a Question," *Ensign,* September 1975, 36–37.

1. Eusebius, *The Ecclesiastical History and the Martyrs of Palestine,* trans. Hugh Lawlor and John Oulton, 2 vols. (London: S.P.C.K., 1954), 1.2.23.
2. Flavius Josephus, *Antiquities of the Jews,* in *Josephus: Complete Works,* trans. William Whiston (Grand Rapids, Mich.: Kregel Publications, 1960), *Antiquities,* 20.9.1.
3. Eusebius, *Ecclesiastical History,* 1.3.10–11 and 3.32.1–4.
4. William Smith, *A Dictionary of the Bible,* rev. ed. (Grand Rapids: Zondervan Publishing House, 1967), s.v. "Simon"; F. N. Peloubet, *Peloubet's Bible Dictionary* (Grand Rapids: Zondervan, 1971), s.v. "Simon."
5. See Stephen and Shirley Smith Ricks, "Jewish Religious Education in the Meridian of Time," *Ensign,* October 1987, 60–62.

Chapter 12

"Knowest Thou the Condescension of God?"

After Lehi recounted to his family his marvelous vision in which he had seen the tree of life, Nephi reported that he was "desirous also that [he] might *see,* and *hear,* and *know* of these things, by the power of the Holy Ghost" (1 Ne. 10:17; emphasis added). Nephi was caught up into an exceedingly high mountain where a grand vision was unfolded before him, and he saw not only what his father had seen but also much more. In the early part of that vision, on two different occasions, the angelic messenger used an unusual phrase—"the condescension of God." In the first instance, Nephi was shown the virgin Mary, and then the angel asked, "Knowest thou the condescension of God?" (1 Ne. 11:15–16). A few verses later, the angel again used the phrase, this time not as a question, but in an imperative command. "And the angel said unto me again: Look and behold the condescension of God!" (1 Ne. 11:26). As Nephi obeyed and looked, he saw the Redeemer of the world. He saw his earthly ministry and its culmination in the death of the Savior (see 1 Ne. 11:26–32).

Later in his writings, Nephi used a phrase similar to that used by the angel. In what is often called the Psalm of Nephi, he said: "O then, if I have seen so great things, if the Lord *in his condescension unto the children of men* hath visited men in so much mercy, why should my heart weep and my soul linger in the valley of sorrow, and my flesh waste away, and my strength slacken, because of mine afflictions?" (2 Ne. 4:26; emphasis added).

By examining the context in which Nephi refers the "condescension of God," we can get a fuller understanding of what is meant by the phrase. The three contexts in which Nephi uses the phrase are the following:

- The birth of Jesus Christ (1 Ne. 11:16)
- The mortal ministry of the Lord (1 Ne. 11:26)
- The mercies of the Savior (2 Ne. 4:26)

Exploring these three contexts of the use of the phrase "condescension of God" can reveal its implications for us today.

The Birth of Jesus Christ

As we read the scriptures that prophesied the coming of Christ into the world, we sense that the ancients had a different perspective on this event than perhaps we in the latter days do. This difference probably stems from the fact that, to them, Jehovah was their God. He was the God with whom they dealt. He was the Lord of all the earth. He was the Almighty, the Lord of Hosts. They viewed Jehovah in a way similar to the way we view God the Father. In the latter days, we start with a view of Jesus in his mortal ministry and think of him secondarily as Jehovah, but to them he was not yet come in the flesh, and so the idea that their God—this almighty, all-powerful, all-knowing being—would come down to earth, take upon himself a body of flesh, and be born of woman left them with a great sense of awe and wonder. For example, after King Lamoni's remarkable conversion, he said with the deepest of reverence, "For as sure as thou livest, behold, I have seen my Redeemer; *and he shall come forth, and be born of a woman,* and he shall redeem all mankind" (Alma 19:13; emphasis added). Paul similarly declared, "But when the fulness of the time was come, God sent forth his Son, *made of a woman,* made under the law" (Gal. 4:4; emphasis added).

Consider the implications of Christ's leaving his position as a member of the Godhead to come to earth, taking upon himself the body of a mortal being, being born of a mortal mother, and living out a life of mortality among his fellow men. In a marvelous passage to the Philippian Saints, Paul wrote, "Let this mind be in you, which was also in Christ Jesus: Who, being in the form of God, thought it not robbery to be equal with God: But made himself of no reputation, and took upon him the form of a servant, and was made in the likeness of men: And being found in fashion as a man, he humbled himself, and became obedient unto death, even the death of the cross" (Philip. 2:5–8).

Paul used two interesting phrases here. He said that though Christ was in the form of God, he did not think it was robbery to be equal with him. Through an examination of the Greek, we get a better sense of what it is he tried to teach us. The New Testament scholar M. R. Vincent, in his *New Testament Word Studies,* indicates that in Greek the word that is translated *robbery* had these different definitions—(1) the act of stealing or robbing something from another; (2) the thing which has been robbed—that is, a piece of plunder; or (3) a prize, something to be grasped and held onto.[1] Thus Vincent indicates that the Greek word *arpagmon,* which the King James Version translates as "robbery," is better thought of as something which is considered a highly prized possession.

Vincent next explained the significance of verse 7, in which Paul used a phrase from the Greek that is translated "made himself of no reputation." Again Vincent indicated that this Greek phrase literally means "emptied Himself."[2] Vincent then added: "The general sense is that He divested Himself of that peculiar mode of existence which was proper and peculiar to Him as one with God. He laid aside the form of God. In so doing, He did not divest Himself of His divine *nature.* The change was a change of *state:* the form of a servant for the form of God."[3]

Trying to reflect more accurately a sense of the Greek, Phillips Modern English Translation renders that passage as follows: "For He, who had always been God by nature, did not cling to his prerogatives as God's equal, but stripped himself of all privilege by consenting to be a slave by nature and being born as a mortal man."[4] In short, Paul reminded us that though Christ had incomprehensible stature, majesty, power and position in the premortal existence, he did not consider that position something that was to be seized and held tightly and not released, but rather, he emptied himself or allowed himself to be taken from that high and holy position and placed into the body of a man with all of its consequent weaknesses and limitations.

This concept deserves examination in more detail. If we are to more fully comprehend the idea of God's condescension, we must first understand who he was before coming to the earth. As we look at Christ as the Creator, we are told in latter-day revelation that the extent of his creations is so vast that they cannot be numbered unto man (Moses 1:33, 35, 37). Enoch stated the same idea in a much more dramatic form when he said the following: "And were it possible that man could number the particles of the earth, yea, millions of earths like this, it would not be a beginning to the number of thy creations" (Moses 7:30).

For much of the world's history, man has had to accept these statements basically on faith, for as we look up in the heavens with the naked eye, we can see approximately six thousand stars. Only in our own century have we begun to sense the vastness of the universe. Sir Edwin Hubble, one of the great astronomers in our time, using the 100-inch telescope on Mount Wilson in California, discovered that what we had thought were clouds of interstellar gas, visible to the eye through smaller telescopes, are actually whole new galaxies of stars. Since then our concept of the universe has expanded tremendously, and astronomers now estimate there are at least one hundred billion galaxies in the known universe, with each of those galaxies averaging around a hundred billion separate stars.[5] With newer, more powerful telescopes, like the 200-inch telescope located on Mount Palomar near San Diego, astronomers can focus on just the tiny portion of the sky encompassed by the bowl of the Big Dipper and count more than a million galaxies there alone![6]

The vastness of space is such that normal measurements do not suffice to describe the distances between stars and galaxies. So astronomers have come up with a measurement called the "light year"—the distance that light, which travels at approximately 186,000 miles per second, will travel in a year's time. That distance turns out to be approximately six trillion miles. Here is an analogy to help us conceptualize the vastness of the universe. Someone calculated that if we took the distance from the earth to the sun, which is 93 million miles, and reduced that in scale down to where it was the thickness of a single sheet of typing paper, the distance from our earth to the nearest star would be a stack of paper 71 feet high! On that same scale, the diameter of the Milky Way, our own galaxy, would be a stack of paper 310 miles high. And if we carried that same scale on to the edge of the known universe, we would have a stack of paper 31 million miles high—a stack of paper that would stretch from the earth nearly one third of the way to the sun.[7]

When we consider the incredible vastness of the numbers of creations, all of which were completed under the direction of the Father by the Only Begotten, we begin to sense the position, the majesty, and the power that were his before his coming to earth. The Doctrine and Covenants gives us even more insight as to his position not only as the Creator but as the sustainer of creation. Speaking of Christ, we read, "He is in the sun, and the light of the sun, and the power thereof by which it was made. As also he is in the moon, and is the light of the moon, and the power thereof by which it was made; As also the light of the stars, and the power thereof by which they were made; And the earth also, and the power thereof, even the earth upon which you stand. . . . Which light proceedeth forth from the presence of God to fill the immensity of space—*The light which is in all things, which giveth life to all things, which is the law by which all things are governed*" (D&C 88:7–13; emphasis added). If this light that emanates from Christ is indeed the law by which all things are governed, the implication is that if somehow that light were extinguished, the entire universe would collapse back into chaos. That is the being of whom we speak. That is who Jehovah was before he came to mortality.

Now we begin to sense the incredible scope of the condescension of Christ in leaving that position, that majesty, that power, and taking upon himself mortality—becoming an infant totally dependent on others, requiring daily nourishment, being subject to the weaknesses of the flesh, feeling pain when he slipped in the carpenter's shop and hit his finger, being vulnerable to suffering and sickness. Imagine the God of the universe being subject to the common cold! But, as Paul said, Christ thought it not robbery that he should leave that position, but rather, he emptied himself of that glorious power and took upon himself all that mortality implies. That is one sense of the condescension of God.

The Mortal Ministry of the Lord

In the vision of Nephi, the second time the angel referred to the condescension of God it was not a question but a command: "Behold the condescension of God!" (see 1 Ne. 11:26). As noted before, after receiving that command Nephi then saw the mortal ministry of the Savior. After seeing John the Baptist, the Twelve Apostles, and Jesus healing all sorts of infirmities, Nephi was again commanded by the angel to look. "And I looked and beheld the Lamb of God, that he was taken by the people; yeah, *the Son of the everlasting God was judged of the world;* and I saw and bear record. And I, Nephi, saw that *he was lifted up upon the cross and slain for the sins of the world*" (1 Ne. 11:32–33; emphasis added). As we look at the mortal ministry of Christ, we see several different aspects of this condescension of God.

The circumstances of his birth, the status with which he came into the world, and the manner in which it was announced all showed great condescension on his part. Considering who the Savior was and what he had been before coming to mortality, one could naturally expect that his birth would have taken place in the grandest, most resplendent palace the world had ever known. One could expect that all mankind would hail him; that kings, potentates, and rulers from every country would come to pay him homage; that they would bring him gifts of wealth, power, prestige, and national alliances. One could even wonder why he chose to come in the age that he did. Had he come in our age, his birth could have been heralded by national television and broadcast over international satellite systems. Estimates say that the Olympics, which are held every four years, are broadcast to more than one billion viewers. Think of the start such coverage would have given to the ministry of the Savior. But instead he was born in a tiny village in the hill country of Judea. Only shepherds, a few wise men, and an old man and woman at the temple were chosen to herald his birth. The only political ruler who did take note of the birth ordered him killed, and Jesus had to flee with his family into a foreign country. When he was finally allowed to return to his native land, he took up residence in another backward village in the hill country of Galilee, where for the next thirty years he quietly spent his life as a carpenter.

He showed condescension in his choice of associations while on earth. Once his formal ministry began, the Savior chose to act in a way that did not indicate his previous position of power, majesty, and status. He chose his leaders and closest associates not from the world's upper crust but from common men—Galileans who were despised even by their own countrymen for being backward and simple. He chose fishermen, a tax collector, a zealot. And that was not all. As he went out among the people, he made no attempt to screen out the unwashed and the unworthy. His whole life was spent dealing and working with those who were what others would define as the dregs of society—lepers, the sick, the diseased, the halt, the maimed, prostitutes, publicans, sinners. He mixed freely among them without the slightest hint of disdain or condescension, although when one considers who he was and where he came from, that alone was a remarkable condescension.

He showed condescension in his patience and restraint when brought before men for judgment. In 1 Nephi 19, Nephi made a statement which, when we consider it carefully, is almost mind-boggling in its horror and irony. "And the world, because of their iniquity, shall judge him to be a thing of naught; *wherefore they scourge him, and he suffereth it; and they smite him, and he suffereth it. Yea, they spit upon him, and he suffereth it,* because of his loving kindness and his long-suffering towards the children of men" (1 Ne. 19:9; emphasis added). The God who created everything was judged to be nothing! And yet he endured it with complete patience. Imagine the being whose power, whose light, whose glory holds the universe in order, the Being who speaks and solar systems, galaxies, and stars come into existence—standing before wicked men and being judged by them as being of no worth or value!

When we think of what he could have done to these men who took him to judgment, we have a new and different sense of his condescension. When Judas led the soldiers and the high priests to the Garden of Gethsemane and betrayed him with a kiss, Jesus could have spoken a single word and leveled the entire city of Jerusalem. When the servant of the high priest stepped forward and slapped his face, Jesus could have lifted a finger and sent that man back to his original elements. When another man stepped forward and spit in his face, Jesus had only to blink and our entire solar system could have been annihilated. But he stood there, he endured, he suffered, he condescended.

He showed condescension in his suffering for our sins. In all the world, there was only one perfectly holy, perfectly sinless being (see Heb. 4:15; D&C 20:22). Only one man lived his very life without a single thought, word, or action that was out of harmony with the will of God. And yet, so that he could bring about our redemption, he stood before the justice of God and paid as though he were guilty of every sin and every transgression ever committed. We cannot begin to quantify or comprehend the vastness of the requirements of that suffering.

Yet, to help us begin to grasp with our finite, mortal minds the enormous price required, consider a few rough indicators of how much sin there is in our world. If you look at the United States alone, there are now more than fifty murders committed every day (that's nearly 19,000 per year). There are more than 21,000 thefts reported every day, and more than 5,500 reported cases of child neglect and abuse.[8] Alma said adultery is the second most serious sin next to murder (see Alma 39:5). Think of how many times in a single day adultery or some other violation of the law of chastity is committed somewhere in the world. How many cases of incest, child abuse, pornography, burglary, robbery? How many times in any one day is the name of God taken in vain? How many times are sacred things profaned? Then multiply these over the span of human history. And that takes into consideration only our world. We know that the Atonement extended to other worlds as well.[9]

Jesus went to the Garden and to the cross and paid in personal suffering an infinite price for all of these horrible, unthinkable things. That gives a completely different meaning to the command, "Behold the condescension of God!"

He showed condescension when he chose to suffer not only for our sins but for the infirmities, sicknesses, and illnesses of mankind. In one of the great discourses of the Book of Mormon, Nephi, speaking of the Savior, said, "For behold, he suffereth the pains of all men, yea, the pains of every living creature, both men, women, and children, who belong to the family of Adam" (2 Ne. 9:21). At first one might think the pains that Nephi referred to are only those caused by sin, but Alma is even more specific and shows that this suffering included other things as well. "And he shall go forth, suffering pains and afflictions and temptations of every kind; and this that the word might be fulfilled which saith he will take upon him the pains and the sicknesses of his people. And he will take upon him death, that he may loose the bands of death which bind his people; and *he will take upon him their infirmities, that his bowels may be filled with mercy,* according to the flesh, that he may know according to the flesh how to succor his people according to their infirmities" (Alma 7:11–12; emphasis added).

Elder Neal A. Maxwell, commenting on this dimension of the Atonement, said:

"Thus, in addition to bearing our sins—the required essence of the Atonement—the 'how' of which we surely do not understand, Jesus is further described as having come to know our sicknesses, griefs, pains, and infirmities as well. Another 'how' we cannot now comprehend! (See Isaiah 53:4; Matthew 8:17; Mosiah 14:4; Alma 7:11–12.) Jesus thus not only satisfied the requirements of divine justice but also, particularly in His Gethsemane and Calvary ordeals, demonstrated and perfected His capacity to succor His people and his empathy for them. He came to know, personally and perfectly, 'according to the flesh' how to help us become more like His fully comprehending Father: 'Great is our Lord, and of great power: his understanding is infinite' (Psalm 147:5).

"Jesus' daily mortal experiences and His ministry, to be sure, acquainted Him by observation with a sample of human sicknesses, grief, pains, sorrows, and infirmities which are 'common to man' (1 Corinthians 10:13). But the agonies of the atonement were infinite and first-hand! *Since not all human sorrow and pain is connected to sin, the full intensiveness of the Atonement involved bearing our pains, infirmities, and sicknesses, as well as our sins.* Whatever our sufferings, we can safely cast our 'care upon him; for he careth for [us]' (1 Peter 5:7)."[10]

Who could even begin to fathom the depths of the suffering and the depths of the pain that the Savior condescended to take upon himself so that he could meet the needs of his children and redeem them? No wonder it could be said, "The Son of Man hath descended below them all" (D&C 122:8).

The Mercies of the Savior

Nephi records one other use of the phrase "the condescension of the Lord": "O then, if I have seen so great things, if the Lord in *his condescension unto the children of men* hath visited men in so much mercy, why should my heart weep and my soul linger in the valley of sorrow?" (2 Ne. 4:26; emphasis added). Consider this context of the word *condescension* as it differs from the context of his coming into this mortal world and the various ways in which he condescended during his mortal ministry.

In the Book of Mormon two great aspects of God's character are described as *mercy* and *justice.* The perfect justice of God requires that every sin and every transgression be recompensed or punished (see Alma 42:16–25). Otherwise, those who have been wronged could cry out that there is no justice. But by the same token, because all men sin and come short of the glory of God (see Rom. 3:23), justice would require that all of us be banned from the presence of God forever because no unclean thing can dwell in his presence (see Moses 6:57). Fortunately God is also a perfectly merciful being and has devised a plan of redemption whereby justice can be paid through the suffering of the Savior and we can be redeemed and brought back into his presence (see 2 Ne. 2:5–7).

Let us consider the quality of mercy. Mercy is an attribute whose very nature requires condescension, because nothing that man could do merits that mercy. In other words, once we have sinned, we have put ourselves beyond the holy nature of God. For him to then extend mercy and love and grace to us, in spite of what we have done, is another great act of condescension.

There are probably several dimensions to this aspect of condescension as well, but two come to mind. It is interesting, considering what he could legitimately ask, how little the Lord requires of us before he responds with his blessings and mercy. For example, as the creator of the heavens and earth and all things that in them are (see D&C 104:14), by every right God could ask that we give everything to him or as a minimum he could ask that he receive nine-tenths and that we live on one-tenth of what we have. But just the opposite is true. He asks only a tenth. Instead of asking us for six days of worship and one day for ourselves, it is just the other way around. And out of a twenty-four-hour day, if we spend even no more than 1/48th of that time—a half an hour—in scripture reading and personal prayer, we will receive immediate and recognizable blessings. So it is in every aspect of our lives. Most of the truly valuable things in this world—life, health, and a beautiful world in which to live—come to us free and without price.

Related to that is the idea of the condescension of God's mercy in our repentance. In the classic story of the prodigal son is a reference after the young man came to himself and realized the foolishness of what he had done. He determined that he would return to his father and ask for his forgiveness. "And he arose, and came to his father. *But when he was yet a great way off,* his father saw him, and had compassion, and ran, and fell on his neck, and kissed him" (Luke 15:20; emphasis added). It was not required that the son come all the way back. The father was watching and went out to meet him while he was yet a long way off.

This principle was illustrated in the example of a man who as a youth rejected the Church and became totally inactive for some twenty years. He paid no tithing and did not go to church. Fairness would seem to indicate that if this man wanted to come back into full fellowship and become a "full" tithe payer, he would be required to pay the twenty years of back tithing and even, legitimately, the interest that would have accrued on that tithing. But such is not the case. The Lord simply teaches that if we turn back, then we can be forgiven and begin again to receive his blessings. That, of course, is the lesson of the parable of the laborers in the vineyard (see Matt. 20:1–16). Even those who went to labor in the vineyard in the final hour of the day were given the same wage as those who had labored all the day long. In the eyes of the world, that is not fairness, but when we understand that God condescends in extending his mercy to unworthy, unprofitable servants, then we see this other dimension of the condescension of God. He condescends in his mercies to us—sinful, unworthy, quick to stray—and lets his arm of love stretch out all the day long.

Implications for Us Individually

It is all well and good to note the various aspects that might be implied by Nephi's phrase "the condescension of God," but what are the individual implications for us? The first is that once we come to understand who God is and what greatness and glory he represents, we ought to be filled with overwhelming reverential awe. The religious-minded person should ideally have God as a common part of his life; but that doesn't mean that God should ever become common. Sometimes in our prayers, we kneel down and, with the business of the day pressed in upon our minds, lightly address the Master of the universe. At times it would be well if we said to ourselves as we begin our prayers, "Wait a moment, remember to whom you are speaking." We should feel a great reverence for who he is and what he is and also gratitude that he should care for us and allow us to communicate with him. Great awe would then fill our hearts as we began to pray.

Indeed, one of the meanings of true humility is to realize just how insignificant we really are in relation to God's power and position. It is interesting that one of the injunctions given clearly and specifically in holy places is that we avoid lightmindedness. The scriptures give us a similar injunction (see D&C 88:121), and we are counseled in numerous places to be filled with soberness when it comes to the things of eternity (see, for example, Jacob 2:2; Mosiah 4:15; D&C 6:19, 35). The Lord himself commanded, "Let the solemnities of eternity rest upon your minds" (D&C 43:34).

A second way in which the phrase "the condescension of God" should affect us has to do with a warning given by Nephi. We have already cited Nephi's sobering comment about how the world judged the Holy One of Israel to be "a thing of naught" (1 Ne. 19:9). Two verses before that, Nephi warned: "For the things which some men esteem to be of great worth, both to the body and soul, others set at naught and trample under their feet. Yea, even the very God of Israel do men trample under their feet; I say, trample under their feet but I would speak in other words—they set him at naught, and hearken not to the voice of his counsels" (1 Ne. 19:7). In other words, if we set aside the counsels of God and refuse to follow them, then we have in reality judged God to be a thing of naught and we trample him under our feet.

As part of our understanding of the condescension of God, then, we should be especially careful to seek to follow the counsel of the Lord. Since much of that counsel comes to us through his servants (see D&C 1:37–38), we must also be earnest in our attempts to follow the Brethren. In this age we have many opportunities to become critical of the Church and its leaders, to put our own desires above the counsel of the Lord, and to reject the warnings of the living prophets. In doing that we may ignore Christ and thus set him at naught.

In a poem by an unknown author, the idea that we can judge Christ by ignoring him was captured in a most sobering form.

When Jesus came to Golgotha,
They hanged him on a tree.
They drove great nails through hands and feet,
They made—a Calvary!
They crowned him with a crown of thorns;
Red were his wounds and deep;
For those were crude and cruel days,
And human flesh was cheap.
When Jesus came to our town,
They simply passed him by.
They never hurt a hair of him!
They merely let him die.
For men had grown more tender now;
They would not give him pain!
They only passed on down the street,
And left him standing in the rain.[11]

A third practical implication that can come from a deeper understanding of the condescension of God is that we finite, imperfect, and very limited human beings do not seek to impose our own agenda on the Lord. In Jacob we are warned,

"Wherefore, brethren, *seek not to counsel the Lord,* but to take counsel from his hand. For behold, ye yourselves know that he counseleth in wisdom, and in justice, and in great mercy, over all his works" (Jacob 4:10; emphasis added). One would think that in recognizing our own finite limitation, we would know better than to seek to counsel the Lord, but how frequently we fall into the trap of trusting more in our own wisdom than in his.

One of the classic examples of that is found in Church history in the loss of the 116 pages of Book of Mormon manuscript translated by the Prophet Joseph Smith. Joseph so wanted to please Martin Harris, who had helped him so much, that he refused to accept the Lord's counsel the first two times it was given. Do we fall into similar traps when we impose deadlines on the Lord as to when we need a prayer answered or when we decide what form we want revelation to come in or what solution we need for a particular problem? We are counseled by Nephi not to trust in the arm of flesh (2 Ne. 4:34). When we trust our own judgment and wisdom instead of God's, we are relying on our own arm of flesh. A true understanding of the condescension of God will help us keep our perspective about our need for him.

In the sacramental prayers on both the bread and water, one of the covenants we make is that we will "always remember him" (D&C 20:77, 79). Is not this perhaps the most profound and important lesson that we should learn from our understanding of the condescension of God? If he in his greatness, power, and glory condescends always to remember us, how much more should we then seek to remember him? It is such a simple thing but can so profoundly affect our lives if the Savior is foremost in our minds. When our thoughts turn to him and we ask ourselves the question, "What would *he* do?" or "What would *he* have me do?" then we begin to accept the condescension of God. He left his high and holy station to come to this world to set the example for us and to guide us back into the presence of the Father. That is the ultimate implication for us, and following him is how we can make the condescension of God become real in our own lives.

Notes

From Bruce A. Van Orden and Brent L. Top, eds., *Doctrines of the Book of Mormon, the 1991 Sperry Symposium* (Salt Lake City: Deseret Book Co., 1992), 80–92.

1. M. R. Vincent, *Word Studies in the New Testament* (MacDill AFB, Fla.: MacDonald Publishing Co., n.d.), 2:878.
2. Ibid., 879.
3. Ibid.
4. Phillips Modern English Translation, as cited in *The New Testament in Four Versions* (Washington, D.C.: Christianity Today, 1965), 611.
5. Kenneth F. Weaver, "The Incredible Universe," *National Geographic,* May 1974, 592.

6. Ibid.
7. Ibid.
8. All figures are based on 1987 or 1988 statistics for the United States only. See 1991 *Information Please Almanac* (New York: Houghton Mifflin Co., 1991), 3.
9. President Marion G. Romney summarized this doctrine in these words: "Jesus Christ, in the sense of being its Creator and Redeemer, is the Lord of the whole universe. Except for his mortal ministry accomplished on this earth, his service and relationship to other worlds and their inhabitants are the same as his service and relationship to this earth and its inhabitants" (as quoted in Robert G. Mouritsen, "I Have a Question," *Ensign*, April 1976, 32).
10. Neal A. Maxwell, *"Not My Will, but Thine"* (Salt Lake City: Bookcraft, 1989), 51; emphasis added.
11. In H. Curtis Wright, *"A Thing of Naught": World Judgment and the Trial of Jesus Christ,* no. 5 in Religious Life Series (Provo: Brigham Young University Extension Publications, 1960), 35.

Chapter 13

"To This End Was I Born" (John 18:37)

In the judgment hall of the Antonia Fortress in Jerusalem, two men faced each other in the early hours of a spring morning—the one a man of the world, supreme political ruler of the province of Judea; the other, a Galilean accused of treason, sedition, and blasphemy, who should have been summarily dismissed and sent to the cross. Pilate had done that very thing numerous times before.

But this man—something in his bearing caused the procurator to pause. "Art thou a king then?" he demanded. And the man from Nazareth, facing death in a few hours, responded, "To this end was I born, and for this cause came I into the world, that I should bear witness unto the truth" (John 18:37).

We cannot possibly argue which portion of Christ's ministry is the most significant, for each aspect of his mission is an integral part of the whole design. It would be safe to say, however, that the events connected with the Last Supper, the Garden of Gethsemane, his arrest and trial, his crucifixion, and his resurrection were the culminating events of his ministry. From the day of his birth and through every step of his ministry, his face was set toward Jerusalem, the cross, and the empty tomb. The following are some random thoughts on the events of those last hours of the mortal life of the Master.

Exertion and Exhaustion

Talking about the physical pain and agony of the Crucifixion is a fairly common thing for us, but too often we overlook the fact that the last twenty-four hours of Christ's life must have been physically, emotionally, and mentally exhausting for him. Think back on a time when you had to go for an extended time without sleep. By the time twenty or so sleepless hours have passed, we tend to get mentally sluggish, emotionally irritable, and physically drained. By the time the Savior died on the cross, he had been without sleep for at least thirty-six hours, possibly more. The disciples had unsuccessfully fought off sleep part way into the night (see Matt. 26:40–45), but he went on through that night and all the next day.

Added to the exhaustion caused by lack of sleep was the physical exhaustion caused by pain. Most of us have had an experience with how a very minor pain, such as a toothache or headache, can drain the body's resources. Imagine the drain that accompanied the incomprehensible agony in the Garden, the physical abuse during the trial, and the scourging by the Romans that flayed strips of skin and flesh from his back.

Many of us have given blood to the Red Cross or to a hospital. Remember how physically drained we felt after that experience and of the cautions we were given for rest and nourishment? In the Garden of Gethsemane, Christ suffered so intensely that he bled at *every* pore (see Luke 22:44; D&C 19:18). What effect would that loss of blood have had in addition to the physical suffering it caused?

Furthermore, Jesus had to exert himself physically during those last twenty-four hours. He walked from the Upper Room, where he had held the Passover with his disciples, to the Garden of Gethsemane, where he was arrested and taken back to the Palace of Caiaphas. From there he was taken to the Antonia Fortress, then to Herod's Palace, then to the Antonia Fortress again, and finally to Golgotha. That represents nearly five miles of walking up and down some very hilly terrain, and all of it under extreme physical, mental, and emotional duress.

Yet in spite of all of this—no sleep, loss of blood, extensive walking, intense agony, physical abuse—Jesus never once lost his temper, never once lost control of himself or of the situation. In fact, no one could have been more fully composed or in control of himself than was the Master throughout the whole ordeal of his arrest, trial, and crucifixion.

Who Crucified Jesus?

As we review the events of the Savior's arrest, trial, and crucifixion, we should understand who was really responsible for the death of Jesus. Throughout the centuries, Christians have used the accounts of the Crucifixion as justification for their hatred and persecution of the Jews. On the other hand, in more recent times Jewish and Christian leaders who abhor what has happened in the past have tried to put the blame for the Crucifixion solely on the Romans.

A careful reading of the Gospel accounts makes it clear that the primary instigators of the plot to kill the Savior were the Jewish *religious leaders.* They were the ones the Master and his teachings most threatened, and they were the ones who engineered the arrest and the trial before the Sanhedrin and who finally badgered the weak and vacillating Pilate into pronouncing the death sentence. Though Roman hands held the whip and drove the nails, the Roman soldiers were only carrying out the will and careful planning of the Jewish leaders. The Jewish leaders, not the Jewish people as a whole, and not even all of the leaders, were the ones who plotted Jesus' death.

Peter was a Jew. James and John were Jews. Martha, Lazarus, and Zacchaeus—all of the first leaders and disciples of Christianity were Jews. Within a few months of the Crucifixion, over eight thousand people of the Jewish nation had become Christians, including "a great company of the priests" (Acts 6:7; see also Acts 2:41; 4:4). If the Jews as a people are to be blamed for the Crucifixion, then the Jews must equally be given credit for establishing the early Christian church, for Jews as individuals were involved in both.

But doesn't the Book of Mormon prophesy that the Jews would suffer persecution because they crucified Jesus? Not exactly. Some of the Book of Mormon writers did prophesy that the Jews would suffer persecution. The reason for their persecution, however, was not the Crucifixion *per se* but an attitude of the heart. This distinction is an important one. Nephi said: "As for those who are at Jerusalem, saith the prophet, they shall be scourged by all people, because they crucify the God of Israel, *and turn their hearts aside,* rejecting signs and wonders, and the power and glory of the God of Israel. And because *they turn their hearts aside,* saith the prophet, *and have despised the Holy One of Israel,* they shall wander in the flesh, and perish, and become a hiss and a by-word, and be hated among all nations" (1 Ne. 19:13–14; emphasis added).

It is hardness of heart in the Lord's covenant people that brings suffering upon them. It was true of the House of Israel in the Old Testament. It was true of the Nephites and Jaredites in the Book of Mormon. And it was true of some Latter-day Saints in this dispensation (see, for example, D&C 97:25–27; 101:1–8).

We believe that punishment for someone else's sin is unjust (see A of F 1). To suggest that Jews of the twentieth century are being punished by God for what their ancestors two millennia ago did is unthinkable when we understand God's nature. But those who have been called to be God's people are expected to serve him with all their hearts (see Deut. 6:5). When they do not, they bring sorrow and suffering upon themselves.

"None Other Nation . . . Would Crucify Their God"

Another important point has to do with the nature of the Jewish leaders and the conspiracy to kill Jesus. In the Upper Room after he had finished the washing of the feet, Jesus made a rather sobering prophecy—a prophecy that in his own case would be fulfilled in less than twenty-four hours. He said: "If the world hate you, ye know that it hated me before it hated you. If ye were of the world, the world would love his own: but because ye are not of the world, but I have chosen you out of the world, therefore the world hateth you" (John 15:18–19). And then he added: "These things have I spoken unto you, that ye should not be offended. They shall put you out of the synagogues"—now here is the prophecy—"yea, the time cometh, that whosoever killeth you *will think that he doeth God service"* (John 16:1–2; emphasis added).

The men who killed Jesus were evil men. Criminals killed him—but not criminals in the usual sense. They were criminals motivated by religious motives. H. Curtis Wright shared this important insight on the arrest and crucifixion of Jesus:

"To begin with, the conspiracy against Jesus was *inspired by the religious motives of pious public officials* whose sense of virtue had been outraged. We must disagree violently with the bulk of Christian writers who have described the leaders of the Jews as hoodlums and outlaws, rascals and ruffians. . . . They were criminals all right, but of a vastly different piece. They had no use for the seamy side of crime, and they campaigned relentlessly against it. . . . They moved in the upper strata of Jewish high society and lived in the better sections of Jerusalem. . . . They inhabited the country club ionosphere of the city's 'velvet alleys' where they breathed the rarified air of religious piety and unimpeachable integrity. . . . They didn't have an arsenal where they stashed tommy guns and blackjacks and knives and rubber hoses. . . . And there were no handkerchiefs over their faces, no gloves to cover their fingerprints. *They wore instead the robes of righteousness*—the cloak of respectability and public trust, and the mantle of high official office."[1]

That point is an important one to understand. The men who had Jesus put to death were the "spiritual leaders" of Judaism. The great irony—and the scriptural accounts have glimpses of this—is that these men used the law, the very law they claimed so scrupulously to obey, as the weapon to kill Jesus. Even while they swelled with righteous indignation and cried that they were protecting the law from this blasphemous man, they violated that law in a dozen ways.

For example, we know that by Sanhedrin law every trial had to be held in daytime, between the morning and the evening sacrifice. We know that by Sanhedrin law every trial also had to be held in a room of the temple. We know that contradictory testimony between two witnesses brought an automatic acquittal of the accused. We know that a man could not be condemned and executed on the same day. We know that a trial could not be held on the day before a Sabbath lest it not be concluded in one day and have to be carried over. We know that no person could be convicted on the basis of his own testimony. We know—and this is an interesting aspect of Jewish law—that a unanimous verdict of the judges automatically brought about an acquittal for the accused, because they felt he had no advocate in court. All of these aspects of the law were violated in the case of Jesus.[2]

Over and over again the leaders of Judaism trampled the law under foot in order to achieve their objective. And yet, even as they did so, they were adhering to other parts of the law with meticulous exactness. Three references in particular give some insight into the character of the men who conspired to put their Savior to death.

Matthew 27. The arrest had been made, and Jesus had been taken to the palace of Caiaphas. Suddenly Judas realized the magnitude of what he had done, and so, Matthew recorded, Judas took back the betrayal money. "I have betrayed the innocent blood," he said. Their response was "What is that to us?" (Matt. 27:4). In despair Judas cast the pieces of money at their feet, fled from the room, and committed suicide (see Matt. 27:5). The next verse even more fully reveals the hypocrisy of the Jewish religious leaders, these "pious criminals," as Wright called them: "The chief priests took the silver pieces, and said, It is not lawful for to put them into the treasury, because it is the price of blood" (Matt. 27:6). They had no qualms about bribing a man to betray his master. They had no qualms about an illegal conspiracy to kill the Savior. But when they received money they viewed as spiritually tainted, they were horrified at the thought of putting it into the temple treasury, because it was blood money.

John 18. A second indication of the spiritual hardness and inconsistency of these men is found in the Gospel of John. The Sanhedrin knew that, after they had pronounced the judgment and decreed that Jesus must die, they could not crucify him without the help and permission of the Roman officers. So, John recorded, "then led they Jesus from Caiaphas unto the hall of judgment: and it was early; and they themselves went not into the judgment hall, lest they should be defiled; but that they might eat the passover" (John 18:28). The rabbis believed that if a Jew associated with a Gentile, especially just before the Passover, he was defiled and had to go through a long and involved ritual cleansing. So again the irony strikes us. Riding roughshod over illegalities in the trial was all right. Manipulating the Roman procurator to do their dirty work was acceptable. Even killing their Messiah was of no concern. But to come in contact with a Gentile and risk defilement before the Passover? Perish the thought!

John 19. John gave us another insight into the character of the men who, in their observance of the law, maintained their obsession with the letter of it but totally lost its spirit. After the crucifixion of Jesus and the two thieves was done, "the Jews therefore, because it was the preparation, that the bodies should not remain upon the cross on the sabbath day, (for that sabbath day was an high day,) besought Pilate that their legs might be broken" (John 19:31). The Mosaic law said that no dead person could be left on the cross on the Sabbath (see Deut. 21:23). Spitting in his face during a totally illegal trial was acceptable. Whipping the mob into the frenzied chant of "Crucify him! Crucify him!" was all right. And once on the cross, looking up into his agonized face and taunting him to come down were nothing. But to leave the body hanging on a holy day—God would surely be displeased by such irreverence. The body must come down!

When we understand that kind of hardness in the Jewish leaders, we can better appreciate what Jacob said: "Wherefore, as I said unto you, it must needs be expedient that Christ . . . should come among the Jews, among those *who are the more wicked part of the world;* and they shall crucify him—. . . and *there is none other nation on earth that would crucify their God*" (2 Ne. 10:3; emphasis added). Had Zeus appeared to the Greeks, had Molech appeared to the Moabites, had Ra or Amun appeared to the Egyptians, the people would have danced in the streets to welcome him and sung hymns of joyous praise. No other people would have crucified their god. And the great irony is that the religious leaders did it, as Jesus had prophesied, thinking they had actually done God a service (see John 16:2).

Stunned Sorrow or Joyous Exultation?

Imagine for a moment the scene in Jerusalem immediately after the death of Jesus. Tear-stained cheeks, eyes red with grief, voices hushed and shocked, a numbing sense of unreality—what a pitiful, tragic three days that must have been for Jesus' followers. The Master, the worker of miracles, he who had raised Lazarus from death just a few days before, now lay in a borrowed tomb. It was too incredible to believe; yet they had seen the torn hands and feet, handled the cold body.

But a vision given to Joseph F. Smith in 1918 tells us that, at exactly that same time, a scene of vastly different tone was occurring elsewhere (see D&C 138). Even as one group of disciples was hastily preparing the body for burial, another group of disciples was gathered awaiting his arrival from the mortal world: "There were gathered together in one place an innumerable company. . . . I beheld that they were filled with *joy* and *gladness,* and were rejoicing together. . . . While this vast multitude waited and conversed, *rejoicing* . . . , the Son of God appeared. . . . And the saints *rejoiced* in their redemption. . . . *Their countenances shone,* and the radiance from the presence of the Lord rested upon them, and *they sang praises* unto his holy name" (D&C 138:12, 15, 18, 23–24; emphasis added).

The assembly included such righteous people as Adam and Eve, Abel, Noah, Abraham, Isaac, and Jacob—famous Old Testament prophets—and Book of Mormon prophets (see vv. 38–49). Prophets from this dispensation, such as Joseph Smith and Brigham Young, were also allowed to attend in their premortal state in preparation for their future roles in the work of the kingdom (see vv. 53, 56). Those in Jerusalem who, for those three days, could see only death sorrowed; yet those who were dead who saw life rejoiced.

"And He Saw, and Believed"

Finally we come to the Resurrection itself. In the twentieth chapter of his gospel, John described how Mary came early and found the empty tomb. When she reported that to Peter and John, they both ran to see for themselves. "He [John] stooping down, and looking in, saw the linen clothes lying; yet went he not in. Then cometh Simon Peter following him, and went into the sepulchre, and seeth the linen clothes lie, And the napkin, that was about his head, not lying with the linen clothes, but *wrapped together in a place by itself*" (John 20:5–7; emphasis added). Why did John take note of that? "Then went in also that other disciple, which came first to the sepulchre [John], and *he saw, and believed*" (John 20:8; emphasis added). What did he see that caused him to believe the Resurrection had taken place?

In the quick preparation for burial, Joseph of Arimathaea and the women with him would have wrapped Jesus with long strips of linen in the manner of the Middle East. Finally they would have wrapped one strip around and around his face to cover it. It was that which John saw, "not lying with the linen clothes, but wrapped together in a place by itself" (v. 7). Who wrapped it and folded it and laid it aside? I believe that Jesus laid aside his own burial clothes; he folded them up and laid them aside.

I have been able to visit Jerusalem often. Every time I go into the Garden Tomb and see that empty tomb, I thrill again and understand, I think, what John meant when he said, "He saw, and believed." And the deepest thrill of all is to know that some day, because of what happened in the tomb that first Easter morning, we will come forth from the grave and lay aside and fold up our own burial clothes and know that we too will live forever and ever.

"Did Not Our Heart Burn?"

Luke told us something about the Resurrection that is not recorded in the other Gospels. After Christ has appeared to Peter and John and to the women at the sepulchre, "two of [the disciples] went that same day to a village called Emmaus, which was from Jerusalem about threescore furlongs. And they talked together of all these things which had happened. And it came to pass, that, while they communed together and reasoned, Jesus himself drew near, and went with them. But their eyes were holden that they should not know him. And he said unto them, What manner of communications are these?" (Luke 24:13–17).

They were, I am sure, overflowing with the news of the day—what the women had said, what Peter had said, what John had said. It is not surprising then that "one of them, whose name was Cleopas, answering said unto him, Art thou only a stranger in Jerusalem, and hast not known the things which are come to pass there?" (Luke 24:18). In other words, Cleopas seemed to say, "How can you be in Jerusalem and not know what has happened?" So they explained to him how Jesus of Nazareth had been delivered up and killed; and then they reported the startling things that had been told to them that very morning.

Jesus replied, "O fools, and slow of heart to believe all that the prophets have spoken: Ought not Christ to have suffered these things, and to enter into his glory?" (Luke 24:25–26). And then, "beginning at Moses and all the prophets, he expounded unto them in all the scriptures the things concerning himself" (Luke 24:27). Wouldn't you love to have been able to walk along behind the three of them and hear that conversation? I have often wondered to which scriptures he referred. To what things did he point their minds? From which writings of the prophets did he quote? There is no way to know, of course, but here are some possibilities.

He might have referred to Exodus 12, which describes the great Passover and how Israel was delivered from death and from bondage through the blood of the lamb. Would he have reminded them that this was the Passover season, that the true Lamb had just been offered, and that deliverance from spiritual bondage had been brought to pass?

Perhaps Psalm 22 was another scripture he cited. The opening lines are, "My God, my God, why hast thou forsaken me?" (v. 1). Had they been at the cross? Had they heard that last agonized cry? (see Matt. 27:46). A few verses later in that same psalm we read, "All they that see me laugh me to scorn: they shoot out the lip [a Hebrew idiom meaning to mock and ridicule], they shake the head, saying, He trusted on the Lord that he would deliver him: let him deliver him, seeing he delighted in him" (Ps. 22:7–8). Did the disguised Savior gently remind them how some at the cross had mocked him and challenged him to come down if he were truly the Son of God? (see Matt. 27:39–43). And then in verse sixteen, we read: "For dogs have compassed me: the assembly of the wicked have inclosed me: they pierced my hands and my feet." And verse eighteen, "They part my garments among them, and cast lots upon my vesture" (see Matt. 27:35). To anyone who had witnessed the Crucifixion, those prophecies would have been electrifying.

Perhaps he pointed their minds to Psalm 41:9: "Yea, mine own familiar friend, in whom I trusted, which did eat of my bread, hath lifted up his heel against me." Certainly these two men knew by now about Judas's betrayal of the Master.

Or perhaps Psalm 69 may have been another scripture he quoted. Verses twenty and twenty-one read, "Reproach hath broken my heart; and I am full of heaviness: and I looked for some to take pity, but there was none; and for comforters, but I found none. They gave me also gall for my meat; and in my thirst they gave me vinegar to drink." Would these men have seen or heard from other witnesses that a soldier gave Jesus vinegar to drink just before he died? (see John 19:29–30). Did the disciples realize, as John apparently did, that the Savior died of a broken heart?[3] (see John 19:34–35). What remorse they must have felt as they thought how no one, not even themselves, had stayed through the ordeal to comfort the Master.

These and other Old Testament prophecies would have clearly showed that all was part of the grand design. We don't know how long he walked with them, and we don't know how long they talked, and we don't know which scriptures he cited, but we do know that when he left them, the two disciples recalled that teaching moment, saying, "Did not our heart burn within us . . . while he opened to us the scriptures?" (Luke 24:32).

What Can We Ever Do?

Study of these special, sacred scriptures and meditation on all these things can fill us with an overwhelming sense of gratitude for what the Savior did. It can bring us to ask the burning question: "Why would he do this for me?" As the hymn says so beautifully:

> *I marvel that he would descend from his throne divine,*
> *To rescue a soul so rebellious and proud as mine.*[4]

If we truly come to sense that he did all these things because of love for us, I hope we will have another question: "What could I ever do to repay him for what he has done for me?" Over the years, I have come across some quotations and ideas that I think have particular power in answering that second question.

The first is a parable by Elder James E. Talmage called "The Parable of the Grateful Cat." He told the story of a naturalist in the nineteenth century who had been called to a grand estate in Great Britain to be honored for his contributions in the world of science. He left his cottage early in the morning to go for a walk, and while he was out walking, he saw two boys by the lake. He also heard the frantic meowing of a cat; and so, curious, he walked over to see what was happening. When he arrived he saw the two boys with a mother cat and some kittens. The boys were taking each kitten, tying it up in a rag with a rock, and tossing it into the lake. As you can imagine, the mother cat was frantic watching her kittens being drowned. A little upset, the naturalist asked the boys what they were doing. They said that the mistress of the great estate had an old mother cat that she loved, but she didn't want any more cats around. Whenever the mother cat had a litter, the woman hired the two boys, who were children of some of the servants, to take the kittens to the lake and drown them.

The naturalist said that he would make sure the boys didn't get in trouble, and he took the remaining three kittens and cared for them. To the scientist's surprise, the mother cat behaved as if she understood exactly what was happening. As he walked back to his cottage with the kittens, she ran alongside him, rubbed his leg, and purred happily. He took the kittens into his cottage, gave them some milk, and put them in a warm box.

The next day, when all the company was gathered together in the great house to honor the scientist, suddenly the door pushed open. In came the mother cat with a large fat mouse in her mouth. She walked to the scientist and laid the mouse at his feet. In the words of Elder Talmage, here is the marvelous parable that he drew from this story:

"What think you of the offering, and the purpose that prompted the act? A live mouse, fleshy and fat! Within the cat's power of possible estimation and judgment it was a superlative gift. To her limited understanding no rational creature could feel otherwise than pleased over the present of a meaty mouse. Every sensible cat would be ravenously joyful with such an offering. Beings unable to appreciate a mouse for a meal were unknown to the cat.

"Are not our offerings to the Lord—our tithes and our other freewill gifts—as thoroughly unnecessary to His needs as was the mouse to the scientist? But remember that the grateful and sacrificing nature of the cat was enlarged, and in a measure sanctified, by her offering.

"Thanks be to God that He gauges the offerings and sacrifices of His children by the standard of their physical ability and honest intent rather than by the gradation of His esteemed station. Verily He is God with us; and He both understands and accepts our motives and righteous desires. Our need to serve God is incalculably greater than His need for our service."[5]

That is one answer to the question, "What could I ever do to repay Him?" The answer is nothing. Nothing I can do could merit what he did for me. But that is only a partial answer.

The second item is an article from a medical magazine about "belaying" in mountain climbing. The belay system is the way a mountain climber protects himself from falls. Someone climbs up first, gets in a firm, secure position, ties the rope tightly around his waist, and calls down to his partner, "You're on belay," which means, "I have you if you fall." The article told about Alan Czenkusch, a man who ran a climbing school in Colorado for physicians:

"Belaying has brought Czenkusch his best and worst moment in climbing. Czenkusch once fell from a high precipice, yanking out three mechanical supports and pulling his belayer off a ledge. He was stopped, upside down, ten feet from the ground when his spread-eagled belayer arrested the fall with the strength of his outstretched arms.

"'Don saved my life,' says Czenkusch. 'How do you respond to a guy like that? Give him a used climbing rope for a Christmas present? No, *you remember him. You always remember him.*'"[6]

What a profound analogy for us. Like the belayer, the Savior stops our traumatic fall toward spiritual destruction and offers us a safe line back to him. And what can we do to repay him? *Always* remember him. In fact, those very words are the words of the sacramental covenant (see D&C 20:77, 79; 3 Ne. 18:7, 11). Think what an effect *always* remembering the Savior and what he has done for us would have in our lives. So the fuller answer to the question, "What can I ever do to repay the Savior?" is both nothing, and everything.

The complete answer to the question must be this: The way I repay the Savior is to accept what he did and make it a reality in my life.

Notes

From Gerald N. Lund, *Jesus Christ, Key to the Plan of Salvation* (Salt Lake City: Bookcraft, 1991), 29–46.

1. H. Curtis Wright, *"A Thing of Naught": World Judgment and the Trial of Jesus Christ,* no. 5 in Religious Life Series (Provo: Brigham Young University Extension Publications, 1960), 9; emphasis added.
2. For an excellent summary of the illegalities of the trial, see James E. Talmage, *Jesus the Christ,* Classics in Mormon Literature edition (Salt Lake City: Deseret Book Co., 1982), 598–601 (644–48 earlier in editions).
3. See Talmage, *Jesus the Christ,* 620–21 (668–69 in earlier editions).
4. "I Stand All Amazed," *Hymns of The Church of Jesus Christ of Latter-day Saints* (Salt Lake City: The Church of Jesus Christ of Latter-day Saints, 1985), no. 80.
5. James E. Talmage, "The Parable of the Grateful Cat," *Improvement Era,* August 1916, 875–76.
6. Eric G. Anderson, "The Vertical Wilderness," *Private Practice,* November 1979, 17; emphasis added.

Chapter 14

"He Hath Anointed Me to Preach the Gospel to the Poor" (Luke 4:18)

One time at lunch, a friend raised an interesting question: Suppose the Savior were to visit your ward this Sunday, where would he go first? There were several of us at the table, but we all agreed that he might stop first at the bishop's office and say something like "I thought I'd let you know I'm here. I'll be back to see you in a while." Then he'd go to the nursery, where he would kneel, and the children would gather around him. Then we decided he would go next to the Primary.

From there we weren't sure where he would go. Someone said, "I think I know what he'd do next," and he cited a scripture in the book of Luke, chapter four. As the chapter number indicates, the Savior's ministry had just begun. In fact, the beginning parts of chapter four are the temptations of Jesus. Verse thirteen relates that, after the devil had ended all the temptations, Satan departed from the Lord for a season, and verse fourteen says that Jesus returned in the power of the Spirit into Galilee. That is the setting.

In the Synagogue

Verse sixteen begins the scene: "And he came to Nazareth, where he had been brought up: and, as his custom was, he went into the synagogue on the sabbath day." The phrase "as his custom was" reveals quite a bit about the Lord's habits and priorities. As important as the Savior's word was, and as many people as were demanding to be with him, every Sabbath day he was in the synagogue where he should have been.

"And stood up for to read." The Jewish practice was for all the people in the synagogue to sit on benches. However, they never sat to read the scriptures—they stood. The great scroll of the scriptures was opened, and various members of the synagogue would come up and read from the scriptures. Thus the Savior stood to take that privilege.

"And there was delivered unto him the book of the prophet Esaias [or Isaiah]. And when he had opened the book, he found the place where it was written" (v. 17). That last phrase suggests that Jesus went specifically to a scripture that he wanted to read, rather than just choosing a verse at random.

This is what he read from Isaiah on the scroll: "The Spirit of the Lord is upon me, because he hath anointed me to preach the gospel to the poor; he hath sent me to heal the brokenhearted, to preach deliverance to the captives, and recovering of sight to the blind, to set at liberty them that are bruised, To preach the acceptable year of the Lord" (vv. 18–19).

The Messiah "closed the book, and he gave it again to the minister, and sat down. And the eyes of all them that were in the synagogue were fastened on him. And he began to say unto them, This day is this scripture fulfilled in your ears" (vv. 20–21). The implication was obvious—Jesus Christ was suggesting, "I am the fulfillment of what I just read."

The Lord's Ministry

The man in our lunch group who referred to those verses in Luke said, "I think that after the Savior visited the Primary, he would return to the bishop and ask, 'Do you have anyone in your ward with a special need? Do you have anyone who is in particular distress right now? Have you anyone who is deeply sorrowful? I would like to visit them. Then I'll come back and talk with you and other members of the ward to see what other needs you have.'" I too think that is what the Savior would do because that is what he said his calling was.

What, then, was the Savior's ministry, as Isaiah defined it and the Savior announced it? Notice what verse eighteen says, "The Spirit of the Lord is upon me, *because* he hath anointed me to preach the gospel to the poor" (emphasis added). The one word *because* may seem unusual here. The Lord didn't say the Spirit of the Lord is upon me, *therefore* I will teach the gospel to the poor. Nor did he say the Spirit of the Lord is upon me *so that* I can preach the gospel. He said the Spirit of the Lord is upon me *because* I have been anointed to preach to the poor. Perhaps I am reading more into the word than is actually there, but as I read it, I think the

Lord was saying, "*Because* of the challenges inherent in what I have been called to do—to preach to the poor, to reach the broken-hearted, and so on—*because* of that, I have the Spirit." In other words, success in fulfilling those needs necessitates having the Spirit.

The entire phrase, "because he hath anointed me," is also significant. In Greek the verb for "anoint" is *chrio,* from which comes from the word *Christos* or, in English, Christ. In Hebrew the verb for "anoint" is *mashack,* from which comes the Hebrew title *Messhiach* or, in English, Messiah. The titles Christ or Messiah thus mean "the anointed one." So when the Savior said, "he has anointed me," he was identifying himself as the anointed one, the long-awaited Messiah, the Christ. It was very clearly an announcement of who he was.

Isaiah succinctly describes what the Messiah would be anointed to do: "to preach the gospel to the poor." In Greek, two different words for *poor people* are used in the New Testament. One means specifically a person who earns a very meager or scanty wage. The other means someone who is totally destitute. The second word is often applied to beggars because they earn no wage and therefore have to live upon the alms of others. Interestingly, Luke here used the latter word, so that Jesus was saying, "The Lord has anointed me to preach the gospel to those who are totally destitute." Those who are beggars spiritually, who basically have no resources, are the ones the Savior is to provide resources for. (Compare with King Benjamin's reminder in Mosiah 4:19–20 that we are all beggars before God.)

The next phrase, "he hath sent me to heal the brokenhearted," is especially full of hope. How many broken hearts are there in the world? How many of us are sorrowing, suffering from difficult circumstances or challenges? The Lord was sent to heal such people—to make whole those hearts that have been rent asunder.

The word *captive* in the next phrase, "to preach deliverance to the captives," is also a bit peculiar. In Greek it is a combination of two words meaning those who are taken at spear point. So a captive is not just a prisoner, but a prisoner of war. What an apt description. How many prisoners of the great war that started in the premortal existence and continues to our day do we see before us? Appropriately, Nephi spoke of "the captivity of the devil"—it is Satan who takes captive those who have delivered themselves over "to the hardness of their hearts and the blindness of their minds" (1 Ne. 14:7).

Appropriately, such captives are delivered not through mighty power, but through preaching. They have enslaved themselves, and hearing the truth and accepting it can free them. Did not the Lord also say, "Ye shall know the truth, and the truth shall make you free" (John 8:32). Jesus said he was sent to preach deliverance. The word *preach* implies so much more than simply teaching, because preaching in the New Testament involves declaring and bearing testimony of God's word so that the Spirit can validate that testimony as truthful.

The next phrase, "and recovering of sight to the blind," also contains a highly significant word. Jesus did not talk about *giving* sight to the blind, but about *recovering* sight to the blind. These are people who once saw but now are blinded. I suspect that the blinding could come from many kinds of darkness—sin, guilt, shame, low self-esteem, ignorance, and so on. It doesn't really matter what the cause of darkness is if a person cannot see. But in all cases Christ provides the illumination to help us see again.

The final phrase, "to set at liberty them that are bruised," in Greek means literally those who are broken to pieces, those who are battered. The Lord does more than heal broken-hearted people. His mission is to free from abuse those who are battered. This is a great message of hope to those who see no way out from misery.

The Jubilee Year

In verse nineteen, the Lord declared that he was come "to preach the acceptable year of the Lord." That is a difficult phrase because we're not exactly sure what the acceptable year of the Lord is. An alternate translation of the phrase is "to preach the year of the Lord's favor." Thus many biblical scholars feel that the phrase alludes to the jubilee year of the Old Testament, which is the most holy year the Lord has decreed and thus the most favorable, or acceptable, to him. Leviticus 25:8 explains how often a jubilee year was to occur: "Thou shalt number seven sabbaths of years unto thee, seven times seven years; and the space of the seven sabbaths of years shall be unto thee forty and nine years." So every fiftieth year came to be called the jubilee year (from verse eleven: "A jubile shall that fiftieth year be unto you.")

The jubilee year was a special sabbatical year. Every seventh year, the land was to rest—nothing could be planted, cultivated, or pruned. People were to eat only what grew of itself and then only what they needed at the time (see Lev. 25:1–7). The Lord promised that the year before, the sixth year, the land would bear three times its normal yield to feed the people during the Sabbath year: "If ye shall say, What shall we eat the seventh year? behold, we shall not sow, nor gather in our increase: then I will command my blessing upon you in the sixth year, and it shall bring forth fruit for three years" (vv. 20–21).

Verses nine and ten in particular explain some of the unique features of the jubilee year: "Then shalt thou cause the trumpet of the jubile to sound on the tenth day of the seventh month, in the day of atonement shall ye make the trumpet sound throughout all your land. And ye shall hallow the fiftieth year, and proclaim liberty throughout all the land unto all the inhabitants thereof: . . . ye shall return every man unto his possession, and ye shall return every man unto his family."

Israelites were to set any bond servants free, give any slaves their liberty, and forgive any debtors their debts. What sweeping changes in an economy! Imagine the panic that would be sent into the banking community today to say all debts would be forgiven. Imagine too the consequences of property being returned. If a person, perhaps through foolishness or because of poverty, had sold his inheritance, that family property would be restored to him on the fiftieth year.

Though the meaning of the phrase "to preach the acceptable year of the Lord" may seem obscure to us, the imagery the Lord evoked in the minds of the people who heard him was powerful and sweeping. Its import was "I am here. I have been anointed to proclaim the acceptable year of the Lord. This is a jubilee year: a year when we shall set the captives free, when we shall free the debtors from debt, and when we shall restore them to their inheritances."

Isaiah's Prophecy of the Messiah's Ministry

In the synagogue, the Lord quoted from Isaiah 61:1–2.[1] He did not quote all of Isaiah's prophecy, however, or at least Luke does not record that he quoted all of it. The prophecy in Isaiah that refers to what the Messiah would do continues to the end of verse three. It expands further upon the Lord's ministry. Verse two, for instance, tells us that the Messiah was to also proclaim "the day of vengeance of our God." The Lord would preach a spiritual year of jubilee, but at the same time he would proclaim that the day of retribution would fall upon the wicked. Though the world can look to the Savior with great hope, those who refuse to repent and who continue in unrighteousness will have great need to fear the justice of God.

Verses two and three continue with these words about mourning: "To comfort all that mourn; To appoint unto them that mourn in Zion, to give unto them beauty for ashes, the oil of joy for mourning, the garment of praise for the spirit of heaviness." While there is no object after the word *appoint,* the implication from the three phrases that follow, which tell what is to be appointed, suggest that gladness will come to those who mourn in Zion. Such sufferers, then, have the promise that the Savior will comfort them and turn their sorrow to joy.

In Old Testament times during periods of deep, deep grief or tragedy, mourners took off the normal clothes and put on sackcloth, which is made from black, woven goat hair five times rougher than burlap. They then took ashes and put them on their heads and on their bodies. This was the sign of mourning, and that is the imagery Isaiah uses here. The Savior will take away the ashes and give them beauty; instead of mourning, there will be the oil of joy.

The Savior will also exchange "the garment of praise for the spirit of heaviness." Think how many of us have the spirit of heaviness. Too often, we may have this spirit not through faulty pride, but through a faulty sense of insecurity, a sense that God is not pleased with us. So we become heavy in our minds and hearts. Instead, the Savior will use a garment of praise for what we are. Compared to the world's criticism, this will be glorious clothing indeed.

I think I learned in a small way what this means. When one of my sons was sixteen, he seemed to have a gift for getting under my skin. One day, after I had asked him many times to close the garage door because the garage had some things in it I didn't want to show up missing, I gritted my teeth and said, "Son, let me say something to you." He hunched down, expecting an attack.

Right at that moment, a thought suddenly flashed into my mind: "You're always comparing him to what he ought to be, and he always falls short. But have you ever compared him to what he is and has done?" I thought of a good friend whose sixteen-year-old was in a reform school, and I thought of other sixteen-year-olds I had met whose lives were wrecked. So I said to him, "Are you listening?"

"Yeah, I'm listening," he replied.

I said, "I just want to say to you, thanks for what you are. I've never had to hassle you about going to church. You always do your priesthood duties. You didn't date until you were sixteen, and that was your own free will and choice. I've never said this before, and I just thought it was about to time to say thanks for what you are."

He gave me a long, incredulous look and finally said, "Are you kidding me?" I thought, *What a tragedy. He's been criticized so often he doesn't expect praise.* Too often we press on our youth the garment of heaviness rather than the garment of praise.

The final image in Isaiah's prophecy is truly beautiful. Isaiah gives the reason why the Savior would do what he does—why he appoints gladness for joy, why he changes mourning into happiness, why he gives praise instead of heaviness. He does it all so that we "might be called trees of righteousness, the planting of the Lord, that he might be glorified." His purpose is that we might be as sturdy as trees in our righteousness, cultivated by the Lord; not that we might be glorified but that God might be glorified.

By his own direct revelation in the synagogue at Nazareth, Jesus Christ has told us what his ministry is. And we know, because we are trying to be one with him, that it is a shared ministry with his disciples: "Neither pray I for these alone, but for them also which shall believe on me through their word; That they all may be one; as thou, Father, art in me, and I in thee, that they also may be one in us: that the world may believe that thou hast sent me" (John 17:20–21).

His purposes are also ours—that we reach out to the poor, that we touch the brokenhearted, that we seek out those who are bruised, that we find those who are laden with heaviness and lighten that heaviness with genuine praise, that we seek those who mourn, whether from family problems, physical impairments, or mental difficulties, it doesn't matter. We seek everyone at the level of his or her needs. We try to show them what the will of the Lord is for them, and then we help them discover how to implement that will in their lives. That is our mission—whether we are General Authorities, teachers of the incarcerated, or neighbors with simple faith. The wonderful hope the Savior offers may be realized by any one of his brothers and sisters, and we may share in that divine work.

Notes

From Gerald N. Lund, *Jesus Christ, Key to the Plan of Salvation* (Salt Lake City: Bookcraft, 1991), 19–28.

1. The King James Version of the Isaiah passage has some different wording from the KJV in Luke 4, but the meaning is essentially the same. Some translations of Isaiah have wordings that are closer to the passage in Luke.

   KJV Isaiah 61:1–2: "The Spirit of the Lord God is upon me; because the Lord [the he in Luke 4:18] hath anointed me to preach good tidings [same as gospel] unto the meek [sometimes translated poor]; he hath sent me to bind up [referring to wrapping wounds, thus similar to heal] the brokenhearted, to proclaim liberty [same as preach deliverance] to the captives, and the opening of the prison [parallel to set at liberty] to them that are bound [instead of bruised]; to proclaim the acceptable year of the Lord." Though this text leaves out entirely one phrase in the Savior's quote, "and recovering of sight to the blind," some translations include it instead of or in addition to "and the opening of the prison to them that are bound." The ancient Greek translation of the Hebrew Old Testament has the phrase. Remember that the text the Savior was reading from was much, much older than the texts from which the KJV was translated.

Chapter 15

"The Way Is Prepared from the Fall of Man, and Salvation Is Free" (2 Nephi 2:4)

One of the most misunderstood and misinterpreted doctrines in all of Christianity is the doctrine of the Fall of Adam. Elder James E. Talmage said, "It has become a common practice with mankind to heap reproaches on the progenitors of the family, and to picture the supposedly blessed state in which we would be living but for the fall; whereas our first parents are entitled to our deepest gratitude for their legacy to posterity—the means of winning title to glory, exaltation, and eternal lives."[1]

The Latter-day Saint conception of the Fall as a necessary part of the overall plan of redemption stems heavily from the doctrines taught in the Book of Mormon. Probably no one taught that doctrine more clearly and forcefully than did father Lehi to Jacob, his firstborn son in the wilderness. Lehi called his posterity together, possibly just shortly before his death, along with the posterity of Ishmael, and gave them his final blessing. Each family group in turn received counsel and admonitions from the great patriarch (see 2 Ne. 1–4). Oddly enough, the longest of all of these blessings, as recorded by Nephi, is that given to Jacob. And while the others are more like fatherly admonitions and counsel, Jacob's is a major doctrinal exposition.

Lehi's Discussion of the Fall

Lehi's great blessing to his son is so full of doctrine and meaning that virtually every sentence and, in some cases, every word has significance. Thus, first stepping back and examining the overall picture of what Lehi was trying to do would be helpful. In broad terms, he did four things after his introduction: (1) he outlined five fundamental principles that we must adhere to before we can understand the Fall; (2) he discussed the redemption of the Messiah and how the Messiah can redeem men from the Fall; (3) he discussed the Fall in some detail, particularly focusing on why there had to be a fall; and (4) he concluded by exhorting both Jacob and the other members of his family to wisely use their agency and reap the blessings of the Atonement.

In more detail, the outline of these four points is as follows:

I. FIVE FUNDAMENTALS (2 Ne. 2:4–5)
   A. The Spirit is the same yesterday, today, and forever (v. 4).
   B. The way is prepared from the fall of man.
   C. Salvation is free.
   D. Men are instructed sufficiently to know good from evil; that is, the law is given unto them (v. 5).
   E. By the law, no flesh is justified.
      1. By the temporal law, men are cut off.
      2. By the spiritual law, they perish and become miserable forever.

II. REDEMPTION COMETH IN AND THROUGH THE HOLY MESSIAH (2 Ne. 2:6–10)
   A. The Messiah:
      1. is full of grace and truth (v. 6).
      2. offers himself as a sacrifice for sin.
         a. This answers the ends of the law for those with a broken heart and a contrite spirit (v. 7).
         b. Unto none else can the ends of the law be answered.
   B. Therefore, no flesh can dwell in God's presence except through his merits, mercy, and grace (v. 8).
      1. This is so because he:
         a. laid down his life according to the flesh.
         b. took it up again by the power of the Spirit.
         c. brought resurrection to pass.
      2. These things make him the first fruits unto God and allow him to make intercession for all men (v. 9).
      3. This intercession brings all men into God's presence where they:
         a. are judged of him.
         b. receive punishment or happiness (v. 10).

III. WHY THE FALL? (2 Ne. 2:11–26).

A. There must be opposition in all things (v. 11). If there weren't:
   1. there could be no righteousness or wickedness, no joy or sorrow, and so on.
   2. all things would be a compound in one.
   3. there would be no death, no life, no mental functions.
   4. there would be no purpose in the creation (v. 12).

B. If that were true, then:
   1. God's purposes would be destroyed (vv. 12–13).
   2. it would prove that there is no creation and that we do not exist.

C. But we do exist and there is a God, and he created opposition and gave us agency (v. 14).

D. The Fall was part of God's divine plan. To bring about his eternal purposes, God:
   1. set up opposing choices in the Garden of Eden (v. 15).
   2. gave man his agency (v. 16).
   3. made both choices enticing.
   4. allowed Satan to become the enticer for evil (vv. 17–18).

E. Therefore Adam and Eve fell (v. 19).
   1. They were driven out of the Garden of Eden.
   2. All mankind are born under the effects of the Fall (v. 20).

F. The lives of men were prolonged so that they could repent. Mortality became a time of probation (v. 21).
   1. Everyone is lost because of the Fall, so everyone must repent.
   2. If there had been no fall:
      a. Adam and Eve would have remained in the Garden of Eden (v. 22).
      b. all things would have remained in the same state forever.
      c. Adam and Eve would have had no children (v. 23).
      d. Adam and Eve would have remained in a state of innocence, knowing neither good nor evil.

G. Thus we see that the Fall (and all things associated with it) was a reflection of God's wisdom (v. 25).
   1. Adam fell so men could be.
   2. Men are, that they might have joy.
   3. The Messiah redeems men from the Fall (v. 26).
   4. This allows them to be free and to act for themselves.

IV. LEHI'S EXHORTATION AND SUMMARY (2 Ne. 2:27–30)

A. Two fundamental facts of existence:
   1. men are free according to the flesh (v. 27).
   2. all that is expedient is given to them.

B. The choice is simple. We can choose:
   1. the Mediator, who brings liberty and eternal life.
   2. the Devil, who brings captivity and death.

C. Lehi earnestly exhorts his sons to (v. 28):
   1. follow the will of the Spirit and choose eternal life by:
      a. looking to the Mediator.
      b. hearkening to his commandments.
      c. being faithful to his words.
   2. not follow the will of the flesh and choose eternal death, because this (v. 29):
      a. gives the devil power over us.
      b. brings us down to hell where Satan rules.

D. Final testimony that Lehi has chosen the good part (v. 30).

Let us now examine in more detail what Lehi taught to Jacob.

The Five Fundamentals

In the beginning of his blessing to Jacob, Lehi gave five fundamentals that must be understood before he could go on to discuss the fall and the redemption of man.

Fundamental 1: "The Spirit is the same, yesterday, today, and forever" (v. 4). This a significant point, especially for Jacob who lived six centuries before the Messiah came to earth to work out the infinite atonement. From this statement of Lehi, we know that the Atonement is bidirectional. That is, it doesn't matter whether one was born prior to the Savior's coming to the earth or afterwards. One can either look forward or backward to the Atonement and have its redemptive power work in his or her behalf.

Indeed, we learn from other sources that the Atonement is not only bidirectional but literally omnidirectional. In Moses 1:33, for example, we are told that by the Only Begotten Son "worlds without number" were created. Elder Bruce R. McConkie, commenting on that verse, said, "Now our Lord's jurisdiction and power extend far beyond the limits of this one small earth on which we dwell. He is, under the Father, the creator of worlds without number (Moses 1:33) and . . . the atonement of Christ, being literally and truly infinite, applies to an infinite number of earths."[2]

Speaking in the same vein, President Marion G. Romney said, "Jesus Christ is the Lord of the whole universe. Except for his mortal ministry accomplished on this earth, his service and relationship to other worlds and their inhabitants are the same as his service and relationship to this earth and its inhabitants."[3] So, whether we are on this earth or another, in this time or a previous, God is the same yesterday, today, and forever, and the plan of redemption is the same yesterday, today, and forever.

*Fundamental 2: "The way is prepared from the fall of man" (*2 Ne. 2:4). Many places in the scriptures clearly teach that the plan of redemption was prepared long before the Fall (see, for example, D&C 124:33, 41; 128:5; 130:20). This was Lehi's way of reminding his son of a second foundational principle: that the plan to redeem men from the Fall was laid from the very beginning. In other words, when Adam fell, there was no mad scramble in heaven to determine what to do to save men from the effects of the Fall.

*Fundamental 3: "Salvation is free" (*2 Ne. 2:4). Though Lehi gave this statement in three simple words, the concept is profound and important. The best single commentary we have on 2 Nephi 2 is 2 Nephi 9. A careful reading of chapter nine shows that this was *Jacob's own commentary* on the doctrine taught by his father in chapter two. Of particular interest is Jacob's commentary on the concept that salvation is free: "Come, my brethren, every one that thirsteth, come ye to the waters; and he that hath no money, come buy and eat; yea, come buy wine and milk without money and without price. Wherefore, do not spend money for that which is of no worth, nor your labor for that which cannot satisfy" (vv. 50–51).

*Fundamental 4: "Men are instructed sufficiently that they know good from evil. And the law is given unto men" (*2 Ne. 2:5). In the two foregoing sentences, Lehi stated a fundamental principle in two different ways. Lehi was speaking of those who reach accountability, though he did not explicitly state so. Jacob later made this point clearly (see 2 Ne. 9:25–26).

Exactly what did Lehi mean when he said, "Men are instructed sufficiently that they know good from evil" and "The law is given unto men"? We know from other places in scripture that the medium or the means by which this instruction comes to all men is known as the Light of Christ. Through and by the Light of Christ, individuals come to a basic level of understanding of good and evil. Moroni, citing the words of his father, Mormon, said, "The Spirit of Christ is given to every man, that he may know good from evil; wherefore, I show unto you the way to judge; for every thing which inviteth to do good, and to persuade to believe in Christ, is sent forth by the power and gift of Christ; wherefore ye may know with a perfect knowledge it is of God" (Moro. 7:16).

In latter-day revelation, it was revealed to the Prophet Joseph that this "Spirit of Christ" is also known as "the Light of Christ" (D&C 88:7). This light is the power that lights the moon and the stars and the sun, the light that gives life to all things and through which all things are governed (see D&C 88:7–13).

Fundamental 5: "By the law no flesh is justified" (2 Ne. 2:5). In that simple statement lies the primary reason why there must be a Redeemer, and so examining Lehi's fifth fundamental at greater length is essential.

The word *justified* and its cognate forms *justification, justice,* or *just* all have the same basic root meaning. To be "just" means to be right or be in order with God. Therefore to be justified (the process of justification) is defined as the "declaration of right, thus judicial acquittal, the opposite of condemnation. . . . Justification may be defined, in its theological sense, as the nonimputation of sin and the imputation of righteousness."[4]

To understand why Lehi said that by the law, no flesh is justified, or that because of the law, men are cut off, we must first understand the operations of the law of justice. In the Book of Mormon, King Mosiah, Alma, and other prophets discuss this concept of justice in some detail. The law of justice could be simply stated in both its negative and positive forms as follows: (1) for every obedience to the law, there is a blessing; (2) for every violation of the law, there is a punishment (see D&C 130:20–21). The scriptures also clarify that the ultimate blessing coming from obedience to the law is joy and that the punishment coming from violation of the law is misery or suffering (see, for example, 2 Ne. 2:5).

Why was it, then, that Lehi said that *no* flesh is justified by the law? Because no one keeps the law perfectly! If the law of justice were the only thing operating, no one could be justified (declared to be right or just) by virtue of the law alone, because as Paul said, "All have sinned, and come short of the glory of God" (Rom. 3:23; see also Rom. 5:12; 1 Ne. 10:6). So by the law, that is, speaking as though nothing operated but the law itself, men would be cut off both temporally and spiritually. They would be cut off temporally because they do not keep the law perfectly; and they would be cut off spiritually because violation of the law makes one unclean, and "no unclean thing can dwell . . . in his presence" (Moses 6:57; see also 2 Ne. 9:6–10).

Redemption Cometh in and through the Holy Messiah

Once Lehi laid down the fundamental principles, he turned to what could be thought of as a sixth fundamental principle. But because this principle or truth is of such transcendent importance, he set it apart and discussed it at great length. Second Nephi 2:6, wherein Lehi said, "Wherefore, redemption cometh in and through the Holy Messiah," is the natural follow-through from verse five. Simply put, Lehi stated that men are *condemned* by the law but *redeemed* by the Messiah. His qualifying statement about the Messiah—"for he is full of grace and truth"—is interesting in and of itself. In the LDS Bible Dictionary, the following definition is given under the entry "Grace":

"A word that occurs frequently in the New Testament, especially in the writings of Paul. The main idea of the word is *divine means of help or strength,* given through the bounteous mercy and love of Jesus Christ. . . . This grace is an *enabling power* that allows men and women to lay hold on eternal life and exaltation after they have expended their own best efforts. Divine grace is needed by every soul in consequence of the fall of Adam and also because of man's weaknesses and shortcomings."[5]

Lehi's point was that if Christ were not full of this grace or this "enabling power," the redemption would not be possible.

Lehi's next statement was that the Holy Messiah would offer himself as "a sacrifice for sin, to answer the ends of the law" (2 Ne. 2:7). In light of our understanding of the law of justice, we see why Lehi made this statement. Remembering the two principles that constitute the law of justice—i.e., obedience brings joy, violation brings suffering—one could say that there are only two ways to satisfy the demands of that law. The *first* would be to keep the law perfectly; that is, to never violate in any degree the law that is given. The second way would be to pay the penalty for any violations.

This is what the Messiah did, for he met both conditions. Jesus kept the law perfectly. Not once in his entire mortal life did he violate the law in any degree or in any way. He was the Lamb without spot or blemish. He was the ultimate in perfection. Here then was one who, in Lehi's words, was justified by the law. In other words, the law had no claim on him. But Christ did more than this. In 2 Nephi 9:21, Jacob again added commentary to our understanding of what his father taught: the Messiah "suffereth the pains of all men, yea, the pains of every living creature, both men, women, and children, who belong to the family of Adam." So not only did Christ keep the law perfectly for himself, but he suffered the penalty for all violations as though he himself were guilty of them.

Lehi indicated that the sacrifice answering the ends of the law was given only for those who have "a broken heart and a contrite spirit." Then he added, "unto *none else*" can that be done (2 Ne. 2:7). To better understand why Lehi made this statement and what it fully means for us, let us examine the doctrine of grace and works.

Members of the Church, particularly missionaries, have often been called upon to defend the belief that the way people live (or their works) plays a critical role in their salvation. Protestants, especially evangelical Christians, cite several references from Paul's writings to indicate that a man is saved by grace (see Acts 16:31; Rom. 3:28; 10:13; Gal. 2:16; Eph. 2:8–9). Those statements by Paul have created some awkwardness in the minds of some Latter-day Saints, especially missionaries, about the issue of salvation by grace. The diagram below, though faulty, has been used by some to help answer those questions.

GRACE AND WORKS—ONE EXPLANATION

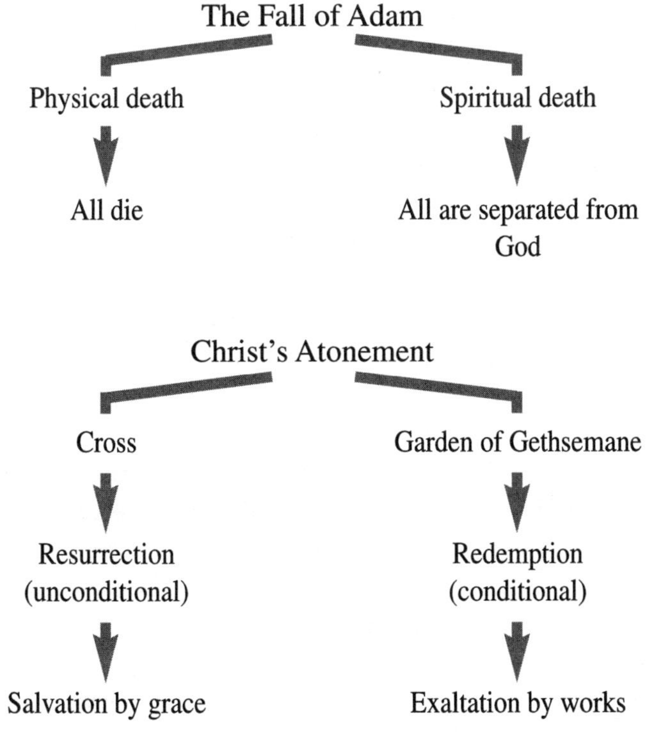

Those using this diagram explain it by saying that through the Fall of Adam there were two deaths that came upon mankind. One is physical death, which is the separation of the body and the spirit. All of Adam and Eve's posterity are subject to mortality and will die. But there is also a spiritual death. This is defined as being cut off or separated from the presence of God. Because Adam and Eve were cast out of the Garden of Eden, all men are born in a state of separation from the presence of God, or in a state of spiritual death.

The diagram goes on to show how Christ's redemption covers both aspects of the Fall. On the cross, the Savior gave up his life but then took it up again, thus overcoming physical death and providing the resurrection. Since no one has to do anything to be resurrected, one could say that this is an unconditional blessing. This explains how we are "saved by grace" without any works on our part. We need do nothing; the grace of Christ resurrects everyone.

But, the explanation continues, there is a second part of the redemption that cannot be overlooked. This part was done in the Garden of Gethsemane. Here the Savior took upon himself the sins of the world and suffered for all mankind. This suffering provided the redemption, but this redemption is *not* unconditional. Here men must do things to have the redemption operate in their behalf. This could be thought of as exaltation by our works. Thus, the conclusion runs, we are saved (resurrected) by grace, but we are exalted (redeemed) by our works. This is a neat and attractive explanation. *The only difficulty is that it has four major doctrinal problems.*

The first doctrinal problem in this explanation is assuming that salvation is different from exaltation. With very few exceptions, the scriptures almost always use the words *salvation* and *exaltation* synonymously. For example, in Doctrine and Covenants 6:13, the Lord says, "If thou wilt do good, yea, and hold out faithful to the end, thou shalt be *saved* in the kingdom of God, which is the greatest of all the gifts of God; for there is no gift greater than the gift of *salvation"* (emphasis added). Resurrection, wonderful as it is, is not the greatest gift of God; eternal life, or exaltation, is (see D&C 14:7). To imply that salvation means only resurrection cannot be supported by scripture.

The second doctrinal problem is the idea that the cross covered only the effects of physical death and that the suffering in the Garden covered only the effects of spiritual death. Such an explanation is not justified by scripture either. The agony in the Garden and the suffering on the cross were both integral parts of the atoning sacrifice. Nowhere do we find indications that the cross alone overcame physical death or that the Garden alone overcame spiritual death.

The third problem is the idea that our works exalt us. As we have seen, one of

Lehi's fundamental points is that no man can be justified, or saved, on the basis of works alone. Only by the merits, mercy, and grace of the Holy Messiah (see 2 Ne. 2:8) are we saved. Righteous works *do* exalt us, but *they are the Savior's works,* not our own (by the simple fact that we cannot fully satisfy the law by our works alone). This is what Nephi meant when he said, "For we know that it is by grace [with which quality the Messiah is filled—see 2 Ne. 2:6] that we are saved, after all we can do" (2 Ne. 25:23).

The fourth problem is the idea that overcoming that part of spiritual death (which resulted from the fall of Adam) is conditional upon how we live. Our second Article of Faith states, "We believe that men will be punished for their own sins, and not for Adam's transgression." To make coming back into the presence of God (overcoming spiritual death) conditional, when the fall of Adam originally caused our separation from him, would mean we suffer punishment for Adam's transgression; and such is not the case. Let us now redo the chart so that it reflects not only what father Lehi taught, but what the other scriptures also teach.

The upper part of the previous chart is correct. The fall of Adam did bring two deaths into the world—physical death and spiritual death. But so far as it applies to Adam's fall, Christ's redemption is unconditional and applies to all. In other words, since we did nothing to be under the effects of the Fall, except come through the lineage of Adam, it is not fair (or just) that we should have to meet any conditions in order to have those effects taken from us.

In 2 Nephi 2:8, Lehi said, "[He] layeth down his life according to the flesh, and taketh it again by the power of the Spirit." Lehi mentioned both the suffering of the flesh and the suffering of the spirit as necessary to bring about the resurrection of the dead. This resurrection is unconditional, and all become immortal. But in verse ten, Lehi went further and said, "Because of the intercession for all, *all men come unto God;* wherefore, *they stand in the presence of him,* to be judged of him according to the truth and holiness which is in him" (emphasis added).

That is a pivotal point. Not only does Christ's redemption bring about resurrection for all without condition, it also brings all men to the judgment bar where they are brought into the presence of the Lord to be judged. If we are brought back into the presence of God, then spiritual death, or the separation from God that came because of Adam's fall, is at that point overcome. What does a person have to do to have this happen? Absolutely nothing. It is unconditional. Thus the Savior automatically redeems us from both effects of the fall of Adam.

The Fall of Me

Now, however, we must consider Lehi's fourth fundamental point. As he said, "Men are instructed sufficiently that they know good from evil" (2 Ne. 2:5). If we know good from evil and then sin (which, according to Paul, all men do), then we must talk about a second fall. This is not the fall of Adam. This is *one's own personal fall.* This fall, which our own, not Adam's, transgression brings about, requires redemption as surely as mankind needed redemption from the consequences of Adam's fall. We'll term this the "fall of me." This diagram charts what happens as the result of the "fall of me."

Once a person reaches the age of accountability and sins through the use of his agency, he becomes unclean. Unless something happens, when he is brought back into God's presence at the judgment, he will not be allowed to stay. Now, since we have no one to blame for this except ourselves, our redemption becomes conditional upon our actions. This is what Lehi meant when he said that the sacrifice that the Messiah offered to satisfy the ends of the law is viable only for those with a broken heart and a contrite spirit. This condition, which comes through faith and

THE MESSIAH REDEEMS MEN FROM THE FALL

("We believe that men will be punished for their own sins"—A of F 1:2)

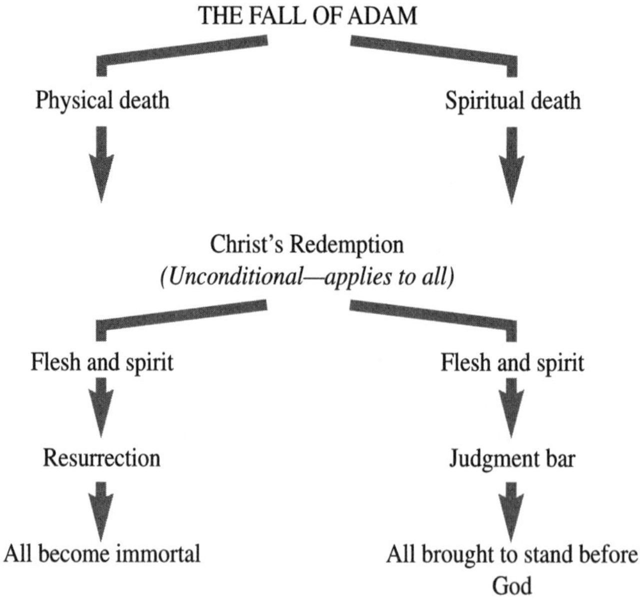

HE OFFERETH HIMSELF UNTO THOSE WITH A BROKEN HEART

The Fall of Me

(Happens to all who become accountable—see Rom. 3:23)

Broken heart and contrite spirit	Hard heart and a proud spirit
↓	↓
Priesthood ordinances	No priesthood ordinances

Christ's Redemption

(Conditional)

Mediation and intercession	No intercession
↓	↓
His suffering answers ends of the law	I suffer for my sins
↓	↓
Justice is paid	Justice is paid
↓	↓
I am sanctified from sin and perfected	Resurrected to lesser kingdoms
↓	↓
Fulness of joy	Joy, but not a fulness of joy

godly sorrow (see 2 Cor. 7:9–10)—or in other words, repentance—brings one to participate in the redemptive ordinances: baptism, confirmation, receiving the priesthood, and the temple ordinances.

Those who refuse to make this new sacrifice (see 3 Ne. 9:20) are characterized in the scriptures as having a hard heart and a proud spirit. These are conditions that lead one to reject the priesthood ordinances. These conditions may also exist, in some cases, even though the outward ordinances may have been performed. In other words, some members of the Church who have been baptized and confirmed, who have received the Holy Ghost and perhaps even temple ordinances, have not exhibited broken hearts and contrite spirits. They go through the outward motions only and therefore experience no validity in those ordinances, no saving power.

What happens, though, to a person who does meet the conditions of a broken heart and a contrite spirit? The left side of the diagram shows the process. The words Lehi used are "mediation" and "intercession" (2 Ne. 2:9–10, 27). The Messiah's mediation and intercession are applied to those with broken hearts and contrite spirits, and his suffering, both on the cross and in the Garden, and his perfect obedience to law answer the demands of the law of justice. Or in Lehi's words, his life and death serve as a "sacrifice for sin" (v. 7). The demands of the law are thus met; in other words, justice is paid, not robbed (see Alma 42:25). The person is sanctified from sin and perfected.

Lehi's statement that the Messiah's merits and not our own merits save us is beautifully supported in the Doctrine and Covenants, wherein the Son says:

"Listen to him who is the advocate with the Father, who is pleading your cause before him—Saying: Father, *behold the sufferings and death of him who did no sin,* in whom thou wast well pleased; behold the blood of thy Son which was shed, the blood of him whom thou gavest that thyself might be glorified; Wherefore, Father, spare these my brethren that believe on my name, that they may come unto me and have everlasting life" (D&C 45:3–5; emphasis added).

What happens, then, to those who do not meet the basic conditions of having a broken heart and a contrite spirit? The right side of the diagram illustrates this. For those hard of heart and proud of spirit who refuse to accept redemptive ordinances, Christ's redemption becomes inoperative. He does not make intercession in their behalf, and he clearly explains so in a modern revelation:

"Surely every man must repent or suffer. . . . Therefore I command you to repent—repent, lest I smite you by the rod of my mouth, and by my wrath, and by my anger, and your sufferings be sore—how sore you know not. . . . For behold, I, God, have suffered these things for all, that they might not suffer if they would repent; *But if they would not repent they must suffer even as I"* (D&C 19:4, 15–17; emphasis added).

Either way, justice is paid. The price of suffering is met. But whereas the Messiah's atoning sacrifice paid the price for the humble and obedient, the rest must pay the price themselves. And how much is that price we would pay ourselves? We don't know exactly, but the Lord described his own suffering: "Which suffering caused myself, even God, the greatest of all, to tremble because of pain, and to bleed at every pore, and to suffer both body and spirit—and would that I might not drink the bitter cup, and shrink" (D&C 19:18). No wonder he commands, "Confess your sins, lest you suffer these punishments of which I have spoken" (D&C 19:20), and urges us to "preach naught but repentance" (D&C 19:21) so that others would not suffer as he did.

Why the Fall?

After laying the foundational principles firmly in place, Lehi was ready to turn his attention to the question of the Fall and why it had to happen. Not surprisingly, the Fall has caused a great deal of confusion and misinterpretation, for on the surface it raises some difficult questions. Though Lehi did not pose these questions openly, he seemed to sense them and proceeded to answer them with a marvelous chain of logical reasoning. Lehi's linchpin argument in explaining why the Fall was necessary is summarized in the well-known scripture "For it must needs be, that there is an opposition in all things" (2 Ne. 2:11). How pivotal this is to Lehi's whole line of reasoning in this chapter can be seen from how much time—verses eleven through fifteen—he spends defending and explaining that statement. Lehi used an interesting chain of reasoning to substantiate his statement. If it were put into a diagram, it would look something like this:

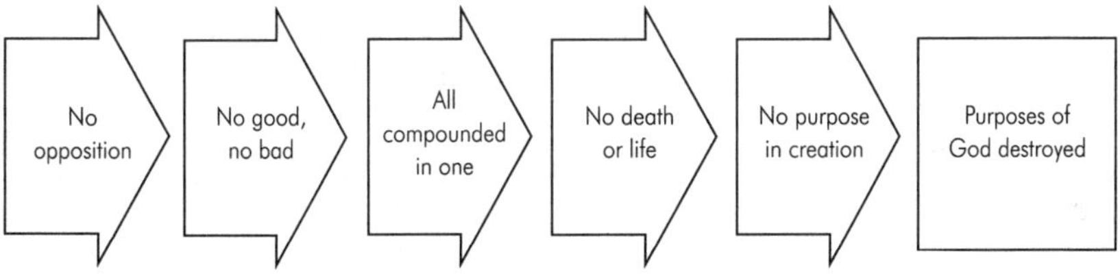

In Moses 1:39, we learn that God's purposes have to do with bringing to pass the immortality and eternal life of man. Therefore, if God's purposes were destroyed, the whole plan of salvation would become meaningless.

Then, as though he had not made his point strongly enough, Lehi started again and put it in other words, reiterating a similar line of reasoning. Again if that were diagram, it would look like this:

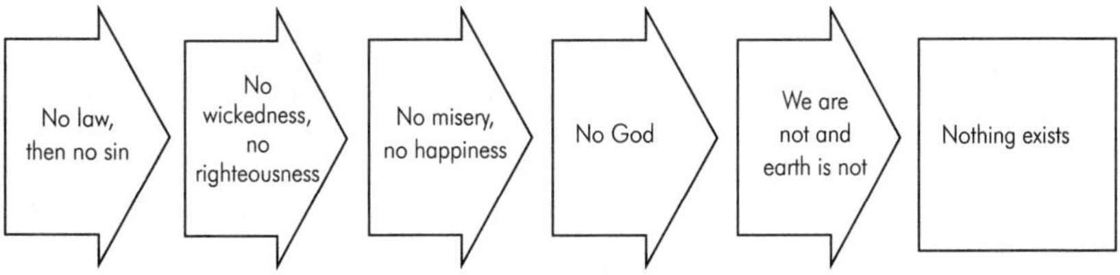

If there is any one thing we can be certain of, it is our own existence. So working backwards from that irrefutable evidence, Lehi showed that God exists and therefore has created all things, and that, as he explained it in 2 Nephi 2:14, includes "both things to act and things to be acted upon."

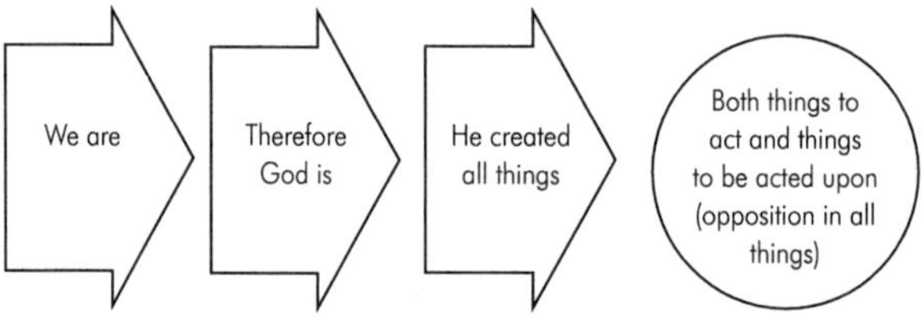

To sum up Lehi's chain of reasoning in just two sentences: In order for God to bring about his purposes with man (their immortality and eternal life), there had to be opposition or opposing alternatives. If there were no opposition, men could not be exalted because there would be no accountability.

This brings us to an important question—if opposition is necessary, why didn't God just create a world of opposition? Here, other scriptures help us understand why this could not be so. Moroni, citing his father's teaching, indicates that "all things which are good cometh of God; and that which is evil cometh of the devil" (Moro. 7:12).

The Prophet Joseph Smith, in the *Lectures on Faith,* indicated that one of the prerequisites for a man to have faith is to have an understanding of the nature, attributes, and *perfections* of God.[6] He then commented, "What we mean by perfections is, the perfections which belong to all the attributes of his nature."[7] From these and other sources we conclude the three following points: (1) creating anything imperfect or unholy is contrary to the nature of God; (2) enticing men to violate law or to do evil is contrary to the nature of God; and (3) if God had created a world in which there was opposition, sin, and evil, then we could hold him responsible for such conditions.[8]

Therefore, the creation of the world (and man) was done in a perfect, holy, and innocent state. To have done otherwise would have been contrary to the nature of God, which sets up an interesting problem. Opposition is necessary to man's progression, but God could not create it and be true to his perfect nature.

The Fall Was Part of God's Divine Plan

Lehi explained how this dilemma was resolved. Note the following points that he made: (1) In verse fifteen, he indicated that God created our first parents and all things that were created. (2) God set up an opposition from the beginning, even the opposition of the forbidden fruit to the tree of life. (3) In verse sixteen, Lehi indicated that God gave agency unto man. (4) If man were to be truly free to act for himself, or in other words, if there were to be truly opposite choices (or opposition), he must be enticed by those choices. (5) Since God cannot entice man to make bad choices, Satan was allowed to come to earth and entice men to do evil (see 2 Ne. 2:17–18). This final point is validated in other latter-day revelation. To the Prophet Joseph Smith, the Lord said:

"It must needs be [note the same language here that Lehi used] that the devil should tempt the children of men, or they could not be agents unto themselves; for if they never should have bitter they could not know the sweet—Wherefore, it came to pass that the devil tempted Adam, and he partook of the forbidden fruit and transgressed the commandment" (D&C 29:39–40).

The positive side of the option given to Adam was clearly enticing in and of itself. The Garden of Eden was a beautiful and alluring place in which to live. Flowers and trees flourished and brought forth fruit spontaneously. There was neither death nor sorrow, nor was there wickedness. But how could the opposite be made enticing so that true opposition could exist? This is why Satan and his angels were cast down to earth and allowed to function.

Lehi made five important points as to why the Fall happened and how the Fall helped the Lord fulfill his divine plan of redemption: (1) opposition is necessary for man's progression (v. 11); (2) the Lord set up opposing choices (v. 15); (3) he gave man his agency (v. 16); (4) in order to make that agency operative, both choices had to be enticing (v. 16; D&C 29:39); and (5) God allowed Satan, who makes the negative option sound as enticing as the positive, to operate in the Garden and in this world.

Once Lehi established why the Fall had to take place, he discussed the results of the Fall for us. He pointed out that, since the Fall had taken place and men were born into the world under the effects of that fall, this life became a state of probation or a time to prove ourselves. He indicated that the days of the children of men were prolonged so they might repent and begin to bring into operation the full plan of redemption (see 2 Ne. 2:21). Lehi further emphasized the importance of the Fall by pointing out what would have happened if the Fall had never taken place (see vv. 22–23). He stated that Adam and Eve would have remained in the Garden of Eden. In particular, all things that were created would have remained in the state they were in prior to the Fall, which was a state of perfection, innocence, spontaneous multiplication, with no death or sorrow. Also Adam and Eve would have had no children. And "they would have remained in a state of innocence, having no joy, for they knew no misery; doing no good, for they knew no sin" (v. 23).

When one examines the four conditions that resulted from the Fall, it becomes evident that all of these are conditions necessary for the progression of mankind toward godhood. They are necessary for man to prove himself and to become accountable before God. Therefore, again noting that if there had been no fall, the purposes of God would have been frustrated, Lehi concluded: "All things have been done in the wisdom of him who knoweth all things. Adam fell that men might be; and men are, that they might have joy. And the Messiah cometh in the fulness of time, that he may redeem the children of men from the fall" (2 Ne. 2:24–26).

Lehi's Exhortation

With the fundamental facts laid out and an explanation given as to why the Fall was necessary, Lehi made his final moving exhortation to Jacob and his other sons (see vv. 27–30). First, he indicated that men are free according to the flesh and all that is expedient is given unto them. That provides a simple yet profound formula:

freedom (agency) + knowledge = accountability

Without accountability, there could be no sin or punishment. Without accountability, God could not make men gods, for there would be no merit in doing good if there were no other choice than to be good. But God set up both conditions required to have accountability.

Second, Lehi noted that the choice is really simple. As King Benjamin pointed out, there are many ways to commit sin, so many in fact that they cannot be numbered (see Mosiah 4:29). But in Lehi's thinking, all choices, all options, all alternatives come down to one basic ultimate choice. It is this: "Men are free according to the flesh; and all things are given them which are expedient unto man. And they are free to choose liberty and eternal life, through the great Mediator of all men, or to choose captivity and death, according to the captivity and power of the devil" (2 Ne. 2:27).

Third, he exhorted his sons to follow the will of the Spirit and choose eternal life by doing three things: (1) looking to the Mediator, (2) hearkening to his commandments, and (3) being faithful to his words (see v. 28). The other alternative is to follow the will of the flesh and choose eternal death, which gives the spirit of the devil power over us and brings us down to hell, where Satan rules (see v. 29).

Finally Lehi closed his blessing to his son Jacob with his own testimony. He said simply, "I have chosen the good part, according to the words of the prophet" (v. 30).

Elder James E. Talmage said that it has become common, even among Christians, to heap reproaches upon Adam and Eve for the Fall. But he concluded that we instead owe them a great deal:

"Our first parents are entitled to our deepest gratitude for their legacy to posterity—the means of winning title to glory, exaltation, and eternal lives. But for the opportunity thus given, the spirits of God's offspring would have remained forever in a state of innocent childhood, sinless through no effort of their own; negatively saved, not from sin, but from the opportunity of meeting sin; incapable of winning the honors of victory because [they would be] prevented from taking part in the conflict. As it is, they are heirs to the birthright of Adam's descendants—mortality, with its immeasurable possibilities and its God-given freedom of action. From Father Adam we have inherited all the ills to which flesh is heir; but such are necessary incident to a knowledge of good and evil, by the proper use of which knowledge man may become even as the Gods."[9]

Lehi's marvelous blessing to his son Jacob provides much of the reason why this is the case. In one couplet, he caught the essence of it all: "'Adam fell that men might be; and men are, that they might have joy" (2 Ne. 2:25).

Notes

From Monte S. Nyman and Charles D. Tate, Jr., eds., *The Book of Mormon: Second Nephi, The Doctrinal Structure* (Provo, Utah: Religious Studies Center, Brigham Young University, 1989), 81–104.

1. James E. Talmage, *The Articles of Faith,* Classics in Mormon Literature Edition (Salt Lake City: Deseret Book Co., 1984), 63 (70 in earlier editions).
2. Bruce R. McConkie, *Mormon Doctrine,* 2d ed. (Salt Lake City: Bookcraft, 1966), 65.
3. Marion G. Romney, "Jesus Christ, Lord of the Universe," *Improvement Era,* November 1968, 46.
4. Samuel Fallows, *The Popular and Critical Bible Encyclopedia and Scriptural Dictionary,* 3 vols. (Chicago: The Howard-Severance Co., 1905-6), 2:1009.
5. Bible Dictionary, LDS Edition of the King James Version, s.v. "Grace"; emphasis added.
6. See Joseph Smith, *Lectures on Faith* (Salt Lake City: Deseret Book Co., 1985), 3:4.
7. Ibid., 5:1.
8. See Daniel H. Ludlow, "Question/Answer," *The New Era,* September 1973, 14.
9. See Talmage, *Articles of Faith,* 63–64 (70 in earlier editions).

Chapter 16

"Then Is His Grace Sufficient for You" (Moroni 10:32)

When the Apostle Paul was imprisoned at Philippi, a distressed jailer asked him, "What must I do to be saved?" Without referring to obedience or repentance or good works, which he himself had so often spoken of, Paul simply answered, "Believe on the Lord Jesus Christ, and thou shalt be saved" (Acts 16:30–31).

But in a church that also has many ancient and modern scriptural passages stressing works of righteousness and the importance of obedience to the laws and ordinances of the gospel, scriptural passages like Acts 16:31 often give rise to confusion. "As far as I'm concerned," one missionary said to his companion, "when somebody starts quoting Paul on salvation by grace, I just quote James on faith without works being dead [see James 2:17–26] and try to get off the subject as quickly as possible." Another time, a Sunday School teacher confessed to his class of teenagers, "Before I joined the Church, I quoted the words of Paul to everyone. Now I just kind of steer away from what he said. I know now how important good works are, so I put the emphasis there."

Paul's Defense of Salvation by Grace

Understanding these reactions isn't difficult. Paul's ringing defense of salvation by grace and his emphatic denunciation of justification through works of the law seem almost to run counter to our third Article of Faith: "We believe that through the Atonement of Christ, all mankind may be saved, by obedience to the laws and ordinances of the Gospel."

The problem in understanding Acts 16:31 isn't that Paul de-emphasized the atoning sacrifice of the Savior, but rather that he apparently de-emphasized the need for works. What missionary hasn't been confronted with Paul's statement to the Saints in Rome: "If thou shalt confess with thy mouth the Lord Jesus, and shalt believe in thine heart that God hath raised him from the dead, thou shalt be saved" (Rom. 10:9). Furthermore, in both Galatians and Romans, he pointedly rejected any idea that justification comes through works of the old law: "Knowing that a man is not justified by the works of the law, but by the faith of Jesus Christ, even we have believed in Jesus Christ, that we might be justified by the faith of Christ, and not by the works of the law: for by the works of the law shall no flesh be justified" (Gal. 2:16; see also Rom. 3:20, 28).

Did Paul indeed reject the value of works for the disciple of Christ? Or was he simply reacting to the Jewish Christians who insisted that adherence to the law of Moses was necessary if one were to be saved? And, for us in the latter days, does Paul's theological position coincide with that revealed in latter-day scripture?

Church members typically seek to synthesize Paul's teachings with Latter-day Saint theology in two different ways. The first suggests that by "the law" Paul meant only the law of Moses. Without a doubt, there is merit in this. Some Jewish Christians insisted that Christianity still required obedience to Mosaic principles like circumcision, the dietary laws, and the observance of certain festivals. Paul combatted that doctrine strongly, saying that no matter how strictly a person kept the law of Moses, it of itself would not bring salvation. The power of salvation comes only through Christ because of his atonement.

However, to limit Paul's meaning to the law of Moses alone would not be quite accurate. Paul rejected the adequacy of the Mosaic code in and of itself for salvation, but he made it broader than that too. For example, in warning the Ephesians about concluding that a man is saved by works, he makes no reference to the law: "For by grace are ye saved through faith; and that not of yourselves: it is the gift of God: not of works, lest any man should boast" (Eph. 2:8–9). So while this explanation is somewhat correct, it does not go far enough.

The second typical explanation tries to divide the effects of the Atonement between physical death and spiritual death. According to this theory, the resurrection saves all from physical death—it is salvation by grace and is not dependent on anything we do. However, if we wish to overcome spiritual death and enter back into God's presence, we must be obedient to laws and principles. This is *exaltation by works*. Thus, according to this explanation, we are *saved* by grace and *exalted* by works.

This argument, however, has some fallacies, as discussed more fully in the chapter titled "The Way Is Prepared from the Fall of Man, and Salvation Is Free." The most obvious fallacy is the assumption that *salvation* and *exaltation* mean different things. While the resurrection of the dead is certainly an integral part of the plan of salvation, and it is unconditional and independent of men's works, the term *salvation,* as used in the scriptures, does not mean physical resurrection alone. As Elder Bruce R. McConkie has pointed out, salvation is usually *synonymous* with exaltation: "*Salvation* in its true and full meaning is synonymous with *exaltation* or *eternal life* and consists in gaining an inheritance in the highest of the three heavens within the celestial kingdom. With few exceptions this is the salvation of which the scriptures speak. It is the salvation which the Saints seek."[1]

Those who are uncomfortable with Paul's statements about grace and salvation should bear in mind that the same teachings are found in other scripture as well. Nephi, for example, nearly echoes Paul's words to the Ephesians when he says, "For we know that it is by grace that we are saved, after all we can do" (2 Ne. 25:23). And Lehi's explanation of the Atonement to Jacob is remarkably similar to Paul's explanation of justification by faith in Romans 3, even down to the phrase "by the law no flesh is justified" (2 Ne. 2:5). Likewise, Doctrine and Covenants 20:30–31 points out that both justification and sanctification come by grace.

Sin, Transgression, and the Law of Justice

How, then, are the principles of grace and works to be understood in relationship to each other? To come to that understanding, we must first look at some related concepts: the concepts of sin and transgression, of justice, and of the Fall. The concept of sin, first of all, rests upon the concept of law. If there were no law, there could be no sin (see 2 Ne. 2:13; Alma 42:17), because "sin is the transgression of the law" (1 Jn. 3:4). However, for purposes of understanding the Atonement better, drawing a distinction between two important variations in how the law may be violated might be helpful.

A person may violate the law in spite of his knowledge of it; that is, he breaks the law deliberately. But others may violate the law because they are unaware of its existence (ignorance) or because they do not have sufficient maturity to understand the implications of disobedience (lack of accountability). For clarification, let us use two terms to delineate the important differences in breaking the law. Any violation of the law that is willful and knowing, we shall call "sin." But any violation that results either from ignorance or lack of accountability, we shall call "transgression." The scriptures do not distinguish between these two terms consistently, but such a distinction may help us understand some important points about the Atonement.

For example, it helps us understand why children under the age of accountability cannot sin (see D&C 29:47). Any parents who have observed their children's behavior know that they often violate laws of the gospel. They hit brothers and sisters, demonstrate extreme selfishness at times, and can be unmercifully cruel to playmates. But while these are "transgressions," they are not "sins," because as Mormon points out, children are "not capable of committing sin" (see Moro. 8:8). Much the same is true of those who have reached adulthood but have had relatively little or no opportunity to learn the principles of righteousness. They also violate the laws of God, sometimes horribly so, as in the case of many primitive peoples, but they are of necessity judged differently because they do not "sin" in the sense of rebelling willingly and deliberately against God[2] (see Rom. 2:12; D&C 82:3).

Standing alongside the concepts of sin and transgression is the law of justice, which implies consistency in reward and punishment. In other words, there would be no justice if one person could violate the law and escape its punishment while another was punished for the same act. Elder McConkie points out that "justice demands that a penalty be paid for every violation of the Lord's laws."[3] The opposite, or positive side, of that idea is that there is a reward for keeping the Lord's laws (see D&C 130:20–21). If punishments and rewards were not consistent throughout the universe and in all of eternity, justice would be violated. Briefly stated, then, the law of justice is that every violation of a law entails a punishment (ultimately suffering and misery) and every obedience of a law entails a reward (ultimately joy and peace).

Also embodied in the concept of justice is the idea that men are punished only for those things they themselves are guilty of. This would make it unjust to punish one man for another's sin; likewise, if through ignorance or lack of accountability, there is no guilt, meting out punishment would be unjust.

Having discussed sin, transgression, and justice, we have enough groundwork to better understand some of the important aspects of the atoning sacrifice of the Savior. One important application of the Atonement is to the fall of Adam. We know that it would be unjust for a person to be punished for violations he did not commit. Thus, all mankind being punished for Adam and Eve's disobedience would be unjust—it would be contrary to the law of justice. So regardless of the kinds of lives individuals have led, the effects of the fall of Adam—physical and spiritual death (i.e., the separation from God's presence)—are overcome for all souls who come to earth. Because of the Atonement, everyone will be resurrected and overcome physical death; and through the power of Christ, all will be brought back into the presence of God for the period of judgment and the assignment of glory (see 1 Cor. 15:22; 2 Ne. 9:38). Thus both physical death and that spiritual death resulting from Adam's fall are therefore removed through Christ.

However, *remaining* in the presence of God is a different, though related, matter. First, there is the case of those who are guilty of transgression but not of sin (in the sense we defined these terms). Where there is no knowledge or accountability, meting out punishment would be unjust. Nevertheless, justice demands payment for *every* violation of the law, whether the violation be sin or transgression. So the atonement of Christ automatically redeems children who die before they reach the age of accountability, and they are brought back into the presence of God (see D&C 137:10). Also, Jesus suffered the penalties of the law for those who violated the law without knowing it: "Where there is no law given there is no punishment; and where there is no punishment there is no condemnation; and where there is no condemnation the mercies of the Holy One of Israel have claim upon them, because of the atonement; for they are delivered by the power of him. For the atonement satisfieth the demands of his justice upon all those who have not the law given to them" (2 Ne. 9:25–26).

Second, there is the case of those who sin knowingly, which is the case for all who reach the age of accountability (see Rom. 3:23). Though the Atonement has removed the effects of Adam's fall, our own personal falls will create another form of spiritual death. This is separation from God because of our own uncleanness and not because of Adam's fall. In other words, when we sin we become alienated from God. Our separation in this case is the result of our own actions.

The Doctrine and Covenants clearly points out that we could enter back into God's presence in this life if we would but purify ourselves from sin (see D&C 67:10; 88:68; 93:1; see also Ether 3:13). This purification from sin strongly involves the role of faith and works: faith leading to works of repentance and obedience is indispensable to the achievement of such a high and holy privilege. Even so, is it really by *our* works that we are saved from spiritual death? Again, Paul and the other prophets indicate no. And to understand this, we must once again look at the law of justice.

Remembering that every violation of the law brings punishment or suffering, there are only two ways possible to meet the demands of the law of justice. Either one keeps the law perfectly and never gets in debt to the law, or else one must pay the debt of suffering. The law is very exact. Even if it is violated only once, the violator is in its debt and must suffer the consequences. Perhaps this is why James wrote, "For whosoever shall keep the whole law, and yet offend in one point, he is guilty of all" (James 2:10). We can see why both Paul and Lehi warned us that no one can be justified by the law: no one (with one exception) has ever kept the law perfectly. Every soul is in debt to the law, "for all have sinned, and come short of the glory of God" (Rom. 3:23).

The Need for Grace

In Greek, the word translated as *grace* in the New Testament means "goodwill, loving kindness, favor." It implies "the idea of kindness which bestows upon one what he has not deserved."[4] In the scriptural sense of the term, for a man to be justified (brought back into a proper relationship with God) by his own works is impossible, because no one keeps the law perfectly.

This was the very mistake that the Pharisees fell into with regard to the Mosaic law. We sometimes smile at their tremendously careful attempts to define the law and what was acceptable to it; but if a person holds that individuals are brought into the proper relationship with God by their works alone, then that person's position is similar to the Pharisees' view. If the tiniest infraction of the law puts one's relationship to God in jeopardy, then one must be extremely careful about any violation. The early rabbis simply carried that idea to its extreme.

For example, the law said, "Keep the Sabbath day holy." Very well then, what does that mean in terms of my behavior? Well, for one thing, I mustn't do any work. All right, but what exactly could be considered as work? Gardening? Cleaning the house? Could I rearrange the furniture? What happens, for instance, if my house should catch fire on the Sabbath? Is it "work" to take things out and save them from destruction? Are these ridiculous questions? Not if you're seeking justification by the law. And so, with great precision, the rabbis enumerated what could and could not be saved if a person's house were endangered by fire on the Sabbath. They even defined how much food could be saved, depending on what time of day the fire occurred. If it broke out on Friday evening (the Jewish Sabbath went from sundown Friday to sundown Saturday), one could save enough for three meals; if Saturday morning, two meals; and if Saturday afternoon, only one.[5] These are the kinds of logical conclusions we are forced to make if we seek justification by the works of the law alone.

To better see why such attempts are ineffective, let us analyze a parable given by Elder Boyd K. Packer, in which he refers to the spiritual jeopardy of all those who are born on this earth:

"There once was a man who wanted something very much. It seemed more important than anything else in his life. In order for him to have his desire, he incurred a great debt.

"He had been warned about going into that much debt, and particularly about his creditor. But it seemed so important for him to do what he wanted to do and to have what he wanted right now. He was sure he could pay for it later.

"So he signed a contract. He would pay it off some time along the way. He didn't worry too much about it, for the due date seemed such a long time away."[6]

Thus, having entered mortality in a state of innocence, people begin to sin and lose their perfect worthiness. They incur a debt (a burden of sin), which, unless paid in full, will extend into the eternities—"the spiritual death, which is separation from the presence of our Heavenly Father."[7] Under these circumstances (disregarding the Atonement for the moment), even if they suddenly realized that they had cheated themselves of the opportunity to go back to God's presence and had stopped increasing their debts (that is, they stopped committing sin and became obedient), there is still no way that they could ever qualify to return to the Father. Even if they committed only one sin (which is unrealistic, of course, for we sin many times), they still could not get back.

Full payment is the condition for admittance, and no exceptions can exist—justice is perfectly exact. Ceasing to sin merely stops the increase in the burden of debt—it does not generate the means to repay. There is, of course, an advantage in keeping the burden of sin (the debt to the law) as small as possible; nevertheless, at the commission of the first sin, a person loses his ability to return to God. Elder Packer continues: "As it always does, the day came, and the contract fell due. The debt had not been fully paid. His creditor appeared and demanded payment in full." The debtor's dilemma was acute:

"'I cannot pay you, for I have not the power to do so,' he confessed.

"'Then,' said the creditor, 'we will exercise the contract, take your possessions, and you shall go to prison. . . . '

"'Can you not extend the time or forgive the debt?' the debtor begged. . . . 'Will you not show mercy?'

"The creditor replied, 'Mercy is always so one-sided. It would serve only you. If I show mercy to you, it will leave me unpaid. . . .

"' . . . Mercy cannot rob justice.'

"There they were: One meting out justice, the other pleading for mercy. Neither could prevail except at the expense of the other. . . .

"Both laws, it seemed, could not be served. They are two eternal ideals that appear to contradict one another. Is there no way for justice to be fully served, and mercy also?

"There is a way! . . . But it takes someone else. And so it happened this time.

"The debtor had a friend. He came to help. He knew the debtor well. . . . He wanted to help because he loved him. He stepped between them, faced the creditor, and made this offer.

"'I will pay the debt. . . .

"' . . . You demanded justice. Though he cannot pay you, I will do so. You will have been justly dealt with and can ask no more. . . . '

"And so it was that the creditor was paid in full. . . .

"The debtor, in turn, had been extended mercy. Both laws stood fulfilled. Because there was a mediator, justice had claimed its full share, and mercy was fully satisfied."[8]

Once the debt was established, then, outside payment had to be introduced from somewhere or our debts would have stood forever. Thus it is that only in the sacrifice of the Only Begotten Son, who had no sin, could we be delivered from this sad state.

Christ—the Source of Unlimited Reserves

The Savior could effect our deliverance for two important reasons. First, he met the demands of the law of justice for himself because *he kept the laws of God perfectly.* In other words, Christ was justified by his works. He avoided the debt altogether and qualified himself to return to the Father—the only one of all mankind to do so. Second, he met the demands of the law for all of the rest of mankind. He himself owed no debt to the law, but he went before it and in essence said: "I am perfect and therefore owe you no suffering. However, I will pay the debt for all mankind. I will undergo suffering that I might pay the price for every transgression and sin ever committed by any man."

In the Garden of Gethsemane and on the cross, Christ paid the price by suffering for every sin as though he himself had committed them, satisfying fully the law of justice. Such suffering is beyond the power of any mortal man to endure. We can't understand how he did it, only that he did and that "through Him mercy can be fully extended to each of us without offending the eternal law of justice."[9] In terms of Elder Packer's parable, he generated sufficient payment to satisfy the debt of every other man. He met the demands of the law for himself through obedience and for all others through suffering.

Alma told his son Corianton that mercy could not rob justice, or else "God would cease to be God" (Alma 42:25). That is the case with the merciful love of the Father and the Son. In fact, mercy paid justice! Their love said to justice, by virtue of the price paid in the Garden, "Here is payment for the wrongs committed. You are paid in full. Now let the captives go free."

In one of the most beautiful images in all of scripture, we find the solution to that awful dilemma we all face as sinners. We are standing before the bar as defendants, facing the great judge, God the Father. Our Advocate with the Father steps forward, not to refute the charges or to hold up a record of our good works to counterbalance our guilt, but to plead our case in a different manner:

"Listen to him who is the advocate with the Father, who is pleading your cause before him—Saying: Father, behold the sufferings and death of him who did no sin, in whom thou wast well pleased; behold the blood of thy Son which was shed, the blood of him whom thou gavest that thyself might be glorified; Wherefore, Father, spare these my brethren that believe on my name, that they may come unto me and have everlasting life" (D&C 45:3–5).

Nothing man could do for himself could bring him past the judgment bar successfully without such an Advocate. That is why eternal life is always a gift, and those who receive it do so by "inheritance." It is interesting to note that the word *inherit* and its cognate words are used seventy-eight times in the Doctrine and Covenants, while the word *earned* and its related words are not used once.

What Must We Do?

The sacrifice that pays the debt and frees us from the results of our own spiritual death, though it comes to us through the grace and goodness of God, does not mean we do nothing. What, then, are we to do if Jesus Christ has done so much for us? Here are the steps: they are first, have faith in the Lord Jesus Christ, then repent, then be baptized for the remission of sins. If we truly move through those steps—mentally, spiritually, and physically—then we are prepared for the reception of the Holy Ghost. When we are given the *gift* (there's that word again) of the Holy Ghost, we have overcome spiritual death to a degree, for we have come into the presence of one member of the Godhead. The Holy Ghost's role, of course, is to help purify, guide, teach, and strengthen us so that we can fully overcome spiritual death by coming back into the presence of the Father and the Son—another way of saying that his role is to help us endure to the end.

Now with all this in mind, remember that Paul said we are justified *by* faith (see Gal. 2:16; Rom. 3:28), which is the first principle of the gospel. In other words, faith is the principle that activates the power of the Atonement in our lives, and we are put back into a proper relationship with God (justification) as faith activates that power. There are marvelous implications in this concept, and perhaps another analogy can help us see more clearly the role faith and works have in relationship to salvation:

Each of us is like a powerhouse on a mighty river. The powerhouse has no power residing in itself; the potential power rests in the energy of the river. When that source of power flows through the generators of the power plant, power is transferred from the river to the power plant and sent out into the homes (lives) of others. The atonement of Christ is the power in the river. Faith is the generators that can harness that power. The power to achieve justification does not reside in us. We require the power of the atonement of Christ flowing into us. If no power is being generated, we do not—indeed, cannot—turn the generators by hand (justification by works); but rather, we make an effort to remove those things that have blocked the power from flowing into the generators (working righteousness as a result of faith).

With this analogy, we can more clearly understand why the scriptures stress that faith *includes* works (see James 2:17–26). Righteous works in themselves do not save us because none of us can work perfectly enough to earn salvation. The atoning power of God saves us. Obedience, commitment, and repentance—these are the works of faith that open up the channels so that the power of the atoning sacrifice of Christ can flow into us, redeem us from sin, and bring us back into the presence of God. Disobedience and wickedness dam those channels. (How literal is the word *damnation!*) Thus, each of us determines whether we will be able to seek the gift and power of the Atonement in our behalf.

There is no need to go to extraordinary lengths to apologize for Paul or try to explain away his statements on salvation by grace. We *are* saved by grace—saved by Christ's love from physical and spiritual death; saved by Christ's love from Adam's fall and our own; saved from sin and transgression by the grace or gifts of God. The atoning power of God unto salvation is a freely available gift from him—but our works of righteousness, welling up from fountains of faith, are essential to bring the gift into power in our lives. Sin brings alienation from God. The more we sin, the greater the alienation and the more difficult it becomes to effectively tap the power of God, which alone is sufficient to save us from our sins.

President Joseph Fielding Smith has summarized the relationship between grace and works as follows:

"So Paul taught these people—who thought that they could be saved by some power that was within them, or by observing the law of Moses—he pointed out to them the fact that if it were not for the mission of Jesus Christ, if it were not for this great atoning sacrifice, they could not be redeemed. And therefore it was by the grace of God that they are saved, not by any work on their part, for they were absolutely helpless. Paul was absolutely right.

"And on the other hand, James taught just as the Lord taught, just as Paul had taught in other scripture, that it is our duty, of necessity, to labor, to strive in diligence, and faith, keeping the commandments of the Lord, if we would obtain that inheritance which is promised to the faithful. . . .

"So it is easy to understand that we must accept the mission of Jesus Christ. We must believe that it is through his grace that we are saved, that he performed for us that labor which we were unable to perform for ourselves, and did for us those things which were essential to our salvation, which were beyond our power; and also that we are under the commandment and the necessity of performing the labors that are required of us as set forth in the commandments known as the gospel of Jesus Christ."[10]

Thus, we can with Paul fervently exclaim that "the wages of sin is death; but the gift of God is eternal life through Jesus Christ our Lord" (Rom. 6:23). We should continue to stress the importance of faith, of repentance, of obedience and strive with all our hearts to be full of faith and demonstrate good works in our lives. But we should never lose sight of the great overriding fact of the grace of our Lord and Savior and the wholly *central* part it plays in our atonement and salvation.

Moroni, in the closing words of the Book of Mormon, teaches the relationship between the grace of Christ and the need for our righteous efforts. Note how he keeps distinctly clear what it is that perfects us, and yet what must happen in our lives to bring that about:

"Come unto Christ, and be perfected in him, and deny yourselves of all ungodliness; and if ye shall deny yourselves of all ungodliness, and love God with all your might, mind and strength, then is his grace sufficient for you, that by his grace ye may be perfect in Christ; and if by the grace of God ye are perfect in Christ, ye can in nowise deny the power of God.

"And again, if ye by the grace of God are perfect in Christ, and deny not his power, then are ye sanctified in Christ by the grace of God, through the shedding of the blood of Christ, which is in the covenant of the Father unto the remission of your sins, that ye become holy, without spot" (Moro. 10:32–33).

Notes

From "Salvation by Grace or by Works?" *Ensign,* April 1981, 16–23.

1. Bruce R. McConkie, *Mormon Doctrine,* 2d ed. (Salt Lake City: Bookcraft, 1966), 670.
2. Joseph Smith, *Teachings of the Prophet Joseph Smith,* sel. Joseph Fielding Smith (Salt Lake City: Deseret Book Co., 1976), 218.
3. McConkie, *Mormon Doctrine,* 406.
4. Carl Ludwig Wilibald Grimm, *A Greek-English Lexicon of the New Testament,* trans. Joseph Henry Thayer (Grand Rapids, Mich.: Zondervan, 1962), s.v. "charis [grace]."
5. See Misknayoth [The Oral Law], "Tractate Sabbath," 16:2.
6. Boyd K. Packer, "The Mediator," *Ensign,* May 1977, 54.
7. Ibid., 56.
8. Ibid., 54-55.
9. Ibid., 56.
10. Joseph Fielding Smith, *Doctrines of Salvation,* 3 vols., comp. Bruce R. McConkie (Salt Lake City: Bookcraft, 1954–56), 2:310-11.

Chapter 17

"Ye Are Still Indebted unto Him" (Mosiah 2:24)

In preparing to write about divine indebtedness and the atonement of Jesus Christ, I reread the magnificent closing sermon of the great and righteous King Benjamin. I pored over it, looking for relationships, outlining the major concepts, and watching for patterns in King Benjamin's thinking. Because of that experience, I have decided to follow a similar approach in this chapter. I intend to examine the message of the king, look at its antecedents, outline its structure, note relationships within that structure, watch for patterns in the words and phrases he chose to use, and explore some of the implications for us today of what he taught. I wish to let this great sermon speak for itself on the relationship between our debt to God and the atoning sacrifice of our Savior.

A Righteous King Bids Farewell to His People

In order to understand the full impact of King Benjamin's address, we must examine the setting that drew it forth. Mormon, writing some four centuries later, informed us about King Benjamin and the circumstances that led to his last great sermon (see W of M 1:12–18; Mosiah 1:1–2:8). Benjamin did not inherit a comfortable situation when he became the king of the Nephite peoples. It was a time of war, with armies of the Lamanites coming down against the Nephites. King Benjamin led his people in battle, wielding the sword of Laban with his own hand. Thousands were killed, and eventually the Lamanites were driven out of the land (see W of M 1:13–14).

But the external threat to the Nephite society was not the only problem. During the kingship before Benjamin's reign, the Nephites had incorporated the Mulekite people, whose language was different and whose knowledge of Jehovah and the Mosaic law had been corrupted. Teaching them a new language and a new religion and having that settle in would have been difficult and time-consuming (see Omni 1:14–19). Mormon said that besides the wars with the Lamanites, there were "contentions among his [Benjamin's] own people." Mormon also explained that there were "false Christs," "false prophets," and "false preachers and teachers" among the people. "Many dissensions" also arose, and the people were described as stiffnecked (W of M 1:12, 15–17).

This was the society over which Benjamin ruled, and these were the people he led. Benjamin, however, was not content with that state of affairs. With the assistance of holy prophets, whom he sustained, and through his own personal righteousness, King Benjamin brought a complete turnaround among his people. In two sweeping sentences, Mormon summarized Benjamin's greatness: "King Benjamin, by laboring with all the might of his body and the faculty of his whole soul, . . . did once more establish peace in the land" (W of M 1:18). "Now there was no more contention in all the land of Zarahemla, among all the people who belonged to king Benjamin, so that king Benjamin had continual peace all the remainder of his days" (Mosiah 1:1). By "peace," Mormon almost certainly meant here far more than the mere absence of war.

Mormon did not tell us how many years King Benjamin's reign lasted, though it seems to have been a lengthy one (see, for example, Mosiah 2:12, 16, 19), but oh, what a reign it must have been! When the people learned that the king was turning the kingdom over to his son, when they heard that this would be the last speech of their beloved king, a vast crowd gathered, as Mormon explained, to "give thanks to the Lord their God, who had brought them out of the land of Jerusalem, and who had delivered them out of the hands of their enemies, and had appointed just men to be their teachers, and also a just man to be their king, who had established peace in the land of Zarahemla, and who had taught them to keep the commandments of God, that they might rejoice and be filled with love towards God and all men" (Mosiah 2:4).

There must have been a tremendous outpouring of love and gratitude toward the king. Even Benjamin seemed unprepared for the huge multitudes that responded to the proclamation to come and hear their king. When the multitude spilled out beyond the temple courtyard, a tower was built. But even that was not sufficient, and Benjamin had to have his words written and sent to those who could not hear his voice (see Mosiah 2:7–8).

Surely as the throngs came, Benjamin would have been inundated with people seeking to thank him for all that he had done. He must have had a constant stream of people grasping his hand, saying, "Thank you for what you are. Thank you for what you've done for us." Praise and thanks for his goodness and greatness must have rained upon him like a tropical downpour.

Many men might be tempted in the face of such praise to say in their hearts, "Yes, you are right. I have done well." But Benjamin would have none of that. He would not let the credit and praise rest with him. He epitomized the counsel of the apostle Paul to every man "not to think of himself more highly than he ought to think" (Rom. 12:3). To God went the glory. These were his opening thoughts as he spoke to his people:

"I have not commanded you to come up hither that ye should fear me, or that ye should think that I of myself am more than a mortal man. But I am like as yourselves, subject to all manner of infirmities in body and mind; yet I have been chosen by this people, and consecrated by my father, and was suffered by the hand of the Lord that I should be a ruler and a king over this people; and have been kept and preserved by his matchless power, to serve you with all the might, mind and strength which the Lord hath granted unto me" (Mosiah 2:10–11).

Benjamin also undoubtedly felt an urgency to deliver a special message, one of great hope and deliverance that an angel had declared to him. The message, he stated, was another reason he had called his people together. Benjamin described this experience thus:

"The things which I shall tell you are made known unto me by an angel from God. And he said unto me: Awake; and I awoke, and behold he stood before me. And he said unto me: . . . I am come to declare unto you the glad tidings of great joy. For the Lord hath heard thy prayers, and hath judged of thy righteousness, and hath sent me to declare unto thee that thou mayest rejoice; and that thou mayest declare unto thy people, that they may also be filled with joy" (Mosiah 3:2–4).

This, then, is the context from which we must examine King Benjamin's last address to his people, asking ourselves why he would choose a theme of indebtedness to God.

Our Indebtedness to Our Heavenly King (Mosiah 2:18–26)

King Benjamin first gave what might be termed a brief "stewardship report" to the people whom he had served. And what a report that was! We learn that King

Benjamin was a man of honor and justice. He had not suffered his people to be placed in prisons or to practice slavery. He had not allowed crime or any kind of wickedness. He had labored with his own hands so as not to lay burdensome taxes on his people, and he had not sought to enrich himself by taking from the people (see Mosiah 2:12–14).

How his people must have loved him! Peace, security, honesty, justice, prosperity, righteousness—these were the legacies that he left for them. The long and melancholy history of monarchies clearly testifies how few kings there have been who could give such a stewardship report as this at the end of their earthly reign.

Hastily, lest he be misunderstood, the king noted that this report was not an attempt to boast of his accomplishments, but only an acknowledgment that his service to his people had merely been an extension of his desire to serve God (see Mosiah 2:16). Then, in what is surely one of the finest, most beautiful, and most succinct lessons on Christian service ever given, he stated the pivotal lesson of his own righteous life. If ye would learn anything from me, he said, learn this one lesson: "When ye are in the service of your fellow beings ye are only in the service of your God" (Mosiah 2:17).

King Benjamin's stewardship report and the resulting lesson on service led him naturally to the concept of divine indebtedness. He had already noted that any success he had enjoyed came only through the grace and sustaining power of God. So their praise of him was misdirected. "If I, whom ye call your king," he pointed out, "do merit any thanks from you, O how you ought to thank your heavenly King!" (Mosiah 2:19). This provided the basis for King Benjamin's concept of divine indebtedness. It is a lesson as applicable today as when given to the Nephites gathered in their tents in the Land of Zarahemla.

A careful look at Mosiah 2:20–25 reveals the structure of King Benjamin's primary thoughts about our indebtedness to God. It would go something like this capsulized into outline form:

I. Our Indebtedness to God (Mosiah 2:20–25)
   A. God has done the following for Benjamin's people (v. 20):
      1. created them
      2. kept and preserved them
      3. caused them to rejoice
      4. granted that they should have peace.
   B. He continues to:
      1. preserve them day to day by giving them breath (v. 21)
      2. allow them to live and to move and to do as they will

    3. support them from one moment to the next
    4. grant unto them their lives (v. 23).
C. So even if they should:
    1. render all the thanks and praise their souls possess (v. 20) and
    2. serve him with their whole souls (v. 21),
D. they would still be unprofitable servants.
E. But all he requires in return is to keep his commandments (v. 22).
F. If they do, he immediately blesses them (v. 24).
G. Conclusions:
    1. Two reasons for our indebtedness to God:
        a. he created us and grants us life (v. 23)
        b. when we keep his commandments, he blesses us more, which only increases our indebtedness (v. 24).
    2. Man has nothing about which he can boast.
    3. Man is not even so much as the dust of the earth (v. 25).

Our Gratitude for Creation

King Benjamin initially emphasized one aspect of God's graciousness, that God is responsible for our creation. By this, Benjamin seemed to have meant not just the making of our own bodies, but the whole of creation—the heavens, the earth, and all that in them are. That simple fact alone should be basis enough for our unending gratitude. When a man creates something through his own labor—a work of art, a building, a piece of furniture, great music—we say that it is his. In other words, we recognize that he has claim upon it, that he has stewardship over it, that he has the right to do with it as he wishes.

By that same principle, we should acknowledge that because all that we see and know comes from the labor of God's hands, it is his. Therefore, whatever we have, or take, or use, or enjoy puts us automatically in his debt. In a revelation to the Prophet Joseph Smith, the Lord clearly stated that this is indeed the case: "For it is expedient that I, the Lord, should make every man accountable, as a steward over earthly blessings, *which I have made* and prepared for my creatures. I, the Lord, stretched out the heavens, and built the earth, *my very handiwork;* and *all things therein are mine"* (D&C 104:13–14; emphasis added). Note the possessive phrases used in those verses: "which I have made," "my very handiwork," "all things therein are mine." As the Psalmist said, "The earth is the Lord's, and the fulness thereof; the world, and they that dwell therein" (Ps. 24:1).

Think for a moment how that simple concept would alter people's thinking if they would really accept it. We clutch things to our bosom and say, "These are mine." Individuals rob, cheat, and steal, or they manipulate and maneuver so they may be able to claim things as their own. Figuratively, the rich sit on their velvet thrones, drinking from golden goblets, and ignore the desperate sufferings of the poor because they think that what they have received belongs solely to them. Nations go to war over lands that they did nothing to create.

If we truly believed that God was the owner of all things, that man was only a user and a borrower, our approach to life would alter drastically. A classic illustration of that principle was the man Job. After facing devastating losses of family, property, and health, he stated simply, "Naked came I out of my mother's womb, and naked shall I return thither: the Lord gave, and the Lord hath taken away; blessed be the name of the Lord" (Job 1:21). Henry B. Eyring spoke of this natural human tendency to forget all that God has done for us: "We so easily forget that we came into life with nothing. Whatever we get soon seems our natural right, not a gift. And we forget the giver. Then our gaze shifts from what we have been given to what we don't have yet. . . . The remembrance urged upon us by King Benjamin can be ours. *Remembrance is the seed of gratitude.*"[1]

Because some miracles are so commonly seen, we accept them as commonplace—an infant's birth, the coming of spring, the glory of a forested mountain range, the silent and undirected healing process within the human body, the never-ending procession of glorious sunrises and sunsets, the infinite variety and minute beauty of something so simple as snowflakes showering upon the earth in countless billions.

Those who try to duplicate nature in the laboratory still feel awestruck when they compare their own marvelous inventions with those of nature itself. In a *National Geographic* article on the recent development of new high-tech materials, Thomas Canby discussed such mind-boggling advances as ceramic ball bearings so tough that they leave dimples on an anvil when hammered by a blacksmith, but they do not break; a metal that actually hardens as its temperature rises; cement sheets thin and light enough that they are used in hang glider fabric; plastics so flexible that they can be stretched as much as a thousand percent and grow stronger in the process! After quoting a scientist who said that his goal was to develop materials that respond as nature does, the author concludes: "[Their goal is to be] like nature. For materials scientists, the perfection of a tree, a bone, a spiderweb remain a distant goal."[2]

Numerous passages in scripture clearly state our obligations of feeling gratitude and giving thanks to God for all he has given. In language similar to that of the Ten Commandments (Thou shalt not steal, thou shalt honor thy parents, and so on), the Lord says: "Thou shalt thank the Lord thy God in all things" (D&C 59:7). A few verses later, he said, "In nothing doth man offend God, or against none is his wrath kindled, save those who confess not his hand in all things, and obey not his commandments" (D&C 59:21).

In March of 1832, the Lord tied thankfulness to both spiritual and temporal results when he said, "He who receiveth all things with thankfulness shall be made glorious; and the things of this earth shall be added unto him, even an hundred fold, yea, more" (D&C 78:19). When we consider the richness of creation, God's inestimable abundance given freely to man, his power that sustains life, and the continual outpouring of those blessings when we are obedient, we ought to have no difficulty understanding why King Benjamin chose the word *indebtedness* to describe our state.

Unprofitable Servants

Now we come to two statements in King Benjamin's address that many Latter-day Saints may find a little troublesome. Unlike Calvinism and some other Christian sects, we do not look upon man as inherently evil. A crucial concept in our theology is that we are literally children of our Heavenly Father. "I am a child of God," we sing, "and he has sent me here."[3] We speak positively about the need for self-esteem and self-reliance. We speak of our potential to become gods, a concept so daring as to cause many Christians to recoil at our boldness.

So how do we reconcile these ideas with King Benjamin's powerful "if" statements? He says that even *if* we should render all the praise and thanks our souls are capable of, and even *if* we should serve him with our whole souls, we would still be "unprofitable servants" (Mosiah 2:20–21). Even more pointed (some might say more devastating) is his answer to his own rhetorical question: "Can ye say aught of yourselves?" Answer: "Ye cannot say that *ye are even as much* as the dust of the earth" (Mosiah 2:25; emphasis added). Let's examine these two points one at a time, for they are pivotal in our understanding of the concept of divine indebtedness and the Atonement.

The Savior used the phrase "unprofitable servants" in a short parable he taught in response to the disciples' plea to him, "Increase our faith" (Luke 17:5):

"Which of you, having a servant plowing or feeding cattle, will say unto him by and by, when he is come from the field, Go and sit down to meat? And will not rather say unto him, Make ready wherewith I may sup, and gird thyself, and serve me, till I have eaten and drunken; and afterward thou shalt eat and drink? Doth he thank that servant because he did the things that were commanded him? I trow not. So likewise ye, when ye shall have done all those things which are commanded you, say, We are unprofitable servants: we have done that which was our duty to do" (Luke 17:7–10).

In some ways, this parable is no less troublesome than King Benjamin's statement. However, focusing on the word *profit* will help us better understand the concept of unprofitable servants. The word implies personal gain or benefit. *Profit* means an increase in assets or status or benefits.

That is the crux of the concept of man being an unprofitable servant. God is perfect—in knowledge, power, influence, and attributes. He is the Creator of *all* things! What could any person—or all people together for that matter—do to bring profit (that is, an increase in assets, status, or benefits) to God?

A nineteenth-century scholar, commenting on this parable, stated that concept eloquently, when he noted that no man "can work righteousness, in the smallest degree, beyond those powers which God has given them; and justice and equity require that they should exert those powers to the uttermost in the service of their Maker; and, after having acted thus, it may be justly said, *They have done only what it was their duty to do.* The nature of God is illimitable, and all the attributes of that nature are infinitely glorious: they cannot be *lessened* by the *transgressions* of his creatures, nor can they be *increased* by the uninterrupted, eternal *obedience,* and unceasing *hallelujahs,* of all the intelligent creatures that people the whole vortex of nature. When ages, beyond the power of arithmetic to sum up, have elapsed, it may be said of the most pure and perfect creatures, 'ye are unprofitable servants.' Ye have derived your being from the infinite fountain of life: ye are upheld by the continued energy of the Almighty: his glories are infinite and eternal, and your obedience and services, however excellent in themselves, and profitable to you, have added nothing, and can add nothing, to the absolute excellencies and glories of your God."[4]

That we are his children and he loves us is undeniable, and that situation puts us in a status far above any of his other creations. But we must somehow disabuse ourselves of any notion that we can bring personal profit to God by our actions. That would make God indebted to men, which is unthinkable. So this explains King Benjamin's ringing "ifs." Even *if* we were to serve him with all the power of our souls, even *if* we should render thanks with that same power (which very few, if any, of us ever do), we would still be unprofitable servants.

Less Than the Dust of the Earth

The comment that we are even less than the dust of the earth may, on the surface, seem a little more difficult to resolve. Has man no worth at all, as that would imply? An experience Moses had has an interesting parallel to King Benjamin's thinking here. Benjamin concluded that man is less than the dust of the earth immediately after he noted that God is the creator and sustainer of men. About a thousand years earlier, the prophet Moses was caught up in heavenly vision and was shown the creation of "the world . . . and all the children of men" (Moses 1:8). Then the heavenly power withdrew, and Moses was left to himself. When he recovered a little from the experience, his first words were "Now, for this cause I know that man is nothing, which thing I never had supposed" (Moses 1:10).

Something about the majesty and infinite awesomeness of the creation reminded both King Benjamin and Moses of man's puny and finite nature. Even when we sense our smallness, however, are we really *less than* the dust? The "less than" concept is what particularly stings. Nothingness is one thing, *worthlessness* quite another. On the surface, however, that is exactly what King Benjamin's phrase "ye cannot say that ye are even as much as the dust of the earth" (Mosiah 2:25) seems to imply. Let us examine the phrase and its uses in the scriptures for clues that may aid our understanding.

To begin with, "dust of the earth" is a scriptural phrase implying far more than mere dirt particles. We are told that man was created from the dust of the earth (see Gen. 2:7). Perhaps another word that would come close to what is implied by dust would be "the *elements* of the earth." In Latter-day Saint theology, we certainly do not believe that God pulled together a pile of mud, formed it into the shape of a man, and breathed life into it. A more accurate statement would be to say that God created the human body from the elements of the earth. Benjamin said then, to paraphrase, that we are not even as much as those elements.

Interestingly, Mormon is the one who gives us the clues to help us better understand King Benjamin's statement. Benjamin's words, as well as the angel's message that the king delivered to his people, had such a powerful impact upon the people that they fell to the ground.[5] Mormon commented significantly, "They had viewed themselves in their own *carnal state,* even less than the dust of the earth" (Mosiah 4:2; emphasis added). What a significant clue! The carnal or natural man is what is less than the dust of the earth. King Benjamin apparently agreed. One of the first things he stated as he continued his address after his people had fallen to the ground was that his people had been awakened to a sense of "[their] nothingness, and [their] worthless and fallen state" (Mosiah 4:5). Here again man's worthlessness is mentioned in the context of his fallen state.

Note that King Benjamin said that lack of humility (or not remembering our own nothingness) leads us to a state he called "the natural man," a state he also described as being "an enemy to God" (see Mosiah 2:37; 3:19). In a similar vein, President Ezra Taft Benson specifically defined pride as enmity against God. "The central feature of pride is enmity—enmity toward God and enmity toward our fellowmen. *Enmity* means 'hatred toward, hostility to, or a state of opposition.' It is the power by which Satan wishes to reign over us. Pride is essentially competitive in nature. We pit our will against God's."[6]

This leads us to Mormon's later specific explanation of why man is less than the dust of the earth:

"How quick [are men] to be lifted up in pride; yea, how quick to boast, and do all manner of that which is iniquity; and how slow are they to remember the Lord their God, and to give ear unto his counsels, yea, how slow to walk in wisdom's paths!

"Behold, they do not desire that the Lord their God, who hath created them, should rule and reign over them; notwithstanding his great goodness and his mercy towards them, they do set at naught his counsels, and they will not that he should be their guide.

"O how great is the nothingness of the children of men; yea, even they are less than the dust of the earth.

"For behold, the dust of the earth moveth hither and thither, to the dividing asunder, at the command of our great and everlasting God" (Hel. 12:5–8).

There is the key. Benjamin said that all God asks of us as payment on our indebtedness to him is that we obey his commandments. But the natural man or fallen man is disobedient. Even the elements of the earth respond to God's voice, but fallen man does not. He proceeds on his own sinful way, ignoring God's goodness to him and the indebtedness we owe to him. Therefore, man is even less than the dust of the earth.

King Benjamin made a second point in almost the same breath as his "less than" statement: "But behold, it belongeth to him who created you" (Mosiah 2:25). This is a profound chain of reason: (1) God created all things including the dust (or elements) of the earth, (2) man is made of those elements, and (3) therefore even man's body belongs to God. This again is a reflection on our willful nature: the dust of the earth obeys God's voice, but we, who are God's as much as the dust is, do not listen or follow.

Indebtedness and Atonement (Mosiah 2:26–3:27)

Benjamin inextricably linked our indebtedness and the Atonement. By emphasizing the concept of man's nothingness, he made the two concepts dependent on one another. If that interdependency were outlined according to Benjamin's teachings, it would look something like this:

I. Man by Himself Is Nothing (2:19–25)
  A. Therefore, we are indebted to God (vv. 19–21, 23–24).
  B. As payment, all that is required is obedience (vv. 22, 24).
II. A Warning against Disobedience (2:26–41)
  A. King Benjamin discharged his obligation to warn the people (vv. 26–30).
  B. He gave a charge to keep the commandments under the new king (v. 31).
  C. All must take care that they don't obey evil spirits (vv. 32–35).
    1. He who does and dieth in his sins is damned (v. 33).
    2. This is a just wage for transgressing knowingly.
    3. All have been taught by prophets and scriptures (yet another reason for our indebtedness to God) (vv. 34–35).
  D. If you knowingly transgress:
    1. You withdraw from the Spirit (v. 36).
    2. You receive no guidance on life's path.
    3. You become an enemy to God (v. 37).
    4. The Lord has no place in you.
    5. And don't repent, you will experience guilt, shame, pain, and torment (vv. 38–39).
  E. King Benjamin called on all to consider the two choices:
    1. The awful situation of transgressors (v. 40).
    2. The blessed state (temporal and spiritual) of the obedient (v. 41).
III. The Message of the Angel (3:1–27)
  A. Glad tidings of great joy (vv. 1–11).
    1. God to come to earth and minister to men (vv. 5–8).
    2. He will be crucified and resurrected (vv. 9–10).
    3. He atones for those who ignorantly sin (v. 11).
  B. Wo to the rebellious (those who transgress knowingly) (vv. 12–13).

C. The Law of Moses and the Atonement (vv. 14–15).
   1. Law of Moses was given because of the hardness of Israel's hearts (v. 14).
   2. The Mosaic law pointed to Christ (v. 15).
   3. But without the Atonement, it had no power to save.
D. The Atonement (vv. 16–23)
   1. Little children are atoned for (v. 16).
   2. No other means but through Christ (v. 17).
   3. Men are damned unless they become as children and believe in Christ (v. 18).
   4. The natural man is an enemy to God and will be unless he (v. 19):
      a. yields to the enticings of the Holy Spirit.
      b. puts off the natural man.
      c. becomes a saint through the Atonement.
      d. becomes as a child.
E. When knowledge of the Atonement spreads, none will be blameless but children (vv. 20–21).
F. Those who reject his words are damned, and their punishments just (vv. 23–27).

With this outline we clearly see that, once Benjamin established the concept of divine indebtedness, he moved immediately to the ultimate proof of our ingratitude—our disobedience—and the consequences of it. From there, he turned naturally to the only cure for those consequences, namely, the Atonement. In fact, the previous concepts establish a natural foundation for the concept of grace, though Benjamin never uses the word itself. The definition of grace as found in the LDS Bible Dictionary states that it is the "divine means of help or strength given through the bounteous mercy and love of Jesus Christ. . . . This grace is an enabling power that allows men and women to lay hold on eternal life and exaltation *after they have expended their own best efforts.*"[7]

Note that last phrase. It is another way of saying exactly what King Benjamin was saying, namely that, even if we thank him with all our souls, even if we serve him our whole lives (another way to describe "best efforts"), we would still be unprofitable servants. Because of this awful state we are in, there must be a higher source of help, some "enabling power" that takes us in our utter helplessness and lifts us to the point where we can overcome our carnal and fallen natures and become the sons and daughters of God.

After establishing our indebtedness to God, King Benjamin then joyfully reported the glad tidings of great joy (the word *gospel* means good news or glad tidings) that the angel had given him and asked him to share with his people. In the visitation, as Benjamin related, the angel had shown him the Savior's ministry. A discourse on the inability of the Law of Moses to save (outside of the Atonement) immediately followed, and then the angel turned directly to the Atonement and its saving power. Without Christ and his saving power, individuals are damned; they are destined to remain in their fallen state as natural and carnal, as enemies to God. But through the grace, or enabling power, of Jesus Christ, they can put off the natural man and become saints, sanctified and holy, thus able to return to God's presence.

Indebtedness and atonement—the two are interwoven in King Benjamin's thinking. The Atonement is both another reason for our indebtedness and the means by which we escape from being servants of sin. According to Benjamin, there are four things that create our indebtedness:

1. He created us and all that we have (2:20–21).

2. He preserves us from moment to moment (2:21).

3. All he asks in return is that we keep his commandments, which if we do, he immediately blesses us, only adding to our indebtedness (2:22–24).

4. He has sent the Savior and provided us a way to overcome our sins and be saved (3:17–19).

Obtaining and Retaining a Remission of Sins (Mosiah 4:1–30)

The two concepts of indebtedness and atonement, as delivered by King Benjamin, had a tremendous impact on the people. They cried for mercy and asked that the atoning blood of Christ be applied in their behalf so their sins could be forgiven (Mosiah 4:2). The Lord granted their request, and Mormon wrote that they received a remission of their sins (v. 3).

King Benjamin, filled with joy at what had happened, returned to the exact same theme with which he began. He talked about how the people could retain the remission of sins they had just experienced. Here, as in the first part of his address, the concept of indebtedness still heavily flavored his thinking. In fact, his opening thought summarized the context of his previous words. Note his chain of reasoning:

A. The knowledge of God has awakened you to a sense of your nothingness and your fallen state (v. 5).

B. A knowledge of God's goodness and of the Atonement leads to trust in God, diligence in keeping the commandments, and continuing in faith to the end (v. 6).

C. These are what lead to salvation (v. 7).

D. There is no other way (v. 8).

E. We retain a remission of sins by remembering God's goodness and our own nothingness and unworthiness (v. 11).

F. This remembrance will influence all we do and lead us to eternal life (vv. 12–30).

Thus the key to the whole process of salvation is remembering, and the primary focus of our remembrance is (1) God's goodness and greatness, (2) our own nothingness, and (3) God's greatest gift, that of his own Son to make us whole. President Ezra Taft Benson said:

"The Prophet Joseph said at one time that one of the greatest sins of which the Latter-day Saints would be guilty of is the sin of ingratitude. I presume most of us have not thought of that as a great sin. There is a great tendency for us in our prayers and in our pleadings with the Lord to ask for additional blessings. But sometimes I feel we need to devote more of our prayers to expressions of gratitude and thanksgiving for blessing already received. We enjoy so much. Of course we need daily blessings of the Lord, but if we sin in the matter of prayer, I think it is in the lack of our expressions of thanksgiving, for blessings that we receive daily."[8]

How simple a thing, this matter of gratitude. Perhaps that is why so many so easily overlook it. But in the matchless address of this humble, righteous monarch, we are taught the profound consequences that can result from gratitude or lack of it. Benjamin did not seek to invoke a sense of hopelessness when he noted that we are less than the dust of the earth. He sought instead to instill a sense of humility and, more especially, a sense of our utter and total dependence upon God for all that we have, all that we are, and all that we can be.

Notes

From "Divine Indebtedness and the Atonement," in *The Book of Mormon: Mosiah, Salvation Only through Christ,* Fifth Annual Book of Mormon Symposium (Provo, Utah: Religious Studies Center, Brigham Young University/Salt Lake City: Bookcraft, 1989).

1. Henry B. Eyring, "Remembrance and Gratitude," *Ensign,* November 1989, 12, 13; emphasis added.
2. Thomas Y. Canby, "Reshaping Our Lives: Advanced Materials," *National Geographic,* December 1989, 781.
3. *Hymns of The Church of Jesus Christ of Latter-day Saints* (Salt Lake City: The Church of Jesus Christ of Latter-day Saints, 1985), no. 301.
4. Adam Clarke, "Matthew to the Acts," in *The New Testament of Our Lord and Savior Jesus Christ,* vol. 5 of Adam Clarke, *The Holy Bible . . . with Commentary and Critical Notes,* 6 vols. (Nashville: Abingdon Press, n.d), 468; emphasis in original.

5. A careful reading of Mosiah 3 shows that all but verses one and two are a direct quote of the message delivered by the angel. That is also confirmed in Mosiah 4:1.
6. Ezra Taft Benson, "Beware of Pride," *Ensign,* May 1989, 4.
7. Bible Dictionary, LDS Edition of the Bible, King James Version, s.v. "Grace"; emphasis added.
8. Ezra Taft Benson, *God, Family, Country* (Salt Lake City: Deseret Book Co., 1974), 199.

Principles of Growth and Progression

Chapter 18

"Faith in the Lord Jesus Christ"

Even without the fourth Article of Faith, which lists "faith in the Lord Jesus Christ" as the first principle of the gospel, it would be obvious to anyone opening the standard works that faith is a pervasive, all-encompassing principle. The word itself and its cognate forms are found hundreds of times. Its importance in the plan of salvation could best be summarized by Paul's statement that "without faith it is impossible to please him: for he that cometh to God must believe that he is, and that he is a rewarder of them that diligently seek him" (Heb. 11:6). Joseph Smith, commenting on that verse, said, "If it should be asked—Why is it impossible to please God without faith? The answer would be—Because without faith it is impossible for men to be saved; and as God desires the salvation of men, he must, of course, desire that they should have faith; and he could not be pleased unless they had, or else he could be pleased with their destruction."[1]

Clearly, then, faith is at the center of all that we do and teach in the gospel of Jesus Christ. Unfortunately, however, in the Church we occasionally find some whose attitude seems to be that, since it is the first principle of the gospel, it is also a simple principle, easily comprehended and left behind as one moves on to more complicated and challenging areas of study. However, this is not the case. Elder Vaughn J. Featherstone has summed up, as well as any, the challenge of studying faith as a concept:

"What a great thing it is if we understand what faith is. What is faith? How does it work? Do you have total faith? When we come to a full and total understanding of faith, then I think we ought to move on to repentance. When we understand that totally, then we should move through the principles. But I doubt we will ever really get through an understanding and complete knowledge of faith in a life-time. I don't care how intellectual you are, or how long you study, I doubt you will ever come to an end of the study of faith, the first principle of the gospel. The gospel is so simple that a fool will not err therein, but it is so beautiful and so sophisticated that I believe the greatest intellectual can make a study of faith and never come to an end of understanding."[2]

Faith—A Principle of Power

If a typical Church group were to give a one-word synonym for *faith,* the usual answers would be *belief, trust, assurance, hope,* and so on. Joseph Smith's *Lectures on Faith* gives a different definition for faith, one that has profound implication for our understanding. In the first lecture, commenting on Hebrews 11:3, the Prophet said: "Faith is not only the principle of action, but of power also, in all intelligent beings, whether in heaven or on earth. Thus says the author of the epistle to the Hebrews (11:3):

"'Through faith we understand that the worlds were framed by the word of God, so that things which are seen were not made of things which do appear.'

"By this we understand that the principle of power which existed in the bosom of God, by which the worlds were framed, was faith; and that it is by reason of this principle of power existing in the Deity, that all created things exist; so that all things in heaven, on earth, or under the earth exist by reason of faith as it existed in HIM.

"Had it not been for the principle of faith the worlds would never have been framed, neither would man have been formed of the dust. It is the principle by which Jehovah works, and through which he exercises power over all temporal as well as eternal things. Take this principle or attribute—for it is an attribute—from the Deity, and he would cease to exist.

"Who cannot see, that if God framed the worlds by faith, that it is by faith that he exercises power over them, and that faith is the principle of power? And if the principle of power, it must be so in man as well as in the Deity? This is the testimony of all the sacred writers, and the lesson which they have been endeavoring to teach to man."[3]

That faith is a principle of power is evident in scripture. As we look in the standard works and find examples of men with faith, we find in virtually every case demonstrations of tremendous and marvelous power. We read about Enoch, for example, speaking the word of the Lord, and the earth trembling and the mountains fleeing! (see Moses 7:13). We see Joshua saying, "Sun, stand thou still"; and the sun obeys! (see Josh. 10:12–14). Or we find Peter spying a lame man near a gate of the temple—a man with a congenital birth defect who had been unable to walk for the forty years of his life. Peter said simply, "In the name of Jesus Christ of Nazareth rise up and walk." The record states, "And he leaping up stood, and walked, and entered with them into the temple, walking, and leaping, and praising God" (Acts 3:1–10). Faith is the power by which God speaks, creating worlds, solar systems, and universes. So when we speak of faith, we speak of tremendous power, not only physical power, but even power that can save a man from temporal and spiritual death.

Requirements for Developing Faith

In the third lecture on faith, Joseph Smith described what is necessary for people to have faith sufficient to bring them salvation:

"Let us here observe, that three things are necessary in order that any rational and intelligent being may exercise faith in God unto life and salvation.

"First, the idea that he actually exists.

"Secondly, a *correct* idea of his character, perfections, and attributes.

"Thirdly, an actual knowledge that the course of life which he is pursuing is according to his will. For without an acquaintance with these three important facts, the faith of every rational being must be imperfect and unproductive; but with this understanding it can become perfect and fruitful, abounding in righteousness, unto the praise and glory of God the Father, and the Lord Jesus Christ."[4]

Looking at these three requirements carefully, we can see that each of the three involves knowledge; that is, we have *an idea* in the first one, *a correct idea* in the second one, and *an actual knowledge* in the third one. If a sequence were designed depicting an individual's movement toward salvation, it would look something like this:

In other words, if we are to achieve salvation, we must have faith; and if we are to have faith, we must have knowledge. This is a crucial thing to know about faith and the means to develop it, and yet it raises a troubling question. If we say that knowledge is the requirement or prerequisite of faith, someone will invariably ask, But if knowledge leads to faith, how do you explain Alma 32, wherein Alma describes the process of faith leading to salvation as having faith first, which *then* leads us to a perfect knowledge?

After carefully rereading Alma 32 and studying the *Lectures on Faith,* I have come to some tentative conclusions about faith. Suppose, for instance, that faith in Jesus Christ is a *process* rather than simply a concept? Suppose that the same word is used by different prophets to describe different phases or stages of the process? Could that explain what seems to be a different use of the same term? And if that is true, can the process be described? Do the scriptures describe it? I believe that they do and that the best descriptions of that process are found within the Book of Mormon itself. In an attempt to describe this process, I have developed a paradigm, or model, of what the process of faith in Jesus Christ is.

Some words of caution need to be given, however, before we begin looking at the model itself. First, one danger of any model is that it tends to oversimplify. This is of value in one way, because the simplification helps us to conceptualize or grasp the relationships of a complex subject. But when we begin to apply the model closely to reality, we find that it may not hold up in all cases. Exceptions will exist that do not truly fit the model. The paradigm of faith included in this chapter is only to help people conceptualize a grand and complex subject. Second, Elder Featherstone's comment that the study of faith can be pursued without ever reaching the end of understanding suggests that the model presented here should be refined or adapted as an individual pursues a deeper understanding of faith. Third, the model is based heavily on three major sections in the Book of Mormon dealing with faith in Jesus Christ: Alma 32, Ether 12, and Moroni 7. Thus, understanding the paradigm is based in part upon a thorough study of those chapters.

The Process We Call Faith

One of the challenges in describing or discussing faith is the idea that faith is a process involving various stages of development. A prophet may use the word *faith* to speak of faith as a whole or to refer to any one of the different stages of the process. This presents a challenge in studying the scriptures, and sometimes even results in confusion. Joseph Smith, for example, said that faith is power; Alma said that faith is hope. Both, however, can be easily understood if we use the process model of faith.

The tendency for prophets to use one word—*faith*—to discuss different aspects of faith makes it difficult to delineate the different stages of the process. After some consideration, I decided that, rather than try to generate new terms—terms the prophets did not use—I would instead use the basic word with a number, thus describing the stages of the process as Faith 1, Faith 2, and so on. In addition, it seems to me that each stage of faith always contains three basic components: hope, action, and confirmation. Again, because these may differ somewhat in their nature, depending on which level of the process of faith a person is at, I have chosen to designate these with subscripts too: Hope 1, Hope 2; Action 1, Action 2; Confirmation 1, Confirmation 2; and so on.

To begin, let us examine Alma 32. I have concluded after studying the chapter that it describes the initial process of the development of faith in Jesus Christ, or, in terms of our nomenclature, the development of Faith 1. Remember that Alma was speaking to the Zoramites, or, more precisely, a group of Zoramites who had been expelled from the congregations of the Zoramite churches because of their poor, lower-class status. The Zoramites had apostatized from the Nephites—they worshiped idols and had developed a proud and perverted way of worshiping (see Alma 31:8–23, 31). In other words, Alma was not speaking to members of Christ's church in the sermon recorded in Alma 32. Rather, he was speaking to a group who had just begun the process of developing faith. This situation has some important implications for Alma's discussion of faith.

When Alma spoke to these Zoramite poor, he seemed to have used the terms *faith* and *perfect knowledge* in a peculiar sense; that is, in a sense different from the normal usage of the terms. He equated faith with a hope or desire to believe what is not known to be true. Notice what he said in verse twenty-one of Alma 32: "Now as I said concerning faith—faith is not to have a perfect knowledge of things; therefore if ye have faith ye hope for things which are not seen, which are true." Notice that he said, "If ye have faith ye hope." In other words, he seemed to be defining faith as a hope or desire that the things he was telling them were true. He also limited his definition of faith to hoping for things that are actually true. That suggests that hoping for things that are untrue will not bring the results he described in the rest of the sermon.

Alma's use of the term *perfect knowledge* is revealed in verses eighteen to thirty-four. In verse eighteen he said, "If a man knoweth a thing he hath no cause to believe, for he knoweth it." In verse thirty-three, after telling the Zoramites how to experiment with the word, which he compared to a seed, he said that, when they begin to see it "swell" and "grow" in them, they must *know* that the seed is good. In other words, they didn't have to *hope* or desire to believe that it is good; they would know that it was good. Therefore he said in verse thirty-four, "Your knowledge is perfect in that thing." Obviously, he was not talking about perfect knowledge in any grand or universal sense; and he made that clear in verses thirty-five and thirty-six by saying that, once they had tasted this light, their knowledge was not perfect in an ultimate sense.

Notice also in Alma 32 that Alma gave two prerequisites for the development of faith (the very first level of faith). These prerequisites are, first, humility (see v. 16) and, second, hearing the word (see v. 23). If we are not willing to humble ourselves and make the experiment, we can never develop faith. Even more fundamental, if we do not have the word of the Lord on which to experiment, if we do not have knowledge or information on which to begin to believe, we cannot have faith. (For additional references, see also Moro. 7:24–25; Rom. 10:13–17.)

Level One: Faith or Hope

At each stage of faith, we must move through three components to reach the next level. Note the diagram of the first level of faith, or Faith 1, on the following page. The three components are shown in their proper relationship to one another.

Hope 1, or the initial level of hope, would be the beginning step for the whole process. This level of hope is really nothing more than the desire or wish that something be true. It is as though we are motivated to say, "I want to know if this is true." Notice in verse twenty-seven, Alma said, "Even if ye can no more than *desire* to believe" (emphasis added). If we have Hope 1, then we will be motivated to Action 1, which is the second step of the process, the second component of faith. At the first level of faith, this action may be no more than a willingness to try to ascertain whether the word we have heard is true.

Moroni taught a valuable concept about this level of faith when he wrote, "I would show unto the world that faith is things which are hoped for and not seen" (Ether 12:6). This is essentially what Paul told us in Hebrews 11:1. In this case, faith, or the ability to trust in something not seen, is quite clear. We cannot "see" that the word we have heard is true; that is, we do not have empirical proof (proof based upon observation or experience) of the truthfulness of the word. Therefore, we must act on faith: we must trust or hope for something to be, although it is not yet based on seen evidence.

Moroni continued the verse by writing, "Dispute not because ye see not, for ye receive no witness until after the trial of your faith." In every case, in every level

FAITH 1—HOPE

CONFIRMATION 1—EVIDENCE BECAUSE OF FEELINGS

Empirical evidence—inner feelings; may be difficult to verbalize, but still real (v. 35)

"It will begin to swell" (v. 28)

"It beginneth to enlarge my soul, . . . enlighten my understanding, . . . be delicious to me" (v. 28)

Based on this evidence, you "must needs know that [it] is good" or true (v. 33). Then you have perfect knowledge (that is, empirical knowledge), and your faith (that is, your hope that it is true) becomes dormant (see vv. 34–35).

Trial of Faith (Ether 12:6)
Investigator Level

ACTION 1—WILLINGNESS TO TRY TO FIND OUT IF IT IS TRUE

Trial of faith

"Experiment upon my words" (v. 27)

"Awake and arouse your faculties" (v. 27)

"Exercise a particle of faith" (v. 27)

"Give place for a portion of my words" (v. 27)

"Do not cast it out by your unbelief" (v. 28)

HOPE 1—DESIRE TO BELIEVE SOMETHING IS TRUE

I want to know if this is true, "even if [I] can no more than desire to believe" (v. 27)

PREREQUISITES

1. Humility (v. 16)
2. Hearing the word (v. 23)

(See also Moro. 7:24–25; Rom. 10:13–17)

Note: Unless otherwise indicated, references in this chart are in Alma 32.

of the development of faith, there must be a trial of faith. That is, we are tested to see whether we will act on the basis of the hope that is in us. We have to show that we are motivated to behave according to the truths the Lord has given us, before we have actual evidence that these things are true. Notice again what Alma told the Zoramite poor in Alma 32:27–28: "If ye will awake and arouse your faculties, even to an experiment upon my words, and exercise a particle of faith, yea, even if ye can no more than desire to believe, let this desire work in you, even until ye believe in a manner that ye can give place for a portion of my words. . . . If ye do not cast it [the word] out by your unbelief, . . . it will begin to swell within your breasts." Notice the verbs of action that he used: *awake, arouse, exercise, desire, give place, not cast out.* We must act on our desire (which desire I call Hope 1) to know if the word of the Lord is true. This initial level of action (Action 1) is basically one of will, one of deciding to try to find out if the word is true.

When we act by experimenting, awaking, exercising, and so on, we are led to the third component of faith, which is a confirmation of our hope. This initial level of the faith process would be called confirmation. Alma described this kind of evidence through feelings. Though this evidence is available only to the feelings, it is still empirical, or real, evidence. It may be difficult to put into words, but that doesn't lessen its reality. Notice how Alma described this evidence through one's feelings, "It will begin to swell within your breasts; . . . it beginneth to enlarge [the] soul; yea, it beginneth to enlighten [the] understanding, yea, it beginneth to be delicious" (v. 28).

Based on this real, though difficult to express evidence, we can say, as Alma did in verse thirty-three, "Ye must needs *know* that the seed is good" (emphasis added). In other words, we now have knowledge based on empirical evidence. Alma called this "perfect knowledge." That perfect knowledge gained through the trial of faith and confirmed by real evidence then does away with the faith described by Alma (to the nonfaithful Zoramites), the faith that is a hope or desire to believe what is not known to be true. Since we have come to *know* that the word is good, we no longer need to *hope* that it is good. Perfect knowledge takes away, or swallows up, faith, as Alma used the term.

When we move through the trial of faith (hope that moves us to act, which leads to a confirmation of that hope), we can say that we have achieved the first stage of faith. These preliminary steps are at an investigator level: we are investigating whether something is true. Alma's description and discussion fit the Zoramite needs perfectly. Typically, we would hypothesize that when a person begins the process of developing and entering into Faith 1, described so perfectly by Alma, he will likely get confirmation quite rapidly. This is an experience missionaries see countless times. When people truly humble themselves upon hearing the word of God and experiment upon that word (for instance, seeking to know through prayer whether something is true), very often the confirmation, the swelling, the feeling of truthfulness, the almost indescribable sensation that this is good come quickly, and they know that the word of the Lord is a good seed.

Level Two: Faith or Knowledge

When we have achieved Faith 1, have we achieved all that there is to have? Obviously not. Alma himself encouraged the people to continue on once they had received this "perfect knowledge." He told them to nourish the seed that was starting to grow until it became a great tree providing them with the fruit of eternal life (see vv. 25–43). In other words, once we have Faith 1, we can move on to the next level of the process in developing faith. The second stage of faith (Faith 2), diagrammed on the following page, is a level of faith entailing belief and knowledge.

Once again there are the three components: Hope 2, Action 2, and Confirmation 2. In the second level of hope, we have more than a desire to know if something is true. Now our attitude could be described not as "I want to know if this is true," but as "I desire this truth." As Moroni stated it, we may "with surety hope for a better world" (Ether 12:4). This is a major step upward from the Faith 1 level. In his sermon to the Zoramites, Alma did not discuss in detail this second level of faith (probably because of the nature of his audience). But others did. Besides Moroni's statement in Ether 12:4 above, we find statements like these from Mormon: You "shall have hope through the atonement of Christ . . . to be raised unto life eternal" (Moro. 7:41); or, "Without faith [could this be Faith 1?] there cannot be any hope" (Moro. 7:42).

When we move into this second level of hope (Hope 2), where we begin to sincerely believe in the things we have heard rather than simply desiring to believe, we will then be motivated to action again. However, this action (Action 2) is on a higher level than that of Faith 1 and could be defined as a willingness to live the truths we believe to be true. Whereas we had previously acted to find out if the Lord's word was true, now we act to incorporate into our lives the truths we have learned. Here again we find in operation the principle in Ether 12:6: we must have our faith tried; we must prove by our actions that the hope in us truly is sincere and serious. Notice what Moroni said about this hope: it makes "an anchor to the souls of men, which would make them sure and steadfast, always abounding in good

FAITH 2—BELIEF AND KNOWLEDGE

Trial of Faith (Ether 12:6)
Conversion or Testimony Level

CONFIRMATION 2—EVIDENCE ON A BEHAVIORAL LEVEL

Empirical evidence—more outward proof, easier to identify and verbalize, though still much on the feeling level

"Because of your diligence and your faith . . . with the word in nourishing it, . . . by and by ye shall pluck the fruit thereof" (Alma 32:42)

"Thus by faith, they did lay hold upon every good thing" (Moro. 7:25)

"For if they . . . have faith in me, then will I make weak things become strong unto them" (Ether 12:27)

ACTION 2—WILLINGNESS TO LIVE THE TRUTHS ONE BELIEVES TO BE TRUE

Trial of faith

"Which hope cometh of faith, maketh an anchor to the souls of men, which would make them sure and steadfast, always abounding in good works" (Ether 12:4)

"They who have faith in him will cleave unto every good thing" (Moro. 7:28)

"But if ye will nourish the word . . . it shall take root" (Alma 32:41)

HOPE 2—BELIEF OR A MORE SURE HOPE

I desire this truth

"Wherefore, whoso believeth in God might with surety hope for a better world" (Ether 12:4)

"Ye shall have hope through the atonement of Christ . . . to be raised unto life eternal" (Moro. 7:41)

"Without faith [Faith 1] there cannot be any hope" (Moro. 7:42)

CONFIRMATION 1

works" (Ether 12:4). In his letter on faith, hope, and charity, Mormon said, "They who have faith in him will cleave unto every good thing" (Moro. 7:28). This seems to be what Alma meant when he said, "If ye nourish [the word] with much care it will get root" (Alma 32:37).

When we operate at the Action 2 level, we again undergo the trial of faith. We must show that we are willing to trust in things not seen. When we do so, we receive confirmation (Confirmation 2), specifically evidence on a behavioral level. This empirical evidence is more outward than that received in Confirmation 1, where the evidence consisted mostly of inner feelings (although Confirmation 2 still includes many feelings). Such evidence is easier to identify and to put into words. It would involve statements such as "Yes, my prayer was answered" or "I can see that this principle works in my life." Such confirmation leads us to say not "I believe . . ." but *"I know* the gospel is true." The word has grown to the point where we can actually begin to taste the fruits of it in our lives (see Alma 32:42). In Moroni 7:25 we read, "Thus by faith, they did lay hold upon every good thing."

Now that we have examined the first two levels of faith, we begin to appreciate the profound implications of the discussion of faith and works James the apostle gave. If we do not have works joined to our faith, then our faith is dead, "being alone" (see James 2:17). If we have the hope or desire that something is true (Hope 1) but refuse to act on that hope, we will receive no confirmation, and our faith, even at this early stage, will be dead. The same is true in level two. Once we believe that something is true but refuse to live the truth, then we have faith without works, and our faith dies. We will receive no confirmation. The confirmation comes only after the trial of faith. But in this second level, our trial is not on an investigator level; we are tried on a higher level involving conversion, or testimony.

Level Three—Faith or Power

Now we are prepared to look at the next level of faith, which brings us to faith as Joseph Smith defined it. We could say that Faith 3, diagrammed on the next page, is the power level of faith. Once again we are describing a major step upward from the previous level, and once again we find all three components operating as in the previous levels.

Hope 1 is to hope that something is true, and Hope 2 is to believe that it is true. After having gone through the process of Faith 2, however, we have confirmation and knowledge that the things we cannot see are indeed true. This makes a new level of hope possible. Hope 3, the third level of hope, could be described as a

FAITH 3—POWER

Trial of Faith (Ether 12:6)
Power Level

CONFIRMATION 3—EVIDENCE ON MANY LEVELS OF EXPERIENCE

Empirical evidence—experiences through feelings, knowing, and senses (though these may be hard to visualize, they are irrefutable kinds of evidence, including hearing, visualizing, touching, and demonstrating of power)

"All they who wrought miracles wrought them by faith" (Ether 12:16)

"There were many whose faith was so exceedingly strong . . . who could not be kept from within the veil, but truly saw with their eyes the things which they had beheld with an eye of faith" (Ether 12:19)

"It is by faith that miracles are wrought, and it is by faith that angels appear" (Moro. 7:37)

"Whatsoever thing ye shall ask the Father in my name, which is good, in faith believing that ye shall receive, behold, it shall be done unto you" (Moro. 7:26)

ACTION 3—WILLINGNESS TO DO WHATEVER GOD REQUIRES

Trial of faith

"Let us here observe, that a religion that does not require the sacrifice of all things never has power sufficient to produce the faith necessary unto life and salvation. . . . When a man has offered in sacrifice all that he has for the truth's sake, not even withholding his life . . . he does know, most assuredly, that God does and will accept his sacrifice. . . . Under these circumstances, then, he can obtain the faith necessary for him to lay hold on eternal life" (Joseph Smith, *Lectures on Faith,* 6:7).

HOPE 3—KNOWLEDGE AND ASSURANCE OF THINGS NOT SEEN

I have the truth and desire to use it to become like God

"A more excellent hope" (Ether 12:32)

"A perfect brightness of hope" (2 Ne. 31:20)

CONFIRMATION 2

knowledge and assurance of things not seen. At this level, our attitude is reflected by this statement: I have the truth, and I desire to use it to become like God. This is, I believe, what Moroni meant by the phrase "a more excellent hope" (Ether 12:32). This desire seems to also describe what Nephi meant by "a perfect brightness of hope" (2 Ne. 31:20). When our hope is this strong, when we truly have knowledge and assurance of unseen things, we move into more committed action (Action 3). This higher level of action could be described as a willingness to do whatever God requires of a person. This, again, is a great trial of faith. Action 3 may involve a wide range of behaviors, including working on a Church welfare project or taking care of a sick neighbor's children. It may be something as trying and challenging as God's request to Abraham that he sacrifice his only son.

In our development of faith, if we have reached this point of hope or knowledge but refuse to act accordingly, then, as James said, "as the body without the spirit is dead, so faith without works is dead also" (James 2:26). We have failed the trial of faith and will receive no confirmation of our hope. Notice the quotation by Joseph Smith from the *Lectures on Faith* included in the diagram. He said that only a willingness to sacrifice whatever God requires brings the knowledge that allows us to obtain the faith required for salvation.[5]

If we operate at this level of action, we would expect that confirmation of this hope would be forthcoming, and such is the case. We could describe this level of confirmation (Confirmation 3) as evidence on many levels of experience. It can not only involve experiences of inner feelings and knowledge, but also include experiences available to the senses, such as visions, visitations of angels, the demonstration of power in miracles, speaking in tongues, and the like. These may still be hard to express in words (in the sense that words are inadequate to describe them), but they are irrefutable kinds of evidence, demonstrations that the honest person cannot deny.

Notice the promises cited under the Confirmation 3 level in the diagram. This is what the Lord meant when he said, "These signs shall follow them that believe" (Mark 16:17). This power level of faith also helps us to better understand what the Lord meant when he said: "Faith cometh not by signs, but signs follow those that believe. Yea, signs come by faith, not by the will of men, nor as they please, but by the will of God. Yea, signs come by faith, unto mighty works, for without faith no man pleaseth God" (D&C 63:9–11).

I believe that understanding the process of Faith 3 also gives us added insight as to why those who seek signs to bolster faith are called "a wicked and adulterous generation" (Matt. 16:4). A person who wants to build his faith only on the basis of confirmation or evidence, without living the principles, seeks to circumvent the trial of faith that Moroni described. That is, he wants to have confirmation without paying the price of hope and action. And this "adulterates" or pollutes the proper relationship in the developmental process of faith. Satan seems to understand the significance of this and often prompts his servants to demand a sign, to demand faith without paying any price (see, for example, Jacob 7:13; Alma 30:43; Ether 12:5).

Level Four—Faith or Perfection

In level three of faith, or the power level, we looked to the faith shown by the people in the scriptures whom we typically characterize as having great faith. Many people might think of this as being the highest level of faith, but I feel that there is a fourth level of faith, which could be described as the perfection level.

Once again, this is a major step upward. We have to be a little more speculative as we describe this level of the process of faith because relatively few have achieved it; and those who have seem reticent (by direction of the Spirit) to talk about it in much detail. But I believe again that it involves our three components of hope, action, and confirmation, as diagrammed on the following page.

In level three, hope involved knowledge and assurance. How could one come to a higher level than that? I suggest that Hope 4 is the actual knowledge that one will become like God, and it can be characterized by the attitude, *I desire to be as God is.* Two scriptures come to mind: "The more sure word of prophecy means a *man's knowing that he is sealed up* unto eternal life" (D&C 131:5; emphasis added); and "If ye do these things, *ye shall never fall*" (2 Pet. 1:10; emphasis added), which is Peter's promise to those who were laboring to make their calling and election sure.

When someone has reached this level of faith in mortality, his calling and election is made sure, and he is told by the more sure word of prophecy that he will be exalted. Imagine the level of hope or desire that such a revelation would create in him. Such hope would lead him to the fourth or highest level of action (Action 4)—the level where his life becomes more and more godlike until he is made perfect and becomes worthy to become a god. Whether the phrase "trial of faith" adequately describes Action 4 is not important. What is important is to know that the person must still live at a level of action commensurate with the level of hope within him. When he does so, he will receive a level of confirmation also commensurate with his level of action. In the highest level of confirmation

FAITH 4—PERFECTION

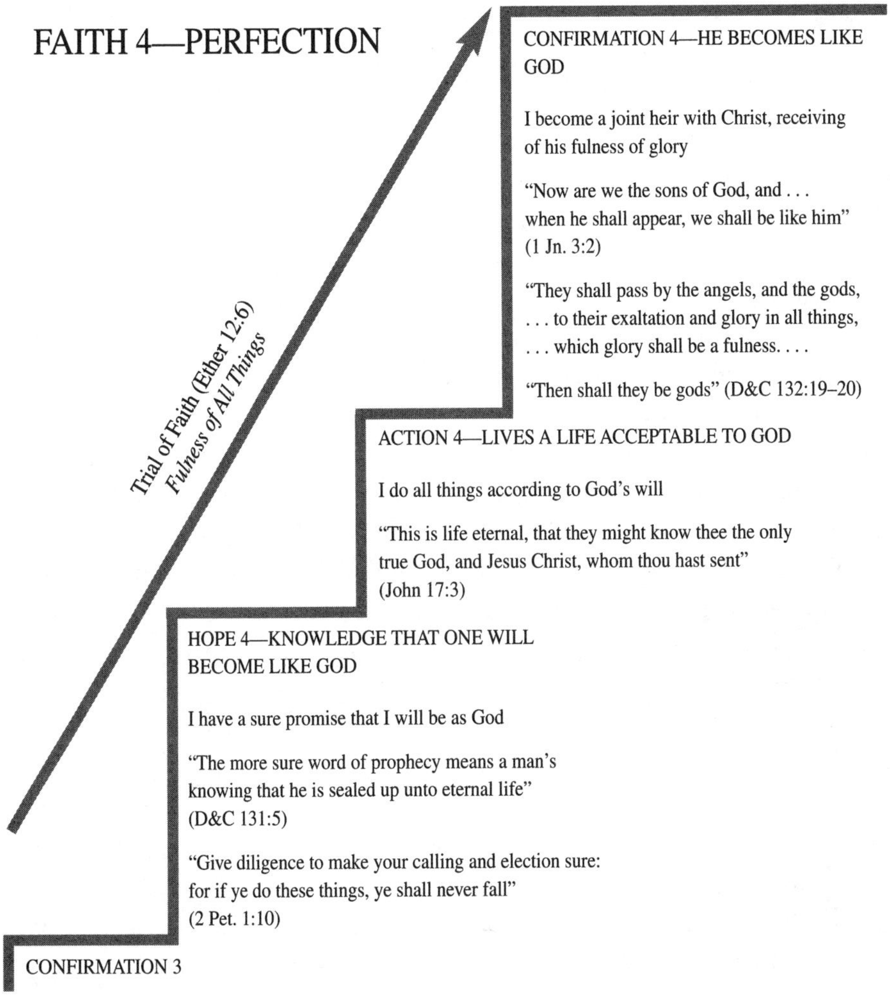

(Confirmation 4), a man receives the ultimate proof of the truths of the gospel—he is made a god!

As discussed at the beginning, the paradigm of the four levels of faith in Jesus Christ is inadequate to describe all the complexities of faith. Certainly it needs further clarification and refinement. But I have found it to be tremendously helpful as I think through what the prophets have said about faith. When Joseph Smith said faith is power, he was obviously speaking about a different level of faith than when Alma said to experiment upon his words so that faith could be swallowed up in perfect knowledge.

I also find it helpful to think of the three components—hope, action, and confirmation—at each level of faith, for I find the three principles operating in the lives of those who demonstrate faith. These principles also have relationship to repentance, baptism, and enduring to the end. Often we risk the danger of becoming sign seekers by talking of having one's calling and election made sure. As we talk about this important concept, we must clearly define the price to be paid so we do not end up testing God. Rather, we should operate according to the level of knowledge and hope that the Lord has granted us. Then we will receive a greater and greater confirmation until Jesus Christ makes us joint heirs with him, and we become gods. I firmly believe that this is the process that we must follow in our lives if we are to find that power. Joseph Smith said this:

"All the saints of whom we have account, in all the revelations of God which are extant, obtained the knowledge which they had of their acceptance in his sight through the sacrifice which they offered unto him; and through the knowledge thus obtained their faith became sufficiently strong to lay hold upon the promise of eternal life, and to endure as seeing him who is invisible; and were enabled, through faith, to combat the powers of darkness, contend against the wiles of the adversary, overcome the world, and obtain the end of their faith, even the salvation of their souls."[6]

Until now, we have not said anything about charity, though faith, hope, and charity are clearly interwoven, interdependent concepts (see 1 Cor. 13; Moro. 7:44–48). We can understand the interrelationship of faith and hope fairly clearly through the paradigm, but where does charity enter in? As I have pondered this, I find a profoundly moving answer—charity enters in at every level, every aspect, every point. The pure love of Christ validates every level of action to make it productive. This seems to be what Paul meant when he said that one can prophesy or give alms or do numerous other things, yet such actions are meaningless if not done because of a love for God and fellowman. Charity is what lights our hope, strengthens our will, deepens our confirmation. It suffers long, endures much, is properly motivated, hopes for all things, and endures all things. I have not shown charity in the paradigm because it would need to be shown everywhere, for it permeates the whole process of faith and salvation. Mormon explained it thus:

"Charity is the pure love of Christ, and it endureth forever; and whoso is found possessed of it at the last day, it shall be well with him. Wherefore, my beloved brethren, pray unto the Father with all the energy of heart, that ye may be filled with this love, which he hath bestowed upon all who are true followers of his Son, Jesus Christ; that ye may become the sons of God; that when he shall appear we shall be like him, for we shall see him as he is; that we may have this hope; that we may be purified even as he is pure" (Moro. 7:47–48).

Notes

From "An Exploration of the Process of Faith as Taught in the Book of Mormon," in *The Second Annual Church Educational System Religious Educators' Symposium: A Symposium on the Book of Mormon* (Provo: Brigham Young University Religious Studies, 1978), 74–80.

1. Joseph Smith, *Lectures on Faith* (Salt Lake City: Deseret Book Co., 1985), 7:7.
2. Vaughn J. Featherstone, "As If They Would Ask Him to Tarry a Little Longer," in *Speeches of the Year, 1975* (Provo: Brigham Young University Press, 1976), 375.
3. Smith, *Lectures on Faith,* 1:13–17.
4. Ibid., 3:2–5.
5. Ibid., 6:7.
6. Ibid., 6:11.

Chapter 19

The Mysteries of God Revealed by the Power of the Holy Ghost

In what must surely rank as one of the great visionary experiences in all of scriptural literature, the young prophet Nephi, very possibly still in his teenage years, had unfolded for him the grand vistas of the future (see 1 Ne. 2:16). The time was six hundred years before the coming of Christ. The place—at least the place where it began—was three days' journey south of the northern tip of the Gulf of Aqaba on the Red Sea, alongside the eastern shoreline. Today the location would be part of the territory of Jordan. Lehi simply called it the valley of Lemuel (see 1 Ne. 10:16).

The Vision of Nephi

Whether Nephi wrote an account of the vision at the time it happened is not clear. We do know that he kept a record, from which he then wrote upon what we call the small plates of Nephi, some thirty years after the colony left Jerusalem (see 2 Ne. 5:28–31). This is worthy of note, because with that perspective of time, he chose to introduce his account of the vision with some very interesting commentary.

The purpose of this chapter is to examine the seven verses of commentary that Nephi chose to give us as prelude to his record of the vision he had. Let us examine the verses, placing alongside each of them the salient points he seemed to be making.

Nephi's Words	Main Points
"But the Lord knoweth all things from the beginning; wherefore, he prepareth a way to accomplish all his works among the children of men; for behold, he hath all power unto the fulfilling of all his words. And thus it is. Amen" (1 Ne. 9:6).	1. The Lord knows all things. 2. He accomplishes all his works 3. He has all power.

Though these three concepts are not specifically mentioned in the vision, they become pivotal in our understanding of (1) how Nephi could be shown what he saw, and (2) what he saw. We shall say more about these important concepts later in the chapter.

Nephi's Words	Main Points
"And it came to pass after I, Nephi, having heard all the words of my father, concerning the things which he saw in a vision, and also the things which he spake by the power of the Holy Ghost, which power he received by faith on the Son of God—and the Son of God was the Messiah who should come—I, Nephi, was desirous also that I might see, and hear, and know of these things, by the power of the Holy Ghost, which is the gift of God unto all those who diligently seek him, as well in times of old as in the time that he should manifest himself unto the children of men" (1 Ne. 10:17).	4. Lehi saw and spake marvelous things by the power of the Holy Ghost. 5. He received that power by faith. 6. Nephi wanted to *see* and *hear* and *know* the same things by the same power. 7. This power is the gift of God unto all men who diligently seek him.

This seems to be Nephi's way of disclaiming any unique or privileged status from his having seen the vision. He recognized (1) that it came from God; (2) that it came because of faith; and (3) that others of faith can have the same thing.

Nephi's expressed desire "that [he] might *see,* and *hear,* and *know,* of these things" (v. 17; emphasis added) was literally fulfilled. As we look at the language of the vision, the sensory reality of the experience is dramatically underscored. For example, Nephi is commanded to "look" or "behold" approximately forty times in the course of the vision. The pattern wherein the angel or the Spirit says, "Look!" and Nephi then says, "I looked and beheld," is repeated no less than sixteen times (1 Ne. 11:8, 24, 26–27, 32). Nephi uses the phrase "I saw" or "I beheld" almost a hundred times as he recounts the vision, and he uses some form of *see, look,* or *behold* over 175 times in the four chapters or, on the average, 1.33 times per verse.

The Prophetic Experience

It may be of interest to analyze briefly exactly what it was Nephi "saw" or experienced. At least three major kinds of things can be identified:

1. He saw things outside the real world, things whose primary meaning is symbolic. These would include things such as the tree of life (11:8); the rod of iron (11:25); the river of water (12:16) and the great and spacious building (11:35).

2. He saw future events unfolding in a linear fashion, that is, one major item at a time. For example, he saw Mary and the birth of the Savior (11:13–20); the ministry, trial, and crucifixion of Jesus (11:31–33); the Savior's visit to the Nephites (12:6); and many other events that were yet future to Nephi.

3. He saw future events unfolding in a grand sweep; numerous things were happening simultaneously. Good examples of this type of experience would include his seeing "many generations pass away, . . . and . . . many cities" (12:3). In another place he said he beheld "many nations and kingdoms" (13:2). This kind of experience seems analogous to that of Moses when he "discerned" every particle and inhabitant of the earth by the Spirit of God (see Moses 1:27–28).

Nephi's Words	**Main Points**
"For he is the same yesterday, today, and forever; and the way is prepared for all men from the foundation of the world, if it so be that they repent and come unto him.	8. God never changes. 9. The mysteries of God will be revealed to those who seek them.
"For he that diligently seeketh shall find; and the mysteries of God shall be unfolded unto them, by the power of the Holy Ghost, as well in these times as in times of old, and as well in times of old	10. This will be done by the power of the Holy Ghost. 11. No unclean thing can dwell in God's presence.

as in times to come; wherefore, the course of the Lord is one eternal round.

"Therefore remember, O man, for all thy doings thou shalt be brought into judgment.

"Wherefore, if ye have sought to do wickedly in the days of your probation, then ye are found unclean before the judgment-seat of God; and no unclean thing can dwell with God; wherefore, ye must be cast off forever" (1 Ne. 10:18–21).

12. God has prepared a way for men to return to him.

13. These promises hold true in all ages.

How We Get the Mysteries of God and Why

As we compare the points made in these last verses with those made in verse 17, we see several reiterations. And when we tie them to the major premises laid down in 1 Nephi 9:6, we see that Nephi set up an interesting sequence of God's operation. Diagrammed, it could look something like this:

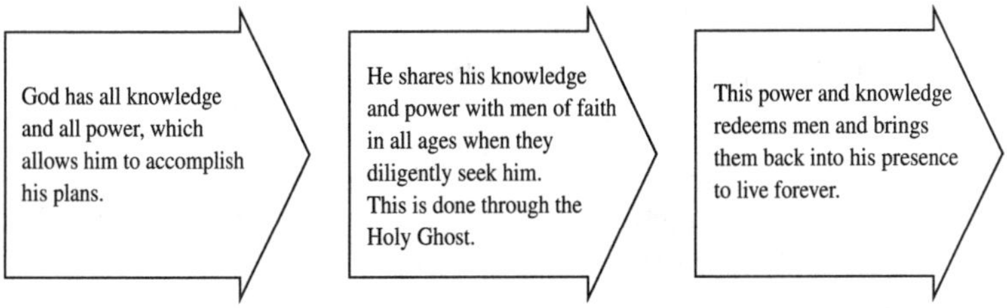

Nephi then concluded his introduction of these principles by bearing testimony: "And the Holy Ghost giveth authority that I should speak these things, and deny them not" (1 Ne. 10:22).

Once a person accepts these premises (or this chain of reasoning, if you will), the vision which follows becomes a logical sequence of what Nephi said. In other words, not only is the vision of Nephi itself proof that God knows all things and will reveal his knowledge to men, but the content of the vision likewise validates that God is working and will continue to work his plan of redemption—through the ministry of the Savior, through the establishment of America, through the coming forth of the Book of Mormon, and so on—so that all who seek him can return to his presence.

Some Challenging Questions

Nephi's logical chain is simple but powerful, and yet it raises numerous questions—not questions of doubt, but questions which seek understanding. To say that God has all power and all knowledge is a staggering concept to the finite mind, especially in our generation, when we are starting to grasp the vastness of the universe around us. When Nephi says the Lord knows all things, does that truly imply that He has all knowledge in the universe?

If so, we cannot help but wonder how God manages to oversee all of his dominions. Even if he is capable of traveling at the speed of light, it still leaves insurmountable time problems.

Let us illustrate with just one example. Abraham told us by means of the Urim and Thummim that the star nearest to the throne of God is called Kolob (see Abr. 3:3). Assuming for a moment that Kolob was in our own Milky Way Galaxy, it still leaves a staggering time question, since our own solar system is approximately thirty thousand light years out from the hub of the Milky Way in one of the spiral arms.[1] Even if we assume Kolob is somewhere near the center of our own galaxy, it would still take a being moving at the speed of light thirty thousand years to travel from Kolob to earth! In other words, if God were moving at the speed of light, he would have had to leave Kolob twenty-four thousand years before the fall of Adam in order to appear to Joseph Smith in the Sacred Grove in the spring of 1820!

The same kinds of time questions surface with prayer. How can a prayer, even if it moves at the speed of light, cross the mind-boggling immensity of space to be heard by our Heavenly Father?

Equally difficult is the question of God's knowledge of the future. Nephi said that God knows everything. Does that include the future? Obviously! He has foretold many events, sometimes millennia before they actually occur. The Savior taught that his Father knows what we need even *before* we ask it in prayer (see Matthew 6:8). One might assume from that that in some cases he might know what we need before *we* even know it! And therein is the difficult question. If God knows whether a person will marry in the temple (or be baptized, or sin, or whatever) before he does it, how can that person be free to exercise agency?

One final question raised by these concepts is, How does the Lord *show* (that is, allow them to see) prophets like Nephi something that hasn't happened yet?

A Question of Time

With a little thought, we see that all of these questions are questions of time. How does God go so far so fast? This really means, How does he do so *in so little time?* Things happening in the future really means they happen in a *time* that has still not happened to us.

There are several scriptures that suggest that God may not be bound by the same system of time as we are. For that matter, these scriptures suggest he may actually *perceive* time differently than we do. For example, Alma told his son Corianton that "all is as one day with God, and time only is measured unto men" (Alma 40:8). In the Doctrine and Covenants, the Lord revealed that "all things are present before mine eyes" (D&C 38:2). There are two definitions of the word *present.* One is geographical. To be present is to be *here.* The other is temporal. To be present is to be *now.* In which sense does the Lord mean "all things are present before mine eyes"? Does he mean all things are *here* before me, or all things are *now* before me? We shall examine some evidence that suggests that both are correct.

Another scripture in the Doctrine and Covenants suggests that past, present, and future are "continually before the Lord" (D&C 130:7). Lael Woodbury, using that scripture as a springboard, speculates that all of these questions on time that trouble us may be due to the fact that our perception of time is restricted:

"You and I don't yet have that facility of viewing time as an essence. But we will. That is part of what it must mean to be exalted. Right now we perceive . . . time as a blind man perceives form in space—sequentially. He explores with his fingers, noting form, texture, contours, rhythms. He holds each perception in his mind, one by one, carefully adding one to the other, until he synthesizes this concept of what that space object must be like. You and I don't do that. We perceive a space object immediately. We simply look at it, and to a certain degree we "know" it. We do not go through a one-by-one, sequential, additive process. We perceive that it is, and we are able to distinguish it from any other object. I'm suggesting that God perceives time as instantaneously as we perceive space. For us, time is difficult. Lacking higher facility, we are as blind about time as a sightless man is about space. We perceive time in the same way that we perceive music—sequentially."[2]

A Question of Relativity

There is something in the human psyche that rebels at seeing the future, something that hasn't happened yet, as happening now. Every logical fiber of our being rejects it, for every experience we have had contradicts it. But again, just in our generation, some scientific theories of space and time have been widely accepted that seem just as strange to our experience. One such theory is Albert Einstein's theory of relativity. It has some fascinating implications for our understanding of the attributes and nature of God.

It will be left to those more qualified than I to explain this theory. Suffice it to say that the unexpectedness of the ideas about time and space that were merely introduced by Einstein and others makes clear that the universe is very different from our naive notions. God's ability to see and know the future and how he was and is able to show his prophets future events such as those described in Nephi's visions may well be explained by properties of time and space that are even more surprising than those proposed by Einstein.

Modern scripture supports the idea that *time* is relative, that is, there is no absolute standard of time that exists throughout the entire universe. Abraham was told that one revolution (or day) on Kolob equals a thousand of our years (Abr. 3:4). If one were to carry the ratio down to smaller units of time, we see some interesting implications.

Kolob Time	**Earth Time**
1 day	1,000 years
1 hour	41.67 years
1 minute	253 days
1 second	4.22 days
.25 second	1.1 days
.01 second	1 hour

Think of the implications of that. While a person on Kolob takes a two-hour nap, a person on earth is born, lives to the age of eighty, and dies before the other awakens. One blink on the part of a Kolobian and he misses one whole day of ours.

That God's power is limitless is made clear in the scriptures. This is the incredibly awesome power that allows him to say, "I . . . spake, and the world was made" (D&C 38:3; see also Gen. 1:3). It is the power that can move a mountain or take note of even a sparrow's fall (see Ether 12:30; Matt. 10:29–31).

This concept gives added significance to Nephi's basic premise, which could now be turned around to read: God "prepareth a way to accomplish all his works among the children of men" precisely and specifically because (1) he "knoweth all things from the beginning" and (2) "he hath all power" (1 Ne. 9:6). That is a marvelous summary of God's attributes, but equally miraculous to Nephi is the fact that God willingly shares that knowledge and power with faithful men of all ages. As Nephi so powerfully bore witness, "For he that diligently seeketh shall find; and the mysteries of God shall be unfolded unto them, by the power of the Holy Ghost, as well in these times as in times of old, and as well in times of old as in times to come; wherefore, the course of the Lord is one eternal round (1 Ne. 10:19).

Notes

From Monte S. Nyman and Charles D. Tate, Jr., eds., *The Book of Mormon: First Nephi, The Doctrinal Foundation* (Provo, Utah: Religious Studies Center, Brigham Young University/Salt Lake City: Bookcraft, 1988), 151–60.

1. This is only an assumption for purposes of illustration. The scriptures give no clue as to the actual location of Kolob. It could just as easily be in a galaxy millions of light years from our own.
2. Lael J. Woodbury, "Continually Before the Lord," Church Educational System Commissioner's Lecture Series, 1974, 5–6.

Chapter 20

Revelation and Reason: A Productive Harmony

There are times in one's life that may seem trivial or only marginally important at the moment they happen, but as the years roll on, they prove to have been like the switch points on a railway line. In a fast-moving train, one is hardly aware of passing over those points where two lines are joined, separated by no more than an inch or two of space. Yet, depending on how the switch is thrown, one can end in destinations as divergent as New York and Los Angeles.

As I have reflected on the factors that have shaped my testimony of the gospel, several such switch points stand out as having been of particularly profound importance to me. Describing three of those influences may well be the best way to express my personal testimony of the gospel of Jesus Christ.

A House of Learning, a House of Faith

I grew up in a home that was fairly typical of mid–twentieth century America. My father was a pipe fitter at the Garfield Smelter at the southern tip of the Great Salt Lake. We lived in a small house on three and a half acres in the western part of Murray, Utah, which at that time was a mostly rural part of Salt Lake County. We lived simply but comfortably, though I suppose by today's standards we would have been below the poverty level and would have qualified for all sorts of benevolent help from the government. Despite our poverty, my mother believed strongly that her occupation was the care and nurturing of her children, and throughout my growing-up years she never worked outside the home.

My father always said he was an "uneducated" man. He did well in high school, but unfortunately, three weeks after he was accepted into the engineering program at the University of Utah, Black Thursday—October 24, 1929—struck and the nation was plunged into the Great Depression. That dashed any hopes for "higher education," and my father became a laborer for the rest of his life. Only much later did I come to realize that his self-imposed title of "uneducated" could not have been more undeserved.

Just a year ago, while visiting with an ailing uncle—the brother that was closest to my father in both age and temperament—I learned something about my father I had not known before. My uncle told me that while my father was in high school, the math teacher in an adjoining town found a trigonometry problem in the textbook that he was unable to solve. Perplexed, he asked other math teachers in the area for help. They were stumped as well. He asked the math teacher at my father's school for help, but he could not solve it either. "Let me give it to Jewell Lund," he said. "He's the best math student I've got." Within a day or two, Dad had solved the problem on his own. It was such an event in that rural community that it made the front page of the weekly newspaper.

It was that analytical tenacity, coupled with an abiding curiosity and inquisitiveness, that characterized my father's whole life of informal education. And he bequeathed that gift to us. Books were always a part of our lives. He loved to learn and to know and encouraged us to feel the same way. He constantly pushed us to think critically and logically. He demanded not negativism, but an examination of the rationale behind what was being postulated. What were the assumptions? Were those assumptions logical? Was the thinking consistent? Did it square with known truth?

In most homes, the dinner hour is a time for quiet talk and relaxed visiting. In our home, the "amen" of the blessing signaled the opening of the debate. One of us would raise this topic or that, and away we went. It was always vigorous, frequently intense, and occasionally downright heated. (I only realized that this was not normal for all families when I brought my wife-to-be to our home for dinner for the first time, and she threatened my life if I left her alone in that forensic fray for one moment.) We never had to agree with Dad in these discussions, but we quickly learned that we had better be prepared to defend our positions properly or else abandon them.

The thing that kept this demanding scrutiny from becoming mere intellectual gymnastics was my father's deep love for the gospel and the scriptures. He often stressed the fact that the scriptures were called the standard works because they are "the measure by which you judge all things." And we learned to do so. Everything we read and learned about was couched in terms of and laid up against the gospel plan. He would note simple things in nature that bore silent witness to the hand of God. We would compare the principles and doctrines of men to the principles and doctrines of God.

I mention my upbringing because occasionally I have had people say to me, "Well, you were raised a Mormon. It's only natural that you would accept your theology without question." I just smile. That may be true in some homes, but it was not in mine. The gospel was put to the same intense scrutiny and debate as any other topic. But here again, this scrutiny came from a foundation of faith, not skepticism. "Whatever God says is right," Dad would often say. "If something God says or does doesn't make sense to you, it's because of your limitations, not God's."

My mother's contribution in shaping this wonderful gift of inquiry was as enormous as my father's, though in a much less dramatic way. My mother has always been a gentle, patient woman. Her temperament is such that she raised her voice in anger only when her children, particularly three teenaged sons, drove her to it, and that was rarely. Not that we did not try, but her capacity for patience was prodigious.

Mom has always been a peacemaker in the fullest sense of the word. Her nature was not to plunge into those verbal duels that were so much a part of our life. She would mostly sit and listen. Occasionally, when we would begin to defend our intellectual turf too vigorously, she would quietly note that we had stopped listening. That always pulled us up short. Or she might make us all feel a little sheepish by noting some core principle we had totally overlooked, or by making a simple declaration of faith that brought the discussion back to its proper moorings.

Only now do I fully understand how important her gentle balance was for us in that climate of inquiry, which could easily have become only strident. She was always there to remind us that one could disagree without being disagreeable. My father taught us to combine reason with revelation, and that was a superlative gift. But my mother did something equally important. She showed us how to keep our balance so that rationalism did not become radicalism.

Teaching, a Lifelong Love

A second influence began with a simple question at the end of a religion class at BYU. "Jerry," the professor asked, "have you ever considered teaching seminary?" I had not, but the idea had instant appeal to me. I enrolled in the training classes and within the year was teaching seminary for the Church Educational System. To that point I had been working toward a career in social work, with an eye toward working with juvenile delinquents. Talk about a switch point!

I have now completed my thirty-fourth year with CES, serving as a teacher in both the seminaries and the institutes of religion, as a curriculum writer, and as an administrator. For the last three decades I have been privileged to devote my full occupational time to studying, teaching, and writing about the gospel of Jesus Christ. Day in and day out, it has been a requirement of my employment to immerse myself in the scriptures. For more than thirty years I have pored over them, studied them, drawn lessons from them, answered questions about them and from them. I have examined them with telescope, microscope, calipers, and slide rule. Whether taking the macro or the micro view of the scriptures, I have found in them an incredible, wonderful, miraculous depth and consistency that cannot be fully plumbed. Over and over I have been asked to teach or to write about a particularly dismaying block of scripture—blocks like Leviticus, Chronicles, or Philemon. "There is nothing much of importance in that particular block," I would say to myself. But, given little choice, I would dive in. And there is where my father's training would begin to pay off. "The problem is not with God," I would remember. "It is your own limitations that make his word difficult." Again and again I would be stunned at the richness of the ore to be mined from that ground I had assumed was barren.

A "Non-Christian" among Christians, a Gentile among Jews

As I neared the completion of a master's degree in sociology at BYU, I began looking in earnest at various graduate programs around the country. I had enjoyed my studies in sociology and was committed to a doctorate in that same field. My wife and I took an opportunity to visit several major midwestern universities with strong doctoral programs in sociology. When we returned home some ten days and three thousand miles later, we were sure of two things. First, we discovered we were quite naive about the world out there, and particularly about the world of higher education. Second, we knew a doctorate in sociology was not for us.

Still desirous of pursuing a doctoral degree, I began to look at programs in either biblical studies or Near Eastern studies. After considerable examination, I applied for and was accepted at the Claremont Graduate School in southern California. At that time, Claremont was considered one of the preeminent schools in this field in America. Though my wife and I had always facetiously stated that there were two places we did not want to go—hell and Los Angeles, and we weren't sure in which order to list them—life has a way of working its will on you. We volunteered to go to California for CES to teach in the institutes of religion. One year later, in September 1969, I was standing in the registration line at Claremont with my tuition check in hand.

The program at Claremont was impressive. For the doctorate, in addition to the base languages for a Ph.D., it was required that a person have a working knowledge of Hebrew, Greek, Aramaic, Akkadian, and Ugaritic. Unfortunately, I had also learned that while they had an impeccable academic reputation, the program in biblical studies was in the mainstream of liberal theological thought. For example, some of the faculty there had been prominent in the development of the "death of god" movement that had swept theological circles during the sixties. I felt some misgivings about this kind of program, but I had my acceptance in hand and I wanted an advanced degree.

As I stood there in the California sunshine, waiting for my turn at the cashier's window, the misgivings went from a disquieting whisper to a deafening roar. Three places away from the cashier's window I suddenly asked myself, "What are you doing here? This is not what you want." I gulped a little, turned on my heel and left, tearing up my tuition check as I walked away. And with that, in what very much seemed at the time like a frivolous if not downright foolish decision, the switch was thrown and I started down a different track entirely.

Still wanting to do something in biblical studies, I began to look around southern California to see what else was available. I investigated everything that had anything close to my interests. I still smile when I think of the bewildered look on the face of the dean of admissions at a Baptist theological seminary when I tried to explain why a Mormon was interested in studying the Bible with the Baptists. Finally, I learned of a small private school in Los Angeles called Pepperdine University. It offered a master's degree in the New Testament. The Church of Christ, which owned and operated Pepperdine and several other schools of higher education, had a fine reputation for conservative biblical scholarship. I applied, was accepted, and, one year after walking away from Claremont, began my studies at Pepperdine.

The Church of Christ and Mormonism go back a long way together. Thomas Campbell and his son, Alexander, began the movement that eventually founded the Churches of Christ throughout America. One of their centers of influence was in the Kirtland, Ohio, area. When Parley Pratt and other missionaries came through

Kirtland, they met with Sidney Rigdon, who was a Campbellite minister. The message of the Restoration struck a responsive chord among the Campbellites, and hundreds joined the Church. Not surprisingly, a strong feeling of antipathy on the part of the Campbellites resulted, which has continued to this day. The Church of Christ still believes that the LDS Church is a source of serious error and deception. It was common during my stay at Pepperdine to see notices on the bulletin boards announcing anti-Mormon seminars or classes for the religion faculty and students. Along with other denominations, they label us "non-Christian." With almost all the religion faculty at Pepperdine drawn from the ranks of Church of Christ ministers and with virtually every student in the graduate religion program preparing for the Church of Christ ministry, I was the only "non-Christian" in a devoutly Christian graduate program.

After a couple of semesters of studying the New Testament, I wanted to do some studies in the Hebrew language as well. There were a few community education classes close to home, but these were conversational Hebrew and moved at a very slow pace. Finally, I found a little college in Hollywood called the University of Judaism, which was run by the conservative branch of Judaism. Like Pepperdine's graduate program, the University of Judaism catered primarily to students who wanted to prepare themselves for the religious life. But I applied, was accepted, and, along with my studies at Pepperdine, attended Hebrew classes in Hollywood. Once again I found myself a minority of one. Not only was I a "non-Christian" in a Christian school, but now I was also a Gentile among the Jews.

But I am happy to say that while my enrollment in both schools caused numerous raised eyebrows, I was accepted graciously and treated with courtesy and respect in every case. By the time I had finished the equivalent of a master's degree in New Testament studies and three semesters of Hebrew, I knew that my choice to walk away from Claremont was a wise one. As the years have gone on and life has unfolded, I can see so clearly that my decision that day was another one of those profoundly important "switching" moments in my life. What a grand thing my experience at both of those universities proved to be. I could write a whole treatise on how those years at Pepperdine and the University of Judaism affected my testimony, but I will briefly note only a few examples.

First, I learned very quickly that Latter-day Saints do not have a corner on sincere devotion and service to God. I think of a black student at Pepperdine with whom I came to be friends. He ran a neighborhood ministry in the heart of Watts and was hated by some of his own people for being a "whites' honkey." I stood in awe of his love for the Savior and his courage in serving him. I think of my biblical

Hebrew teacher who invited us to attend a conservative synagogue service one Saturday. One of the students offered him a ride. The young instructor quietly indicated that he honored the restriction of his faith that forbade lighting fires on the Sabbath. Since an automobile engine ignites the gasoline in order to run, he could not ride in an automobile without violating that commandment. Instead, he and his wife and two little boys walked the four miles back and forth. It was not done in a boastful or self-righteous manner. It was just a quiet willingness to sacrifice comfort to principle.

Second, I learned how to study the Bible. I learned the full meaning of taking an exegetical approach to scripture study. (*Exegesis* comes from the same root as *exodus* and means "to draw out," suggesting that through exegesis one draws out the meaning of a scriptural passage.) The Churches of Christ accept the Old Testament but believe that it was fulfilled when Christ came. The New Testament is the basis for their belief, and they study it with an intense passion. In my studies at Pepperdine, I learned how to study the linguistic, historical, cultural, and contextual settings of scripture. We analyzed and criticized and dissected and debated. I wrote fifteen- and twenty-page papers on two or three verses of scripture. Over and over I was filled with wonder at the power of the scriptures, at their incredible consistency, and at the marvelous inspiration of Peter and Paul and John and the other early writers.

Third, with all of that academic emphasis, I also came to more fully appreciate two statements I had heard repeatedly in our church. I learned just how strongly the world feels that one cannot preach the gospel unless one has been trained for the ministry. That was the primary qualification for service in the minds of these sincere and wonderful young ministerial students and their teachers. Academic expertise was the prime qualifier, not priesthood authority or revelatory experience. I also saw just how successful the adversary has been over the centuries in teaching the philosophies of men mingled with scripture. It always intrigued me that it was stated that way, and not the other way around—that is, scripture mingled with the philosophies of men. By the time I was through with my studies there, I understood that the first was the better description of what had happened: The philosophies of men took first priority.

Fourth, and most important, I came to learn just how much we owe to Joseph Smith and the Restoration. I learned what a rich treasure-house of doctrine we have in the Book of Mormon and other latter-day scriptures. Over and over I saw examples of the simplicity of the doctrine restored under the hand of the Prophet. I came to know firsthand how the Book of Mormon restored many of the "plain and precious truths" that had been stripped out of the Bible by careless transcribers and designing priests.

One day in a class on the book of Revelation, we ended up in a major discussion about the "natural paradox," as the professor called it, found in Revelation 2:26–27. As part of the promise to the faithful who endure to the end, the Lord said they would receive "power over the nations," "rule them with a rod of iron," and break the nations to "shivers." "Do you see the paradox?" the professor asked. "The image is that of a tyrant, smashing nations to pieces like clay pots, but the promise is given to the faithful. How do you reconcile faith and tyranny in the same breath?" I wanted to tell him that the Book of Mormon makes it clear that the rod of iron is a symbol for the word of God, and that the faithful were leading with God's word, not some tyrannical weapon. But since references to the Book of Mormon and Joseph Smith were not warmly received at Pepperdine, I bit my tongue.

On another occasion, I wrote a long exegetical treatise on Peter's references to Christ's visit to the spirit world (1 Pet. 3:18–20; 4:6). I dug into the writings of the early patristic fathers (those who wrote within a few years of Christ's death) and found that they clearly taught the idea of doing work for the dead. I cited Paul's writings. I explained the theological logic behind the position. When my professor (a fine man and a wonderful teacher who was the Church of Christ minister over a large congregation in Glendale, California) handed me back the paper, he said something like this: "Jerry, I know what you Mormons believe about vicarious work for the dead. I know about your work in the temples. And frankly, I will have to admit that it makes sense. The scriptures are with you. The patristic fathers are with you. Logic is with you." Then he shook his head. "But I can't accept it. I just can't accept it." To say such experiences came every day would be a bit of an exaggeration, but they came nearly every week. It was a wonderful academic experience that constantly reaffirmed my testimony rather than calling it into question. Time after time during the three years that I studied at Pepperdine and the University of Judaism I saw evidence of the truthfulness of the Church and of God's work.

A Witness of the Truth

There they are—three influences that have had a profound effect on me and on my feelings about the gospel of Jesus Christ. I was raised in a home of faith, but one in which inquiry and reason were championed. I have spent thirty years studying and teaching the scriptures and the gospel. And I was privileged to examine the Bible under the tutelage of some very fine scholars and teachers. There were, of course, other important influences, but those three have proven to be the most important. Together they have combined, in what one person called a great "confluence of influence," to build my testimony. Because of those three factors, I now can boldly declare my witness:

I know that God the Father lives and that Jesus Christ is our Redeemer and Savior. I know that God is a loving, caring Father. He not only hears and answers prayers and shows an almost incomprehensible degree of long-suffering for my stumblings, but he also nurtures us and guides our steps, helping to pull those "switches" that send us down tracks we did not even know were out there. I know that he so loved the world that he sent his Only Begotten Son, a being of such perfection that even a lifetime of study only begins to lift the curtain enough that we catch the slightest glimpse of his majesty and power. The foundations for this testimony of the Father and the Son were laid during my early childhood years by wonderful parents. But a lifetime of searching, studying, questioning, teaching, trusting, and learning have only shown me all the more how truly God and Christ live and how profoundly they are involved in my life.

The scriptures are a repository of miraculous truth and power. The words of God have withstood every scrutiny, shone brightly through every challenge, brought power and wisdom and peace through every examination I have given them. The hand of God is evident throughout the standard works. They are like a great, interwoven tapestry of truth. The principles and practical guidelines weave through the whole fabric with an absolutely incredible complexity, consistency, and genius of design. The scriptures are simply a miracle. There is no other adequate word to describe them. No human hand could have produced their power and their wisdom.

Joseph Smith was called of God, labored under his direction, and surely stands high among the list of noble and great ones God chose to do his work. The work of the Restoration in this dispensation is of such magnitude, such majesty, and such scope that it can be described only as "a marvelous work and wonder." I have studied the writings of some of the world's most learned men and women, people with enough letters behind their names to provide a serious game of Scrabble. They are brilliant, erudite, scholarly, and articulate—but compared to Joseph Smith, they are like children beginning a study of the alphabet. I have learned that God's prophets are not only his servants, but truly become his spokesmen. What a statement of confidence that God should say of them, "whether by mine own voice or by the voice of my servants, it is the same" (D&C 1:38).

The Church of Jesus Christ of Latter-day Saints is the only "true and living" church on the face of the earth. I have come to admire and respect other faiths and the people who sincerely hold to those faiths, but oh how keenly has it been made manifest to me that this is His church! It is filled with struggling, quick-to-falter Saints, but the organization reflects the divine hand of God and it is led by his Son. It moves forward in the face of swirling change and intense opposition. Again and again I have had carried into my heart the witness that the Brethren who lead it are doing God's work and are his servants. The Church is indeed the stone cut out of the mountains without hands, and I know that it will continue to roll forth until it fills the whole earth. I am humbly grateful that my Father saw fit to send me to a home where the Church would become part of my daily life.

Finally, and perhaps most important because it is the validation of all of the above, I bear witness of the reality of the Spirit's whispered guidance. In my earlier years as a teacher I used to say that I believed the Holy Ghost spoke to us daily. I am sure now that hourly would be a much more likely description. I know that he comforts, testifies, enlightens, guides, verifies, prompts, warns, directs, compels, restrains, leads, and witnesses to me. I know that it was his voice during all those years with my parents, and during all those years of teaching, and during all those months of study and learning in California, that over and over whispered to me, "This is true! This is true!"

What an unthinkable gift, to be given the presence of a member of the Godhead as a personal guide and companion. And I thank my God for it and the testimony that is the result of that influence.

Note

From Susan Easton Black, ed., *Expressions of Faith: Testimonies of Latter-day Saint Scholars* (Salt Lake City: Deseret Book Co./F.A.R.M.S., 1996), 55–66.

Chapter 21

The Voice of the Lord

Personal revelation is a matter of vital importance to every Latter-day Saint. When we are baptized and confirmed members of the Church, we are commanded to receive the gift of the Holy Ghost. When you think about it, that is an incredible gift. Imagine receiving a member of the Godhead as our personal companion. We are told that our mission in life is to "come unto Christ, and be perfected in him" (Moro. 10:32). But that is not a simple thing. Life is too complex to provide a rule book that covers every situation. Instead, the Lord has given us the Holy Ghost to serve as our teacher, watchman, mentor, and guide.

I believe that one of the most important challenges of our mortal probation is learning to hear, recognize, and then follow the voice of the Lord. I would like to say that again: One of the most important—if not the most important—challenges in learning how to come unto Christ and to be perfected in him is to learn to hear, to recognize, and then to follow the voice of the Lord.

Part of that challenge is that there is sometimes confusion in the minds of some about personal revelation. Others have important questions about how it works or what it is like. Have you heard statements such as these: "How do I know if an impression is really from the Lord or if it is just my own emotions?" Or "I never seem to have a spiritual experience." Or "I have prayed again and again about this. Why isn't the Lord answering me?"

Let me give just one quick example of how the area of personal revelation can sometimes get confusing. When I was teaching in the institutes of religion in southern California, there was hardly a semester that went by that I didn't have an experience like this: One of my students would come to me (usually a girl) and report that the boy she had been dating (sometimes seriously, sometimes casually) had received a "revelation" that they were to marry. I won't ask for a show of hands how many here have faced a similar declaration, but I know, from my own experience, it would be more than a few of you. Carlfred Broderick, a renowned LDS family therapist, dubbed these as "hormone revelations."[1]

The interesting thing to me was that often the girl felt intimidated by such a declaration, feeling that she needed to accept the "Lord's will" even though she found the prospect somewhat distasteful. (In some cases it was *downright* distasteful.) Some were even a little shocked when I boldly explained that unless they received an independent confirmation from the Lord, they should feel no pressure to accept the boy's request.

Today I should like to address three questions about personal revelation:

- What is the voice of the Lord like?
- How can I distinguish between true and counterfeit revelation?
- What can I do to enhance my ability to hear, recognize, and follow the voice of the Lord?

What Is the Voice of the Lord Like?

There are two scriptures in the Doctrine and Covenants that are particularly helpful in describing what the voice of the Lord is like and how it works with us. The first is in section 85, wherein the Lord says, "Thus saith the still small voice, which whispereth through and pierceth all things" (D&C 85:6).

Note the descriptive phrases used here. The voice is still. It is small. And it whispers. When you think about that, it becomes clear that hearing the voice of the Lord has inherent challenges. It would be much simpler if the Lord spoke in a voice of thunder or used a microphone and 80-megawatt speakers. Then there would be no doubt. But he does not. He whispers. His voice is still and small. Elder Boyd K. Packer said this about the nature of the Lord's voice:

"The Spirit does not get our attention by shouting or shaking us with a heavy hand. Rather it whispers. It caresses so gently that if we are preoccupied we may not feel it at all. . . .

"Occasionally it will press just firmly enough for us to pay heed. But most of the time, if we do not heed the gentle feeling, the Spirit will withdraw and wait until we come seeking and listening."[2]

The second scripture that tells us what the voice of the Lord is like is found in section 8, a revelation given through the Prophet Joseph Smith to Oliver Cowdery. In that section the Lord defined what revelation is and how it comes:

"Yea, behold, I will tell you in your mind and in your heart, by the Holy Ghost, which shall come upon you and which shall dwell in your heart.

"Now, behold, this is the spirit of revelation" (D&C 8:2–3).

"In your mind and in your heart"—think about that for a moment. If the Lord spoke something to our mind, how would it come? We would probably describe it as coming to us as "thoughts." If he tells us something in our hearts, we would probably describe that as coming as "feelings."

Thoughts and feelings—these are the most common ways the Lord gives his children personal revelation. And therein lies another challenge. Every one of us is a veritable stream of thoughts and feelings. Every day our minds are constantly occupied with thoughts, and we are filled with various emotions. In the midst of that torrent of thought and feeling, the Lord from time to time inserts a thought or a feeling that comes from him. How do we tell the difference? Revelation is rarely preceded by a drumroll or by the announcement "The following thought or feeling will be from the Lord."

There is yet one other thing we need to note when we talk about what the voice of the Lord is like. It has to with revelation that does not come from the Lord. Note what Elder Packer said about counterfeit revelation:

"Be ever on guard lest you be deceived by inspiration from an unworthy source. You can be given false spiritual messages. There are counterfeit spirits just as there are counterfeit angels. . . .

"The spiritual part of us and the emotional part of us are so closely linked that it is possible to mistake an emotional impulse for something spiritual. We occasionally find people who receive what they assume to be spiritual promptings from God, when these promptings are either centered in the emotions or are from the adversary."[3]

If something is counterfeit, it means that it resembles the original so closely that it is difficult to distinguish which is the true and which is the false. So it is with counterfeit revelation. On the surface it may feel real. It may appear to be from the Lord. We may even have very strong feelings about what we have received. But this alone is not proof it is from God. Note that President Packer warns that we must ever be on guard against being deceived by our emotions or by revelation from an unworthy source. That suggests that counterfeit revelation is not a rare thing.

This shouldn't be too surprising to you, should it? If you were Satan and knew that personal revelation was absolutely essential for a person striving to come unto Christ, wouldn't you try to sow confusion and deception about it? Which brings us to our second question.

How Can I Distinguish between True and Counterfeit Revelation?

Personal revelation comes in many different ways and forms. It may vary from one person to another, and therefore it is difficult to set down rigid rules that cover every situation. But the Lord has not left us without guidance in this matter. Through the scriptures and the statements of his modern prophets, we find principles that can help us determine how to decide if revelation comes from the Lord or from another source. I would like to briefly outline five of those guidelines or principles to you today. There are others, but these have proven to be particularly helpful to me.

Principle 1: It is God who determines all aspects of revelation.

By definition, revelation is the communication of the mind and will of the Lord to his children. If you think about that for a moment, then you will understand that revelation is always unidirectional. It comes only from God to us. We may communicate back and forth with God in a two-way process, but revelation always comes in one direction. We never reveal anything to God.

Since all revelation comes from the Lord, then it is reasonable that he should set all of the parameters of that revelation. Those parameters include (a) to whom a revelation is given; (b) what content is given in the revelation; (c) when the revelation comes; and (d) in what form the revelation may be given. Sometimes, with the best of intentions, we inadvertently seek to tell the Lord how he should conduct his business. We may feel a particular urgency about a question and press the Lord for an answer by a certain deadline. Or we may strongly desire a particular kind of manifestation, such as one of the more dramatic forms of revelation, and be satisfied with nothing less. We may try to tell the Lord how to solve our problems or what answer we would like. But these are not our choices. All aspects of the revelation are determined by the Lord.

Elder Packer counseled against trying to force spiritual things:

"It is not wise to wrestle with the revelations with such insistence as to demand immediate answers or blessings to your liking. You cannot force spiritual things. Such words as *compel, coerce, constrain, pressure, demand,* do not describe our privileges with the Spirit. . . . You can create a climate to foster growth . . . ; but you cannot force or compel. . . .

" . . . [And then comes this warning:] . . . Do not force it or you will open the way to be misled."[4] Note that he says we can create a climate that fosters spiritual growth. Through appropriate action we can influence the process of revelation. We can study and pray, on occasion we can add fasting to our prayers, we can importune the Lord with deep yearnings, we can keep sacred covenants—all of these will help create a climate that fosters spiritual growth. But we must remember that when all is done, it is still up to the Lord to determine when the revelation comes, how it is given, what is revealed, and to whom.

In connection with the principle that God determines all aspects of revelation, I should like to make two other points. The prophet Jacob taught a simple principle with these words: "Seek not to counsel the Lord, but to take counsel from his hand" (Jacob 4:10). Think about that for a moment. God's wisdom is infinitely greater than ours. His knowledge is infinitely more complete. How foolish we are when we presume to tell him how he should do his work.

There is also great wisdom in what some have called the Gethsemane principle. With the utmost earnestness and the deepest of pleadings, the Savior called on his Father in the Garden of Gethsemane to remove the dreaded cup of his coming sacrifice. But that request was followed immediately by these profound words: "Nevertheless not as I will, but as thou wilt" (Matt. 26:39). That should be part of every prayer we utter, every request we take to the Lord. In that simple phrase lies the key to our willingness to let the Lord decide what is best.

Principle 2: The content given in a revelation is more important than the form in which it comes.

Another mistake some make is to covet the more dramatic forms of revelation. God reveals his mind and will to man across a broad spectrum of experiences. These may range from the very direct and dramatic: the appearance of divine beings, open visions, fire from heaven. Or they may be very subtle: quiet premonitions, gentle thoughts, a feeling of peace. The latter are by far the most common. We must be careful that we don't feel that only the more direct forms of revelation are valid. President Spencer W. Kimball warned of this tendency:

"Even in our day, many people . . . expect if there be revelation it will come with awe-inspiring, earthshaking display. . . .

"The burning bushes, the smoking mountains . . . , the Cumorahs, the Kirtlands were realities; but they were the exceptions. The great volume of revelation came to Moses and to Joseph and comes to today's prophet in the less spectacular way—that of deep impressions, without spectacle or glamour or dramatic events.

"Always expecting the spectacular, many will miss entirely the constant flow of revealed communication."[5]

We must learn to be content, not only with what the Lord decides to reveal to us but with what form he chooses to send that revelation. As Elder Packer warned, if we try to force a spiritual manifestation to our liking, we open the way for us to be deceived.

Principle 3: True revelation does not contradict gospel principles or go contrary to established Church policy and procedure.

This principle seems self-evident and hardly worthy of mention, but again and again we hear of cases where the principle is violated. Sensational stories or wild rumors go through the Church like wildfire. Some are almost ridiculous in nature, and yet there are still those who believe them. For example, one story that has been around for years tells of a hitchhiker supposedly picked up by Church members. As they drive along, the hitchhiker tells the people that if they don't have their food storage now, it is too late. Then he mysteriously disappears out of the car. You would think that everyone would be skeptical of such a story, but there are always a few who believe it. In another case a person predicted that the great earthquake foretold in the scriptures was about to hit Utah. For months he was a popular fireside speaker, and tapes of his talk were widely distributed. Do you remember a major earthquake in Utah in recent years? Neither do I. Another man worked out the exact day and date that Christ will come, and that, too, went around the Church like a sensation. The scriptures say that "no man, no, not [even] the angels of heaven" know the day nor the hour of his coming (Matt. 24:36). So where does that leave him? And why aren't we wise enough to see the contradiction? Here is what President Harold B. Lee had to say of such things:

"It never ceases to amaze me how gullible some of our Church members are in broadcasting sensational stories, or dreams, or visions, or purported patriarchal blessings, or quotations, or supposed [entries] from some person's private diary. . . .

" . . . We find that these [things] are finding their way into our Relief Society meetings, into priesthood quorums, firesides, institutes, and seminaries.

"Brethren of the priesthood, you defenders of the faith, . . . cease promoting the works of the devil . . . for they are the works of Satan."[6]

Now, is that strong enough language for you? Here is something equally clear given in an official declaration by the First Presidency:

"When visions, dreams, tongues, prophecy, impressions or any extraordinary gift or inspiration conveys something out of harmony with the accepted revelations of the Church or contrary to the decisions of its constituted authorities, Latter-day Saints may know that it is not of God, no matter how plausible it may appear. . . . Anything at discord with that which comes from God through the head of the Church is not to be received as authoritative or reliable."[7]

Is that plain enough? If the Lord wants to warn the Church about the importance of food storage, he won't do it through a hitchhiker. If you need to be told of a coming earthquake, you won't get that news from an audiotape your neighbor hands you. Let us be wise, brothers and sisters. When there is new doctrine or new procedures to come forth, you will get it in one of three ways:

A formal press conference will be called by the leaders of the Church and an official announcement will be made.

It will be announced through the *Church News,* the *Ensign,* or other official Church organs.

It will be announced in general conference by those in authority.

Otherwise we should be very wary about accepting it ourselves, and also we should not share it with others.

Principle 4: The Lord wants us to use our agency and develop spiritual self-reliance.

In some ways this guideline may at first seem like a paradox. There is no question but what the Lord wants us to rely on him, to turn to him, and to trust in his guidance, counsel, and direction. On the other hand, the scriptures and the prophets warn us about having to be directed in every matter of life. From time to time we meet people who feel that being "spiritual" means that the Lord inspires or confirms every action they take. Everything they do is attributed to the Spirit. In some cases they submit even the most trivial of matters to the Lord for confirmation. When I was a young college student many years ago, I remember a teacher saying something like this: "If you are living by the Spirit, you will even know which brand of toothpaste to buy." I was deeply impressed then and hoped that someday I might reach that level of "spirituality." Today I have a different understanding.

Do these words sound familiar?

"For behold, it is not meet [i.e., it is not proper, it is not good] that I should command in all things; for he that is compelled in all things, the same is a slothful and not a wise servant; wherefore he receiveth no reward" (D&C 58:26).

They should sound familiar. They come from the Lord. It seems to me that if I require spiritual direction in whether to buy Crest or Colgate, I run the risk of being slothful and not wise.

We know from scripture that there are some things that don't matter to the Lord, that he leaves the choice up to us. There are several places in the Doctrine and Covenants where you will find this phrase: "it mattereth not unto me" (see, for example, D&C 60:5, 61:22, 62:5, 63:40). It is clear then that the Lord does not expect us to seek help on every trivial matter. As president of BYU, Dallin H. Oaks spoke of this:

"The Spirit of the Lord is not likely to give us revelations on matters that are trivial. I once heard a young woman in a testimony meeting praise the spirituality of her husband, indicating that he submitted every question to the Lord. She told how he accompanied her shopping and would not even choose between different brands of canned vegetables without making his selection a matter of prayer. That strikes me as improper."[8]

Striking the balance between trust in the Lord and spiritual self-reliance is a delicate matter, but it is clear that the Lord does not want us to be spiritual automatons who are afraid to move without first being told what to do.

Principle 5: A person is not given revelation to direct another person unless they have priesthood or family responsibility for that person.

Some time ago I was speaking at a Know Your Religion lecture in another part of the country. My topic was the same as it is today. Afterward a woman came up and told me that this was the first church meeting she had been to in more than six years and that she had come only at the urging of a friend. Then she told me why. She and her husband had been unable to have children for several years after marriage. Finally she got pregnant, and they looked forward with great joy to having a child. Shortly before the baby was due, she went into terrible contractions and started to hemorrhage. Her husband rushed her to the hospital barely in time to save her life, but not in time to save the baby. You can imagine their devastation.

About a week after the funeral a sister from the ward came to visit this woman. This neighbor told the woman that she had had a dream the previous night in which it had been revealed to her that if the father had taken the time to give his wife a priesthood blessing before he had rushed her to the hospital, the baby would have lived.

"That was when I stopped going to church," the woman told me. "My husband is faithful priesthood holder, but all he could think about that night was saving my life. I decided that if God would let my child die under such circumstances, I wanted nothing more to do with him." Then she said this: "But what that woman told me wasn't from the Lord, was it?"

I shook my head and said no.

What had led her to that conclusion? It came from two quotes I read that night. Let me read them to you now. The first is from an official declaration by the First Presidency: "In secular as well as spiritual affairs, Saints may receive Divine guidance and revelation affecting themselves, but this does not convey authority to direct others."[9]

The second statement comes from Elder Oaks:

"We should understand what can be called the principle of 'stewardship in revelation.' . . . Only the president of the Church receives revelation to guide the entire Church. Only the stake president receives revelation for the special guidance of the stake. The person who receives revelation for the ward is the bishop. . . . Individuals can receive revelation to guide their own lives. But when one person purports to receive revelation for another person outside his or her own stewardship . . . you can be sure that such revelations are not from the Lord."[10]

This young mother began to weep then and said: "I am so glad I came tonight. It is time I came back to the Lord." I am sure the neighbor woman was well-meaning. I am sure that she felt that her dream was from the Lord. But had she understood this principle, she would have known that it wasn't from God because she had no right to direct the lives of that couple.

Remember those cases of "hormonal revelation" that I came across while teaching institute? I told my students that they didn't have to accept another's so-called revelation about marriage unless they received independent confirmation of it for themselves. Why did I feel bold enough to make such a statement? Because it comes under this same principle of not getting revelation to direct another over whom we have no responsibility. Again from Elder Oaks:

"I have heard of cases where a young man told a young woman she should marry him because he had received a revelation that she was to be his eternal companion. If this is a true revelation, it will be confirmed directly to the woman if she seeks to know. In the meantime, she is under no obligation to heed it. . . . The man can receive revelation to guide his own actions, but he cannot properly receive revelation to direct hers. She is outside his stewardship."[11]

That concludes the five principles that can serve as guidelines concerning personal revelation. I hope from these examples that you can see how they provide a standard by which we can judge and measure the processes of personal revelation. They help us better understand how the Lord works with us and also help us weigh which things are truly from the Lord and which may be counterfeit.

This now brings us to the third and, almost certainly, the most important of our three questions.

What Can I Do to Enhance My Ability to Hear, Recognize, and Follow the Voice of the Lord?

There are obviously many answers that could be given to that question: be worthy, earnestly seek the Lord, pray always, follow the Brethren. But I should like to answer in a little different way. To do that, I would like to conduct a brief experiment with you. Turn off the radio, the television, and anything else making noise in the room where you are now sitting and reading this book. I would like you to listen to the silence and see what you can hear.

What did you hear? Could you hear the hum of the air conditioning? The ticking of a clock somewhere nearby? The sounds of traffic from a busy street several blocks away? Had you heard those sounds before? Why not?

Do you see the principle now? If, as we noted before, the Lord's voice is still and small and it whispers, then if our lives are filled with noise, we will find it difficult to hear. Elder Henry B. Eyring made this keen observation:

"Your problem and mine is not to get God to speak to us; few of us have reached the point where he has been compelled to turn away from us. Our problem is to hear."[12]

In our little experiment, only in the silence did we begin to hear the more subtle and quieter sounds. And yet they were there all along. Other sounds cover, mask, or distract us from those quieter sounds. If the voice of the Lord is still and small and whispers to us, then we must find ways to reduce the inner noise in our lives and create times of inner stillness and quiet.

There are many sources of inner noise. Some are obvious. Sin is clearly a major source of spiritual noise. The effect is similar to what loud prolonged noise does to the auditory nerves. Prolonged or even permanent hearing loss can result. I believe this is what Paul meant when he spoke to Timothy about having our "conscience seared with a hot iron" (1 Tim. 4:2). It means we are beyond feeling. Sin rapidly impairs our spiritual senses. It can create tremendous inner noise.

Anger and contention are a major source of inner noise. Remember the story of the Prophet Joseph during the days of translating the Book of Mormon? It was reported that one day he came up to the room to translate but could get nowhere. He then admitted that he and Emma had spoken some disagreeable words earlier. He excused himself and went to make his peace with his wife. After a time he returned and indicated he was now ready to proceed.

Other sources of inner noise are not necessarily bad in and of themselves. Physical tiredness, stress, busyness, apathy, and worry can all create inner noises of their own.

Even outer noise can detract from inner quiet. Noise is endemic in our society. We live in envelopes of outer noise. We play music in our homes and cars, we watch television while we study, we even buy portable tape and CD players so we can carry this envelope of noise with us when we walk or jog. This is not a bad thing, but it may interfere at times with the quiet whisperings the Lord wants to give us. One observer noted that before a revelation could be given to some people, there would have to be something like this: "We interrupt this broadcast to bring you the following message."

Irreverence is a source of inner noise. Elder Boyd K. Packer made this observation in a conference talk:

"Irreverence suits the purposes of the adversary by obstructing the delicate channels of revelation in both mind and spirit. . . .

"Leaders sometimes wonder why so many active members get themselves into such predicaments in life. Could it be that they do not feel what they need to feel because our meetings are less than they might be spiritually?

" . . . Leaders should teach that reverence invites revelation."[13]

Let me mention one other common source of great inner noise, often found even among faithful, obedient people. It is what Elder Eyring on another occasion described as "having your wants too high." When we desperately desire something, it creates a great rush of emotion within us. And high emotion can mask or cover spiritual promptings. Even if the thing we desire is a good thing—such as wanting help for a critically ill family member—our "wants" may be so high that we become unwilling or unable to hear the Lord's will in the matter.

In summary, then, if the voice of the Lord is still and small and it whispers, it shouldn't surprise us that his counsel is "Be still and know that I am God" (D&C 101:16). Only as we are still can we learn to hear the still small voice.

Thankfully, the scriptures and the prophets teach us how to reduce inner noise and create times of quiet and reverence. These will be neither new nor surprising ideas to you, but they are of great importance. I list only a few.

Reading and studying the word of God is a great source of inner quiet. There are many who already understand that principle. Life has left you torn and troubled. Inside you feel like a churning, boiling cauldron of anxiety and unrest. Then you turn to the scriptures. Almost immediately you can feel things begin to change. The churning calms, the agitation melts away, and peace comes in its place. I have experienced that time and time again in my own life.

Prayer is another source of inner quiet and serenity. I am not talking about the perfunctory "I have to do my duty" sort of prayers. I speak of prayers that are filled with yearning. I speak of prayers when your heart swells with gratitude for the almost countless gifts God has given you. I speak of prayers that are consistent, focused, and submissive to God's will.

If irreverence is a great source of static and noise, then we can deliberately set about to increase our own personal reverence. In sacrament meetings we can sit quietly and prepare for the covenant-making process offered there. We can sing the hymns, paying attention to the words so they become a prayer unto the Lord. We can focus on what the speaker is saying and try to understand how the principles being taught apply to us.

Here is a simple thing, and yet one of the most effective ways to attune our inner hearing to spiritual things. In the sacramental covenant we witness to God that we are willing to do three things. One of those, to "always remember him," is repeated in both of the sacramental prayers. If we keep that covenant, what is God's promise back to us? That we shall always have his Spirit to be with us (see D&C 20:77, 79). What a promise! Let me give you a quick example of how that simple promise could bring tremendous inner peace and quiet.

One of the great sources of inner noise in our society is driving the freeways, a challenge that earlier generations did not have to face. In Utah, at the moment, that has become particularly so. After half an hour or more on the freeways, we feel anger and frustration, irritation and impatience. Some even experience rage. By the time we reach our destination we are fuming with anger or trembling with fear. The next time you get in your car to drive the freeway, try this experiment. Pause for a moment and offer this short prayer: "Help me to remember the Savior as I drive today. Help me to try and act as he would act. When that person in front of me is talking on his cellular phone and not paying attention to his driving, help me to remember the Savior and act accordingly. When some knucklehead cuts directly in front of me, help me to not say anything that the Savior would not say." I suggest that it will not only dramatically reduce the inner noise within you, but it will directly bring the promise of the Lord to you: "that they may always have his Spirit to be with them."

Finally, one of the most important things you can do when you are searching to reduce inner noise in your life is to take time to ponder and reflect. Get away from the bustle of life. Find a quiet place and take time to simply sit and think, to listen to your thoughts and feelings, to open yourself to the promptings of the Spirit. Note what the following prophets said they were doing prior to receiving important revelations. Nephi: "I sat pondering in mine heart" (1 Ne. 11:1). Joseph Smith and Sidney Rigdon: "While we meditated upon these things" (D&C 76:19). Joseph F. Smith: "I sat in my room pondering over the scriptures; and reflecting" (D&C 138:1–2). Joseph Smith: "My mind was called up to serious reflection. . . . I reflected . . . again and again [upon the words of James]" (JS-H 1:8, 12).

Sometimes we must deliberately put aside the cares of the world, put aside the rush of our daily lives, and find a quiet place and a quiet time where we can sit and ponder and reflect and meditate—and listen for that still small voice that whispers. Part of that time of pondering will be to deliberately push your wants down. You will remind yourself that it is not your place to counsel the Lord or to try and tell him what is best for you. You will consciously remember the Gethsemane principle mentioned earlier and submit your will to his.

Conclusion

Let me repeat this important point: One of the most important—if not the most important—challenges in learning how to come unto Christ and to be perfected in him is to learn to hear, to recognize, and then to follow the voice of the Lord. Fortunately the Lord has given us his almost incomprehensible gift of the Holy Ghost—a member of the Godhead—to be our constant companion and spiritual guide. If we learn how to distinguish the voice of the Lord from the many other voices and sounds that fill our lives, the promises are incredibly rich. I cite only one such promise:

"For thus saith the Lord—I, the Lord, am merciful and gracious unto those who fear me, and delight to honor those who serve me in righteousness and in truth unto the end.

"Great shall be their reward and eternal shall be their glory" (D&C 76:5–6).

To the realities of that promise I add my own testimony. I have experienced to some small degree the blessings therein promised, and I testify that the quiet revelations of the Spirit have enhanced my life greatly, as they will the lives of any faithful Latter-day Saint who seeks the Lord's voice.

Notes

From an address given 2 December 1997, Brigham Young University, Provo, Utah; in *Brigham Young University 1997–98 Speeches* (Provo: Brigham Young University Publications and Graphics, 1998), 81–90.

1. Carlfred Broderick, *One Flesh, One Heart: Putting Celestial Love into Your Temple Marriage* (Salt Lake City: Deseret Book Co., 1986), 21.
2. Boyd K. Packer, "The Candle of the Lord," *Ensign,* January 1983, 53.
3. Ibid., 55–56.
4. Ibid., 53.
5. Spencer W. Kimball, in Conference Report of Munich Germany Area Conference, 1973, 76–77; emphasis added.
6. Harold B. Lee, in Conference Report, April 1970, 55–56; emphasis added.
7. Joseph F. Smith, Anthon H. Lund, and Charles W. Penrose, "A Warning Voice," August 1913, in *Messages of the First Presidency,* comp. James R. Clark, 6 vols. (Salt Lake City: Bookcraft, 1965–75), 4:285, as cited by Harold B. Lee, in Conference Report, April 1970, 55; emphasis added.
8. Dallin H. Oaks, "Revelation," *BYU 1981–82 Fireside and Devotional Speeches* (Provo: Brigham Young University, 1982), 26.
9. "A Warning Voice," 285–86; emphasis added.
10. Oaks, "Revelation," 25; emphasis added.
11. Ibid.
12. Henry B. Eyring, *To Draw Closer to God* (Salt Lake City: Deseret Book Co., 1997), 29; emphasis added.
13. Boyd K. Packer, "Reverence Invites Revelation," *Ensign,* November 1991, 22.

Chapter 22

"Even So Ye Must Be Born Again" (Moses 6:59)

The scriptures often refer to "the doctrine of Christ" (2 Ne. 31:21), which the Savior clearly defined as follows: "The Father commandeth all men, everywhere, to repent and believe in me. And whoso believeth in me, and is baptized, the same shall be saved; and they are they who shall inherit the kingdom of God. And whoso believeth not in me, and is not baptized, shall be damned. Verily, verily, I say unto you, that *this is my doctrine*" (3 Ne. 11:32–35; emphasis added).

The doctrine of Christ is taught in many places in the scriptures (see, for example, 2 Ne. 31:11–21; 32:1–6; 3 Ne. 11:31–40; D&C 10:63–69), but perhaps nowhere was it more fully and clearly taught than in the very beginning to Father Adam. In Moses 6:48–62, this fuller account ties the first principles and ordinances to the fall of Adam and the atoning sacrifice. In other words, it contains a full discussion of the Father's plan. This is why the closing verse clearly states, "And now, behold, I say unto you: *This is the plan of salvation unto all men" (*v. 62; emphasis added).

The flow chart listed in this chapter is an attempt to help you better conceptualize what is taught in those verses in the book of Moses. Without a careful prereading and constant referral back to the scriptural passages, the chart will not be fully understood. Additional references that help clarify the doctrine are given below some of the boxes on the chart.

It is important to remember that the scriptures, not the chart, contain the reality of these saving truths. The chart is only an instructional device to help you conceptualize those saving truths and doctrines. Only as you immerse yourself in the scriptural sources—carefully, thoughtfully, and prayerfully—will the chart become a meaningful instructional experience.

The analogy of rebirth needs a brief explanation. In Moses 6:59, the Lord indicates that we are born into this world through water, blood, and spirit. In other words, three elements are essential to our birth into mortality. For the first nine months of life, the unborn fetus is totally immersed in the amniotic fluid in the uterus. This watery environment protects the child and allows it to move freely inside the mother. When the "water breaks," the mother knows that birth is imminent. So water is the first essential element.

Blood is the second. The circulatory system develops early in the unborn child. Blood becomes the life-giving and life-sustaining fluid in the tiny new body. Blood has three primary functions: It brings oxygen and food to all parts of the body, it carries carbon dioxide and waste products away, and it protects and fights against infection and disease through the white blood cells.

The third element of our physical birth is the spirit. We are not told exactly when the spirit enters the body, but if the spirit is not present at birth, there will be no life (see Alma 40:11; D&C 93:33–34). Such a baby would be called a "stillborn" child.

The Lord, in simple but significant imagery, likens our spiritual rebirth to our birth into mortality. As it was with our first birth, so it is when we are "born again." Water, blood, and Spirit are again essential. In the water of the baptismal font, we are again totally immersed in a watery environment. In other words, the baptismal font is not only a symbol of the grave, where we bury the old sinful man, but also a symbol of the womb where the newborn spiritual person is given life. The atoning blood of Christ is also required, and like the blood in our bodies, the atoning blood nourishes, cleanses, and protects us from spiritual infection. And finally, the source of life for the reborn spiritual man is the Holy Spirit. If it were not so, the newborn spiritual man would be "stillborn."

One other thought: Does not this concept of rebirth give a wider and deeper dimension to the commandment that we "become as a little child" (3 Ne. 11:37–38; see also Mosiah 3:19) if we are to overcome the natural man and become "the children of Christ, his sons, and his daughters" (Mosiah 5:7)? This is the profound and beautiful imagery of being born again through the water, blood, and Spirit.

"THE DOCTRINE OF CHRIST"

(2 Ne. 31:21; see Moses 6:48–62)

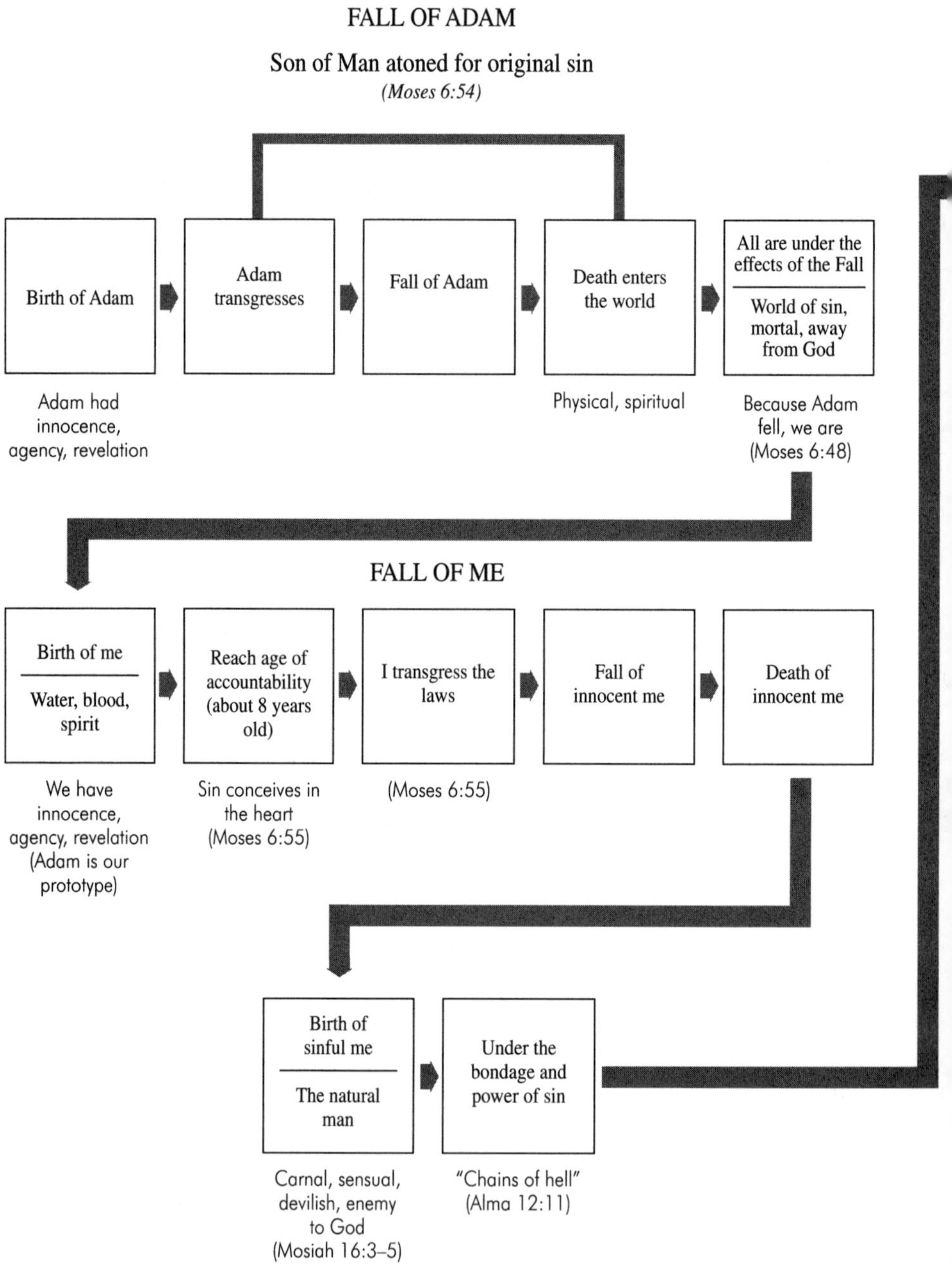

Note: References and text outside the boxes give additional information or clarification.

FIRST PRINCIPLES AND ORDINANCES

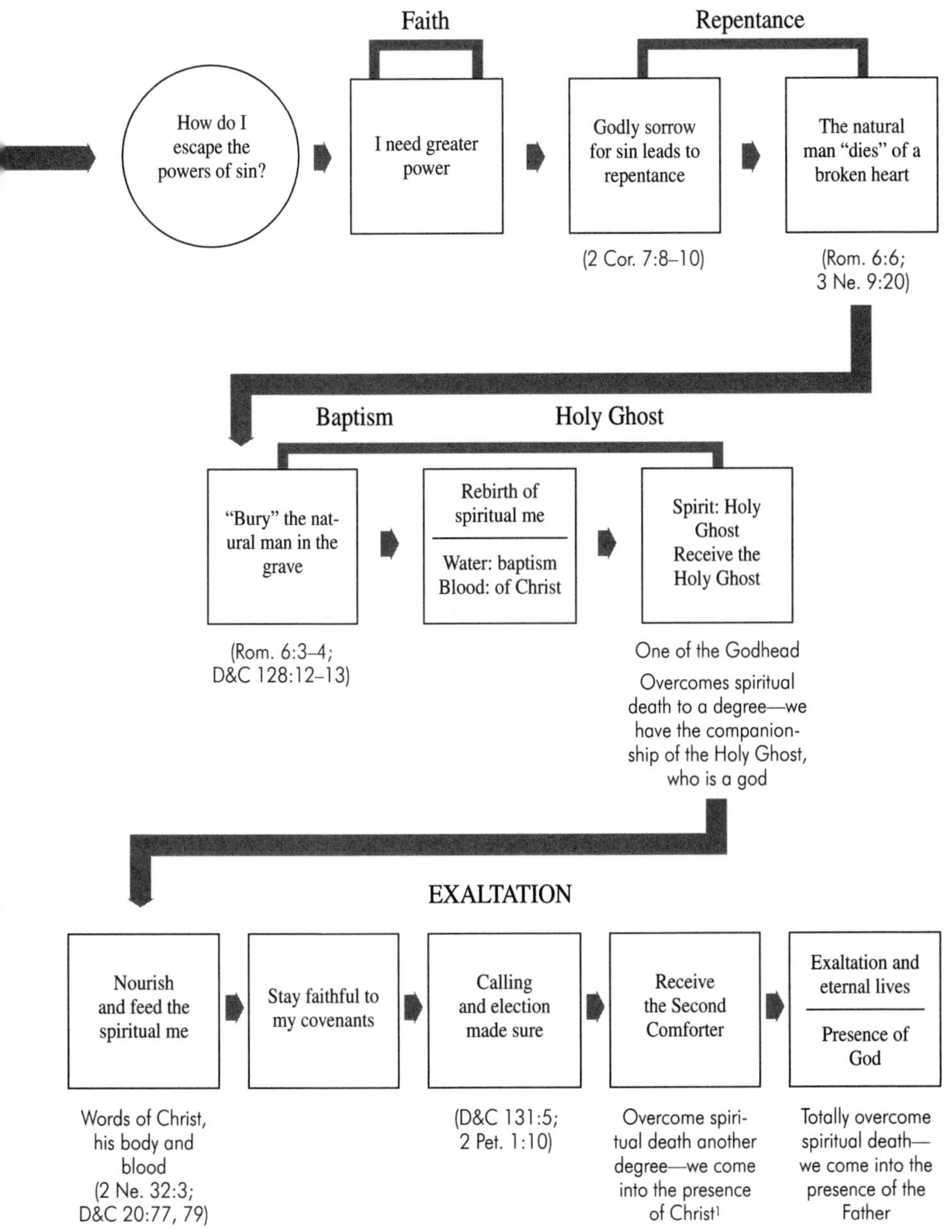

Notes

From Gerald N. Lund, *Jesus Christ, Key to the Plan of Salvation* (Salt Lake City: Bookcraft, 1991), 105–7.

1. *Teachings of the Prophet Joseph Smith,* sel. Joseph Fielding Smith (Salt Lake City: Deseret Book Co., 1976), 150–51.

Chapter 23

"I Would That Ye Should Be Perfect Even As I" (3 Nephi 12:48)

The Savior has given us a commandment, recorded twice in scripture, to be perfect, even as he or his Father in heaven is perfect (see Matt. 5:48; 3 Ne. 12:48; see also 3 Ne. 27:27). Jesus Christ not only has personally offered himself as a savior to fulfill the plan of salvation, but also has been set as a high standard for us to reach. In some way, this latter facet of the Savior's mission is integral to the plan of salvation too. The purpose of the plan of redemption is to bring us exaltation, and the work and sacrifice of the Savior are to lift us past the obstacles to that goal. As the Lord told the Saints, "Ye are not able to abide the presence of God now, neither the ministering of angels; wherefore, continue in patience until ye are perfected" (D&C 67:13).

Being Perfected

Many of us have wondered whether the commandment means we have to be perfect in order to achieve exaltation. Whether we answer this question yes or no depends on how we define the word *perfect.* One definition of *perfect* is "never having flaw or error." In this sense, only one person in all of human history—our Savior—has been perfect. Not once in all his mortal life—not as a child, not as an adult—was he out of harmony with the Father's will. In this sense, we clearly do *not* have to be perfect to be saved. Otherwise, there would be no hope for any of us, for as Paul said, "All have sinned, and come short of the glory of God" (Rom. 3:23).

But *perfect* can also mean "having all flaws and errors removed." Perhaps a clearer question to ask ourselves is "Do we have to be *perfected* to be exalted?" Here the scriptural answer is a resounding yes. In numerous references, the Lord says that no unclean thing can dwell in his presence (see 1 Ne. 10:21; Alma 7:21; 3 Ne. 27:19; Moses 6:57). Obviously, then, we must repent of those flaws identified as sins and become clean before we can be exalted. But what of other flaws—those that don't qualify as sins but are nevertheless imperfections?

The Prophet Joseph Smith said that our very faith rests in knowing that the attributes of God, such as his love, mercy, power, and knowledge, are all held in perfection.[1] An imperfect God would indeed be a contradiction in terms. At some point, then, if we are to become like God, we must be perfect, without any flaw or error. But must we achieve that state in this life? Here the prophets have spoken plainly. In the great sermon known as the King Follett discourse, the Prophet Joseph taught:

"When you climb up a ladder, you must begin at the bottom, and ascend step by step, until you arrive at the top; and so it is with the principles of the Gospel—you must begin with the first and go on until you learn all the principles of exaltation. But *it will be a great while after you have passed through the veil before you will have learned them. It is not all to be comprehended in this world; it will be a great work to learn our salvation and exaltation even beyond the grave.*"[2]

President Joseph F. Smith confirmed this idea:

"We do not look for absolute perfection in man. *Mortal man is not capable of being absolutely perfect.* Nevertheless, it is given to us to be as perfect in the sphere in which we are called to be and to act, as it is for the Father in heaven to be pure and righteous in the more exalted sphere in which he acts. We will find in the scriptures the words of the Savior himself to his disciples, in which he required that they should be perfect, even as their Father in heaven is perfect; that they should be righteous, even as he is righteous. I do not expect that we can be as perfect as Christ, that we can be as righteous as God. But I believe that we can strive for that perfection with the intelligence that we possess, and the knowledge that we have of the principles of life and salvation."[3]

Elder Joseph Fielding Smith spoke with equal clarity on the same subject:

"Salvation does not come all at once; we are commanded to be perfect even as our Father in heaven is perfect. *It will take us ages to accomplish this end, for there will be greater progress beyond the grave,* and it will be there that the faithful will overcome all things, and receive all things, even the fulness of the Father's glory. I believe the Lord meant just what he said: that we should be perfect, as our Father in heaven is perfect. That will not come all at once, but line upon line, and precept upon precept, example upon example, and even then not as long as we live in this mortal life, for *we will have to go even beyond the grave before we reach that perfection and shall be like God.*

"But here we lay the foundation."[4]

While these statements clarify that full perfection is not achievable in mortality, each also suggests that we should always strive for perfection in our lives. Perfection is our eternal goal; it is what we must eventually achieve if we are to become like our Father. A primary purpose of mortality is to come as close to perfection as possible before we die.

Is Perfection a Practical Goal?

The idea of achieving perfection, wonderful as it may be, seems staggering. How many of us have also wondered how to keep perfection as a goal without becoming so discouraged or depressed with our failings that we lose hope and give up trying to perfect ourselves? I would like to suggest eight practical ideas that can help us maintain the balance between eternal goals and mortal realities.

1. Remember that one of Satan's strategies, especially with good people, is to whisper in their ears: "If you are not perfect, you are failing." This is one of his most effective deceptions, for it contains some elements of truth. But it *is* deception nonetheless. While we should never be completely satisfied until we *are* perfect, we should recognize that God is pleased with every effort we make—no matter how faltering—to better ourselves. One of the most commonly listed attributes of God is that he is long-suffering and quick to show mercy. He wants us to strive for perfection, but the fact that we have not yet achieved it does not mean we are failing.

2. Feelings of failure are natural and common to most people. Elder Neal A. Maxwell put it this way:

"I speak, not to the slackers in the Kingdom, but to those who carry their own load and more; not to those lulled into false security, but to those buffeted by false insecurity, who, though laboring devotedly in the Kingdom, have recurring feelings of falling forever short. . . .

"The first thing to be said of this feeling of inadequacy is that it is normal. . . . Following celestial road signs while in telestial traffic jams is not easy, especially when we are not just moving next door—or even across town."[5]

Even such great men as Moses, Enoch, and Gideon were reluctant to believe that they were capable of doing what God called them to do. To their credit, they tried anyway—and, with the Lord's help, succeeded (see Ex. 4:10; Moses 6:31; Judg. 6:15).

3. The Lord himself has warned us about being unrealistic in our expectations. To a young prophet, deeply contrite over losing 116 pages of sacred manuscript, the Lord said, "Do not run faster or labor more than you have strength" (D&C 10:4). And after a lengthy and powerful call to repentance, King Benjamin gave this counsel: "See that all these things are done in wisdom and order; for it is not requisite that a man should run faster than he has strength. And again, it is expedient that he should be diligent, that thereby he might win the prize; therefore, all things must be done in order" (Mosiah 4:27).

4. Remember that the scriptures are replete with examples of great men and women who moved toward perfection *through missteps, in spite of failings,* and *having to overcome* their weaknesses. For example, the author of the second Gospel is the same Mark who earlier had left his missionary service, deserting Paul and Barnabus (see Acts 12:25; 13:13; 15:37–38). The same Corianton who was severely chastized for being immoral on his mission (see Alma 39:3–5, 11) was later listed among the faithful who helped bring peace to the Nephites (see Alma 49:30). Finally, the people of Melchizedek at one point had "waxed strong in iniquity and abomination; yea, they had all gone astray; they were full of all manner of wickedness." But "they did repent" and went to join the city of Enoch (Alma 13:17–18; see JST Gen. 14:34).

5. The Lord not only looks at our works, he also takes into account the desires of our hearts (see Alma 41:3; D&C 88:109; 137:9). This means that even if we don't always perfectly translate our good desires into action, these desires will be included in our final evaluation. Elder Bruce R. McConkie described what it takes to be saved:

"What we do in this life is chart a course leading to eternal life. That course begins here and now and continues in the realms ahead. We must determine in our hearts and in our souls, with all the power and ability we have, that from this time forward we will press on in righteousness; by so doing we can go where God and Christ are. *If we make that firm determination, and are in the course of our duty when this life is over, we will continue in that course in eternity.* That same spirit that possesses our bodies at the time we depart from this mortal life will have power to possess our bodies in the eternal world. *If we go out of this life loving the Lord, desiring righteousness, and seeking to acquire the attributes of godliness, we will have that same spirit in the eternal world,* and we will then continue to advance and progress until an ultimate, destined day when we will possess, receive, and inherit all things."[6]

6. "Hanging in there," in modern vernacular, is one of the most important keys to becoming perfected. This is what the scriptures mean by enduring to the end. Some people live out years of righteousness and then, when life takes a downward turn or becomes boring, tedious, and monotonous, they become discouraged and decide that striving for perfection is no longer worth their effort. After a remarkable life of faith and commitment, King David lost his exaltation because he did not continue in his set course.

Somehow, some of us get it into our heads that if we are not making great, dramatic leaps forward spiritually, we are not progressing. Actually, for most of us, the challenge of living the gospel is that progress comes in almost imperceptible increments. Very seldom can we look back over one day and see great progress. Becoming like God takes years and years of striving, and trying again.

We must also keep in mind that just because we are striving to better ourselves does not mean all problems, challenges, and setbacks will disappear. Elder Gordon B. Hinckley, quoting columnist Jenkins Lloyd Jones, reminded us that life will always have its challenges:

"Anyone who imagines that bliss is normal is going to waste a lot of time running around shouting that he's been robbed. The fact is that most putts don't drop, most beef is tough, most children grow up to be just people, most successful marriages require a high degree of mutual toleration, most jobs are more often dull than otherwise. Life is like an old time rail journey . . . delays, sidetracks, smoke, dust, cinders, and jolts, interspersed only occasionally by beautiful vistas and thrilling bursts of speed. The trick is to thank the Lord for letting you have the ride."[7]

7. To overcome the discouragement we feel as we see our failings and imperfections, we should remember that we learn and progress in spiritual things much the same way we learn and progress in physical things. Parents are not disappointed when their baby first learns to crawl before he walks. It is the natural order of things. Likewise, no one expects a student to understand calculus until he has first learned the numbers, then the laws of addition and subtraction, and then the mysteries of algebra and trigonometry. President Spencer W. Kimball noted that "working toward perfection is not a one-time decision but a process to be pursued throughout one's lifetime."[8] So why is it that we demand instant perfection? Why should we expect to run spiritual four-minute miles until we have jogged hundreds upon hundreds of times around the spiritual tracks of our lives? Why do we expect to work spiritual calculus before we have mastered the spiritual multiplication

tables? And why should we be disappointed when we cannot play spiritual symphonies if we have not yet taught ourselves to play the spiritual scales?

8. Finally and most important, perfection is not left up to us alone. Along the way, the Lord has given us innumerable helps: the ordinances of salvation, the organizations of the Church, the priesthood, the guidance and gifts of the Holy Ghost, repentance and forgiveness, temples, scriptures, home teaching and visiting teaching. The list goes on and on and includes everything the gospel and the Church have to offer.

Even with all this, however, the key to perfection is the Savior himself. If at times we feel weary or think that we can't do enough or do it well enough to be perfected, we have lost sight of the Atonement. We are in a mindset where we think we are supposed to make gods of ourselves. Stated that way, of course, the notion is foolish, but we must remember that Jesus Christ, because of his atoning sacrifice and his power, is the one who makes godhood—and glorification, sanctification, perfection, and everything else that goes with it—possible for us. His is the power behind our quest for perfection. So, though the goal may at times seem intimidating and the work overwhelming, he can say to us, "Come unto me, all ye that labour and are heavy laden, and I will give you rest. Take my yoke upon you, and learn of me; for I am meek and lowly in heart: and ye shall find rest unto your souls. For my yoke is easy, and my burden is light" (Matt. 11:28–30). Remember, the burden of perfecting ourselves is his burden too; and since he is carrying it with us and for us, it is light enough for us to carry.

Perfection is our goal. But let us not be thrown off course when we do not fully achieve it in this life. And most of all, let us, as we strive for that lofty goal, remember the Lord's promise to those of us who so keenly sense our weaknesses and inadequacies: "If men come unto me I will show unto them their weakness. I give unto men weakness that they may be humble; and my grace is sufficient for all men that humble themselves before me; for if they humble themselves before me, and have faith in me, then will I make weak things become strong unto them" (Ether 12:27).

Notes

From Gerald N. Lund, *Jesus Christ, Key to the Plan of Salvation* (Salt Lake City: Bookcraft, 1991), 168–75.

1. See Joseph Smith, *Lectures on Faith,* comp. N. B. Lundwall (Salt Lake City: N. B. Lundwall, n.d.), lecture 4, 1–19.
2. Joseph Smith, *Teachings of the Prophet Joseph Smith,* sel. Joseph Fielding Smith (Salt Lake City: Deseret Book Co., 1976), 348; emphasis added.

3. Joseph F. Smith, *Gospel Doctrine,* 5th ed. (Salt Lake City, Deseret Book Co., 1939), 132; emphasis added.
4. Joseph Fielding Smith, *Doctrines of Salvation,* 3 vols., comp. Bruce R. McConkie (Salt Lake City: Bookcraft, 1954–56), 2:18; emphasis added.
5. Neal A. Maxwell, "Notwithstanding My Weakness," *Ensign,* November 1976, 12.
6. Bruce R. McConkie, "The Seven Deadly Heresies," in *Speeches of the Year, 1980* (Provo: Brigham Young University, 1981), 78–79; emphasis added.
7. As quoted in Gordon B. Hinckley, address given to religious educators, September 1978, 4.
8. Spencer W. Kimball, "Hold Fast to the Iron Rod," *Ensign,* November 1978, 6.

Chapter 24

Some Steps for Achieving Perfection

I would like to explore with you something that I have wrestled with for many years, and just in the last few months I have heard some things that have given me a new perspective and, I think, a new hope that I'd never had before. To begin the chapter, I would like to share with you five statements. The first is by President Marion G. Romney in October conference 1956. I suppose this ought to be on the mirror of every Latter-day Saint in the Church: "No Latter-day Saint should be content to stand day after day in the same place on the way to eternal life."[1] In a way, that's a little discouraging, but what a great concept.

The second statement was made by one of my professors at BYU many years ago. He said something like this: "The terrible predicament with most men is they know what is right but want what is wrong."

The third statement was by Alma to his son, Helaman. After drawing on the symbolism of the Liahona, he said in Alma 37:46, "O my son, do not let us be slothful because of the easiness of the way." I suppose that by "easiness" he does not mean lacking effort, but rather the simplicity of the way.

The fourth statement was by a little boy who was in a bit of an argument with his mother over whether or not he ought to go to sacrament meeting. His mother told him, "We must go. Heavenly Father wants us to go." And the little boy said, "Why do we have to go to sacrament meeting anyway?" His mother answered, "Well, we partake of the sacrament and we remember Jesus, and then we learn more about the gospel." The little boy responded, "Don't we already know more than we live?"

The fifth statement is a little ditty I once overheard. It goes like this:

I want to be good,
And do what I should;
But I can't seem to do it
Whenever I would.

In the case of many active Latter-day Saints, I think the predicament that we are in is that we know what is right and we want what is right, but we can't quite pull it off in our lives.

I was thinking the other day about parents yelling at the children. We know what is right and we want what is right. And yet sometimes, even as we're yelling at them, we find ourselves in the back of our minds saying, *Wait a minute. Stop it. What are you doing? Get hold of yourself.* And it doesn't work.

So if I can, I would like to quickly share with you some principles of spiritual development that I've been trying to articulate for myself. These principles have been very helpful not only in my deciding what to do, but in giving me hope that I can do it. Let me list five principles of spiritual development. The first two of these I'm going to cover very quickly.

Principle number one: To be saved we must be perfect. There is no lesser acceptance for celestialization. One must be perfect because the basic law of God's nature is that no unclean thing can dwell in his presence (see Moses 6:57).

Principle number two: We are physical *and* spiritual beings. We have a dual nature. We sometimes forget that. I used to tell my institute students, especially the young men, "Your problem is that you're running around falling in love with other people's 'houses.' All you're looking at is the 'house' [the body] they live in and you're not nearly as concerned with the person who lives in it." We have two natures—the outer, physical self and the inward spirit, or spiritual being. And to be saved, we must perfect both of those. We cannot be saved without both being perfect (see D&C 93:33–34).

Principle three: If we are going to be saved, two things are necessary. We must have knowledge, but we must also have skill. And this was something that really came home forcefully to me one day. We were at a symposium at BYU for Church educators, and Brother Bruce C. Hafen, the president of Ricks College (now Elder Bruce C. Hafen of the Seventy), spoke to us. He articulated some things that I think are very crucial:

"It is a fact of nature that salvation is a process as well as a goal. Salvation involves growth, development and change. The process implies that in mortality we must learn capacities and skills as well as picked-up information. Nobody knows more about the blessings of paying tithing than somebody who's paid it. . . . Imagine, if you will, an innovative music school that tries a revolutionary new approach to teaching the piano. It's called the 'Think Method.' In this course the piano students don't have to practice. The school would teach all the rudiments. They would describe in detail how to move one's finger. They would go deeply into music theory and music history. They would teach thoroughly how to read music. The students would memorize all the best books that have ever been written on how to play the piano. Let's say the course would last a full baccalaureate four years. Each student would have a project such as memorizing a score of a major concerto. They would be able to close their eyes and the music for both the piano and the orchestra would flow in front of their eyes. They could tell you anything about that concerto. Finally, on graduation day, the 'do-it-without-practice' student comes to the stage to play the concerto for the audience. What do you suppose will happen? Not much. Why? Because some things can be learned only by practice."[2]

Now that really hit home with me as a teacher in religion because I think in the past I have been guilty primarily of emphasizing knowledge. We talk about the importance of skills, but I'm not sure I have ever even concentrated on how to *teach* the skills of gospel living. Normally we just stress the *principles* of gospel living.

Spiritual development principle number four: The process of learning skills is similar in both the physical and spiritual realms. This came as a spiritual revelation to me. I'm a slow learner. Some of you have probably thought through this all by yourself. The other day it occurred to me that the learning process in the spiritual realm is probably in many ways closely parallel to how we learn in the physical realm. Let me stop there and list six observations I have made about how we learn in the physical realm and then apply them to the spiritual.

1. When my son was about fifteen months old, I noticed some things about his physical development. I don't know why I had never articulated this before, but it occurred to me that a person must learn how to make his body obey his will. Let me repeat: *A person must learn how to make his body obey his will.*

I watched my son one day lying on his back in his playpen. We had one of those big, fancy play boxes hanging just over him. It was brightly colored and, I suppose, very attractive to his eyes. As I watched him I could sense that he wanted to reach out and grab hold of that. And you could see him concentrating and his mind telling his body, "Grab that." And yet his hand wouldn't respond. Only gradually did he learn to make his hand obey what his mind told it to do. I watched him go through that kind of a process in crawling and walking. And now he's an adult and runs everywhere.

We saw that same process in his communication skills. One night I was working at the table and he was toddling around and he would say, "Dad," and I would say, "What?" "Mumble, mumble, mumble." And then he would pick up something else and run over and say, "Dad." And I would say, "What?" "Mumble, mumble, mumble." And away he would go. As I watched him, I really believed he was telling me something. But his tongue would not obey what his mind was telling it to say. He had not yet learned to make his tongue obey his mind.

2. This mastery of the body—and *mastery* is what we're after—comes only step by step. First we learn to get even the basic body movements down. Then we learn to crawl. Then to walk, and then to run. That is true of virtually everything we do. Piano players start by learning the scales. A baseball player has got to master some basic skills before he or she can start doing the things he or she wants to do.

3. The learning of any skill is the process of moving from the simple to the complex. Can you imagine me taking a five-year-old and saying, "Honey, when you get into college, you're going to need calculus. So sit down and let me teach you some calculus." Before I can teach calculus I have to teach trigonometry, before trigonometry, algebra, and before algebra, they've got to know the basic math. And that's where a five-year-old is, just basically learning the numbers and then, later, the multiplication tables and so on. That is true in any physical skill you can name. That was the marvelous insight from Elder Hafen's example. We have to develop by moving from the simple to the complex.

4. In the physical realm, the body must not only develop the ability to obey the mind, but it must develop the strength and endurance. One day a former student of mine came to me and we were talking. He mentioned that he ran in the July 24th marathon in Salt Lake City. So I quizzed him a little about it. This young man happened to come in, as I remember, fourth or fifth in his class. I was impressed. So I asked him how he got interested in that. When he had run in high school, he had started running cross-country, and out of that he developed this interest in the marathon. I said, "Well, is this your first year?" "No," he said. "I first ran four years ago." "How did you do?" He said, "I walked the last five miles and crawled the last 100 yards, but I made it. Then," he said, "the next year I ran all the way. Last year I decreased my time fifteen minutes. This year I decreased my time eighteen minutes."

Now what do you suppose he had been doing in between one July and the next July? He knows *how* to run the marathon, he has the *skills;* but he needed to build his body's ability to *endure.* I can go to the top of Emigration Canyon, where the marathon starts, and I can tell my body, "Okay, here we go, body; hang in there until the end." But it's not enough to want it. I have to build skills *and* endurance.

5. Strength and endurance are always increased by pushing against the limits. If I wanted to prepare for the marathon and just jogged around the living room, I probably wouldn't have a lot of success. It is interesting that it is the record book that is largely responsible for people breaking the records. Do you know what I mean by that? When I was in high school, in the football locker room we had a huge sign that had been put up by the coach. It said, "'The four-minute mile is all in your head.'—Roger Bannister." Now maybe you don't remember back then, but at that time in many people's minds the four-minute mile was an impossibility for a human being. The fastest runners were down to 4:04 or 4:02. And Roger Bannister said that the four-minute mile was right there in their heads. A short time later, Roger Bannister became the first person in the history of modern track and field to break the four-minute mile when he ran the mile in 3:59:04 in 1954 in England. Now the world's record for the mile is under 3 minutes and 50 seconds. Why? Because each time a new record is set, it becomes a new mark to try to break. In other words, it becomes a new limit for people to push against. Every time somebody breaks that record, somebody else has to push against that limit. And they drive themselves further and further until they achieve it.[3]

6. The more one develops his skills, his strength and endurance, the more free he becomes to do what he wants. It's easy to say, "I'd like to play in the World Series." I may have the will, but I don't have the capacity. And in the physical realm, I reach that capacity by constantly increasing my skills, my strength, and my endurance.

Let's apply those principles to the spiritual realm for a moment because, as I said, I'm convinced that the two are parallel and very, very similar. Without going through them one by one, let me summarize:

The frustration of most people in the spiritual realm is they expect an instant ability to play a spiritual symphony without first mastering the spiritual scales. They want to work spiritual calculus before they master the spiritual multiplication tables, or they want to run a spiritual marathon without spiritually jogging first.

I am convinced that Satan, understanding this principle, very often encourages us to be discouraged. Is that a proper way to put that? In other words, I read something President Kimball or President Benson or President Hinckley said and I think, *Oh, how could I ever be like that?* Or I say to myself, *All right, now this week I'm going to have meaningful prayers.* And yet at the end of the week I haven't achieved that. And so what do I tend to do? I tend to give up.

If I said to you, "Right now we're going to go out to the track and we're going to run a mile," some of you would not be the least bit surprised if you had to walk four of the eight laps, would you? Then why, in the spiritual realm, do you expect to run a spiritual four-minute mile without working up to it spiritually? We have a tendency to be so hard on ourselves that we end up getting discouraged. Yet that same thing is not true in the physical realm. You don't give up because you can't run four-minute miles the first night you go out on the track. Then why hold ourselves to that standard of ultimate perfection in the spiritual realm? Perfection is what we are eventually striving for, but we should understand we won't get there in one giant step.

So that leads me to *spiritual development principle six:* We reach perfection in a step-by-step process, teaching our spirit to obey our will. You see, I have the same problem in the spiritual realm that I do in the physical. I say to myself, *Don't yell at the children.* But until I teach my spiritual self to obey my will, I can't expect it to obey, just like I can't expect my will to stand up and say, "Run the marathon." It's not going to happen until I have developed some intermediate skills. So let me suggest four steps, four processes that one could go through as we strive to perfection.

1. Start from where you are. Sometimes we get discouraged at how far away from perfection we are. Going back to our running the mile example, some of us would be in such poor physical shape that we would have to walk every lap for a time. Some may even have to hire a taxi to take us a lap or two. Well, the same principle is true spiritually speaking. So, we start from where we are. Even if that position is far down the spiritual scale. Start there and work up.

In Matthew 19, an interesting little interchange takes place between the Savior and a young man. You've heard this story many times, but in that story I think there's some great counsel for us. Let me paraphrase. A young man (starting in verse 16) comes to the Savior and says, "Good Master, what one good thing, what good thing shall I do, that I may have eternal life?" Do you notice the singular? That would be nice, wouldn't it, if we could just go to the Lord and say, "What thing do I have to do?" and he would say, "Do this thing or that and you'll be saved." Then we could say, "All right, exaltation is taken care of." It doesn't work that way. The Lord chides the young man a little bit for trying to impress him with titles and then he says, "If you will enter into life [i.e., eternal life] keep the commandments."

The young man said unto him, "Which?" That is an interesting question. What it sounds like he wants to know is, Which commandments can I *break* and still be saved? If you ask which commandments you have to live to be saved, in a way you're asking to know which ones you *don't* have to live. The Savior answered, "Thou shalt do no murder, Thou shalt not commit adultery, Thou shalt not steal, Thou shalt not bear false witness, Honour thy father and thy mother: and, Thou shalt love thy neighbor as thyself" (vv. 18–19). It seems to me that the Savior is saying, "That's really a question you shouldn't have to ask. The commandments are obvious. You know what they are." And the young man said to him, "All these things have I kept from my youth up: what lack I yet?" (v. 20). Well, I know what my response would have been to that last question—"a little humility." But the Savior simply said, "If thou wilt be perfect, go and sell that thou hast, and give to the poor, and thou shalt have treasure in heaven: and come and follow me. But when the young man heard that saying, he went away sorrowful: for he had great possessions" (vv. 21–22).

Now I've heard many people, particularly in the Christian world, teach that if you want to achieve perfection, you must sell everything you have. Maybe I'm misinterpreting the scripture, but I really believe that if somebody else had gone to the Lord and said, "What lack I yet?" the answer may have been a little different.

I know a young man who perhaps would get a different answer; the Lord might say to him, "Sell your Corvette," and he would go away sorrowing. And the Lord might say to another man, "Give up golf," and he would go away sorrowing because he just couldn't give that up. You see, it doesn't matter much what we are doing if it is stopping us from coming closer to God and following him. Then it becomes a problem for us. When I say start from where we are, we must ask that question: "What lack I yet?" I think it is one of the most profound questions we can ask ourselves, to honestly and sincerely look into our heart and say, "Where do I need to change?" That may be discouraging because most of us who are desirous of being better will grab a pencil and start scribbling furiously. We will have dozens of things we'll want to write down. But remember, we have to start from where we are. We look at the things that we think are really stopping our spiritual progression and then ask ourselves, "Of all of these things, which one probably is having the greatest negative influence on my spirituality?" Then start there and try to change.

2. Set reachable goals of self-mastery. My wife and I were talking about this one day when she was preparing to teach her Young Women class a lesson on the sacrament. We were talking about the deep covenants of the sacrament and the power that comes through the sacrament, and suddenly it occurred to me, "We're asking those girls to run spiritual four-minute miles." So we sat down and outlined some specific beginning steps of mastery. Some of the girls can start at step three, but some may have to start at step one, which is, "Sit quietly and don't talk from the moment the sacrament hymn begins until the deacons sit down." In the case of some of the girls that she had in her class, that would be a major change. But why expect them to master covenants until they can get that basic skill down? You're asking them to run when they haven't even learned to crawl. Once you get that mastered, then move to step 2, "Concentrate on the words of the sacrament hymn." Once that becomes a habitual skill, then three, "Ponder the words of the sacrament prayer." My wife outlined fifteen goals a girl can choose and move through progressively.

I may as well warn you, before we talk about process number three, that the Lord is going to raise the hurdles. He is like a great coach. Let's suppose you are trying to run the high hurdles. The first time you run the track and clear the hurdles, the coach comes up and pats you on the back and says, "That's great," and then he raises the hurdles. Sometimes we get angry with God because he keeps raising the hurdles. I suspect that a great majority of you, when you were little, prayed for some ridiculous little thing—a lost nickel, some little thing you wanted. You went to the Lord and asked in simple faith and the Lord blessed you with an answer. That happened to me as a child. But I don't think that as adults that we typically pray for lost nickels and get answers, because the Lord is saying, "You've reached that hurdle. Now I want you to stretch a little." And so as soon as you get one spiritual skill mastered, the Lord will say, "All right, now let's force you back and let you take another run at it." In the physical realm we develop greatness by pushing against our limits. The same holds true in the spiritual realm.

3. *After you've set reachable goals, plead with God for power to master these goals.* Sometimes we try to do it ourselves. Sometimes we forget that the Lord is there. We need to remember the idea of putting a vertical dimension into your problem-solving efforts (that is, calling upon God) rather than thinking only of the horizontal dimension (that is, relying only on what you can do yourself).

Elder Hartman Rector tells the story of a good man who had a Latter-day Saint wife, and the stake missionaries had been working with him for years to join the Church. He believed it was true and he wanted to join, but he couldn't stop smoking. Hartman Rector, under inspiration, suggested they fast and pray about it. Six stake missionaries, the man, and his wife fasted for two days. To break the fast they all met and knelt in a circle, and one by one they each prayed that this man would be given strength. The man was the last to pray. As he said "Amen," he jumped to his feet and said, "My desire to smoke is gone." And that is the last cigarette he ever smoked. Somehow they introduced a vertical dimension into the relationship. They brought the Lord into it.

So, the process is (1) start from where you are; (2) set an achievable goal; (3) then call on the Lord for power to reach it. Then step number four is very simple. Start over again, only raise the hurdle.

As Marion G. Romney said, we should not be content to stand in the same place day after day. I'm convinced that if we move in that step-by-step fashion, if that is the mode of life we're living, even though we may still be miles from perfection when we die, if we're on the right path and traveling in the right direction, the Lord will then speed up the process and we will see the reality come to pass.

Notes

From an address delivered 17 October 1980, Salt Lake Institute of Religion, Salt Lake City, Utah.

1. Marion G. Romney, in Conference Report, October 1956, 16.
2. Bruce C. Hafen, "On Being Believing," in *A Symposium on the New Testament* (Salt Lake City: The Church of Jesus Christ of Latter-day Saints, 1980).
3. *Guinness Book of World Records,* 1987 edition (Toronto: Bantam Books, 1987), 647.

Chapter 25

What Can We Learn About Becoming Perfect from the Arrest, Trial, and Crucifixion of Jesus?

We have been told many times that there is, in the life of Jesus, a model to which we can turn as we seek to mold and sculpt our own lives into works of perfection. It matters not at which point we focus the eye of scrutiny. Examine the life of Christ as minutely as you wish. No hint of blemished conduct, no trace of lost control, no moment of foolish passion, no spot of crumbling weakness can be found. Jesus is the perfect man. Every moment of his recorded life inspires those who would bring themselves to that level of perfection marked out in the indelible chalk of Christ's own life.

In the trial, arrest, and execution of Jesus we find no exception to this unmatched faultlessness. In those hours of life when he was being ground with merciless pressure, his balance was never threatened, his composure never marred. The betrayal of Judas, the denial of Peter, the gross injustice of his trial, the savagery of the mob, the cowardice of Pilate, even the weeping of his mother at the foot of the cross—nothing could loosen his hold on perfect control; nothing could lessen his total mastery. Christ's marvelous ability to face adversity without loss of balance or faith in God is one of the great lessons we can learn from him.

In addition, he taught by his own example that God's will takes priority over all. Submission to the Father is paramount even if it means pain, ridicule, and death. Obedience must remain firm under all conditions, even unto death, if one is to be found worthy of him (see D&C 98:14–15). Here again, the Son set the perfect example for us. Torture, injustice, the supreme irony of being condemned for blasphemy, the agony in the garden, the sadistically cruel death by crucifixion—all of these combined could not divert him from his determination to do the will of the Father.

Sometimes when circumstances corner a man and leave him no alternative, he may show great courage and strength of will. However, Christ showed those qualities throughout, even though he could have escaped at any moment. The powers of heaven, we are told, are controlled by righteousness (see D&C 121:36). Keeping in mind that his was a perfectly sinless life, fathom, if you can, the powers Jesus had at his command. How pitifully futile the might of Pilate's Roman garrison would have been in the face of the twelve heavenly legions Christ could have summoned but didn't (see Matt. 26:53). How easy it would have been for the one who cast out devils to banish the arrogant high priest. How elementary for one who loosed the tongues of the dumb to stop the tongues of false witnesses. Yet he who brought worlds and galaxies into being stood mute before his mortal accusers. He who stilled the rushing winds and pounding waves of the Sea of Galilee stilled not the stormy cries of "Crucify him! Crucify him!" He who had escaped unharmed from the angry mob at Nazareth (see Luke 4:29–30) faced the small band of arresting soldiers with a simple "I am he" (John 18:5). The awesome, infinite power at his command was not unleashed to spare himself the least pain, the smallest discomfort. His will was irrevocably interwoven with that of the Father's, and nothing deterred him from its accomplishment.

One cannot help but be struck with the tremendous difference between Christ's behavior during those terrible hours and the actions of those around him. Throughout, it becomes clear that Jesus was the *only* one who was not thrown off balance by the passions of that night and the following day. Judas betrayed him, then committed suicide, apparently in a great overflowing feeling of guilty remorse. The armed party sent out to arrest him fell back in fright when he told them he was Jesus. Peter vowed perfect support and then failed miserably as fear washed out his determination. The high priest was thrown into a rage by the calm demeanor of the accused. Pilate, symbol and wielder of Roman might, became a frightened vacillating man when faced with the King of the Jews. Even the hardened Roman soldier was awed by Christ's manner of dying. Throughout, it becomes clear that Jesus was not the victim but the Master.

The tragedies and tests of life strike us all; they are inevitable. But they need not hurtle us down to destruction or defeat. Let the storms descend, let the winds howl in all their fury. By the eloquent testimony of his own life, the Master has shown the true meaning of living in a house built upon the rock.

Note

From "I Have a Question," *Ensign,* July 1975, 31.

Chapter 26

"As God Now Is, Man May Be"

Is President Lorenzo Snow's oft-repeated statement—"As man now is, God once was; as God now is, man may be"—accepted as official doctrine by the Church?

To my knowledge there has been no "official" pronouncement by the First Presidency declaring that President Snow's couplet is to be accepted as doctrine. But that is not a the only criterion for determining whether or not it is doctrine.

Generally, the First Presidency issues official doctrinal declarations when there is a general misunderstanding of the doctrine on the part of many people. Therefore, the Church teaches many principles which are accepted as doctrines but which the First Presidency has seen no need to declare in an official pronouncement. This particular doctrine has been taught not only by Lorenzo Snow, fifth president of the Church, but also by others of the Brethren before and since that time.

In her biography of her brother, Eliza R. Snow explains the circumstances which led Lorenzo Snow to pen the famous couplet: "Being present at a 'Blessing Meeting,' in the Temple, previous to his baptism into the Church; after listening to several patriarchal blessings pronounced upon the heads of different individuals with whose history he was acquainted, and of whom he knew the Patriarch was entirely ignorant; he was struck with astonishment to hear the peculiarities of those persons positively and plainly referred to in their blessings. And, as he afterwards expressed, he was convinced that an influence, superior to human prescience, dictated the words of the one who officiated.

"The Patriarch was the father of Joseph, the Prophet. That was the first time

Lorenzo had met him. After the services, they were introduced, and Father Smith said to my brother that he would soon be convinced of the truth of the latter-day work, and be baptized; and he said: 'You will become as great as you can possibly wish—EVEN AS GREAT AS GOD, and you cannot wish to be greater.'"[1]

Lorenzo Snow was baptized a short time later and began his service in the Church. In the spring of 1840 he was called to serve a mission in the British Isles. Before his departure he was in the home of a Church member who was preaching a sermon on the parable of the laborers in the vineyard (see Matt. 20:1–16). According to Elder Snow, "While attentively listening to his explanation, the Spirit of the Lord rested mightily upon me—the eyes of my understanding were opened, and I saw as clear as the sun at noonday, with wonder and astonishment, the pathway of God and man. I formed the following couplet which expresses the *revelation,* as it was shown me, and explains Father Smith's dark saying to me at a blessing meeting in the Kirtland Temple, prior to my baptism. . . .

"As man now is, God once was:

"As God now is, man may be.

"I FELT THIS TO BE A SACRED COMMUNICATION, WHICH I RELATED TO NO ONE EXCEPT MY SISTER Eliza, until I reached England, when in a confidential private conversation with President Brigham Young, in Manchester, I related to him this extraordinary manifestation."[2]

President Snow's son LeRoi later told that the Prophet Joseph Smith confirmed the validity of the revelation Elder Snow had received: "Soon after his return from England, in January, 1843, Lorenzo Snow related to the Prophet Joseph Smith his experience in Elder Sherwood's home. This was in a confidential interview in Nauvoo. The Prophet's reply was: 'Brother Snow, that is a true gospel doctrine, and it is a revelation from God to you.'"[3]

The Prophet Joseph Smith himself publicly taught the doctrine the following year, 1844, during a funeral sermon for Elder King Follett: "God himself was once as we are now, and is an exalted man, and sits enthroned in yonder heavens! . . . It is the first principle of the Gospel to know for a certainty the character of God, and to know that we may converse with him as one man converses with another, and that he was once a man like us; yea, that God himself, the Father of us all, dwelt on an earth, the same as Jesus Christ himself did."[4]

Once the Prophet Joseph had taught the doctrine publicly, Elder Snow also felt free to publicly teach it, and it was a common theme of his teachings throughout his life. About ten years before his death, while serving as the President of the Quorum of the Twelve, President Snow incorporated his original couplet into a longer poem. He addressed the poem to the Apostle Paul, who had written the following to the Philippian Saints:

"Let this mind be in you, which was also in Christ Jesus:

"Who, being in the form of God, thought it not robbery to be equal with God" (Philip. 2:5–6).

Part of the poem reads:

The boy, like to his father grown,
Has but attained unto his own;
To grow to sire from state of son,
Is not 'gainst Nature's course to run.
A son of God, like God to be,
Would not be robbing Deity.[5]

Numerous sources could be cited, but one should suffice to show that this doctrine is accepted and taught by the Brethren. In an address in 1971, President Joseph Fielding Smith, then serving as President of the Quorum of the Twelve Apostles, said:

"I think I can pay no greater tribute to [President Lorenzo Snow and Elder Erastus Snow] than to preach again *that glorious doctrine* which they taught and which was one of the favorite themes, particularly of President Lorenzo Snow. . . .

"We have been promised by the Lord that if we know how to worship, and know what we worship, we may come unto the Father in his name, and in due time receive of his fulness. We have the promise that if we keep his commandments, we shall receive of his fulness and be glorified in him as he is in the Father.

"This is a doctrine which delighted president Snow, *as it does all of us.* Early in his ministry he received by direct, personal revelation the knowledge that (in the Prophet Joseph Smith's language), 'God himself was once as we are now, and is an exalted man, and sits enthroned in yonder heavens,' and that men 'have got to learn how to be Gods . . . the same as all Gods have done before.'

"After this doctrine had been taught by the Prophet, President Snow felt free to teach it also, and he summarized it in one of the best known couplets in the Church. . . .

"This same doctrine has of course been known to the prophets of all the ages, and President Snow wrote an excellent poetic summary of it."[6]

It is clear that the teaching of President Lorenzo Snow is both acceptable and accepted doctrine in the Church today.

Notes

From "I Have a Question," *Ensign,* February 1982, 39–40.

1. Eliza R. Snow, *Biography and Family Record of Lorenzo Snow* (Salt Lake City: Deseret News Co., 1984), 9–10.
2. Ibid., 46-47; emphasis added. Brigham Young was President of the Quorum of the Twelve at the time.
3. LeRoi C. Snow, "Devotion to a Divine Inspiration," *Improvement Era,* June 1919, 656.
4. Joseph Smith, *Teachings of the Prophet Joseph Smith,* sel. Joseph Fielding Smith (Salt Lake City: Deseret Book Co., 1976), 345–46.
5. As cited in Snow, "Devotion to a Divine Inspiration," 661.
6. Address on Snow Day, given at Snow College, 14 May 1971, 1, 3–4; emphasis added.

Chapter 27

Our Legacy: Faith, Covenant, and Power

As you know, the year 1997 was the sesquicentennial celebration of the pioneers' arrival in the Salt Lake Valley in 1847. We have had a chance to reexamine our heritage, that priceless legacy that has been passed down to us, whether through blood lineage—through our own ancestors—or through those who are our spiritual ancestors. One thing began to bother me, however, as the year of the sesquicentennial celebration progressed. I am sure you heard many of the stories of those pioneers and their endurance of suffering and their great sacrifice. Some of those are deeply moving, almost unbelievable. Let me just mention a few stories in quick review in order to set up the point I would like to discuss.

The Suffering Saints

I think of Elizabeth Horrocks Jackson, who was part of the Martin handcart company. She and her husband were converts from England. She had three little children. Somewhere near Red Butte, Wyoming (near present-day Casper), they were caught in a terrible blizzard, and her husband collapsed, soaking wet and freezing cold. A few nights later at about midnight she woke up and realized that he was lying dead beside her. She cried out for those nearby to help her, but they were too weak and exhausted to do anything before morning. And so she had to lie there during the night without sleep, knowing that here she was now a widow, stranded in the wilderness of America with three children.[1]

I think of Jens and Elsie Nielson, two converts from Denmark. Jens was a well-to-do farmer. He and his wife joined the Church and, of course, wanted to come to Zion. They came across in that same year, only they were assigned to the James Willie handcart company. By the time they reached the sixth crossing of the Sweetwater, they were out of food. They had been living on less than four ounces of flour for more than two weeks. They learned that the rescue wagons were close by, just seventeen miles away. The only problem was that in their exhausted and very poorly clad condition, they had to pull up over what is called Rocky Ridge in order to get there. They rose that morning and started. The last of them did not arrive until twenty-seven hours later, in the midst of a howling Wyoming blizzard. Jens Nielson's feet were frozen so badly that he would walk with a limp for the rest of his life. Partway up one of those hills Jens collapsed in the snow. Their son had already died, and another girl they were bringing with them had also died. Jens collapsed in the snow and said to Elsie, "I cannot go farther. You leave me and go on alone." And Elsie said, "Ride. I can't leave you. I can pull the cart." Weeping that he had to rely on his wife, he climbed into the cart and she pulled him the rest of the way into camp. The amazing thing is that Jens Nielson was six feet two inches tall and weighed about 220 pounds. Elsie Nielson was four feet eleven and weighed about 98 pounds.[2]

Drusilla Hendricks lived just outside of Far West in 1838. One night there was a knock on the door, and some of the brethren of the Mormon militia asked her husband, James, to get his rifle and ride with them. Some of the mob had kidnapped three of the brethren and were taking them back to Jackson County to execute them. As James got his rifle and started for the door, Drusilla, trying to be brave, said, "Now, James, don't you go getting yourself shot in the back." The brethren rode all night. The next morning they came upon Crooked River and, not realizing that the mob was camped just across the river in a thicket of willows, they started to ford the river. A picket guard saw them coming and opened fire. David W. Patten, a member of the Quorum of the Twelve, took a ball in the stomach and died that afternoon, the first apostle killed in this dispensation. Patrick O'Bannion was hit in the face and killed instantly. James Hendricks, seeing that he was under fire in the middle of the river, turned to run for cover, and a ball caught him in the back of the neck and he dropped in the water, paralyzed from the neck down.

Drusilla Hendricks had six children, the oldest ten years old. For the next six years she had to not only earn a living for those children, knitting mittens, making gingerbread and ginger beer to sell on holidays, but also she had to lift her husband every time he had to move. In her own words she said, "I had to lift my husband at least 50 times a day and in doing so I had to strain every nerve."[3]

A man named Stillman Pond, who left Nauvoo late in September 1846, headed for Winter Quarters with his wife and eight children. By the time he reached the halfway point, he was so sick with dysentery that for the last hundred and fifty miles he was too weak to sit in the wagon seat, so he drove his wagon by looking through a knothole in the front running board and driving it with his arm up and over the running board, holding the reins. By the time January 1847 came his wife and all but one of his eight children had died. He had lost almost every single member of his family.[4]

We could go on and on with such stories. Martha Pane Jones Thomas was driven out of Far West in the winter of 1838. In one very poignant paragraph, she writes, "The snow was about six inches deep. The children all barefoot, except the oldest boy. To hear them crying at night with their feet cracked and bleeding was a grievous sight for a mother to bear." And then she concludes, "I would often grease them and put on clean stockings, instead of making them wash them when going to bed."[5]

When we sing "Come, Come, Ye Saints," it is traditional in the Church that on the fourth verse we lower our voices and sing with hushed reverence, "And should we die before our journey's through . . ." But I'll tell you the verse that impresses me. It's the second verse: "Why should we mourn or think our lot is hard? 'Tis not so; all is right."[6] Why should they mourn? I can give you about ten thousand reasons. I could go on and on listing reasons for complaining.

A Legacy of Suffering?

One of the things that bothered me as I read those stories and heard others tell them or share them was that I started hearing things like this: "I don't know if I could do that." "I don't know if I would have been strong enough." "I wouldn't have made a very good pioneer." One day after a member of my ward said that, I remembered an experience I had had when my wife and I were in Israel many years ago. We were at the historic Wailing Wall and one of our number noticed a young Jewish boy at the western wall, in the attitude of prayer. When he finished, my colleague struck up a conversation with him, and in the course of the conversation he learned the boy was American. He had come to Israel to worship at the Wailing Wall. And then my colleague said, "Do you believe as a Jew that you're part of a chosen people?" He said, "Of course." And then my colleague said, "For what were you chosen?" The young man's answer was tragic: "We were chosen by God for suffering. God needed somebody to pour his suffering upon and he chose us."

Why did I think of that story when this woman in our ward said, "I don't know if I could have done that; I don't know if I would be strong enough"? It occurred to me—we talk about our legacy, but is *that* our legacy, a legacy of suffering and endurance? Surely there's something greater than that. Then I started to be bothered by something else. You don't have to read very far in Church history before troublesome questions start to hit you. I am not talking about the kind that are related to the history itself, but questions about why God does what he does. If this is really God's work, as we believe it is, and if the Latter-day Saints are really his people, which we believe we are, and if he is truly all powerful and loving, then questions arise regarding these historic events.

Why did 1856, the year the Martin and Willie handcart companies were so delayed and so long in coming, have the worst winter in known memory—with one of the earliest major blizzards that could be remembered? Now, I am not expecting the Lord to make it sunshine all the way across Wyoming in October. That would be a miracle. But the worst winter in known memory? One member of the rescue parties said, "I've crossed this road forty-nine times, and this is the worst I have ever seen it." Why didn't God temper the weather? These were faithful people. They were answering the call to come to Zion. They had given up everything in their lives. Why didn't he temper the weather until they could get to Salt Lake?

When Brigham Young said, "This is the right place—drive on," where was he? Do we remember? He was lying in a wagon so sick that he couldn't sit up. Here's the prophet of the Church, who with great faith has led all these people. He has twelve thousand people to worry about. And he is very ill by the time they reach the valley. He was not even the first one to enter the valley. Erastus Snow, Orson Pratt, and John Brown arrived first. Why not Brigham? Didn't he deserve that?

In 1846, when the call came to go west, why did the Lord not excuse Drusilla Hendricks? She had a paralyzed husband and six children. Why didn't He say, "Drusilla, you've had a tough enough time. Just stay here in Nauvoo." But the Lord didn't excuse her, and she went.

Have you ever thought about the calendar of the exile? Let me just briefly review it. The Latter-day Saints moved from New York to Ohio in January and February. When they were driven out of Jackson County, Missouri, it was November and December. When they were driven out of Kirtland, it was December and January. When they were driven out of Far West, January and February. And when they were driven out of Nauvoo, February and March. Do you notice anything missing there? One June would have been wonderful! A July, or even a May would be nice. Why? Why does the Lord allow the persecution to happen, and at the worst possible time for movement?

Martha Pane Thomas, the one who talks about the bleeding feet of her children, was eight and a half months pregnant. She had to leave Far West, carrying a child, shepherding the others. Why didn't the Lord take mercy on her? Why doesn't he interfere? Why doesn't he intervene?

Here is another question that struck me one day. Brigham Young left Nauvoo in mid-February of 1846. It took them one hundred and thirty days—four months—to reach Winter Quarters. Those who didn't leave in February but waited until May made the same journey in about three weeks. Why didn't the Lord say, "Brigham, if you leave in February the rains are going to come and the roads are going to be one huge bog. So just wait until May. You'll go so much faster." But no, in February Brigham was out there leading that group on their muddy trek. (In fact, I love Brigham's sense of humor. In his history he records that they "only hit one mud hole, but it was six miles long."[7] And that's the way it was.)

Our Priceless Heritage

These comments that people make about suffering and these questions that arose began to change my feelings about what our legacy is. I have come to believe that the legacy that we have been given, this priceless heritage, as President Faust called it,[8] is not a legacy of suffering and endurance; it is a legacy of faith and covenant and power.

Let's consider the 136th section of the Doctrine and Covenants. This section was given through Brigham Young (the only revelation in the Doctrine and Covenants given to Brigham Young) on January 14, 1847. The Saints are languishing in Winter Quarters. They are preparing to leave the following spring because they could not get far enough that first season. The Lord tells President Young how to organize, how to accomplish what must be done. Then, in verse 4, we have this important statement: "And this shall be our covenant—that we will walk in all the ordinances of the Lord." Think about that. We are not going to covenant that we are going to endure. We are not going to covenant that we will take whatever comes. We simply covenant that we will walk in the ordinances with faith.

Why is the price so high? Why are we tested so thoroughly? We find part of the answer in section 98 of the Doctrine and Covenants. Do you want to read a troublesome scripture? This is very sobering—and incidentally, section 98 was given at the very moment the Saints in Jackson County, Missouri, were being driven from their homes. The men had fled into hiding because the mob was out to kill them. When they couldn't find the men, the mob drove all the women and children from their beds. They didn't let them stop for clothing, for shoes; they just drove them out into a winter's night. They drove them twenty-five miles across the prairie in a sleet storm. Lyman Wight said that when they came back to the village and found their wives and children gone, they had no trouble following where they went because they could easily see the bloody footprints in the snow.[9]

In this setting, here is what the Lord said in section 98, verses 13 and 14: "Whoso layeth down his life in my cause, for my name's sake, shall find it again, even life eternal. Therefore, be not afraid of your enemies, for I have decreed in my heart, saith the Lord, that I will prove you in all things, whether you will abide in my covenant." And then come these sobering words: "even unto death." The Lord says, "even unto death, that you may be found worthy." And then comes this: "For if you will not abide in my covenant ye are not worthy of me" (D&C 98:15).

Now that, I submit, is hard doctrine. Why would the Lord require so much of his people? Why is it that Joseph Smith has to languish for six months in jail while his people are suffering on the plains? Why doesn't the Lord just smite the Missourians? One blast of his nostrils and we'd have an empty place in the center of America. But he doesn't. And out of those questions I began to see things I had never seen before.

One lesson I learned is to remember what God's purpose is. You see, God's purpose may not be to make sure that Brigham Young is first in the Valley. Do you think God really cares who is named in the history books as being the very first one in the Salt Lake Valley? I don't think so. I am not sure he really cares a lot about a number of things that matter a great deal to us. What is he doing? He is preparing us for eternal life. "This is my work and my glory—to bring to pass the immortality and eternal life of man" (Moses 1:39). Now you know what that means. Eternal life is God's life. He wants us to be like him. He wants us to be as he is.

Now we can begin to sense why the Lord does what he does. Can you imagine having a God who gives in under pressure, who gives in when the going gets tough? Can you imagine having a God who, when things go wrong, says, "Oh, I don't know what to do, this is just too tough for me. I can't go on." Of course not—and he is seeking to build a people who will be like him.

Their courage, their determination to carry on, was what made these early pioneers so wonderful. That's what their legacy is. They had a clear vision of what God was about with them. They never lost sight of what he was trying to do. And out of that vision of the covenant, they developed great faith, and from their great faith came tremendous power.

Examples of Spiritual Power

Let me give you some examples of what I mean. You've heard the story, I am sure, of what is called the Day of Power in Nauvoo, when Joseph Smith rose from his sickbed and went down to visit the bedsides of many people suffering with malaria. He healed one after the other, even raising some from the dead. Those are marvelous events—but notice the quiet power that came into the lives of these lesser known people when they also kept the covenant.

Elizabeth Horrocks Jackson, who lay that night with her hand on her husband's dead cheek, wrote a few days after that ordeal: "It will be readily perceived that under such adverse circumstances I had become despondent. I was six or seven thousand miles from my native land, in a wild, rocky, mountain country, in a destitute condition, the ground covered with snow, the waters covered with ice, and I with three fatherless children." The night she wrote this, the ground was too frozen for them to drive their tent pegs in, so she got a single blanket, wrapped it around her, put her baby on her lap, put her two other children under one arm, and sat with them through the long night of a Wyoming blizzard. During that time, the temperature was recorded at somewhere around zero. Unfortunately, there was no weather man there to calculate the wind chill factor. This is what Elizabeth says: "When I retired to bed that night"—retired, sitting on a rock with her three children—"I had a stunning revelation. In my dream, my husband stood by me and said—'Cheer up, Elizabeth, deliverance is at hand.'"[10] She woke up greatly comforted by that thought but not knowing what it meant. Within eight hours, someone in the camp cried out. They looked to the west, and there were the first of the wagons coming to rescue them. Do you think her faithfulness had anything to do with her ability to have her husband come to her?

One of my favorite stories is about a woman named Ellen Breakell Neibaur. She was an English girl. She married a German, Alexander Neibaur, who had come to England to study dentistry. They were in Preston, England, when Heber C. Kimball went on his first English mission. Ellen and Alexander were converted. Eventually they came to America and settled in Nauvoo. When it came time to leave on the westward journey, the Neibaurs were extremely poor. It took all of their money to buy a team and wagon and enough supplies to get them through. She didn't even have enough money to buy a pair of shoes, so she wrapped her feet in rags and came all the way across the plains barefoot. After they reached Salt Lake, traveling in the second company with Brigham Young in 1848, her husband became a teacher. She took in laundry. For the next eight years, any time she could save a penny or two she put it aside. After eight long years, she finally had reached the point where she could buy a pair of commercially made shoes from a mail order house. She ordered a pair of high-top patent leather button shoes. They arrived sometime in September 1856.

Just a few days later, on October 4, a company led by Franklin D. Richards of the Quorum of the Twelve rode into Salt Lake with some very disturbing news. They said, "President Young, we have two more handcart companies stranded out on the plains, with over a thousand people." Brigham Young was stunned; three companies had already come in safely, and he assumed that was it for the season. He had no idea there were more, so he had called all the supply wagons back to Salt Lake. The news reached him on Saturday afternoon, October 4. In general conference on the next day, October 5, Brigham Young stood up and said, "I will now give this people the subject and the text for the Elders who may speak to-day and during the conference. It is this. On the 5th day of October, 1856, many of our brethren and sisters are on the plains with handcarts, and probably many are now seven hundred miles from this place, and they must be brought here, we must send assistance to them. The text will be, 'to get them here.'"[11] President Young then called for teams, wagons, food, and clothing to help those who were stranded. And Ellen Neibaur, after eight years of waiting, had not lost sight of what the covenant was and what mattered. She took that brand-new pair of shoes down to the wagon team and gave them to the rescue effort.

It was customary, when a new company came into the Valley, for all the Saints to go out and line the streets and greet them. When this particular company came in, everyone went out to greet them, because this was the first of the two besieged handcart companies to be rescued. Ellen Neibaur went out. Normally the Saints watched the faces of the people coming in to see who they were. What do you think Ellen Neibaur was watching that day? She wasn't looking at faces. She was looking at feet. She wanted to know who had gotten her shoes.

Now, here comes the beautiful end to this true story, a great example of faith and covenant, and an example of the power that follows. When Ellen Neibaur saw her shoes, she looked up and, to her absolute amazement, wearing them was an old friend from Preston, England, who had joined the Church since Ellen had left England! Ellen's sacrifice had helped to save her friend's life and had helped her come to the Valley safely.[12] That is the lesson we can learn from these wonderful, wonderful people.

Here is another example from the life of Drusilla Hendricks, who had given so much effort to care for a crippled husband. When they reached Winter Quarters in July 1846, her oldest boy, William, aged sixteen, was able to drive the team. She finally had a child old enough and strong enough to help with her husband and her other children.

Then Captain James Allen from the United States Army rode into camp and said, "We're looking for five hundred volunteers for the Mormon Battalion," and young William Hendricks said, "Mother, I want to go." Not surprisingly, she said she didn't want him to go. She had already sent one man to war, and he had come back crippled. She adamantly refused to give in until the morning of the mustering when the men were preparing to march out. I would like to share with you from her own journal what happened. She said, "I went to get some flour from the wagon, and as I stood on the tongue the whispering of the Spirit said to me, 'Do you not want the greatest glory?' I answered in my natural voice, I was so surprised. 'Why, of course.' 'Then how can you get it without making the greatest sacrifice?'"

Many of us at that point would try to remind the Lord: Don't you remember what's been going on these last six years with me? But she said, in effect, "Lord, what lack I yet?" And then the Spirit whispered, "Let your son go in the Mormon Battalion." So she returned to camp. William looked at her and said, "Mother, can I go?" And she said, "Yes." And then, weeping because she couldn't bear the thoughts of losing her son, she went about her duties. Her journal records, "I went to milk the cows. I thought they would shelter me in my tears. I knelt down and told the Lord if he wanted my child to take him, but I begged him that he would spare his life. Then a voice, that same spiritual voice that spoke to me before answered me saying, 'Drusilla, it shall be done unto you as it was unto Abraham when he offered Isaac on the altar.'" And then she concluded her account: "I don't know whether I milked or not, for all I felt was the presence of the Lord."[13]

Pure Steel

Faith, covenant, power. That's the legacy we've been given. Joseph Smith taught, "God hath said that he would have a tried people that he must purge them as gold."[14] That is what God is doing with these people; he is creating gold.

I was in a Church history class some years ago and another student asked, "How did Brigham do it? He brought all these people from all over the world, different languages, different cultures, different economic levels, and he colonized the whole western part of the United States! How did he do it?" I will never forget the answer of the professor. He said, "You have to remember something. By the time they reached the Valley, most of the physically weak had died and most of the spiritually weak had apostatized. What Brigham had left was pure steel."

That pure steel was further strengthened by covenant. In September 1846, while in Winter Quarters, Brigham Young learned that the poor Saints who were still in Illinois had been driven out of Nauvoo and were languishing on the western banks of the Mississippi River. He called the brethren together and reminded them that in the temple they had covenanted that they would not leave any of the poor behind. He then said: "Now is the time for labor. Let the fire of the covenant, which you made in the House of the Lord, burn in your hearts like flame unquenchable, till you, by yourselves or delegates, have searched out every man . . . [to] rise up with his team and go straightway and bring a load of the poor from Nauvoo."[15] The Saints responded generously to his plea.

It was the fire of the covenant burning in their hearts that gave us the rich legacy we now enjoy.

That's the true legacy of the pioneers. And that leads me to an understanding of the challenge of our generation: to have that fire of the covenant burning in our hearts and to never lose sight of that spiritual direction and power that drove our pioneer ancestors so faithfully and sustained them as they endured so much.

Notes

From an address given at a devotional luncheon for the wives of General Authorities, Salt Lake City, 14 April 1998.

1. *Leaves from the Life of Elizabeth Horrocks Jackson Kingsford* (Ogden, Ut.: n.p., 1908), 5–7.
2. Albert R. Lyman, "Bishop Jens Nielson," unpublished manuscript, 4. Copy in author's possession. The size difference between Jens and Elsie was related to the author by the couple's descendants.
3. "Drusilla Dorris Hendricks: 'Mother's Little Christian,'" in Leonard J. Arrington and Susan Arrington Madsen, *Sunbonnet Sisters* (Salt Lake City: Bookcraft, 1984), 29–30.
4. Kate B. Carter, *Heart Throbs of the West,* 12 vols. (Salt Lake City: Daughters of the Utah Pioneers, 1939–51), 2:108–9.
5. In Richard N. Holzapfel and Jeni Broberg Holzapfel, *Women of Nauvoo* (Salt Lake City: Bookcraft, 1992), 11.
6. *Hymns of The Church of Jesus Christ of Latter-day Saints* (Salt Lake City: The Church of Jesus Christ of Latter-day Saints, 1985), no. 30.
7. *Manuscript History of Brigham Young* (Salt Lake City: Elden J. Watson, 1971), 106.
8. James E. Faust, in Conference Report, October 1992, 117.
9. As cited in B. H. Roberts, *The Missouri Persecutions* (Salt Lake City: Bookcraft, 1965), 107.
10. *Leaves from the Life of Elizabeth . . . Kingsford,* 8.
11. As cited in LeRoy R. Hafen and Ann W. Hafen, *Handcarts to Zion* (Lincoln: University of Nebraska Press, 1992), 120.

12. "Ellen Breakell Neibaur, Wife of Alexander Neibaur," unpublished manuscript compiled by Jolene Smith Davis. Copy in author's possession.
13. Arrington and Madsen, *Sunbonnet Sisters,* 30–31.
14. Joseph Smith, *History of The Church of Jesus Christ of Latter-day Saints,* 7 vols., 2d ed. rev., ed. B. H. Roberts (Salt Lake City: The Church of Jesus Christ of Latter-day Saints, 1932–51), 3:294.
15. Journal History, 28 September 1846, as cited in Susan Easton Black and William G. Hartley, eds., *The Iowa Mormon Trail: Legacy of Faith and Courage* (Orem, Ut.: Helix Publishing, 1997), 163.

Chapter 28

"If Ye Are Prepared Ye Shall Not Fear" (D&C 38:30)

When a group of Latter-day Saints were asked what one question they would most like to ask of the Savior about his second coming, three questions came up again and again. Not surprisingly, "When will it be?" was the most-asked question. The second took various forms but had essentially the same intent: "What is life going to be like before he comes and then when he comes?" The third most-asked question was "How do I prepare myself so I will be ready?" Although the answers to the first two questions are of great interest, the answer to the third question is probably of greatest immediate importance. The nature of Christ's coming is described with the paradoxical phrase "the great and dreadful day of the Lord" (D&C 110:14; emphasis added; see also v. 16).

How can something be both great and dreadful at the same time? Yet that is part of the reality of Christ's return to the earth and the judgments that usher it in. In many respects, the future holds things that are horrible and dreadful—war, wickedness, earthquakes, storms, famine, disease. On the other hand, the future also holds many things that will make it a great day—the establishment of Zion, the return of the lost tribes, the great council at Adam-ondi-Ahman, the return of Christ to the earth, a thousand years of peace and prosperity.

So what determines whether it will be a great day or a dreadful day for us as a people and as individuals? What makes the difference of whether we look forward to the future with fear and anxiety or faith and anticipation? There may be several answers to those questions, but one thing is clear. Whether the Lord's return will be great or dreadful for us will depend largely on whether or not we are prepared.

The Lord has specifically commanded us, "Prepare yourselves for the great day of the Lord" (D&C 133:10). And in another revelation he gave this wonderful promise: "If ye are prepared ye shall not fear" (D&C 38:30). That promise may apply in many situations, but it certainly has particular relevance when we talk about the Second Coming.

Many people, especially those along in years, are certain that they will not live long enough to see the Second Coming. Does preparation really matter that much for them? Of course it does. Taking the broader perspective, remember that every one of us will be alive when Christ comes again to the earth. In many cases, our bodies will have died and will lie waiting in the grave, but the spirit part of us, the part that gives us personality, character, individuality, will still be living. Thus the Lord's admonition that if we are prepared we shall not fear applies to everyone. If we are to be properly prepared for what the future holds, we must gain knowledge and understanding and prepare both temporally and spiritually.

Gain Knowledge and Understanding

President Jedediah M. Grant of the First Presidency asked the following question and then gave the answer: "Why is it that the Latter-day Saints are perfectly calm and serene among all the convulsions of the earth—the turmoils, strife, war, pestilence, famine and distress of nations? It is because the spirit of prophecy has made *known* to us that such things would actually transpire upon the earth. We *understand* it, and view it in its true light. We have learned it by the visions of the Almighty."[1] It is knowledge and understanding that make the difference in whether we view the future with anxiety or anticipation.

Just before his death, the Savior was on the Temple Mount in Jerusalem with his disciples. The temple built by Herod was one of the wonders of the ancient world—great walls, massive stones, beautiful gates. It was a marvel of engineering and architecture. As they walked along, the disciples commented on what a wonderful building it was. Then the Savior turned to them and said, "See ye not all these things? verily I say unto you, There shall not be left here one stone upon another, that shall not be thrown down" (Matt. 24:2). They left the Temple Mount, crossed through the Kidron Valley, and went up on the Mount of Olives. The temple and all of Jerusalem lay before them. The disciples, troubled by the Savior's stunning declaration, said, "Tell us, when shall these things be? and what shall be the sign of thy coming, and of the end of the world?" (Matt. 24:3).

The Savior's reply, because it was given on the Mount of Olives, has come to be known as the Olivet Discourse. It is one of the most complete discussions of the Second Coming that Jesus himself gave. In the Doctrine and Covenants version of the Olivet Discourse, the Savior said that after the disciples had heard about all the signs of the times, "they were troubled" (D&C 45:34). That should be of interest to us today. Just hearing about those events that were still centuries away troubled them. It is not surprising that we who live in the day when those signs are being fulfilled should also be troubled. But the Lord specifically commanded his disciples, "Be not troubled" (D&C 45:35). And then he told them why. "And I said unto them: Be not troubled, for, when all these things shall come to pass, ye may know that the promises which have been made unto you shall be fulfilled" (D&C 45:35).

President Marion G. Romney noted the importance of knowledge in that scriptural admonition: "It was in the light of Christ's foreknowledge of this glorious consummation that he said to his disciples, 'be not troubled.' . . .

"I hope we are all familiar with these words of the Lord and with his predictions concerning other coming events, such as the building of the new Jerusalem and the redemption of the old, the return of Enoch's Zion, and Christ's millennial reign.

"Not only do I hope that we are familiar with these coming events; I hope also that we keep the vision of them continually before our minds. This I do because upon a *knowledge* of them, and an assurance of their reality and a witness that each of us may have part therein, rests the efficacy of Christ's admonition, 'be not troubled.'"[2]

At least two kinds of knowledge and understanding will be particularly valuable to us as we prepare ourselves for what is to come.

Understanding the Prophetic View of the Future

After telling the disciples that they were not to be troubled, the Lord referred to a proverb common in the Holy Land in his day: "It shall be with them like unto a parable which I will show you—Ye look and behold the fig-trees, and ye see them with your eyes, and ye say when they begin to shoot forth, and their leaves are yet tender, that summer is now nigh at hand" (D&C 45:36–37).

It is an interesting fact of nature that the fig tree is one of the last of all the trees to come into leaf. That part of its nature is so dependable that it became a common thing in the Middle East to say that if the fig tree was in leaf, then summer was now come, or in other words, the cold weather was over.

The Lord continued by comparing the leaves of the fig tree to the signs of the times: "Even so it shall be in that day when they shall see all these things, then shall they know that the hour is nigh. And it shall come to pass that he that feareth me shall be looking forth for the great day of the Lord to come, even for the signs of the coming of the Son of Man" (D&C 45:38–39). Thus the Lord himself has specifically counseled us to watch for the signs of the times. Like the leaves of the fig tree, these prophetic signs will signal that his coming is approaching.

Many of the events that are prophesied for that time are not pleasant. Some of what the world will bring upon itself through its own wickedness is terrible and depressing. If that were all we could look forward to, we could honestly say, "I hope I die before those things happen." But the Lord has given us considerable detail about future events—even about the terrible things—so that when they come to pass, those who understand and know the prophecies will see them as the fulfillment of God's word. They will see them as proof that his great plan is rolling forward.

Joseph Fielding Smith, then a member of the Quorum of the Twelve Apostles, gave a series of lectures in Salt Lake City shortly after World War II began. After describing some of the terrible things associated with the battle of Armageddon, Elder Smith said: "I know these are unpleasant things. It is not a pleasant thing even for me to stand here and tell you that this is written in the Scriptures. If the Lord has a controversy with the nations, He will put them to the sword. Their bodies shall lie unburied like dung upon the earth. That is not nice, is it, but should we not *know* it? Is it not our duty to read these things and *understand* them? Don't you think the Lord has given us these things that we might know and we might prepare ourselves through humility, through repentance, through faith, that we might escape from these dreadful conditions that are portrayed by these ancient prophets?"[3]

Unpleasant or not, however, those who are watching and waiting for the signs can better prepare for what is to come. How can we watch for those signs unless we have studied the scriptures and listened to the modern prophets carefully? Through them the Lord has told us about what is going to happen. We should know what they say. We should understand their words so that we can prepare for and live through those times without a loss of faith. It is upon our knowledge and understanding of those prophetic events that a large part of our personal preparation rests. In a proclamation made to the world shortly after the Saints arrived in Utah, the First Presidency stated: "Of the day and the hour of the coming of Christ no man knoweth. It is not yet, neither is it far off; there are prophecies yet to be fulfilled before that event takes place; therefore let no man deceive the Saints with vain philosophy and false prophecy; for false prophets will arise, and deceive the wicked, and, if possible, the good; but while the wicked fear and tremble at surrounding judgments, the Saints will watch and pray; and, waiting the final event in patience, will look calmly on the passing scenery of a corrupted world, and view transpiring events as confirmation of their faith in the holy gospel which they profess, and rejoice more and more, as multiplied signs shall confirm the approach of the millennial day."[4]

Understanding the World around Us

In Doctrine and Covenants 88, a revelation directed to those in the School of the Prophets, the Lord gave a very specific and direct commandment to study and learn about "things that pertain unto the kingdom of God, that are expedient for you to understand; Of things both in heaven and in the earth, and under the earth; things which have been, things which are, things which must shortly come to pass; things which are at home, things which are abroad; the wars and the perplexities of the nations, and the judgments which are on the land; and a knowledge also of countries and of kingdoms" (D&C 88:78–79).

The judgments that will precede the coming of Christ and prepare the world for the millennial reign will have a profound effect upon the nations of the world. Eventually, there will even be an end to "all nations" (D&C 87:6). Can such things come to pass without a profound change in the political situation as we know it today? Already great changes are taking place around the world. For those watching with eyes of faith, things that make daily headlines or the evening television news are seen as at least partial fulfillment of things prophesied centuries ago. But how can we see the hand of the Lord in these things if we do not keep abreast of world events and know what is going on around us? For example, in recent years we have seen dramatic changes in what used to be the Soviet Union. Is the hand of God in such events? More than sixty years ago, Elder Melvin J. Ballard of the Quorum of the Twelve Apostles made a most remarkable statement about Russia: "I am sure also that God is moving in Russia. . . . I can see God moving also in preparing the way for other events that are to come. The field that has gone to wild oats needs to be plowed up and harrowed and prepared for a new seed. So in Russia. It may seem appalling to us, but it is God breaking up and destroying an older order of things, and *the process will be the accomplishment of God's purposes within a very short period of time,* which normally may have taken generations. But that people will come back, for I bear witness that there are thousands of the blood of Israel in that land, and God is preparing the way for them."[5]

More recently, President Thomas S. Monson also spoke of what has been happening in that part of the world: "In the month of May, my wife and I were in the historic city of Berlin. We boarded a taxi and asked that the driver take us to the Berlin Wall. When the driver failed to respond to the direction provided, again the desired destination was given. Still no movement. Then he turned toward us and, in halting English, explained, 'I can't. The wall is *kaput*—gone!' We drove to the Brandenburg Gate. We viewed its restoration. We gazed from West Berlin to East Berlin, now one Berlin, and reflected on the events which followed the wall's demise: a new mission of the Church established in Poland, another in Hungary, yet another in Greece, and a mission reestablished in Czechoslovakia. And now, official recognition of our Leningrad Branch in the Soviet Union. Who, except the Lord Himself, could have foreseen these historic events? It was He who declared, 'This gospel of the kingdom shall be preached in all the world for a witness unto all nations.' (Matt. 24:14.) Surely the purposes of the Lord continue to unfold to our view if we but have eyes that truly see and hearts that know and feel."[6]

In summary, then, one important thing that we can do to prepare ourselves for the Second Coming is to gain greater knowledge and understanding. Part of that knowledge will come directly from the scriptures and what the modern prophets have said and are saying to us. But the Lord has also commanded us to be knowledgeable about the world around us and the unfolding events that are all part of his great plan, leading up to the return of his Son to earth to reign as King of kings.

Prepare Temporally

Get together with a group of Latter-day Saints, mention getting oneself prepared for the Second Coming, and it is almost certain that talk will quickly turn to food storage. That is not wrong, of course, but if the discussion stays focused only upon home storage, it will be woefully inadequate, even if the discussion is limited to preparing oneself temporally for Christ's return.

Natural disasters have struck with increasing frequency in recent years—the great earthquakes in Armenia, California, China, and other parts of the world; great storms, such as Hurricane Andrew in Florida and Hurricane Iniki in Hawaii; devastating floods in Europe and Asia and the midwestern United States. We see long lines at grocery stores as people try to purchase food and safe water. It is not surprising that when such disasters hit, our minds immediately jump to the importance of having a year's supply of food and clothing and fuel. And one can hardly say enough about the importance of this principle. For example, President Ezra Taft

Benson declared: "The revelation to produce and store food may be as essential to our temporal welfare today as boarding the ark was to the people in the days of Noah."[7]

But the signs of the times include political, social, and economic events that will try the preparedness of individuals and families in different ways. Economic turmoil is common in our day. Recession, depression, widespread unemployment, runaway inflation—any one of these can be as disastrous for an individual or a family as a major earthquake. War and widespread social upheaval are becoming the norm in some countries. Major storms can seriously affect food supplies or transportation. Even normal life has a way of testing the limits of our physical, mental, emotional, and spiritual health from time to time.

When we speak of being prepared temporally, food storage is an important part of that preparation, but it is only a part, one aspect of the greater principle of self-reliance. President Spencer W. Kimball explained that principle clearly: "The responsibility for each person's social, emotional, spiritual, physical, or economic well-being rests first upon himself, second upon his family, and third upon the Church if he is a faithful member thereof.

"No true Latter-day Saint, while physically or emotionally able will voluntarily shift the burden of his own or his family's well-being to someone else. So long as he can, under the inspiration of the Lord and with his own labors, he will supply himself and his family with the spiritual and temporal necessities of life."[8]

The Church has defined six areas in which we need to develop self-reliance: education, health, employment, home storage, resource management, and social, emotional, and spiritual strength (these six areas are detailed in materials published by the Welfare Services Department of the Church). When some of the future judgments strike, our self-reliance in these areas may be sorely tested. If we have properly prepared ourselves in such balanced and well-rounded ways as outlined by the Church, then surely we shall be able to claim the promise "If ye are prepared ye shall not fear."

There are at least three reasons why temporal preparation will be so important in the days that lie ahead:

1. *The Church may be cut off from normal avenues of transportation, commerce, and social interaction.* Recent natural disasters have shown us how fragile and complex are the infrastructures that support our day-to-day living. When an earthquake strikes and freeway overpasses collapse, the traffic flow, the ability to get to work or school, the flow of food and goods into a city, can be seriously disrupted if not stopped altogether. That can put a whole city into immediate crisis.

Widespread social disruption, such as a riot or civil war, can cut a whole people off from the normal avenues of supply, security, and protection.

Both as a church and as individual members of the Church, we are heavily dependent on current social structure for the normal functioning of our lives. Yet in a revelation given in March 1832, the Lord made this statement: "Behold, *this is the preparation wherewith I prepare you,* and the foundation, and the ensample which I give unto you, whereby you may accomplish the commandments which are given unto you; That through my providence, notwithstanding the tribulation which shall descend upon you, *that the church may stand independent* above all other creatures beneath the celestial world" (D&C 78:13–14; emphasis added).

That seems to be one main reason why the welfare program of the Church was organized: not only to meet the needs of those who are poor but also to move the Church toward greater independence. Harold B. Lee, when he was president of the Church, recounted an experience he had had in the earliest days of the Welfare Program. He had been asked by the General Authorities to go to the various stakes and talk about the importance of getting the program in place. "In one of those meetings, the thought came to me, 'I wonder what this [the welfare program] is all about?' And there came to me something that has stayed with me to this day, 'There is no person who knows the real purpose for which this Welfare Program is being instituted. But hardly before sufficient preparation has been made, the real purpose will be revealed, and *when that time comes it will challenge every resource of the Church to meet it.*'"[9]

In the welfare session of the April 1975 general conference, Marion G. Romney of the First Presidency made a similar statement: "I do not want to be a calamity howler. I don't know in detail what's going to happen in the future. I know what the prophets have predicted. But I tell you that the welfare program, organized to enable us to take care of our own needs, has not yet performed the function that it was set up to perform. *We will see the day when we will live on what we produce.*"[10]

A year earlier, also in a welfare session of general conference, President Spencer W. Kimball said: "I remember when the sisters used to say, 'Well, but we could buy it at the store a lot cheaper than we can put it up.' But that isn't quite the answer, is it, Sister Spafford [Relief Society General President]? Because *there will come a time when there isn't a store.*"[11]

Therefore, one of the important reasons for being temporally prepared—and this is in all aspects of self-reliance, not just food storage—is that in the coming calamities we may see groups of Church members cut off from the normal structure of society which provides so many of their daily needs. We may also see the day when as a Church we must be independent of the world and be able to carry on with nothing but our own resources.

2. *We shall have to help others in the coming calamities.* A second reason why our personal and family preparedness will be especially critical has to do with another effect that is prophesied to happen. As wickedness increases and iniquity abounds (see D&C 45:27), or when the predicted judgments descend upon the world, many people will look to the Church for peace and security. And when they do, many will come with few or no resources. That means that they will need help and could become a severe demand on the resources of the Church and its members.

In the scriptures, the city of Zion and the stakes of Zion are described in terms that should give the Saints some consolation. The New Jerusalem, for example, will be "a land of peace, a city of refuge, a place of safety for the saints of the Most High God" (D&C 45:66). The Lord also said that the Saints would gather to the stakes of Zion "for a defense, and for a refuge from the storm, and from wrath when it shall be poured out without mixture upon the whole earth" (D&C 115:6).

Such conditions—peace, safety, refuge, defense—clearly will attract others who are not members of the Church. Good people will seek those conditions. The Lord specifically noted that in coming years, people will flock to the Saints for safety. Speaking of the city of Zion, he said: "And it shall come to pass among the wicked, that every man that will not take his sword against his neighbor must needs flee unto Zion for safety. And there shall be gathered unto it out of every nation under heaven; and it shall be the only people that shall not be at war one with another" (D&C 45:68–69).

Obviously, this scripture suggests a state of widespread and probably lasting social chaos. In such conditions, thousands, perhaps tens of thousands, of people will join with the Saints in an attempt to escape the horrible things going on around them. The modern prophets have also talked about such possibilities. In 1856, President Heber C. Kimball, speaking of the handcart companies, asked: "Is this the end of it? No; there will be millions on millions that will come much in the same way, only they will not have hand carts, for they will take their bundles under their arms, and their children on their backs, and under their arms, and flee; and Zion's people will have to send out relief to them, *for they will come when the judgments come on the nations.*" About a year later, he returned to that same theme and said: "It behooves us to be saving and to prepare for the time to come. The day will come when the people of the United States will come lugging their bundles under their arms, *coming to us for bread to eat.*"[12]

Orson Pratt, of the Quorum of the Twelve Apostles, who was told in a specific revelation that he was to prophesy and it would be given him by the power of the Holy Ghost what he should say (see D&C 34:10), also saw a time when there would be thousands of people coming to the Church for help: "They [the world] will read her laws, and say, 'Our laws are as nothing, our wisdom as foolishness, our words like the tow that is exposed to the devouring flame; we are broken asunder, torn into fragments, and ready to crush under our own weight; but your laws, government, and officers are all good, righteous, just, and true; surely the God of Israel is in your midst. Come, let us go up to Zion, let us hear from the wise legislators of Zion, and let us hear the laws proclaimed therein; let us learn of the wisdom that dwells in the servants of the Most High.' And they will come up with their armies, and their mighty men, and their judges, and their rulers, and kings will come to the brightness of her rising, and *the Gentiles will come like a flowing stream,* and the gates of Zion will be open day and night, and never be shut."[13]

Elder Pratt said later: "A flowing stream is one that runs continually; and the Gentiles will, in that day, come to us as a flowing stream, and we shall have to set our gates open continually, they will come as clouds and as doves in large flocks. . . .

"The people will see that the hand of God is over this people; they will see that He is in our midst, and that He is our watch-tower, that He is our shield and our defence, and therefore, they will say, 'Let us go up and put our riches in Zion, for there is no safety in our own nations.' Those nations are trembling and tottering and will eventually crumble to ruin, and those men of wealth will come here, not to be baptized, but many of them will come that have never heard the servants of God; but they will hear that peace and health dwell among us, and that our officers are all peace officers, and our tax-gatherers men of righteousness."[14]

If large numbers of people come in who have not made the proper temporal preparation—or who have had to abandon whatever temporal preparation they had—that will be a great drain on the resources of the Church. They will need to be fed and clothed and housed. The clear implication is that if we as individual members of the Church have prepared ourselves temporally and properly, we will be able to help those in need rather than ourselves being a drain on the resources of the Church.

3. *The Church cannot meet the needs of everyone who is unprepared.* A third reason why our temporal preparation will be important is that it is not possible for the Church, as an organization, to care for everyone's needs if there is widespread social disruption. The Welfare Program was not created for that purpose. Two of

its foundational principles are self-reliance and personal and family preparedness. Occasionally we will hear comments like, "Well, if things get really bad, I can always turn to the Church for help." Such misplaced hope not only is contrary to gospel principles but it will likely be impossible in every case. In the welfare session of the April 1976 general conference, Victor L. Brown, then Presiding Bishop of the Church, summarized possible conditions the Church might face and described the Church's ability to handle the needs of people in those conditions:

"Let me share the panorama of conditions that could befall each of us individually and the Church collectively. I would like you to see what might happen under three hypothetical but potentially real conditions.

"Condition One is characterized by a relatively stable economy, modest unemployment, and only limited natural disasters—a condition much like that which we now experience in this and many other countries. Only a small number of families or individuals in the Church would need to call upon their bishops for temporary health, emotional, or economic assistance. For those families or individuals unable to fully care for themselves, we would use our production projects, storehouses, employment efforts, and fast offering funds to help meet their needs. Appropriate health and social services capabilities of the Church would support the priesthood in administering to these special needs. Our present state of Church preparedness allows us to meet the claims on the Church which Condition One seems to imply.

"Condition Two is characterized by more serious health, social, and economic stress. This could include a depressed economy with serious unemployment, or perhaps localized natural disasters. Society would be unstable and disunited. In order for the Church to meet the needs of those who could not care for themselves, we would be required to produce the maximum from our production projects, reduce the variety of items produced and distributed, provide broad-scale work opportunities, and organize special quorum relief efforts. Health and social services would be needed in many places. Clearly, the material resources of the Church would be taxed heavily to meet this burden, particularly if Condition Two lasted very long or were very widespread.

"Under Condition Three, circumstances would be very serious. The economy would be very depressed, perhaps even suffering a near breakdown. Unemployment would be widespread. There would probably be widespread social disunity. This condition could be the result of either economic problems such as severe crop loss, broad-scale natural disasters, or possibly international conflict. *Under such circumstances, the Church, relying on its present resources, would very likely not be able to provide any more assistance than that rendered under Condition Two, and therefore could not meet the total welfare needs of the people. . . .*

" . . . Therefore, if the time comes that we move out of Condition One into a widespread Condition-Two situation, we are well beyond the current capacity of the Church alone to meet the temporal needs of the Saints.

"I would like to stress that this preparedness includes more than temporal preparedness. Particularly in Conditions Two and Three we would encounter social disunity, worry, fear, depression, and all the emotional stresses that accompany such economic and social conditions. Health conditions would be precarious. Families and individuals would need to be prepared emotionally and physically to weather this condition. Members would have greater need than ever to rely on each other for strength and support. . . .

" . . . Our temporal salvation will come only in following the counsel of the Brethren to be prepared as families and individuals, as wards and as stakes. As we apply their counsel, we make of Zion a refuge and a standard of righteous living as commanded by the Lord."[15]

If faithful members of the Church who have prepared themselves and their families for whatever calamities, setbacks, or disasters may strike, whether widespread or individually, are able to cope with those challenges and problems without having to draw upon the resources of the Church, the capability of the Church to help those in need would be greatly expanded. Thus, not only are we fulfilling a commandment of the Lord to be self-reliant ourselves, but we could also become a great blessing to our fellowmen. Preparing ourselves in all six areas of temporal self-reliance is one important thing we can do so that we can claim the Lord's promise, "If ye are prepared ye shall not fear."

Prepare Spiritually

In the closing chapter of the first book of Nephi, Nephi detailed some marvelous prophecies about the events of the last days. He talked about terrible conditions in Babylon, or the world, in which the people will be warring among themselves, every nation will be warring against the house of Israel, and the fulness of the wrath of God will be poured out upon the children of men (see 1 Ne. 22:13–16). But in the midst of that terrible picture are some marvelous promises. Note what Nephi said: "Wherefore, he will *preserve the righteous* by his power, even if it so be that the fulness of his wrath must come, and the *righteous be preserved,* even unto the destruction of their enemies by fire. Wherefore, *the righteous need not fear;* for thus saith the prophet, they shall be saved, even if it so be as by fire. . . . For behold, *the righteous shall not perish;* for the time surely must come that all they who fight against Zion shall be cut off. And *the Lord will surely prepare a way for his people. . . .* And *the righteous need not fear*" (1 Ne. 22:17–22; emphasis added).

The key word Nephi used here is *righteous.* The promises of deliverance and protection are for the righteous.

The scriptures and the modern prophets make it clear that of the three areas of personal preparation—knowledge and understanding, temporal preparation, and spiritual preparation—spiritual preparation is the most critical. President Ezra Taft Benson said in 1981: "We will live in the midst of economic, political, and spiritual instability. When these signs are observed—unmistakable evidences that His coming is nigh—we need not be troubled, but 'stand in holy places, and be not moved, until the day of the Lord come' (D&C 87:8). *Holy men and women stand in holy places,* and these holy places consist of our temples, our chapels, our homes, and stakes of Zion."[16]

Unfortunately, in some cases, spiritual preparedness is the most neglected area of preparation. During the winter of 1976–77, a severe drought had set in the western United States. Scarcely any snow had fallen through December. In the news was constant talk of a severe water shortage if things did not change. The reaction in Utah and surrounding states with high concentrations of Latter-day Saints was an interesting one. One news report indicated that wheat—primarily for home storage—was normally trucked from Idaho into Utah at the rate of one semi-truck load per week. Suddenly the rate jumped to three semi-truck loads per day! Another television news broadcast reported that purchase of food storage items jumped 800 percent in January 1977. Newspapers reported that people were taking out loans and mortgages on property to add to their food supplies.

It would be interesting to know if at that same time there was a resulting rise in the concern about one's spiritual readiness. Did family prayer jump 800 percent during that same period? Was there a significant increase in the holding of family home evening or personal scripture study? Did temple attendance go up sharply? In short, as we rushed to beef up our food storage, was there also a great turning to the Lord and an increased desire to put one's spiritual life in order?

Remember the question people would most like to ask the Savior about his second coming? Most would ask, "How do I prepare myself for what is coming?" In a way, we already have the Savior's answer to that question—the Olivet Discourse, found in Matthew and other places. Some may think Matthew 24 contains the full discourse, but a careful reading of chapter 25 shows that Jesus continued his teaching to the disciples through chapter 25, ending with three parables whose very context was Christ's second coming. That assertion is borne out by the opening words of chapter 25: "And then, at that day, before the Son of man comes, the kingdom of Heaven shall be likened unto . . ." (JST Matt. 25:1). Then follow the three parables: the parable of the ten virgins, the parable of the talents, and the parable of the sheep and the goats. These parables do not discuss the signs of the times *per se* but rather relate to our spiritual condition. In that sense, they could be thought of as parables of spiritual preparation. So, in a way, we already have the Lord's answer to the question, "How do I prepare myself for what is to come?"

The Parable of the Ten Virgins (Matthew 25:1–13)

The well-known parable of the ten virgins draws on the wonderful imagery of a wedding celebration in the Middle East. George Mackie, a Christian minister who spent much of his life in the Holy Land, described what a wedding ceremony was like in Palestine in the nineteenth century. In it we see the rich imagery of the parable of the ten virgins.

"Oriental [Near Eastern] marriages usually take place in the evening. . . . The whole attention is turned to the public arrival of the bridegroom to receive the bride prepared for him and waiting in the house among her female attendants. . . .

"As the hours drag on their topics of conversation become exhausted, and some of them grow tired and fall asleep. There is nothing more to be done, and everything is in readiness for the reception of the bridegroom, when the cry is heard outside announcing his approach.

"The bridegroom meanwhile is absent, spending the day at the house of one of his relatives. There, soon after sunset, that is between seven and eight o'clock, his male friends begin to assemble. . . . The time is occupied with light refreshments, general conversation and the recitation of poetry in praise of the two families chiefly concerned and of the bridegroom in particular. After all have been courteously welcomed and their congratulations received, the bridegroom, about eleven o'clock, intimates his wish to set out. Flaming torches are then held aloft by special bearers, lit candles are handed at the door to each visitor as he goes out, and the procession sweeps slowly along toward the house where the bride and her female attendants are waiting. A great crowd has meanwhile assembled on the balconies, garden-walls, and flat roofs of the houses on each side of the road. . . . The bridegroom is the centre of interest. Voices are heard whispering, 'There he is! there he is!' From time to time women raise their voices in the peculiar shrill, wavering shriek by which joy is expressed at marriages and other times of family and public rejoicing. The sound is heard at a great distance, and is repeated by other voices in advance of the procession, and thus intimation is given of the approach half an hour or more before the marriage escort arrives. . . . As the house is approached the excitement increases, the bridegroom's pace is quickened, and the alarm is raised in louder tones and more repeatedly, *'He is coming, he is coming!'*

"Before he arrives, the maidens in waiting come forth with lamps and candles a short distance to light up the entrance, and do honour to the bridegroom and the group of relatives and intimate friends around him. These pass into the final rejoicing and the marriage supper; the others who have discharged their duty in accompanying him to the door, immediately disperse, and the door is shut."[17]

In the time of Christ, olive oil was used as the fuel for lamps. Some of those lamps, particularly those carried outside at night, were small. Made of clay or brass, they were filled with olive oil, in which a wick was laid and then lit to provide light. Because these lamps were small enough to fit in the palm of the hand, they obviously contained only a small amount of oil. They would generally burn for about an hour without renewing the supply.

A careful study of the parable shows that the key element is the oil for the lamps. All of the ten were virgins. All of the ten had lamps. What distinguished the five wise virgins from the five foolish ones was the extra supply of oil they carried. In the Doctrine and Covenants, the Lord gives us the key for understanding what the oil symbolized: "At that day, when I shall come in my glory, shall the parable be fulfilled which I spake concerning the ten virgins. For they that are wise and have received the truth, *and have taken the Holy Spirit for their guide,* and have not been deceived—verily I say unto you, they shall not be hewn down and cast into the fire, but shall abide the day" (D&C 45:56–57; emphasis added).

Olive oil is a wonderful symbol for the power of the Holy Ghost. He is a source of light and truth. His influence is sometimes described in terms of burning and fire. For example, we speak of the burning of the bosom that sometimes accompanies his presence (see D&C 9:8). The scriptures also refer to the "baptism of fire" or of the Holy Ghost (D&C 33:11). So the oil in the parable symbolizes having the light, or the power, of the Holy Ghost in our lives.

Once we understand that symbolism, the message of the parable is clear. We must have the influence of the Spirit with us if we are to be prepared for the Bridegroom's coming. President Spencer W. Kimball commented at some length on the meaning of this parable for our day: "I believe that the Ten Virgins represent the people of the Church of Jesus Christ and not the rank and file of the world. All of the virgins, wise and foolish, had accepted the invitation to the wedding supper; they had knowledge of the program and had been warned of the important day to come. They were not the gentiles or the heathens or the pagans, nor were they necessarily corrupt and reprobate, but *they were knowing people who were foolishly unprepared* for the vital happenings that were to affect their eternal lives. . . .

"Hundreds of thousands of us today are in this position. Confidence has been dulled and patience worn thin. It is so hard to wait and be prepared always. But we cannot allow ourselves to slumber. The Lord has given us this parable as a special warning.

"At midnight, the vital cry was made. . . . At midnight! Precisely at the darkest hour, when least expected, the bridegroom came. When the world is full of tribulation and help is needed, but it seems the time must be past and hope is vain, then Christ will come. The midnights of life are the times when heaven comes to offer its joy for man's weariness. But when the cry sounds, there is no time for preparation. . . . In the daytime, wise and unwise seemed alike; midnight is the time of test and judgment. . . .

"The foolish asked the others to share their oil, but spiritual preparedness cannot be shared in an instant. . . .

"The kind of oil that is needed to illuminate the way and light up the darkness is not shareable. How can one share obedience to the principle of tithing; a mind at peace from righteous living; an accumulation of knowledge? How can one share faith or testimony? How can one share attitudes or chastity, or the experience of a mission? How can one share temple privileges? Each must obtain that kind of oil for himself. . . .

"In the parable, oil can be purchased at the market. In our lives the oil of preparedness is accumulated drop by drop in righteous living. Attendance at sacrament meetings adds oil to our lamps, drop by drop over the years. Fasting, family prayer, home teaching, control of bodily appetites, preaching the gospel, studying the scriptures—each act of dedication and obedience is a drop added to our store. Deeds of kindness, payment of offerings and tithes, chaste thoughts and actions, marriage in the covenant for eternity—these, too, contribute importantly to the oil with which we can at midnight refuel our exhausted lamps."[18]

That is the real oil crisis of our generation, not the one that we sometimes see at the gas pumps. And *crisis* may not be too strong a word, considering how important it will be to have the Spirit with us in the days that lie ahead.

President Harold B. Lee quoted extensively from a statement by President Heber C. Kimball that directly referred to the imagery of the parable of the ten virgins: "I want to say to you, my brethren, the time is coming when we will be mixed up in these now peaceful valleys to that extent that it will be difficult to tell the face of a Saint from the face of an enemy to the people of God. Then, brethren, look out for the great sieve, for there will be a great sifting time, and many will fall—for I say unto you there is a *test,* a test, a TEST coming, and who will be able to stand? . . .

"Let me say to you, that many of you will see the time when you will have all the trouble, trial and persecution that you can stand, and plenty of opportunities to show that you are true to God and his work. This Church has before it many close places through which it will have to pass before the work of God is crowned with victory. To meet the difficulties that are coming, it will be necessary for you to have a knowledge of the truth of this work for yourselves. The difficulties will be of such a character that the man or woman who does not possess this personal knowledge or witness will fall. If you have not got the testimony, live right and call upon the Lord and cease not till you obtain it. If you do not you will not stand.

"Remember these sayings, for many of you will live to see them fulfilled. The time will come when no man nor woman will be able to endure on borrowed light. Each will have to be guided by the light within himself. If you do not have it, how can you stand?"[19]

From this we can conclude that perhaps the single most important thing that we can do in preparing ourselves for the Second Coming is to live so that we can have the power of the Holy Ghost in our lives to guide us, to help us to avoid deception, to give us testimony, and to prepare us for whatever is to come.

The Parable of the Talents (Matthew 25:14–30)

The parable of the talents, the second parable given by the Savior in Matthew 25, is well known, although not often associated with preparing ourselves for the Second Coming. It has an important lesson for anyone seeking to live the gospel, but the context in which it was given—the Olivet Discourse—gives it special meaning in relation to preparing spiritually for the Savior's return.

In the parable, a man about to take a journey into a far country calls three servants together and delivers to them some of his goods. To one he gives five talents; to another, two; and to another, one. That is done "according to [their] several ability." Then the master takes his journey, leaving the servants to carry on. The first servant through diligent effort doubles the investment given him. When the master returns and learns that this servant now has ten talents, the master is greatly pleased and says to him, "Well done, thou good and faithful servant: thou hast been faithful over a few things. I will make thee ruler over many things: enter thou into the joy of thy lord" (Matt. 25:21). When the second servant reports that he too, through his diligent effort, has doubled the investment given to him, the master says exactly the same thing to him. That clearly indicates it was not the original amount that mattered but the effort to magnify it. We can assume, then, that if the servant to whom one talent had been given had also been diligent in the use of what the Lord had given him, the Lord would have said exactly the same thing to him as well. Only when the servant makes excuses is the master angry with him, calling him a "wicked and slothful servant" (Matt. 25:26).

Once again, remembering that this parable was given as part of Christ's answer on how to prepare for his second coming, what do we learn from the parable of the talents? Statements from two of our modern prophets help us see what the Savior was trying to teach us with this parable.

President Joseph Fielding Smith linked the parable to the obligations of priesthood holders: "Each man holding the priesthood should learn his duty from the Parable of the Talents. . . . We are under obligation as men holding the priesthood to put to service the authority which we have received. If we do this, then we shall have other responsibilities and glory added, and we shall receive an abundance, that is, the fullness of the Father's kingdom; but if we bury our priesthood, then we are not entitled to receive any reward—we cannot be exalted."[20]

And President Spencer W. Kimball talked about the meaning of the parable for all Church members: "The Church member who has the attitude of leaving it to others will have much to answer for. There are many who say: 'My wife does the Church work!' Others say, 'I'm just not the religious kind,' as though it does not take effort for most people to serve and do their duty. But God has endowed us with talents and time, with latent abilities and with opportunities to use and develop them in his service. He therefore expects much of us, his privileged children. The parable of the talents is a brilliant summary of the many scriptural passages outlining promises for the diligent and penalties for the slothful."[21]

What is the lesson of this parable for those who wish to better prepare themselves spiritually? We are to use those things the Lord has bestowed upon us—gifts, talents, abilities, goods, services—in furthering his work. That is what is meant by the principle of consecration. It is a principle often taught in the scriptures. For example, in the Sermon on the Mount, the Savior said: "Seek not the things of this world but seek ye first to build up the kingdom of God, and to establish his righteousness" (JST Matt. 6:33). And an oft-repeated charge given to early leaders of the Church was to "seek to bring forth and establish the cause of Zion" (D&C 6:6; see also 12:6; 14:6).

And here is an interesting point. When we take this second charge—to strive to use whatever we have been given to further God's work—then we also fulfill the lesson of the first parable and add oil to our supply. Note how Nephi directly connected the effort to build Zion to having greater power through the Spirit: "And blessed are they who shall seek to bring forth my Zion at that day, for they shall have the gift and the power of the Holy Ghost" (1 Ne. 13:37).

If we are diligent in consecrating to his service whatever the Lord has blessed us with, not only shall we be greatly blessed spiritually now but when the Lord comes he shall say to us, as he said to the first two servants in the parable, "Well done, thou good and faithful servant."

The Parable of the Sheep and the Goats (Matthew 25:31–46)

The parable of the sheep and the goats, the last parable given by the Savior on the Mount of Olives, is another well-known and often-cited parable that is not often directly related to preparing for the Second Coming, although that is the context in which it was given. It compares the final judgment to a shepherd's separating his flock. In the Near East, shepherds commonly allow sheep and goats to graze together, but when it comes time for sale, shearing, or other purposes, the sheep and the goats are separated. So shall it be at the Judgment.

In the parable, those compared to the sheep are asked to sit at the right hand of God. To them, the king says, "Come, ye blessed of my Father, inherit the kingdom prepared for you from the foundation of the world: for I was an hungred, and ye gave me meat: I was thirsty, and ye gave me drink: I was a stranger, and ye took me in: Naked, and ye clothed me: I was sick, and ye visited me: I was in prison, and ye came unto me" (Matt. 25:34–36).

Surprised at the Savior's comments, those on his right hand asked, "Lord, when saw we thee an hungred, and fed thee? or thirsty, and gave thee drink? When saw we thee a stranger, and took thee in? or naked, and clothed thee? Or when saw we thee sick, or in prison, and came unto thee?" (Matt. 25:37–39). The Lord's answer summarizes a most important gospel principle: "Verily I say unto you, Inasmuch as ye have done it unto one of the least of these my brethren, ye have done it unto me" (Matt. 25:40).

Those who are put on the left hand of God (those compared to the goats) are dismayed, and they demand to know why they are so placed. Again the Lord explains, this time saying that they did not do any of those things for him.

This parable teaches a third area of spiritual preparation, which is that we must serve our fellowmen as though we were serving Christ. Like the doctrine of consecration, the doctrine of service to our fellowman is taught in numerous other places in the scriptures. For example, in the Lord's preface to the Doctrine and Covenants, the Lord specifically linked how we will be judged to how we have treated our fellowmen (see D&C 1:10). King Benjamin taught that when we serve our fellowman, we are serving God (see Mosiah 2:17).

Modern prophets have taught the same principle. Christian service was often stressed by President Spencer W. Kimball:

"None of us should become so busy in our formal Church assignments that there is no room left for quiet Christian service to our neighbors."[22]

"Recently [the Church] established the new consolidated schedule which is aimed at enriching family life even further, together with greater opportunity for individual and family gospel scholarship *and for more Christian service.* We are trying to provide more time and emphasis on Christian service, so that our example can be more powerful in the world and so that those who are so worthy of attention might get more attention than they sometimes have in the past."[23]

"How much easier it is to understand and accept [the gospel] if the seeker after truth can also see the principles of the gospel at work in the lives of other believers. No greater service can be given to the missionary calling of this Church than to be exemplary in positive Christian virtues in our lives."[24]

These three wonderful parables show us how to prepare ourselves spiritually for the Second Coming. First, we live so that we will have the influence of the Holy Ghost to give us testimony and guide us (the lesson of the five wise virgins). Second, we render service to the Church and kingdom of God, doing all we can to further the cause of Zion and aid the Lord in doing his work (the lesson of the talents). Third, we show we love God by loving and compassionately serving our fellowman (the lesson of the sheep and the goats).

Conclusion

We prepare ourselves for Christ's second coming by gaining greater knowledge and understanding; by becoming temporally self-reliant in education, health, employment, home storage, resource management, and social, emotional, and spiritual strength; and by increasing our spirituality so that we have the Spirit, consecrating the things with which the Lord has blessed us to build his kingdom, and serving our fellowman. When we have made such preparation, then surely we will better understand the Lord's promise: "If ye are prepared ye shall not fear" (D&C 38:30).

President Brigham Young gave some marvelous advice about what our focus should be as we strive to be better prepared for Christ's coming: "Are you prepared for the day of vengeance to come, when the Lord will consume the wicked by the brightness of his coming? No. Then do not be too anxious for the Lord to hasten his work. *Let our anxiety be centred upon this one thing, the sanctification of our own hearts,* the purifying of our own affections, the preparing of ourselves for the approach of the events that are hastening upon us. *This should be our concern, this should be our study, this should be our daily prayer,* and not to be in a hurry to see the overthrow of the wicked. . . . Seek not to hasten it, but be satisfied to let the Lord have his own time and way, and be patient. *Seek to have the Spirit of Christ,* that we may wait patiently the time of the Lord, and prepare ourselves for the times that are coming. This is our duty."[25]

Notes

From *Watch and Be Ready: Preparing for the Second Coming of the Lord* (Salt Lake City: Deseret Book Co., 1994), 192–219.

1. Jedediah M. Grant, "The Hand of God in Events on Earth," *Improvement Era,* February 1915, 286; emphasis added.
2. Marion G. Romney, in Conference Report, October 1966, 51–52; emphasis added.
3. Joseph Fielding Smith, *The Signs of the Times* (Salt Lake City: Deseret Book Co., 1964), 154–55; emphasis added.
4. Brigham Young, Heber C. Kimball, and Willard Richards, First Presidency of The Church of Jesus Christ of Latter-day Saints, Fifth General Epistle, 7 Apr. 1851; printed in *Millennial Star* 13 (15 July 1851): 210.
5. Melvin J. Ballard, in Conference Report, April 1930, 157; emphasis added.
6. Thomas S. Monson, "Days Never to be Forgotten," *Ensign,* November 1990, 67.
7. Ezra Taft Benson, "To the Fathers in Israel," *Ensign,* November 1987, 49.
8. Spencer W. Kimball, in Conference Report, October 1977, 124.
9. Harold B. Lee, address delivered at LDS Church employees Christmas devotional in Salt Lake City, Utah, 13 December 1973, 6; emphasis added.
10. Marion G. Romney, in Conference Report, April 1975, 165; emphasis added.
11. Spencer W. Kimball, in Conference Report, April 1974, 184–85; emphasis added.
12. Heber C. Kimball, in *Journal of Discourses,* 26 vols. (London: Latter-day Saints' Book Depot, 1854–86), 4:106; 5:10; emphasis added.
13. Orson Pratt, in *Journal of Discourses,* 2:60–61; emphasis added.
14. Ibid., 3:16–17.
15. Victor L. Brown, "The Church and the Family in Welfare Services," *Ensign,* May 1976, 111–12; italics in original.

16. Ezra Taft Benson, *The Teachings of Ezra Taft Benson* (Salt Lake City: Bookcraft, 1988), 106; emphasis added.
17. George Mackie, *Bible Manners and Customs* (New York: Fleming H. Revell, 1898), 123–26.
18. Spencer W. Kimball, *Faith Precedes the Miracle* (Salt Lake City: Deseret Book Co., 1972), 253–56; emphasis added.
19. Orson F. Whitney, *Life of Heber C. Kimball* (Salt Lake City: Bookcraft, 1945), 446, 449–50; cited by Harold B. Lee, in Conference Report, October 1965, 128.
20. Joseph Fielding Smith, in Conference Report, April 1966, 102.
21. Spencer W. Kimball, *The Teachings of Spencer W. Kimball,* ed. Edward L. Kimball (Salt Lake City: Bookcraft, 1992), 149.
22. Ibid., 256.
23. Ibid., 493.
24. Ibid., 555.
25. Brigham Young, in *Journal of Discourses,* 9:3; emphasis added.

Excellence in Teaching

Chapter 29

Strengthening the Bridges

The story is told of a naval captain in San Diego, the commander of a battleship, who sailed from the dock out through the harbor and into the open sea. The ship had been away from the harbor for just a few minutes when a huge, very dense fog bank rolled in, so they had to go to radar mode. All of a sudden, the signalman ran onto the bridge to his naval commander and said, "Commander, we've picked something up on the radar: we're on a collision course with another ship." The commander very coolly said, "Well, radio that ship and tell him to move ten degrees starboard" (to the right). So they signaled and sent the message. Right back came the reply: "You are on a collision course; suggest you move ten degrees port"—that is, to the left.

When they showed that message to the commander, he was really upset. So he said, "Send this message back. Tell them that I am a full naval commander, and I am ordering them to move ten degrees starboard." Back came the message, "I am a seaman second class and I am ordering you to move ten degrees port." By now the commander was livid. "Send this message! I am on the bridge of a five-thousand-ton battleship. Demand you move ten degrees starboard." Back came the message: "I'm at the bridge of a lighthouse. Demand you move ten degrees port."

Besides being a delightful story (though probably not true), this has some great messages that apply to all of us who teach in the Church. One of the things we are trying to do is to get our students to move a few degrees—or a lot of degrees—to the right and to avoid some collision courses with some dangerously hard objects.

Elder Neal A. Maxwell, in 1979, made a statement that I think supports the idea that we are on a collision course with some pretty serious kinds of things: "Now we are entering times wherein there will be for all of us as Church members, in my judgment, some special challenges which will require of us that we follow the Brethren. All the easy things that the Church has had to do have been done. From now on, it's high adventure. And followership is going to be tested in some interesting ways."[1]

As I have thought about that statement and the idea of what challenges lie in the future, I have been reminded of some other scriptures. In the first section of the Doctrine and Covenants, there is a sobering statement in verse 35, where the Lord says, "For I am no respecter of persons, and will that all men shall know that the day speedily cometh; the hour is not yet, but is nigh at hand, when peace shall be taken from the earth, and the devil shall have power over his own dominion."

In Doctrine and Covenants 45 there is a prophecy about the future that, when you really think about its implications, is quite sobering:

"And it shall come to pass among the wicked, that every man that will not take his sword against his neighbor must needs flee unto Zion for safety. And there shall be gathered unto it out of every nation under heaven; and it shall be the only people that shall not be at war one with another" (vv. 68–69).

This prophecy suggests to me that the time is coming when a person will have two choices: either he will have to take up personal arms in defense against his neighbor, or he will have to flee to Zion. Anarchy and war and hypocrisy will be widespread when we reach that state.

In 2 Timothy 3, Paul makes another rather sobering prediction to Timothy, who is evidently a young bishop. This is the chapter where Paul says that in the last days perilous times will come. But two verses I had not paid a whole lot of attention to until recently are verses 12–13:

"Yea, and all that will live godly in Christ Jesus shall suffer persecution. But evil men and seducers shall wax worse and worse, deceiving, and being deceived."

Finally, in Revelation 12:17, John prophetically gives another very serious and thought-provoking statement: "And the dragon [which is the symbol of Satan] was wroth with the woman [which is the symbol of the Church], and went to make war with the remnant of her seed."

Think about that. John wrote that Satan will "make war with the remnant of her [the Church's] seed, which keep the commandments of God, and have the testimony of Jesus Christ" (Rev. 12:17).

Then in Revelation 13:7, John said, "And it was given unto him [a wicked beast that serves Satan] to make war with the saints, and to overcome them." I do not think he means to overcome the Church, but to overcome some of the Saints. I think we see that spiritual disaster happening in the lives of many around us—youth, adults, and others.

As I think about that challenge and some of the collision courses that we are on and that our youth are on, I think of a story that was printed in the *Guideposts* magazine a few years back.

A Christian missionary couple were called to Africa to serve deep in the heart of the continent. When they got to the coast, they were told that they would be taking machinery to a missionary center at their outpost in Zaire. They had a whole truckload of heavy machinery. When they got the truck completely loaded, it weighed about eight tons.

That was a problem. The road that led to where they were going passed over many rivers and many streams, and over deep ravines. The bridges were crude, they were made of logs tied together with vines. Some of the bridges had 3T on the sign next to them meaning the limit was 3 tons. Some had 6T. None of them had 8T beside them. The truck was too heavy.

The missionary was deeply concerned, and his wife said, "What are we going to do about all that weight on those bridges? We will have to leave some stuff behind." The missionary said, "There isn't anything I can do to lighten the load. I'll just have to reinforce the bridges." So that is what they did. They started out, and at each bridge they would stop and, with considerable work, sometimes dangerous work because the rivers were infested with crocodiles and poisonous snakes, they would cut down trees, strengthen the bridge, and rebuild it to the point where it could carry the eight tons. And thus they delivered the supplies.[2]

I have thought a lot about that in terms of our youth today because, as I look down the future and glimpse what the Lord has shown us and told us about what is coming, I see no way to lighten the load for the students. Think about the challenges the Church has given us, which includes the youth: to teach the world, every nation, kindred, tongue, and people; to perfect the Saints, more than ten million of them, when only about 45 percent of them go to sacrament meeting on any given Sunday; and to redeem the dead. Do you think of the staggering audacity of each of those objectives? It is pretty sobering, is it not?

In a little book published by the Church called *From You to Your Ancestors,* we get a small glimpse of the enormity of this latter task. The book indicates that somewhere around fifty-two million people die each year. We do vicarious work for about five million people in the temples each year. This means each year we fall

93.5 percent behind in the work for those who die, and that's not to count the billions who died before![3]

We expect the youth to teach the world, perfect the Saints, and redeem the dead—and all in a day of increasing wickedness, spreading warfare, and collapsing social order. No wonder it is sobering. I just do not know any way that you are going to take any part of that load off the truck. I do not think we can do it, so it seems to me that our only option is to strengthen the bridges.

How can we strengthen the bridges for our youth? And how can we strengthen those who are teaching and who are, in some ways, the bridges for the bridges?

In that same talk by Elder Maxwell, given in 1979, he said: "Now I know the realities of the classroom—some of the time your best efforts will be met with indifference [if you are lucky]. I know also, however, that for many of your students you are in fact planting little intellectual and spiritual time bombs, and the implantation is so subtle that you'll wonder if in fact you have connected at all. And then someday, when circumstances are right, there will be in them an explosion of reminding relevancy from that implantation from your instruction. And there will be a few—there always are—in the classroom for whom you will become particularly powerful as you awaken in them and stir within them this desire to deepen their personal scholarship."[4]

Now let me give you a statement from another talk by Elder Maxwell, given in 1983. It is a little lengthy, but it is relevant to what we are talking about. He said:

"I hope, even in your modesty, that you [as religious educators] have some sense of your place in Church history. With the exception of your students who are blessed with especially dedicated and teaching parents or the occasional able teacher of long tenure in a ward or branch, you spend more time teaching the gospel to your students than does anyone else. Moreover, the rising generation, those seedling Saints who sit before you—ordinary as they may seem on a dull day—are being especially prepared for unique service to the last days of this dispensation. To a significant degree, you are trusted with the shaping of their religious education—a very genuine compliment to you and a blessing to them.

"Even so, I have no desire to dramatize unduly your influence on your students. Some of the concepts you teach so carefully will be blown away. . . . Still other principles will go unnourished and will be scorched by the heat of the sun and will wither. Yet some of your students will remember and apply what you have taught. . . .

"Meanwhile, what you teach will sometimes make the behavioral margin of difference in the lives of your students—whether expressed in a parked car, in the terror of a future battlefield, in the loneliness of a hospital room, or in quiet Christian service. There will be no notice taken of this, your causality, on the six o'clock news. There will be no letter to the editor in praise of you. But even so, you will have had a share in such victories because you will have cared for your students, for the gospel you teach them, and, especially for the Savior who is the Center of it all."[5]

That is an interesting challenge in our time and age. Later in his address, with that marvelous ability he has to capture imagery, Elder Maxwell said: "Though drenched in destiny, they [your students], cannot yet feel the moisture of their own possibilities."[6] They *are* drenched in destiny, even though they don't know it.

So our question is, how do we help them strengthen the bridges? There is a section in the Doctrine and Covenants that, though it may not have been written for us, has great application and great help and great teaching. It is section 38, given on the second day of 1831 through the Prophet in Fayette.

I would like to walk through this section, applying it to what we do with the students and the challenges they face, the bridges they have to cross, and the obstacles that are in the seas they will have to travel. The section begins this way: "Thus saith the Lord your God, even Jesus Christ, the Great I Am, Alpha and Omega, the beginning and the end" (v. 1).

Each of these words is weighted with meaning about this being who is speaking to us, this glorious God who is addressing us. He continues, I am "the same which looked upon the wide expanse of eternity, and all the seraphic hosts of heaven" (v. 1).

Imagine what comprehension it would take to look upon the whole expanse of eternity and all the seraphic hosts of heaven, before the world was made.

I am "the same which knoweth all things" (v. 2).

It seems to me that he is saying, "I know where all the lighthouses are for your people. I know the challenges they are going to face. I know the rivers and ravines they must cross. I know what traps they are going to fall into. And how do I know this?"

"For all things are present before mine eyes" (v. 2).

This is an interesting concept because there are two definitions for the word *present.* One is to be in the same geographical location, or "here." Another is to be in the same time, or "now." Does the Lord mean "all things are *here* before mine eyes" or "all things are *now* before mine eyes"? I think there's a good chance both are true.

Now let's skip down to verse 7:

"Behold, verily, verily, I say unto you that mine eyes are upon *you.* I am in your midst and ye cannot see me. But the day soon cometh that ye shall see me, and know that I am" (vv. 7–8; emphasis added).

The scriptures tell us when the Second Coming takes place all men will see him together (see D&C 101:23).

"For the veil of darkness shall soon be rent, and he that is not purified shall not abide the day" (D&C 38:8).

Now think about that in terms of teaching. We as teachers, we as the spouses, and we as students—if we are not purified, we shall not abide that day. We will see him, but we will not abide the day.

"Wherefore, [now is the time to] gird up your loins and be prepared. Behold, the kingdom is yours, and the enemy shall not overcome" (v. 9).

As sobering as the challenges are, as powerful as Satan is in this day and age, God says the kingdom is ours, not Satan's, in spite of what he boasts. And God promises the enemy shall not overcome.

"Verily I say unto you, ye are clean, but not all" (v. 10).

When I first read that, I thought, *That is really true. There are many in the Church who are not clean.* I was thinking of it as the group—that not all of us are clean. And suddenly it occurred to me that in our language *you* can be either singular or plural. We can talk about *you,* referring to several people, or we can talk about *you,* referring to one person. I asked myself, *Does that fit? Could he be speaking singularly here: "Verily I say unto you [Jerry Lund], ye are clean, but not all"?* The answer was sobering. I think there is some application there.

And yet even though you (individually or collectively) are not completely clean, he continues: "There is none else with whom I am well pleased" (v. 10)—no other group besides the Church.

"For all flesh is corrupted before me; and the powers of darkness prevail upon the earth" (v. 11).

Your students are swimming in that darkness. Your students are bringing it home on videocassettes. They are getting it in the high school and the junior high. I have a fourteen-year-old daughter. On vacation a couple of weeks ago, we started talking about the challenges she faces, and I asked her about drugs in her junior high school. She said, "Oh, yeah. They're all over the place. I could get them any day of the week I want. Even down to seventh grade." And one of my other children piped up and said, "You could probably find them at the elementary schools, too, if you looked a little harder."

Our children are swimming in darkness. It does prevail upon the earth. So much, in fact, that the Lord says it "causeth silence to reign, and all eternity is pained" (v. 12).

That is a tremendous amount of wickedness, enough to pain all of eternity.

"And the angels are waiting the great command to reap down the earth [to get rid of the filth and the trash and clean up the mess and prepare for the Second Coming], to gather the tares that they may be burned; and, behold, the enemy is combined" (v. 12).

Whether the various organizations engaged in evil know it or not, all of Satan's forces are united to fight against the work. All the forces of hell are combined to fight against God and his work.

"And now I show unto you a mystery, a thing which is had in secret chambers, to bring to pass even your destruction in process of time, and ye knew it not; but now I tell it unto you, and ye are blessed [speaking of us again as a church], not because of your iniquity, neither your hearts of unbelief; for verily some of you are guilty before me, but I will be merciful unto your weakness. Therefore, be ye strong from henceforth" (vv. 13–15).

We are talking about building stronger bridges. "Be ye strong from henceforth," he says. And again comes the admonition, in spite of the sobering weight of the challenges that face us: "Fear not, for the kingdom is yours" (v. 15).

And then he says in verse 16: "And for your salvation I give unto you a commandment" (v. 16).

As I read through the next few verses looking for the commandment, I had a hard time finding it. But on closer examination, I found not one commandment, but ten commandments. Since they apply so directly to us, I call these the ten commandments of teaching. Let's go through these one at a time.

"Hear My Voice and Follow Me"

This is found in verse 22: "Wherefore, hear my voice and follow me."

In some of our seminary and institute classes, we spend a lot of time talking about hearing the voice of the Lord. Unfortunately, this voice is still and it is small and it whispers. Wouldn't it be wonderful if the Holy Ghost used eighty-megawatt amplifiers and five-foot speakers so that every time he spoke the whole room would shake? There would be no mistaking where it was coming from. But instead the voice is still and it is small and it whispers. It cannot be forced, but it comes to us every day, every hour.

I really believe that the second major way the Lord's voice speaks to us is through the scriptures. One of the best ways to hear the voice of the Lord and follow him is to immerse yourself in the scriptures. Read them. Study them. Ponder them. Notice the Lord's words: "Feast upon them" (see 2 Ne. 31:20). "Treasure them up" (see JS–M 1:37). If we do that, if we heed this commandment to "hear my voice," we can partake of the promise in Doctrine and Covenants 38:22: "Wherefore, hear my voice and follow me, and you shall be a free people, and ye shall have no laws but my laws when I come, for I am your lawgiver, and what can stay my hand?"

There is the concept of power again—even though we are up against a tremendous combined evil force, nothing can stay the hand of the Lord if we are with him.

"Teach One Another"

In Doctrine and Covenants 38:23, we have commandment number two: "But, verily I say unto you, teach one another according to the office wherewith I have appointed you."

There are two other places in the Doctrine and Covenants where the Lord uses this same phrase: "Teach one another." Both are in section 88. First, in verse 77 we read: "And I give you a commandment that you shall teach one another." Then in verse 118 we find the phrase again: "And as all have not faith, seek ye diligently and teach one another."

Now let's look at those two verses and see what we are commanded to teach one another. In verse 77 we are told to teach one another "the doctrine of the kingdom," and in verse 118 we are to "teach one another words of wisdom."

I have thought a lot about this. I'm not suggesting that every time a group of us Latter-day Saints gather together we take all the smiles off our faces and say, "Now, don't anybody talk about anything but the scriptures." But are we teaching one another the doctrine of the kingdom? Are we teaching one another out of the best books? Wives, are you teaching your husbands? Husbands, are you teaching in your homes? Let me give you an actual example of how you wives can teach your husbands.

Some years ago, we were wrestling with the question of what really constitutes scripture mastery for a teacher. When we use the phrase "He is a master teacher of the scriptures," what do we mean? We were trying to pin that down so we could talk more about it. I wrestled with different definitions for two or three days and was really frustrated because none of them was very satisfying. That night I happened to mention it to my wife. I said, "How do you define mastery of the scriptures?" With hardly a thought she said, "When you can call upon the scriptures without specific prior preparation." When you are in class and have prepared something else and a student raises his hand and says, "What does this mean, Brother Jones?" and you can call up answers at will from the scriptures, that is scripture mastery. My wife taught me that day, and I have remembered it. It was a significant experience.

Your students can teach you. Teaching one another does not always imply teacher to student. Some of the great insights of my life have come from students and the comments they have made or the insights they have picked up. Teaching one another can happen in other times and places as well.

"Let Every Man Esteem His Brother as Himself"

Commandment number three for teachers is, "And let every man esteem his brother as himself" (D&C 38:24). This commandment is so important that the Lord stresses it again in the next verse: "Let every man esteem his brother as himself."

I have had an interesting experience lately. I do not know whether the Lord has a sense of humor or just a great sense of justice, but I have been talking about teaching and telling others how to do it for the last five years. We moved this last January into a new home and a new ward. Presently, I serve on the Youth Correlation Committee of the Church, which means that I do not have to take any other Church callings. They recommend that we do not take anything major, but they leave it at our option if we want to take callings that do not involve large blocks of time. We had not been in that ward for three weeks before a member of the bishopric came over and said, "We'd like you to teach Sunday School." I smiled. Then he said, "The thirteen-year-olds." I quit smiling because my daughter is in that class, and I knew what it was like. This was the terror class of the ward—fifteen thirteen-year-olds. They had had six teachers in the previous few weeks, each quitting for one reason or another. Three of the teachers had quit before their first class period was over. They just said, "That's it," walked out, found the bishopric, and said, "I quit!"

I remember I almost said to this counselor in the bishopric, "Well, Brother, I'm on the Youth Correlation Committee, and they ask us not to take other callings." At that moment, a thought ran through my mind: *Sure, go ahead. You tell everybody else what to do and how to teach, but you don't do it.* All those things ran through my mind, and I thought, *Come on, hypocrite,* and so I found myself saying, "Yes, I'll do it."

I am telling you, that has been one of the most frustrating experiences of my life. First of all, class is held in a tiny room; it is the smallest room in the building. I have fifteen thirteen-year-olds crammed in there, one sitting on top of the other. Second, they are totally unimpressed by what I do for a living. The fact that I teach thousands of teachers all over the world means nothing to them. And frankly, after two very disastrous experiences, I became intimidated and violated all of the very principles I had been teaching. I decided I would hook them with gimmicks. I did not say that straight out to them, but I decided to start a little scripture chase. I figured a little competition, fun and games, would do it. It went from total disaster to absolute chaos, and then I started to repent.

The first thing I started to remember is something about esteeming your brother as yourself. I was frustrated with those young people. They were good kids, every one of them, but I was getting so I resented them terribly. I would go to class well prepared, I would teach them my best lesson—and nothing! If we got through the opening prayer without disaster, I considered it progress. Then I remembered this commandment: "Esteem your brother as yourself" (see v. 24). I knelt down and began to pray to the Lord, "Help me to love these kids." And something began to happen.

The second thing I remembered was some comments from President J. Reuben Clark Jr.—statements about how our students are hungry for the things of the Spirit.[7] My class was hungry all right. They were eating me every time I went into class! It was I who was being chewed to pieces.

So one day in the middle of the lesson I just threw up my hands, and I said, "Hey, this is it. Why should I do this? I mean, I have had it. What do you want out of this class?" The first answer, of course, was "We want a party." So we talked about that, and they laughed and joked.

Then they started to get a little more serious, and finally one of the girls, one of the worst ones, said, "Stop teaching us what we already know. We've heard what you are teaching again and again."

I said, "What do you want to know?" I expected they would list dating and things like that. Instead, they surprised me by saying, "Teach us about the resurrection. We want to know about patriarchal blessings. What does it mean to be Israel?" So I repented and began feeding them from the scriptures, and it has been one of the great experiences in my life.

I have come to love that class and to love the experience of teaching them. We are having a great experience together because they are now feeding on the gospel. I know of a surety that what President Clark said is true, that the scriptures are food for them. I came to that realization when I began to esteem them as I esteem myself. When I go to a Sunday School class, I do not want to be fed fun and games. I am sick to death of going into a Sunday School class and being entertained for forty minutes; yet that is what I was trying to do to them. If I really esteemed them as myself, I would try to teach them.

"Practice Virtue and Holiness"

In the verse we cited previously, verse 24 of section 38, the Lord gives us the fourth commandment: "Let every man esteem his brother as himself, and practise virtue and holiness before me." As I have read that in the past, I have always focused on the phrase "virtue and holiness." And they are important qualities—qualities we must have if we are to please the Lord. But another word leaped out at me this time, the word *practice.* We are to practice virtue and holiness.

There are two senses in which the word *practice* can be used. One sense is in the same way we use it when we say "He has a dental practice," or "He has a good medical practice." This connotes the doing of something, a profession, a way of life. And certainly verse 24 suggests this. Wouldn't it be wonderful if people said of us, "They have a virtue and holiness practice"? But there is another sense in which the word is used. We say, "Jane needs to practice her piano," or "John needs more practice to really excel at baseball." Can the word *practice* in this sense be used of virtue and holiness? I believe so. Most of us do not strike the perfect life in our first attempt.

Practice, in this sense, means to do something again and again with continual efforts to improve one's performance. While I may not yet have fully achieved virtue and holiness in my life, I can practice it every day.

This concept becomes critical as we teach. Your students have not yet achieved the practice (in the medical or dental sense) of virtue and holiness, but they too can practice it every day. We need to be aware of this so we do not teach and inadvertently breed discouragement.

We need to start where our students are and help them move in small, incremental steps, a day at a time, in order to reach spiritual goals—just like we would help them practice the piano, or batting a baseball, or learning any other physical skills. And so in commandment four I found some great insights—"*practise* virtue and holiness before me" (emphasis added).

"Be One"

After telling us that we should esteem our brothers as ourselves, the Lord gives us the parable of a parent with twelve sons. Would you be a fair parent if you treated one son this way and another son that way for the same behavior? Of course not. After the parable the Lord gives us commandment number five: "Behold, this I have given unto you as a parable, and it is even as I am. I say unto you, be one" (v. 27). Oh, what a great challenge that is! Man and wife are commanded to be one flesh; brothers and sisters are to be one.

In the great prayer in John 17, Christ says we are to look to him and the Father as the model of what it means to be one. In Moses 7:18 he talks about Zion and teaches us that they were of *one* mind and *one* heart. That is what we are trying to achieve.

One of the experiences I truly cherish is working on the *Hold to the Rod* media project for the Church's seminary system. After working together on the project for some time, Steve Jones and I brought Ron Munns in to help with the project. Right off the bat we had him join us for a brainstorming session. For almost two hours Steve and I just went at it. "I don't like this," one would say. "I don't like this," the other would respond. Ron just sat there thinking. "What's going on?" What he came to understand later was that early in the life of the project, Steve and I made a commitment to each other—and I recommend it to husbands and wives, to people in many work situations, or whatever you are. We made a commitment that *no one* had the final say, not me as the division director, not Steve as the producer, not Ron as the manager. You either had to convince the rest of the team or we kept on talking.

The commandment that none of us would impose our will on the other, that we would not move without oneness, has brought many great experiences to us. We still go at it on some things, we still have long discussions, but when we finally come to unity, great results happen. Think of what building that oneness would do for a seminary faculty, or for a Young Women presidency. Great things happen when men and women come together in unity for a righteous cause. I really believe that, and so the Lord says, commandment number five is "Be one" (D&C 38:27).

"Treasure Up Wisdom"

Commandment number six is given in verse 30: "Treasure up wisdom in your bosoms." There are two senses of the word *treasure*. One is in the verb sense, to value something greatly. I think the Lord means that when he says, "Treasure up wisdom"; and notice that he does not tell us to treasure it up in our heads—it is in our bosoms or our hearts.

But there is another sense of the word *treasure,* and that is to build or make a treasure. What do you do with a treasure? You draw from it as you need it. I think the scriptures are that kind of treasure, to be highly valued and to be drawn from as needed. But remember in Doctrine and Covenants 88:118 he said to study words of wisdom "out of the best books." One of the things I have found most helpful in my teaching is to constantly read good books.

Later in section 38 the Lord said, "And if ye seek the riches which it is the will of the Father to give unto you, ye shall be the richest of all people." What riches is he talking about? "For ye shall have the riches of eternity" (v. 39).

One of our commandments, one of our goals should be to seek the riches of the Father—wisdom, understanding, gospel knowledge, power in the priesthood, faith, repentance, all of the gifts he has to offer us. But he couples this commandment with a warning: "The riches of the earth are mine to give; but beware of pride" (v. 39).

"Beware of Pride"

During my years of teaching in the Church Educational System, as I have watched myself and other teachers, I have noticed an occupational hazard of my profession: the better you get, the more likely you are to believe it. The better you become as a teacher, the more often people will come to you and say you were wonderful. And the more they do that, the greater the temptation to say inwardly, *Yeah, I really was.*

Pride does not come only from temporal riches. Most of us have been endowed with great gifts and talents, and the Lord says to seek those gifts and talents, *but*—beware of pride.

In connection with this is the seventh commandment of teaching: "Seek the riches . . . of the Father . . . but beware of pride" (v. 39). I often think of something a very wise (and skilled) teacher told me years ago. I asked him one day how he had become so skilled. He said, "I have learned to say two things in my prayers everyday: 'Lord, I thank thee for the gifts I have,' and 'Help me to remember that these gifts come from thee and that they are to be used in thy cause and thy purpose.'" We are to seek for the gifts, but we must be very, very careful about pride.

"Go to with His Might"

In verses 40 to 42, the Lord gives three commandments in rapid-fire order. "And again, I say unto you, I give unto you a commandment, that every man, both elder, priest, teacher, and also member, go to with his might" (v. 40). That is commandment number eight: As teachers we are commanded to go to with our might.

"Go to with your might." It is not an easy job to be a teacher. I think that the Lord is saying, in his own way, "Pay the price." Pay the price in diligence; do all that is required of you. Pay the price in preparation. If you are putting in half an hour to prepare a one-hour lesson, unless you are far better than anyone I know, you are not going to be succeeding. I wish it came cheaper, but it doesn't. You have to pay a price in caring for those you teach, and that does not come easily either. The Lord says, "The laborer is worthy of his hire" (D&C 31:5). If we truly labor, then we are worthy of what we are paid, and I think the Lord will pay us well.

"Let Your Preaching Be the Warning Voice . . . in Mildness and in Meekness"

In verse 41 of section 38, we find the ninth commandment: "Let your preaching be the warning voice, every man to his neighbor, in mildness and in meekness." I have thought a great deal about that combination of words. One of the things that comes to my mind is an experience I had in my first year of teaching at a school in the Salt Lake Valley. One of my students was a young man who was a member of the so-called "parking lot gang." He was on drugs back when drugs were not so common. He smoked. He drank. I developed a great relationship with that young man and had an excellent rapport with him. He began to come into my office each morning or after school. Day after day, he would tell me all the things he was doing, the girls he was sleeping with, the drugs he was taking. I worked with that young boy for almost a year. As I said, we had a great relationship, great rapport. But not once did I ever say to him, "What you are doing will bring you misery. What you are doing will have an eternal effect on you." I was so concerned about keeping that relationship warm, loving, and supportive that I never warned him. Thoughts of that boy still haunt me. I have never seen him since, but I still think of him when I read, "Let your preaching be the warning voice."

Taken alone, however, that counsel could lead to abuse. We could thunder out repentance daily and drive our students away. So the Lord adds this little caution:

"every man to his neighbor, in mildness and meekness." No pulpit thumping, no scripture bashing.

Let me share with you another experience that I think illustrates the balance between raising the warning voice and doing it in mildness. When I was a junior in high school, our teachers held a dance as part of gym. I did not dance. I am not saying I did not like to dance. *I did not dance.* The reason was that I was deathly afraid of stepping on the girl's toes and making a fool of myself because I did not know how to dance. So during the dance I took my chemistry book and went to the top row of the bleachers and started studying chemistry.

About halfway through the dance, they announced a girls' choice, at which point I promptly buried my head deeper in my book. Then I heard footsteps coming up the bleachers. I can remember refusing to look up and thinking, *Oh, no! Don't do this to me!* But finally there were a pair of legs and a skirt standing before me. I looked up, and she said, "Jerry, would you dance with me?"

I said, "I'm sorry, but I just can't."

Well, you can imagine how she felt. She turned around and started down the bleachers. At this point, the girls' gym teacher, who had been watching the whole thing, came over and took her by the hand. Now the two of them were coming back up the bleachers. I knew this was not going to be pretty. The girls' gym teacher was also my math teacher, so she knew me. She said, "Jerry, this young lady has come all the way up these bleachers to ask you to dance. Now you're really not going to tell her no, are you?"

I said, "Yes, I am. I do not dance."

She said, "I know how you feel, but you can't tell this young lady no."

I said, "Oh yes, I can."

She said, "You *won't* tell this young lady no."

I said, "Oh yes, I will."

She started to get angry and said, "You *will* dance with her."

I said, "No, I won't."

So she took the girl and down the bleachers they went. Of course, the girl was flaming red by now—and as I think of this now, I cringe to think of what it must have meant for her. But I was so wrapped up in my own worry and low self-esteem, I could think of nothing but myself.

I watched the sequence of events that followed from my perch. The teacher dropped the girl off at the bottom of the bleachers and went straight across the gym floor to the coach, who was also my gym teacher. He looked up; she talked; he looked up again. He motioned to me to come down, and I shook my head no. It was at that point that he decided to teach without mildness and meekness.

The coach turned the record player off, went to the microphone, and said, "Could I have your attention, please." The gym immediately quieted down. "Sandra," he said, "has just walked all the way up to the top of the bleachers to ask Jerry Lund to dance. Jerry Lund has said no. How do you feel about that?"

Well, you know what the kids did. "Hey, Jerry," they shouted. "Come on!"

I just shook my head, and then my coach, who was very famous for his temper, got angry. He said, over the microphone, "You will be off those bleachers in thirty seconds or you will take an *F* in this class." And I said, "Coach, flunk away!"

I took an *F* in gym that term. You see, I would rather have taken the *F* than face the pain of being a fool. And when the coach backed me into a corner, there was no way I was going to come out.

Now let me tell you the sequel to that story. Remember, at the time I was a junior in high school. Time passed. I graduated from high school, spent six months in the service, went on a mission, and then attended BYU, where I met a young lady named Lynn. She loved to dance! And guess who ended up taking a dance class? We actually made a trade. I loved to play tennis; she loved to dance. So I took a dance class; she took a tennis class. I learned to dance and even reached the point where I enjoyed dancing.

I have thought of that often. How many times do we try to back people into a corner and force them to do what they ought to be doing? I knew what I ought to do. I did not want to hurt that girl in the least, but my pain was more important to me than her pain. The coach tried to ensure my cooperation through force, coercion, peer pressure, and an attempt to shame me. If he had just loved me enough to try to understand me, maybe great things would have happened.

I think of that experience now when I read, "Let your preaching be the warning voice, every man to his neighbor, in mildness and in meekness." I believe in the power of warning, but I also believe in the power of love.

"Be Ye Clean"

Finally, we come to the tenth commandment. It is actually three commandments, but I think they are the same. "Go ye out from among the wicked. Save yourselves. Be ye clean that bear the vessels of the Lord" (v. 42). What a great final commandment for teachers.

We have a great challenge in front of us. We have students who are sailing head-on toward that point of rock where the lighthouse is, and when we try to tell them to move ten degrees starboard, many of them just say, "Why don't you move ten degrees port?" We need to strengthen the bridges they are going to have to cross. Youth need to be strengthened to carry the load. Teachers need to be strengthened to carry the load. It may be a slow, laborious process. It may take a lot of timber cutting. But I want to bear you my testimony that in the scriptures you can find the wood to strengthen the bridges. I believe that with all my heart. Youth love the scriptures. They love to feast upon them, and I love to feed them as I teach, because it is not me who feeds them, it is the Spirit.

When you get discouraged with the challenge, remember the promise found in Doctrine and Covenants 84:88: "Whoso receiveth you, there I will be also, for I will go before your face. I will be on your right hand and on your left, and my Spirit shall be in your hearts, and mine angels round about you." Now I consider that fairly successful fortification. That is our promise. That is our privilege. I bear that witness to you.

Notes

From an address delivered at a Church Educational System symposium on the Book of Mormon, 13–15 August 1986, Brigham Young University, Provo, Utah.

1. Neal A. Maxwell, "The Old Testament: Relevancy within Antiquity," in *A Symposium on the Old Testament, 1979* (Salt Lake City: The Church of Jesus Christ of Latter-day Saints, 1979), 12.
2. See Virginia Law Shell, "The Bridge," *Guideposts,* January 1975, 10–11.
3. See *From You to Your Ancestors* [basic course in family exaltation], 3d ed. (Salt Lake City: The Church of Jesus Christ of Latter-day Saints, 1983), 2.
4. Neal A. Maxwell, "The Old Testament: Relevancy within Antiquity," 8.
5. Neal A. Maxwell, "Those Seedling Saints Who Sit before You," in *Old Testament Symposium Supplement* (Salt Lake City: The Church of Jesus Christ of Latter-day Saints, 1984), 1.
6. Ibid., 3.
7. See "The Charted Course of the Church in Education," address to religious educators, 8 Aug. 1938, 3; see also *Charge to Religious Educators,* 2d ed. (Salt Lake City: The Church of Jesus Christ of Latter-day Saints, 1982), 4.

Chapter 30

Aha or Ho Hum: Teaching the Old Testament to Make It Live

One of the primary charges given again and again to teachers in the seminaries and institutes is to teach the scriptures. As just one example, in an address to religious educators, Elder Boyd K. Packer said, "And there you have it—your commission, your charter, your objective in religious education. You are to teach the scriptures."[1]

The message is unmistakable: we are to teach the scriptures—not just *with* the scriptures, not just *about* the scriptures, not just *from* the scriptures; we are to teach the scriptures as they have been given to us. And the real challenge is not just to teach the scriptures, but to teach the scriptures *effectively.*

We admit from the outset that teaching the scriptures effectively is a challenge of the highest order, but it is an achievable goal if we are willing to meet certain conditions. Three conditions seem especially important.

Paying the Price in Getting to Know Our Students

There are two reasons why getting to know our students is important. First, when there is a mutual relationship of caring, trust, and respect, learner readiness is enhanced, and the student is more apt to accept the teacher's leadership in the class. Second, and equally important, the teacher who does not know his students—their needs, problems, conceptual levels, and so on—will be handicapped as he prepares and gives his lessons. But getting to know the students requires great commitment from the teacher both in and out of class.

Paying the Price in Preparation Time

A recent informal survey of teachers showed that one of the strong corollaries of high success in the classroom was the amount of time spent in lesson preparation. Effective teachers said that on the average they spent at least two hours of preparation time for each hour of presentation time, whereas those who were having a greater struggle often indicated the ratio was closer to one to one, or often, even less.

Many out-of-class demands compete for a teacher's time, but the fact still remains that excellent presentation requires careful preparation. Without preparation, presentation will be weakened. There are at least three areas in which we need to spend our preparation time.

Time to immerse ourselves in the scriptures. The one thing which should be studied, no matter what else has to be neglected, is the scripture reading block to be covered. It is often tempting to skim that block quickly and then turn to the other resources. But the key to effective scripture teaching is effective scripture study. The other sources are important and valuable, but the promise for meaningful teaching is directly coupled with immersing ourselves in the scriptures (see D&C 84:85).

Time to search, meditate, ponder, and pray. Often the most productive times of preparation are those times in which the teacher ponders the scriptures and the lesson. Some of the best ideas and approaches come out of such pondering. Also, if a question surfaces from the teacher's own study, there must be time to search out the answers. And finally, of course, much of the understanding of difficult passages or concepts is achieved through prayer, which also takes time.

Time to decide how to teach the lesson. While the time we use to study the scriptures may be the most critical time we spend in lesson preparation, taking the time to decide how the scripture block will be taught is very important. A variety of approaches and techniques is critical if the students' interest is to be maintained. Coming up with this variety also takes time.

Paying the Price in Personal Righteousness

When Hyrum Smith desired to go forth and teach the gospel, the Lord gave him some very interesting counsel. In one way or another, at least eight times in eighteen verses, the Lord told Hyrum to keep the commandments (see D&C

11:6–24). Though the Lord was speaking to Hyrum Smith, he concluded by saying: "Behold, I speak unto *all* who have good desires, and have thrust in their sickles to reap" (D&C 11:27; emphasis added).

Herein lies one of the most significant keys to success in teaching. We can know our students well and be loved by them. We can spend hours in meaningful preparation. We can pore over the scriptures endlessly. But unless we also have a commitment to personal righteousness and a determination to keep the commandments, as teachers we will fall short of success. The reason is simple and clearly stated: without the Spirit, a teacher shall not teach (see D&C 42:14). The Lord counsels that if we are to do things in the Spirit, we must practice virtue and holiness continually (see D&C 46:30–33).

When we talk about paying the price in personal righteousness, how righteous must we be before we see results? Obviously, the more personal righteousness we achieve, the greater our spiritual power. But since the Lord responds with blessings as soon as we turn toward him, we do not need to reach perfection before we see results. Certain specific kinds of behavior bring immediate results.

Out of simple things come great spiritual power and blessings in our teaching. We might ask ourselves these questions: (1) Do I have daily personal prayer? (2) Do I study the scriptures daily? (3) Do I have daily family prayer? (4) Do I have meaningful family home evenings each week? (5) Do I conduct personal interviews with my children? (6) Do I go on a date with my spouse weekly?

Techniques and Suggestions

With that much of an introduction to general principles, let us now turn to an examination of practical techniques and suggestions for making the Old Testament live. We will briefly examine eight suggestions for teaching the Old Testament in a way that will enhance the effectiveness of the teaching.

Maintain Variety in Our Teaching

It is an inherent part of human nature that change and variety are desirable in life. Even the most exciting and rewarding activity or the most highly desired thing may dull with repetition. The same holds true in teaching. A teacher may be an outstanding lecturer or storyteller; but let him do nothing but lecture or tell stories, and in a short time he will see increasing "ho hums" among his students. Teaching the scriptures is particularly challenging in this regard. The scriptures are deep and sometimes difficult to understand. Even mature and motivated adults tire after prolonged, intensive study of the scriptures. Teachers should therefore not be surprised that students lose interest when the teacher approaches the scriptures with the same techniques day after day.

Create Learner Readiness

Most of us have heard the expression "a teaching moment." This expression means that moment when a person is particularly teachable. Parent and teachers are often encouraged to watch for such teaching moments. The effective teacher does not just watch for those moments; *he creates them.* In other words, before teaching begins, the effective teacher deliberately does something that make his students ready and receptive.

A masterful example of a teacher who created learner readiness was Ammon on his mission to the Lamanites. When brought before the king, instead of immediately explaining that he had come down to teach him the gospel, Ammon asked that he be allowed to be servant to the king. And he served him with such remarkable faithfulness that when Lamoni (who was hardly an ideal student in the beginning) finally called for Ammon, he was almost insistent that Ammon teach him (see Alma 17–18).

We find both the Lord and his prophets using this principle of creating learner readiness over and over in the Old Testament. The Lord's use of physical objects or actions in teaching is an example of how he created a powerful readiness for learning in his people. The dimensions, layout, and materials used for the tabernacle and its furnishings were all designed to teach. The sacrifices, feast days, and other religious rituals readied the minds of the people for the spiritual lessons the Lord wished to teach. Jeremiah's wearing of the yoke (see Jer. 27:2; 28:10–14) and Ezekiel's shaving off his hair (see Ezek. 5:1–4) are other examples of this technique.

The teacher must ask himself again and again, "What can I do before I actually start into my lesson that will prepare my students to learn this principle or concept?"

It Is Better to Lead Than to Drive

Often the gospel principles taught in the Old Testament tend to be embedded in other material and consequently are not taught as directly and clearly as in some of the other standard works. They are taught through historical stories, symbolic acts, rituals, and so on. Occasionally the teacher may have to directly tell the students what the principle is; but a more effective approach is, first, to lead the students to where the principles are given, and second, to help the students uncover and discover the principle for themselves. Instead of asking, "What do I need to tell my students about this story (or symbol, or example, or whatever)?" the teacher asks, "How can I lead my students to discover this principle themselves?"

Through well-prepared questions, scripture-chaining (making a connected "chain" or list of related references to give a fuller picture), apperceptions (comparing one thing to another to help better understand what something is like; e.g., love is like a fuzzy kitten), chalkboard diagrams, and a myriad of other techniques, the teacher can lead the students into paths where they will discover for themselves the truths he wants them to see. Like the shepherds of the Middle East, the wise teacher realizes it is easier to lead his sheep where he wants them to go than it is to drive them there. Self-discovery of the principles will increase tenfold the chance that the student will then accept that principle and remember it. But if it is to happen, the teacher must give the particular principle a great deal of thought and preparation and planning. If he wishes to use questions, for example, then not only must he formulate good questions, but he also must anticipate student responses and put his questions in a logical order so they lead the students in the desired direction.

Help Our Students Conceptualize the Unknown

One of the things that makes the Old Testament difficult for many students is that it is set in an ancient day and in a culture vastly different from that in which most of our students live. The Old Testament often refers to customs, practices, and events which will seem strange to our students. Unless they have a clear image in their minds of what is described, they will have difficulty understanding the scripture and its application to them.

One of the marvelous things about our human imagination is that we do not have to actually experience something to have it become real and clearly understood. For example, a student who has spent his entire life in the heart of a large city can still understand and visualize such things as plowing fields, herding sheep, or harvesting grain. Through pictures or excellent verbal descriptions, he can picture those activities in his mind.

In a way, the word *conceptualize* may be slightly misleading, for it does not mean just picturing tangible things. There are many intangible concepts which must be understood, too. For example, in ancient times a woman's failure to produce male children for her husband was viewed as a great shame and tragedy, sometimes even as a punishment from God. Until students understand that concept clearly, they will never understand the story of Sarah and Hagar, of Rachel and Leah, or of Tamar and Judah.

The skilled teacher is therefore constantly alert to those places in the Old Testament where students will not have a good conception of what is referred to, and then he will seek to find ways to bridge the gap between the ancient and the modern.

Things to watch for especially include peculiar customs or practices, geographical features, weights and measures, money, objects not familiar to us, historical events familiar to people of the scriptures but not to us, and references to other peoples.

There are many specific ways to help students make this conceptualization, but generally they all fall into one of three main categories: (1) verbal descriptions; (2) audio and visual representations, such as photographs, movies, tape recordings, artistic renderings, models, or replicas; and (3) actual experience. The following are examples of things teachers have done to help students conceptualize the unknown: (1) pace off the dimensions of Noah's ark in an empty field, putting one student at each of the four corners; (2) show illustrations or models of the tabernacle and its furnishings; (3) take an ox yoke to class to show what Jeremiah wore in Jerusalem; (4) show slides of Egyptian gods and the splendor of their civilization to show the setting in which Joseph was placed; (5) let students taste unleavened bread and bitter herbs.

Convey the Reality of History

Closely related to conceptualizing is another technique for making the Old Testament live: helping students realize that the historical record describes real people and real events. Too often, even though we intellectually realize and even believe the events are real, they still have an unreal, abstract sense about them. As teachers, our role is to help students *feel* the reality of those events.

This skill is difficult to describe, but the key is to help students visually and emotionally put themselves in the time and place of the people of the scriptures. The human imagination can do exactly that. Generally, the following suggestions may help students to put themselves in the historical setting and more keenly feel its reality:

Verbally identify things about the physical setting that are known. These are such things as climate, temperature, time of year, countryside, type of building in which the event takes place, and nature of people involved. The amount that is known varies, but don't be limited to what is just given in the actual scripture. For example, the phrase "Dan even to Beer-sheba" (Judg. 20:1) takes on a whole new significance when the student realizes not only that Dan was the extreme north and Beersheba in the extreme south, but also that Dan was built around a huge spring and is very green and lush whereas Beersheba is on the edge of the desert and is barren and hot.

Help the students feel what the participants were feeling by asking such questions as "How would you feel if you were in that position?" For example, ask girls how they would have responded had they been in Rebekah's shoes. A man they've never seen is arranging a marriage for them to a man they have never met who lives several hundred miles away. They will have to leave their family and probably never see them again. Would they hesitate? That question will give far more effect to Genesis 24:58, where Rebekah says, "I will go."

Ask students to consider the personalities involved in the story. Though it is limited somewhat, we still get a fairly clear picture (both in and out of the scriptures) of the power and egos of Egyptian pharaohs. Remembering that power and ego makes the conflict between Moses and the pharaoh of the exodus much more believable.

Point out the consequences or the costs of the choices the people are making. Why did Saul hesitate to go against Goliath? We know from earlier events that Saul had great courage. What could have been in his mind? Or why did Moses start objecting to the Lord's call on Sinai? What were the consequences he had to face if he accepted the call?

There is one caution in this area, and that is this: the teacher should not add things which are not valid. Fictionalizing the scriptures must be avoided. But generally there is much more we know or can learn about a situation besides what is given in the scriptural text alone. This background information helps us tremendously in making history live.

Ask Challenge Questions

Perhaps the single most common technique used by effective teachers is asking questions that stimulate students to want to know. Most of us recognize that there are different levels of questions. Those requiring a simple answer or little thought are not very stimulating. Note the difference between the two questions in each of the following examples.

Genesis 13:5–13: (1) When Abraham and Lot divided up the land between them, who took which part? (2) What insights into the personalities of Lot and

Abraham do we discover from the division of the land, and how do these traits affect each one's future?

1 Samuel 17:1–50: (1) Why did David have the courage to face Goliath? (2) What was the difference between the David who faced Goliath and the David who faced Bathsheba?

Meaningful Scripture Search

Scripture search is actually another form of a challenge question, but it directly involves the scriptures. The easiest way to explain this technique is to illustrate it with some actual examples.

In the account of Abraham "bargaining" with the Lord over the destruction of Sodom and Gomorrah (see Gen. 18:16–33), we learn about Abraham's concern for his fellowman. But in that story there is also a principle taught which is of great significance to every righteous person, even those living today. Read through the following scriptures to see if you can discover the principle: Alma 10:22–23; 16:1–3, 9–10; Hel. 13:12–14; 3 Ne. 8:11; Jer. 5:1.

When Moses saw the burning bush and met the Lord on Mount Sinai, he was called to return to Egypt and free Israel. Though eighty years old at the time, Moses still felt deeply inadequate, and he objected to his calling. In each case, the Lord answered his objections. Now read carefully Exodus 3–4 and list Moses' three main objections. How did the Lord answer each one?

Often, dividing the class into small groups or letting students help each other in these scripture searches can add to the usefulness of the experience. Once the search is complete, allow the class members to share their answers and discuss them as they do so. This will more likely keep them involved with you even as you begin making application from the scriptures.

Explore Scriptural Symbolism

We need not read far into the Old Testament to realize that it is filled with symbolic imagery, likenesses, figurative language, and things which are imbued with deeper meaning than is represented by the object or the act itself. In numerous places the Lord has told us that he used the law of Moses to bear witness of him through types and symbols (see, for example, Gal. 3:24; Mosiah 13:31; Alma 25:15; 34:14). Many of those types and symbols are not immediately evident because they are deeply hidden.

In addition, the pages are filled with similes, metaphors, and hyperboles that are no longer familiar to us, since we live in a culture far removed from that of the

Old Testament peoples. These cultural differences are sometimes bewildering and even frustrating to our students. On the other hand, the Lord seems to use symbols because once the symbols are understood, they have tremendous effect upon the learner. Therefore, if you can help your students discover the meaning of the symbols for themselves (leading them, not driving them), they will find that same effect, and this effect will help the Old Testament come alive for them.

Here are some general rules for interpreting scriptural symbols that will be helpful to you as you work through the Old Testament.

Do the scriptures give the interpretation of the symbol? Often when the Lord uses a symbol he will give its interpretation. Frequently, the explanation is given elsewhere, and so you must go looking for it; but it is there. For example, in the book of Hebrews, Paul explains the spiritual significance of the high priest, the rituals of the Day of Atonement, and some aspects of the tabernacle. A careful study of his comments sheds great light on passages in Exodus and Leviticus.

Does the nature of the symbol give any clues to its significance? Sometimes it is clear why a certain object is used symbolically. We do not have to be overly keen to understand why Jeremiah wore a yoke (see Jer. 27:2): it signified the coming bondage of Israel. But in other cases the significance is not so clear. Why, for example was it forbidden to use leaven with sacrifice, and yet salt had to be part of every sacrifice? (see Leviticus 2:11, 13). When we consider the characteristics of leaven and salt, the spiritual significance becomes clear. Leaven, or yeast, spoils easily and therefore is an appropriate symbol of corruption. Salt, on the other hand, is a preservative and adds flavor to food. To add salt to the sacrifice symbolically suggested that making the covenants was of value and preserved the person from corruption. For those who may not be sure why a particular object is used, there are numerous sources (institute student manuals, Bible dictionaries, commentaries on the Old Testament, etc.) that can help us interpret the symbols more correctly.

Is the interpretation we give to a symbol in keeping with other known teachings, doctrines, and standards of the scriptures? Once we think we understand the interpretation of a symbol, we should measure it against other proven knowledge and usage in the scriptures to double-check whether our interpretation is correct.

It may be surprising how frequently students can discover the meaning of symbols for themselves when they are led through appropriate questions and challenged to think. For example, let's suppose we were talking about the breastplate of the high priest (see Ex. 28:15–29). How would the following questions direct the thinking of our students?

Why did the Lord select jewels and command that the names of the twelve tribes of Israel be written on them? (The jewels became symbols for Israel; cf. D&C 60:4; 101:3.)

Why are jewels an appropriate symbol of God's people? (They are precious, beautiful, reflect light, have to be cut and polished to become beautiful, and so on.)

Whom did the high priest himself represent? (He is a symbol, or type, of the Great High Priest, Jesus Christ.)

Where were the jewels worn? (see Ex. 28:24).

What is the significance of that placement? (It showed that Israel was next to the high priest's heart.)

When students come to those answers through their own pondering and thought, they will be excited to understand the deeper meaning.

Conclusion: The Old Testament Is a Living Book—Teach It That Way

Within the limited scope of this chapter, we cannot fully explore all the ways to teach the Old Testament to make it live. We can only suggest a few ways that this can be done. It is our firm belief, however, that the Old Testament can be taught in ways that make it live when a teacher pays a personal price and makes the effort required to teach it in an exciting way.

Notes

From *A Symposium on the Old Testament* (Salt Lake City: The Church of Jesus Christ of Latter-day Saints, 1983), 105–9.

1. Boyd K. Packer, *Teach the Scriptures* (Salt Lake City: The Church of Jesus Christ of Latter-day Saints, 1978), 5.

Chapter 31

THE BOOK OF MORMON: AN ANCHOR OF HOPE IN A WORLD OF DESPAIR

The Book of Mormon is an anchor of hope in a world of despair.

Let me introduce you to some of the students you may face in the classes you teach as you fulfill your Church callings. As you read these descriptions, you may see yourself in one of them, though perhaps a few years older, or you may see one of your children.

The first is a young man. He is a junior in high school. He is good looking, has a very pleasant personality, is strong in athletics. He is active in the Church, comes from a strong LDS home, and has a desire to be good. In your class he will be silent or perhaps if you push him even rebellious. One of the reasons is that he is functionally illiterate. He reads at a fourth-grade level. If you were to have him read 1 Nephi 1:1–4, he could not understand and probably would have trouble pronouncing words like *afflictions, mysteries, proceedings, commencement,* and *prophesying.* Those words appear in the first four verses of the chapter. Down in his heart he says to himself, *Other people understand this. What is wrong with me? I must be wicked in some way because I can't read the scriptures and understand them.* And he chooses not to participate rather than face the resulting pain and the embarrassment and the ridicule if he tries to read.

The second student, a girl who is a senior in high school, has a cumulative grade point of 3.98. She is attractive, she has a pleasing personality, she is deeply committed to the Church and the gospel. She is what most of you would define as the ideal student. She has just been awarded a full-tuition scholarship to BYU. She has read the scriptures every night since the ninth grade. She keeps a daily journal.

She refused to date until she was sixteen at absolutely no prompting from her parents. She is in every way an ideal young Latter-day Saint.

But the other day her father came into the kitchen while she was at the sink doing the dishes. He said hello, heard a sniff, looked a little closer, and saw tears streaming down her face. When he asked what was the matter, she finally broke down and sobbed and said, "I am not worth anything. I cannot do anything right." So her father started to point out some things, including the full-tuition scholarship, 3.98 grade average, and so on. "But I'm not doing anything that pleases Heavenly Father, you see," she explained. She is deeply saddened by her present state.

Third is another girl who will also be a senior this year. She is overweight and what many people would call plain. She doesn't date very often, perhaps not at all. When she was thirteen, her parents, who were married in the temple, started to have some serious marital problems and two years later were divorced. She feels deep down in her heart that somehow she could have and should have prevented that from happening, so she has great guilt feelings. Presently her mother, who is now the head of the house, works as a nurse, doing the midnight shift at a hospital, so this young lady is alone five nights a week. When she does date, it is with boys who know she is an easy mark and that she will allow some necking and petting. This only adds to her deep feelings of unworthiness and being used. Twice in the last year she has seriously considered committing suicide.

Now I wish I could tell you that such students are the exception, but they are not. Virtually all those who teach youth in the Church will have students like those in your classes. Virtually all of those who are parents have children with great challenges. (You don't need me to tell you that!) And we could easily rewrite the above descriptions to apply to many adults in the Church. We live in an era when loneliness and despair are the primary factors affecting people. This year over a million marriages will end in divorce, leaving more than a million and a half children who are products of broken homes. Many of those will not be able to escape the feeling that it is partly their fault for what their parents have done. Many of the children in the United States now come home from school to empty homes or else are being taken care of during the day by someone other than their parents.

One of the leading causes of death between the ages of twelve and eighteen in the United States, including Utah, is suicide. For some reason young people and women are particularly vulnerable to depression and loneliness and despair, and we see it over and over, even in the Church.

Five Reasons for Low Self-Esteem

I have identified five reasons why I think people have low self-esteem. If we know of those reasons, we can then combat them more effectively.

Number one: The destruction of self-esteem is one of Satan's primary objectives. What is it that motivates Satan? In 2 Nephi 2:18, 27, we are given answers. Satan, Lehi taught, "had fallen from heaven" and thus "had become miserable forever." Accordingly, "he sought also the misery of all mankind. . . . He seeketh that all men might be miserable like unto himself."

These verses point out that Satan is the epitome of the saying, "Misery loves company." His very goal for us is misery. An accompanying goal, as we read in 2 Nephi 2:29, is to reign over people, to put them under his subjection.

I once heard a man say that there are two doors to sin—the front door is pride and the back door is low self-esteem. Many times people sin not because they really want to or because they are rebellious, but because they are so discouraged, so filled with hopelessness, or so desirous of meeting their basic needs that they go after them in unwise ways.

Someone once noted that the majority of sins committed by people are an inadequate or misguided attempt to meet our basic needs. Most sins are not committed by evil people, just misguided people. How many instances of adultery, particularly on the part of women, are motivated more by a desire to be loved and accepted than for physical passion? We are seeking to meet those basic needs and Satan knows that; so he drives it and hammers on it, which brings us to the second reason we have low self-esteem.

Number two: We are listening too much to the world and what it says we need to be happy. We are bombarded with it, and so are our youth and our children. The world is telling us that if we are truly going to be happy, we need three things: material wealth, physical attractiveness, and a fun, exciting lifestyle. If we don't have those things, there is no hope.

Let's briefly look at each of those worldly appeals. I think we all understand material abundance. The father of one of my son's friends just gave him a new car for his sixteenth birthday. Now, that is challenging competition for a father. It is pretty hard for my son to understand why I don't love him that much. It is not hard for me to understand, but it is tough for him.

The marketing of physical attractiveness is aimed primarily at women. In electronic media, in books, in advertisements, women are constantly being presented with models for the ideal physical image. I believe there is going to be a special place in you-know-where for certain advertisers. Take something as simple as toothpaste. A shy, sensitive girl can see a television advertisement for toothpaste and she'll know that if she brushes with that brand she'll find the man of her dreams. Of course, such advertising methods are deceitful lies. And that is what we are competing against day after day.

The exciting lifestyle promoted by the media is just as deceitful. It simply isn't real. Most of us lead ordinary lives and do some mundane, boring things every day. But that doesn't mean we can't be happy, grateful for our blessings, and full of joy as we go about our daily work and interaction with our families. There can be great joy in the little moments of life.

So don't listen to the world. You don't have to be attractive. You don't have to be rich. You don't have to live a constantly exciting life to be happy.

Number three: Members of the Church are trying to reach the ultimate ideal, which is perfection. Now I am going to make a statement, which I will then defend. Perfection is an eternal goal, not a mortal possibility. We need to remember that and we need to help our students remember it.

Someone recently told me, "My fifteen-year-old just came home and said, 'Dad, in seminary they keep telling me that I have got to be perfect, and there is no way I'm going to make it.'" Most of us feel this way. But we needn't. Perfection is not a mortal possibility. It is an eternal goal.

Let me defend that with a statement by Joseph Fielding Smith: "We are commanded to be perfect even as our Father in Heaven is perfect. I believe that the Lord meant just what he said—that we should be perfect—but that will not come all at once but line upon line, precept upon precept, example upon example, and even then not so long as we live in this mortal life, for we will have to go even beyond the grave before we reach that perfection and shall be like God."[1]

That does not mean we should say to ourselves (or others), "I guess I don't need to worry about it." The goal is perfection and we strive for it constantly. But what we need to remember is that we will never make it in this life. We ought to go on working for it and get as close as possible, but when we don't achieve it, we need to learn to not be totally devastated.

In Mosiah 4:27 Benjamin gives us a key: "It is not requisite that a man run faster than he has strength, . . . and all things should be done in order." So keep the balance.

Number four: We feel inferior because we are not perfect. And so we are bound to feel imperfect. That is good logic, isn't it? One of the reasons we feel inadequate is because we are.

You know what the three most guilt-ridden occupations in the world are? You will never come out of these feeling totally good about yourself. The first is being a spouse, the second is being a parent, and the third is being a teacher. So don't be devastated. Teachers will not reach every student. Parents will never do everything right with their children. Wives will never have a husband who is perfectly understanding and sensitive. (Now, husbands, that doesn't mean that you stop trying!)

If our feelings of adequacy are bound up with our lack of perfection, we will surely suffer a degree of low self-esteem.

Number five: You feel so bad about yourself because you are so good. A function of the Holy Ghost is to sensitize you to sin. The more closely you approach godliness the more keenly will you feel your sins and inadequacies. So one of the reasons you feel bad about yourself is that you are so good. If you don't believe that, just go out and listen to the world and watch how insensitive and hardened they have become. No wonder the worldly don't feel guilty about adultery; they are, as Nephi said, "past feeling," and if you are still feeling, that is a good sign. And it is a good sign for your families and for those you serve in the Church.

Creating and Fostering Hope

Having talked about what contributes to low self-esteem, let's discuss how we can teach others (and ourselves) in ways that create and foster hope. So often, even when we teach with the best of intentions, we tend to breed despair in our teaching and as parents.

I once heard Elder Henry B. Eyring give a wonderful talk about teaching with the Spirit. He began his address with a story that just hit me like a sword in the heart. He mentioned a mission president who is a good friend of his. He said as they were talking he had asked the mission president how to better prepare a boy for a mission. He was expecting the mission president to mention that one should teach a boy how to work, teach him to love the scriptures, and so forth. The mission president instead told him that many missionaries come into the mission field not knowing they are accepted and loved and worthwhile, particularly by their fathers.[2]

I thought about my son, fifteen years old, who is a good boy. He does his priesthood duty without me prodding him. He goes to church. When he goes out at night I don't worry about what he is doing. And yet I am constantly on his back. Why? Because he is not doing the little things I want him to get better at. And it occurred to me that I have never said to him, "We really love you and appreciate you."

Here are five keys for fostering and creating hope as you teach the gospel, especially the great truths of the Book of Mormon. I mention the Book of Mormon in particular because that is the scripture that fosters hope perhaps more than any of the others.

Key number one: Deliberately and consistently teach the doctrine of hope. If you want a meaningful experience, get out the full concordance to the Book of Mormon and go through the references on hope. There are some beautiful phrases. Let me give you a few. Moroni 7:3 describes what is called a sufficient hope. Ether 12:4 talks about a surety of hope. Ether 12:32 calls it a more excellent hope. Second Nephi 31:20 describes a perfect brightness of hope. Three chapters, Ether 12, Moroni 7, and Moroni 10, teach hope more clearly than you'll find anywhere else in the scriptures. They teach you that you cannot be saved without hope. Alma 5:7, 10–13 and Alma 22:16 specifically ask the question (and answer it), "How do I get hope in my life?" You ought to study them, internalize them, and then point them out to your children and your students.

Key number two: As you teach the Book of Mormon, teach that in the atonement of Jesus Christ there is power to overcome sin. The Book of Mormon clearly teaches that there is power in sin. It speaks of the captivity of the devil, of the chains of hell, and of instances when Satan had all power over individuals or groups. The Book of Mormon gives a very graphic description of the power of evil. But sometimes as we emphasize that we neglect to teach that the power of the Atonement is sufficient to overcome. And the scriptures teach us how to get that power into our lives. Let me share some examples that can be blessings to our youth—and to all of us.

The first is in Jacob 3:1, where he says, "Behold, I, Jacob, would speak unto you that are pure in heart. Look unto God with firmness of mind, and pray unto him with exceeding faith, and he will console you in your afflictions, and he will plead your cause." Don't you think a teenager would identify with that? The Lord is somebody who really understands me and will plead my cause and will send down justice upon those who seek my destruction. Talk about hope! (Now, you have got to be a little careful or they may be calling down destruction on the opposing football team.) But what a promise.

In Helaman 5:12, Helaman says, "And now, my sons, remember, remember that it is upon the rock of our Redeemer, who is Christ, the Son of God, that you must build your foundation; that when the devil shall send forth his mighty winds, yea, his shafts in the whirlwind, yea, when all his hail and his mighty storm shall beat upon you, it shall have no power over you to drag you down to the gulf of misery and endless wo, because of the rock upon which ye are built." Jesus Christ has power over the devil and all his mighty efforts to harm us spiritually. Through him we can surely cope in this life, and we can cope successfully and with power.

When we or those we love and serve feel they have a glaring weakness, we can review Ether 12:27. If you will humble yourself before me and come unto me in prayer, the Lord says, I will make weak things become strong unto you. What a promise! Or Moroni 7:33: In Christ you will have power to do all things that are expedient. These are tremendous promises of power.

Key number three: Remind your students of God's love for them. A third way to foster hope is to remind people of the love of the Godhead for them. As I watch my son, who has to wear Adidas tennis shoes, Adler socks, and so on, and as I try to say to him that it is ridiculous to pay double the price for clothes with a big label, I have to consider what is behind this insistence on certain brands of clothes. Of course, clothes are not really the issue at all. The issue is one of being accepted and not being looked down on. Though acceptance is important for almost everyone, it is particularly critical for teenagers. And many of our young people are not having their emotional needs met and so they are hurting inside. Most of the rebellion we see in our homes and classrooms is a misguided attempt to meet those basic needs. But we can teach our families and others that the one anchor that will never falter, the one source of never-failing love, is the Godhead. Somehow they need to sense that in God and Jesus Christ and the Holy Ghost there is a living, present reality of love for them that knows them, that cares for them, and that is concerned for them.

Let me share an example of this from 3 Nephi 17. Jesus is among the Nephites. Notice how he begins in verse two: "I perceive that ye are weak." But then look at verses six and seven: "And he said unto them: Behold, my bowels are filled with compassion towards you. Have ye any that are sick among you? Bring them hither. Have ye any that are lame, or blind, or halt, or maimed, or leprous, or that are withered, or that are deaf, or that are afflicted in any manner? Bring them hither and I will heal them, for I have compassion upon you; my bowels are filled with mercy."

What we need to understand in our hearts—and what we need to help our youth to understand—is that if we had been at that meeting with Jesus, we would have felt that love. We sense the same compassionate spirit in 2 Nephi 26:24–28, where the Lord says, in effect, "Do I say unto anybody, depart from me? Do I say to anybody, you cannot have my salvation? I say unto you, nay." He doesn't say to anybody, "Well, you are divorced, so I'm sorry," or "You are a little overweight.

When you lose twenty pounds, come back and see me and we will talk about salvation." The Lord says, "Come to me without money, without price, and buy milk and honey." Then notice 3 Nephi 17:20–21: "Now behold, my joy is full. And when he had said these words, he wept."

Let's go back to Jacob, which is a good concluding scripture for this section: "O all ye that are pure in heart, lift up your heads and receive the pleasing word of God, and *feast upon his love*" (Jacob 3:2; emphasis added). Teach the youth that they have a Father, an older Brother, and a loving Holy Spirit who will help them feel needed and loved and accepted. And accept those truths in your own heart, concerning yourself.

I don't think we want to whitewash in our teaching of the Book of Mormon. The Book of Mormon is specific and clear in teaching the effects of sin. It teaches that wickedness never was happiness. And we all, including our youth, need to know that as well.

I think God punishes people in order to save them. The punishments of God for sin are not given out by an angry God because he is trying to get even. He sends punishments because that is the only way he can turn us around. So even his punishment is a proof of his love. Even in teaching the consequences of sin, it is important that we keep stressing that there is hope and love and encouragement.

Key number four: Use the lives of Book of Mormon people to create hope. Now this is a two-edged sword; we need to be a little careful with this. But in the lives of such people as Alma (both the Elder and the Younger), the four sons of Mosiah, and King Lamoni and his father, you can find dramatic proof that the Lord can reach pretty low to pick a man up. Not many of your students will be worse off than Alma the Elder, Alma the Younger, or Lamoni. You can imagine the hardness of heart you would have to have if, when your servants lose sheep to robbers, you execute them. Yet the Lord can reach down even to someone that deep in sin and touch him. These examples are hope for the hopeless. We can use them in that manner—but we need to remember that they are a two-edged sword. Let me give you an example.

In an earlier chapter I talked about a girl who was a model teenager in every way and yet who inexplicably started fasting every other day. When her father finally was able to learn what was in her heart, he was surprised to hear her say very tearfully, "I don't have a testimony." Her father wondered why she would think that. She said, "Because I have never experienced anything like Alma the Younger, or Paul, or King Lamoni"—who all were very wicked but were given very dramatic experiences that converted them to the gospel.

It is unfortunate, it makes me weep, that inadvertently, we who are teaching the gospel sometimes make our youth feel that if their conversion is not dramatic, if it is not remarkable, then it is not true. When you teach the Book of Mormon, you teach Alma and Lamoni. But you remind them that for every Alma the Younger there were a thousand unnamed Saints who just lived good lives and who lived righteously from the time they were young. For every King Lamoni there were thousands of Lamanites who didn't have to go into a trance or an unconscious state; they just heard his words and believed and were converted.

In teaching the remarkable stories of spiritual rebirth, we need to balance them with something the Lord said in 3 Nephi 9:20: "Whoso cometh unto me with a broken heart and a contrite spirit, him will I baptize with fire and with the Holy Ghost, even as the Lamanites, because of their faith in me at the time of their conversion, were baptized with fire and with the Holy Ghost," and then comes this little phrase, "and they knew it not." They were born again and didn't know it.

We need to remind our young people of that. We need to remind ourselves of that. We can be born again without having to go through an all night and all day experience like Enos, or without falling into a trance like Alma the Younger or Lamoni. That blessing can simply grow out of the way we live. And thus the Book of Mormon can give us hope through the examples of conversions both dramatic and simple.

Key number five: As you teach the Book of Mormon, look for those gems that teach hope. Let me give two examples. First is the song of Nephi. Here is Nephi, one of the great spiritual giants of history, saying, "O wretched man that I am. Why am I torn with sin? Why is it so easily besetting me?" (see 2 Ne. 4). It is important that we all remember that you don't have to be wicked to be torn with those feelings of inadequacy. Here is Nephi struggling with them.

Then, if you read carefully, you will find the key for overcoming that despair. In effect, he says, "Nevertheless, I remember the kind of experiences I have had. The Lord loves me. I have seen visions, I have been led by the Spirit." The next time we feel we are wicked and terrible, the next time one of our youth feels inadequate, we need to look at the world and see where it is. And we will see that we are head and shoulders above so many who are lost and floundering.

Here is a second example: Alma 34:32–34 is a scripture often used by teachers to hammer the student into the ground on the subject of procrastination. But it is very instructive to see how Elder Bruce R. McConkie dealt with that scripture: "If we keep two principles in mind we will thereby know that good and faithful members of the Church will be saved even though they are far from perfect in this life.

These two principles are (1) that this life is the appointed time for men to prepare to meet God—this life is the day of our probation; and (2) that the same spirit which possesses our bodies at the time we go out of this mortal life shall have power to possess our bodies in that eternal world."[3] Elder McConkie is quoting Alma 34. Instead of taking that negatively and saying, "Boy, you had better repent; you had better stop procrastinating," he says these are the two keys to *hope:* first, in this life you are trying to prepare to meet God—preparing by doing good things and wanting to do good things—and second, if you now have good desires, those same good desires will be with you when you leave this life and go to the world to come. Teach to bring hope, and work to gain that hope yourselves.

Notes

From an address given at the Church Educational System symposium on the Book of Mormon, 21 August 1982, Brigham Young University, Provo, Utah.

1. Joseph Fielding Smith, *Doctrines of Salvation,* 3 vols., comp. Bruce R. McConkie (Salt Lake City: Bookcraft, 1954–56), 2:18.
2. Henry B. Eyring, address given at the Book of Mormon summer inservice meeting for the Granite District, Church Educational System, Taylorsville, Utah, 10 August 1982, 1–2. Unpublished transcript in possession of the author.
3. Bruce R. McConkie, "The Seven Deadly Heresies," *1980 Devotional Speeches of the Year* (Provo: Brigham Young University Press, 1981), 78.

Chapter 32

A Stone Cut Out

As I thought about the subject of Church history, I thought back to when I was a seminary student. They made a very popular television series about the days when I went to high school. It was called *Happy Days.* I graduated in 1957 in the days of greasers, ducktail haircuts, and Cadillacs with fins. They were called the idyllic fifties, and in many ways they were.

I worked in a movie theater when I went to high school. I can still remember clearly one movie that came to town. Some of you have probably seen this now on video. It was called *The Moon Is Blue* with William Holden and Audrey Hepburn. I can still remember that movie because it made headlines before it got to the little theater where I worked. This was the raciest movie that had yet been put out by Hollywood, according to some. There were two lines that got it that kind of ranking. The first was when William Holden was sitting on the couch with Audrey Hepburn and he leaned over and was kind of nuzzling her ear. All of a sudden, she pulled back—she was kind of an innocent young thing—and she said, "Are you trying to seduce me?" I can still remember, as an usher in that theater, hearing an audible gasp from the audience. The other shocking line? She said, "I think I'm pregnant." That was the first time the word *pregnant* had been used openly in a movie.

That is why I say I think it was the idyllic fifties. As someone once said, "We've come a long way, baby," since then.

Just for curiosity I went back and did a little checking. In 1957 the Church had a membership of 1.5 million. It had been just ten years prior to that when we crossed the one million mark for the first time. There were 251 stakes in 1957.

Since then we have added more than 2,000 new stakes. There were 2,500 missionaries set apart in 1957. At the time of this book's release, there are 30,000 missionaries set apart each year worldwide, and currently there are about 60,000 missionaries serving worldwide. I can also remember that we were electrified when the fourth temple in a three-year period was announced in the *Church News.* We had seen the Swiss, the Los Angeles, the New Zealand, and finally the London temples announced. The headlines then talked about the "new era" of temple building. Now, in April 1999 President Hinckley announced plans for the Church's one hundredth temple, the Nauvoo Temple. More have been announced since then.

When I was a ninth grader in seminary, Sir Edmund Hillary climbed Mount Everest for the first time in history, and October general conference was televised beyond the Salt Lake Valley for the first time in history. When I was in the tenth grade, Utah colleges were in such desperate financial straits that the state tried to give these colleges, formerly owned by the Church, back to the Church. Dixie College, Snow College, and Weber State College were offered back to the Church. The Church did not really get excited about that, but they said if that was what was wanted, they would accept them. A referendum was held and fortunately, we think, the people voted *no* on the referendum, and the state kept them.

When I was in the eleventh grade in seminary, Brigham Young University campus wards and stakes were formed for the first time. Ricks College became a two-year school, and work on Utah's first interstate highway system began. (Some things never change.) When I was a twelfth grader, general conference was cancelled because of a flu epidemic, the only time in history that I know of.

I say all of this because if you have a teaching calling in the Church currently, and if you are teaching seniors in high school, your students will see even further changes. If the growth rate that has been seen in the Church since I graduated from high school continues for the next twenty years, when your seniors are attending their thirtieth-year reunion, the Church will have 31 million members and there will be 11,500 stakes.

Some ten years ago I was privileged to be in a Church Educational System meeting where Elder Richard G. Scott spoke. It was a thrilling experience. He said not once but three different times, speaking of areas such as Russia, China, and India: "We are no longer talking about *if* the doors will open. We are not even any longer talking about *when* the doors to those countries will open. They are open now. The only question is *how* do we enter?" Just look at what has happened in the last ten years since Elder Scott spoke. The Berlin Wall has fallen, governments of the Eastern Bloc countries have been reorganized, and missionaries have entered the former Soviet Union. And we are seeing doors open to the Church in such places as India, Vietnam, and China.

I do not know specifically what the next thirty years are going to bring, but we know in broad terms what the future holds. From the scriptures I can tell you some of the things the young students you are teaching can look for in the future. They can look for Adam-ondi-Ahman and Armageddon (see Dan. 7:9–10, 21–22; D&C 116; Rev. 16:16). They can look for the time when the Dead Sea becomes a living sea (see Ezek. 47:1–12). They will see worldwide war and, some time in the future, millennial peace (see D&C 87:1–2; 101:26). The scriptures promise that our children will see Babylon seeming to reign supreme, and someday they will also see Babylon supplanted (see D&C 1:35; Rev. 18). The world has seen and will see the ten tribes return (see D&C 133:26–32). We shall someday see the Zion of Enoch come down from heaven and fall upon the necks of the Zion of Joseph and Brigham and Spencer and Ezra (see D&C 84:100). We will see a temple in Jerusalem and a temple in Jackson County (see D&C 124:36; 84:3–4). I am not saying these things will happen in the next thirty years, but we know that they are things that are coming, things that we are to prepare for, things we are to prepare our students for.

One of the things your students have to look forward to was described by Lorenzo Snow. Every time I read this, I long to live to see those times. Speaking to a group of temple workers, President Lorenzo Snow said, "Many of you will be living in Jackson county and there you will be assisting in building the Temple; and if you will not have seen the Lord Jesus at that time you may expect Him very soon, *to see Him, to eat and drink with Him, to shake hands with Him and to invite Him to your houses as He was invited when He was here before.*"[1] Can you imagine that, sisters, to someday have your husband come home and say that the Savior will be coming to dinner? Remember the poem that asked what we would do if Jesus came to our house. Would we run around putting the unacceptable magazines under the table? Dust where it has not been dusted? Pull out the Bible? Well, according to President Snow, having Jesus visit in the home may be a very real possibility for some of the young people we will be teaching either now or in the future.

In the book of Daniel is the scripture from which I take my title for this chapter. In Daniel 2, we read that Nebuchadnezzar had a dream and none of his wise men could interpret it. He sentenced them to death. Daniel stepped forward and under inspiration gave him the interpretation. I would like to read four verses starting in verse 34.

Daniel said, "Thou sawest till that a stone was cut out without hands, which smote the image upon his feet that were of iron and clay, and brake them to pieces."

And then in verse 35 he said, "And the stone that smote the image became a great mountain, and filled the whole earth." And then as he gives the interpretation, in verse 44, it continues: "And in the days of these kings shall the God of heaven set up a kingdom, which shall never be destroyed: and the kingdom shall not be left to other people, but it shall break in pieces and consume all these kingdoms, and it shall stand for ever." Finally in verse 45, he again points out that the stone is cut out "without hands."

As we look at those scriptures, there are five elements that the Lord seems to stress: That the stone is cut out. That it is done so without hands—that is, it is not a mere human endeavor. That it eventually fills the earth. That it will break and consume all other kingdoms as it rolls forth. That it will stand forever.

So I hope we as teachers in the Church can teach the scriptures and the stories of our history with power. Somebody once described a good historian as someone who is obsessed with minutia. Oh, how I appreciate our Church history experts. I am also working on a personal project in Church history and, oh, how I appreciate the historians who paid attention to minute details of our history.

But as you teach Church history to your families and other young people, do not get caught up so much in detail that the grand picture is lost. Do not count the buffalo chips on the prairies; count the evidences of the hand of God in the lives of his people. I do not want my children to memorize the ordination dates of the First Quorum of the Twelve as much as I want them to know we still have living apostles and prophets today. I would rather have the students feel the power of the word in their own lives than be able to recite the contents of the 138 sections of the Doctrine and Covenants from memory. As teachers, we need the detail, but our students need the grand picture.

Remember what Nephi said to his brothers. He said, "I did liken all scriptures unto us" (1 Ne. 19:23). That is what we must also do when we teach. We must liken the stories and examples and lessons of our history to ourselves and to our students.

Sometimes as we teach the Old Testament or the Book of Mormon, we feel to cry out, "You fools, you blind idiots! Couldn't you see the foolishness of your ways?" In a way, we will do the same in Church history. For example, when we read the story of Simonds Ryder, who fell into apostasy because the Prophet did not spell his name correctly, we think, "You idiot! Where is your good sense?" What about the future, say thirty, forty, a hundred, even a thousand years from now? Will that generation look back at our time and our generation and say, "You fools! Why couldn't you see?"

Our purpose is to help our students be those who are looked to with inspiration.

Our goal should be to have future generations read our students' journals and use them to teach future Church history classes and fill them with awe and inspiration. I have always had a feeling for the grandeur of the Lord's hand in history, for all the great events of the coming forth of the priesthood, the organization of the Church, and so on, but there is also something about the tiny, little, seemingly insignificant things in the lives of individuals, some of whose names we do not know, that really has an impact on me.

I would like to note four lessons that I would love my children to learn when they study the history of our Church and the revelations in the Doctrine and Covenants. The first is choices. The second I call "the Lord's forge." Third, "be still and know." And fourth, "the stone rolls on." Now, let us discuss each one.

Choices

Something came into my hands quite by accident as I was preparing for a Church history tour some years ago. Brother George Talbot of BYU Travel Study handed me a book of Benjamin Franklin's thoughts. One of the first pages I opened to contained the following statement by Benjamin Franklin. He said:

We stand at the crossroads,
each minute,
each hour,
each day,
making choices.

We choose
the thoughts
we allow ourselves to think,
the passions
we allow ourselves to feel,
and the actions
we allow ourselves to perform.

Each choice
is made in the context
of whatever value system
we've selected
to govern our lives.

In selecting that value system,
we are,
in a very real way,
making the most important choice
we will ever make.

Those who believe there is one God
who made all things
and who governs the world by his Providence
will make many choices different
from those who do not.

Those who hold in reverence
that being who gave them life
and worship Him through
adoration,
prayer,
and thanksgiving
will make choices different
from those who do not.

Those who believe
that mankind are all of a family
and that the most acceptable
service of God
is doing good to man
will make many choices different
from those who do not.

Those who believe
in a future state
in which
all that is wrong here
will be made right
will make many choices different
from those who do not.

Those who subscribe
to the morals of Jesus
will make many choices different
from those who do not.

Since the foundation of all happiness
is thinking rightly,
and since correct action
is dependent on correct opinion,
we cannot be too careful
in choosing the value system
we allow to govern
our thoughts and actions.

And to know that God governs
in the affairs of men,
that he hears and answers prayers,
and that he is a rewarder of them that
diligently seek Him,
is, indeed,
a powerful regulator
of human conduct.[2]

As I read those words, I thought, *What better three concepts could one hope for his children or his students to know: That God governs in the affairs of men. That he hears and answers prayers. And that he is the rewarder of those who seek him.*

Let me just quickly run through some simple examples of choices that come to us out of the stories of Church history. My wife shared this one with me. Her fourth great-grandmother was named Lucy Sally Downey, of whom we know virtually nothing except for her genealogical data. But, oh, what a story is told in that data! Let me just read through some items from her pedigree chart. She was born 31 March 1804 in Sheldon, Vermont. She married David McOlney on 3 April 1826. She had a stillborn child in 1827, and somewhere in the interim they moved to an area around Toronto, Canada, where a missionary named Parley P. Pratt came to visit. Whether she was one of the group that John Taylor had taught and prepared there, we do not know. The next thing on the record is that she has four children, one of whom is my wife's third great-grandmother. But then on the genealogical sheet comes the following:

Joseph McOlney, *born* Nauvoo, Hancock County, Illinois, 28 August 1841; *died* 7 September 1841.

Adeline McOlney, *born* Nauvoo, Hancock County, Illinois, May 1843; *died* 23 August 1843.

Hiram McOlney, *born* Nauvoo, Hancock County, Illinois, 26 May 1845; *died* 12 June 1845.

And finally, an entry for her son who had been *born* in 1829; *died* in Nauvoo, Hancock County, Illinois, 23 August 1845.

In addition to having a stillborn child, she lost these four children—all dead in less than four years.

As we stood on a point of land in Nauvoo and gazed across the Mississippi River, two questions came to my mind. What brought those people to this point? And then immediately came another question. What drove them across the river? One would think a woman, after losing four children, had every right to say, "Brother Brigham, I'm sorry. I've given enough."

We have no other record of Lucy Sally Downey. We do not know why she did not give up, why she did not quit. But here is a quote from her daughter's diary, which may be a partial explanation:

"I heard the Prophet Joseph Smith preach on many occasions. I saw and heard him when he made his farewell address to the Nauvoo Legion. I saw the body of our beloved Prophet after he was martyred. . . .

"I was present when Brigham Young spoke to the saints and the mantle of the Prophet Joseph Smith fell upon him, for his voice and appearance were that of the Prophet and we felt and knew that he was the one to lead the church."[3] That is from her daughter, but I assume those emotions were also true of her mother.

The final entry for Lucy Sally Downey McOlney reads simply: "Died 20 August 1846, Council Bluffs, Pottawatamie County, Iowa." She left Nauvoo. She left four children in the cemetery there. She knew Brigham Young was the one called of God to lead the Church, and so she followed him. But only to Winter Quarters, where she joined her children in death. Those were the choices she made. I often wonder what she would now say if we could go into the spirit world and interview her and ask her, "Lucy, how do you feel about your choices now?" It would be an interesting response. Oh, please teach my children to make those kinds of choices if it comes to that.

Here is another interesting example of choices. Calvin R. Stephens shared with us a couple of entries from some local newspapers in the Palmyra area of 1829 and 1830. Let me just read two.

This is from the *Rochester Advertiser and Telegraph,* 31 August 1829: "The Book of Mormon has been placed in our hands. [This was written 31 August 1829. It is an interesting claim since the Book of Mormon was not published until March of 1830.] A viler imposition was never practiced. It is an evidence of fraud, blasphemy, and credulity, shocking both to christians and moralists. The author and proprietor is Joseph Smith, Jr., a fellow who by some hocus pocus acquired such influence over a wealthy farmer . . . that he later mortgaged his farm for $3,000 . . . for [the] printing and binding of 5000 copies."

This one is from a paper called *The Gem,* dated 15 May 1830. This is a great example to build your confidence in the unerring accuracy of mass media: "An ignoramus near Palmyra, Wayne County, 'found' some 'Gold Plates' as he is pleased to call them. . . . The book comes before the public under the general title of the 'Book of Mormon' arranged under different hands, something as follows, the Book of Mormon—containing the books of Nephi, Nimski, Pukei, and Buckeye—and contains some four or five hundred pages."

Let me compare those reactions, or choices, if you will, with an entry from the autobiography of a young girl named Mary Elizabeth Rollins. This is the same young girl who, when she and her sister saw the Church printing shop in Independence being destroyed by the mob, ran and at personal threat to their own lives saved several copies of the Book of Commandments. Here is what she wrote about the Book of Mormon: "We learned that Brother [Isaac] Morley had the Book in his possession—the only one in that part of the country. I went to his house just before the meeting was to commence, and asked to see the Book. . . . As I looked at it, I felt such a desire to read it, that I could not refrain from asking him to let me take it home and read it, while he attended meeting. . . . He finally said, 'Child, if you will bring this book home before breakfast tomorrow morning, you may take it.' . . . When I got into the house, I explained, 'Oh, Uncle, I have got the "Golden Bible."' . . . We all took turns reading it until very late in the night—as soon as it was light enough to see, I was up and learned the first verse in the book. When I reached Brother Morley's they had been up for only a little while. When I handed him the book, he remarked, 'I guess you did not read much in it.' I showed him how far we had read. He was surprised, and said, 'I don't believe you can tell me one word of it.' I then repeated the first verse, also the outlines of the history of Nephi. He gazed at me in surprise and said, 'Child, take this book home and finish it, I can wait.'"[4]

What an interesting contrast of choices. Two journalists, supposed objective reporters, who choose to react to the Book of Mormon in one way, and a young girl who made a very different choice. This is the same girl—if we wish to talk about the influence of choices on young people, this is a great example—who with her family was driven from Independence when it was winter time. The Mormons got to the Missouri River and ferried across. The mobs were behind them and the threat to their lives was very real. Some of the families had no money to pay to cross the river. This put them in a very precarious position. I would like to read again from the life and testimony of Mary Elizabeth Rollins Lightner about what then happened:

"While we were camped on the banks of the Missouri River waiting to be ferried over, they found there was not money enough to take all over. One or two families must be left behind, and the fear was that if left, they would be killed. So, some of the brethren by the name of Higbee thought they would try and catch some fish, perhaps the ferryman would take them, they put out their lines in the evening; it rained all night and most of the next day, when they took in their lines they found two or three small fish, and a catfish that weighed 14 pounds. On opening it, what was their astonishment to find three bright silver half dollars, just the amount needed to pay for taking their team over the river. This was considered a miracle, and caused great rejoicing among us."[5]

What a great lesson about the consequences of choices.

Here is another example. Parley P. Pratt tells the story of a blind woman in Canada on that same mission I previously mentioned. She was a teacher who had gone so blind that she could no longer teach. She was a widow. Parley went in and cured her in a most miraculous way. And then what follows is very much what followed with the healing by the Savior of the man born blind (see John 9).

The people of her church came to her and began to say such things as, "Tell us how this happened." And she would say, "Well, this man named Parley Pratt healed me." "Well, it must be of the devil." And she would say, "Well, how could it be of the devil? Does the devil cure blind people?" This was very much the gist of the conversations. As I was reading that story for the first time, I was so inspired. What a great example of faith, I thought. But then comes the final line of Elder Pratt's account:

"Such contentions and discouragements as these, poured into the ears of a poor mother from day to day, together with railings, lyings, and various sophistry and slander, soon caused her to waver, and like thousands of other poor, weak mortals, she shrank back into the net of sectarian delusion, and was seen by the Saints no more."[6] An interesting choice. Compare that with Catherine Spencer, wife of Orson Spencer. Orson Spencer was a Baptist preacher who was very well educated, and so was she. She was the favorite daughter of a very wealthy family who disowned her when she joined the Church. As they were preparing to be driven out of Nauvoo, she was very ill so Orson wrote to her parents and asked if they would at least consider taking her in until he found a home in the West and could send for her. A letter came back, and this I quote from her parents, "Let her renounce her degrading faith and she can come back, but never until she does." Orson Spencer read that letter to his wife, Catherine. She asked that the Bible be brought to her. When it was, she turned to the book of Ruth and read to her husband from chapter 1, verse 16: "Intreat me not to leave thee, or to return from following after thee: for whither thou goest, I will go; and where thou lodgest, I will lodge: thy people shall be my people, and thy God my God."[7]

And so they crossed the river. She became more and more ill. She was lying on beds that were soaked from the rain. She finally begged for the privilege of dying in a home. They found a nearby house where the man was kind enough to take her in, and there Catherine Spencer died.

An unnamed woman cured of blindness makes a choice. A woman of wealth and culture makes another choice. How significant are our choices.

Here is yet another simple but eloquent example of choices. Brigham Young wrote the following single entry in his diary in 1846: "I was very busy through the day in preparing for the burial of Brother Little, and rolling out in the morning."[8]

Do you know what makes that entry so poignant? Brother Little was Brigham's nephew. Over some time, he had watched him grow sick and then finally die. But Brigham simply says, "We prepared him for burial and then rolled out in the morning."

Let me give one last example of choices. There is an interesting article in the *National Geographic* of August 1986 on life and death on the Oregon Trail. It talks about the pioneers. It mentions the Mormons, but primarily focuses on the Oregon and California immigrants. Let me just read two excerpts from that very interesting article that provide another interesting illustration of choices.

One man "passed a man by the side of the road who had been attacked by cholera, when his company, panic struck, inhumanely left him to die one hundred and fifty miles from any house. He had a sack of provisions by his side, and lying on the ground, could hardly speak. . . . He could not be moved . . . All I could do for him was to bring him one of my pint tin cups full of water. . . . We learned by a man on horseback the next day, that he had recovered [and was following along behind us.]"[9] His company had left him to die.

Here is another paragraph that is kind of interesting, from that same article: "Two brothers grew to detest each other so much that they sawed their wagon in half, then fought over who would get which end. Finally one hitched up to the tongue and drove off with his cart, leaving his brother on the prairie 10 miles from timber with one yoke of oxen & the hind wheels of a wagon. . . . This trip is not boy's play.'"[10]

Now contrast those choices with this one found in the *History of the Church,* dated January 1839: "On motion of President Brigham Young, it was resolved that we this day enter into a covenant to stand by and assist each other to the utmost of our abilities in removing from this state, and that we will never desert the poor who are worthy, till they shall be out of the reach of the exterminating order of [these people]." And then later comes a short little entry by the Prophet. "President Brigham Young got eighty subscribers to the covenant the first day, and three hundred the second day."[11]

There are so many interesting choices that can be made. Our students and you and I, daily and hourly, face the same kinds of choices. The Doctrine and Covenants and the stories of Church history are a way to help them make those choices correctly. Section 58 says:

"It is not meet that I should command in all things. . . .

"Verily I say, men should be anxiously engaged . . . of their own free will, and bring to pass much righteousness" (vv. 26–27).

Use the scriptures and stories of the Doctrine and Covenants to build in our young people that kind of ability to choose.

The Lord's Forge

Now I would like to talk about the Lord's forge. There are two really interesting scriptures that I would like to read with you. The first one is in 3 Nephi.

"Behold I have created the smith that bloweth the coals in the fire, and that bringeth forth an instrument for his work. . . .

"No weapon that is formed against thee shall prosper. . . . This is the heritage of the servants of the Lord, and their righteousness is of me, saith the Lord" (3 Ne. 22:16–17).

The second scripture is in the book of Jeremiah. This is not a happy time for Jeremiah and his people. The Lord says to Jeremiah:

"Arise, and go down to the potter's house, and there I will cause thee to hear my words.

"Then I went down to the potter's house, and, behold, he wrought a work on the wheels.

"And the vessel that he made of clay was marred in the hand of the potter: so he made it again another vessel" (Jer. 18:2–4).

Can you picture that? The potter turning the potter's wheel, shaping the vessel with his hands, then all of a sudden he slips and the jar is marred. What do you do with it? You just kind of scrunch it all in and start over. Jeremiah continues:

" . . . So he made it again another vessel, as seemed good to the potter to make it.

"Then the word of the Lord came to me, saying,

"O house of Israel, cannot I do with you as this potter? saith the Lord. Behold, as the clay is in the potter's hand, so are ye in mine hand, O house of Israel" (vv. 4–6).

These are two powerful metaphors. We are as raw clay in the hands of the potter, and we are an instrument formed in the fire of the Lord's forge. Just what can we learn from the Doctrine and Covenants and Church history that relates to these two metaphors?

Let us start with James Covill. This is not one of the great looming tragedies of scripture, but it is an individual tragedy. If you look at the heading to section 39 in the Doctrine and Covenants, you see this is a revelation given to James Covill at Fayette. Let us start in verse 7:

"Now, behold, I say unto you, my servant James, I have looked upon thy works and I know thee.

"And verily I say unto thee, thine heart is now right before me at this time; and, behold, I have bestowed great blessings upon thy head;

"Nevertheless, thou hast seen great sorrow, for thou hast rejected me many times because of pride and the cares of the world.

"But, behold, the days of thy deliverance are come, *if* thou wilt hearken to my voice, which saith unto thee: Arise and be baptized, . . . and you shall receive my Spirit, and a blessing so great as you never have known" (vv. 7–10; emphasis added). Notice the date on the heading of section 39. It is 5 January 1831.

Once I watched a blacksmith forging a horseshoe. He took the red hot shoe out of the fire and was shaping it with a hammer against the anvil. Suddenly the horseshoe shattered and a piece went flying off. I remember that he held it up and you could see the flaw in the metal that had caused it to shatter. And the blacksmith said, "When the metal is flawed like that, there ain't nothing to do but throw it back in the fire."

Look at Doctrine and Covenants 40 now, which is dated January 1831. We are not given a specific day, but at the most it could not be more than three weeks since section 39 and the Lord's great promise to James Covill. Here, just three weeks later, at most, is what the Lord said:

"Behold, verily I say unto you, that the heart of my servant James Covill was right before me, for he covenanted with me that he would obey my word.

"And he received the word with gladness, but straightway Satan tempted him; and the fear of persecution and the cares of the world caused him to reject the word" (D&C 40:1–2).

I read that and remembered the words of the blacksmith: "When the horseshoe is flawed like that, there ain't nothing to do but throw it back in the fire."

Could this not be a partial answer to why the Saints underwent so many trials—one exodus after another in winter, mobbings, persecutions, ridicule? He was out to forge steel so hard it could become an instrument for his purposes. And if the metal is flawed, sometimes it must go back into the fire. If the clay is marred, the potter may have to put it back on the potter's wheel and start again. This is tough doctrine, particularly for young people. There are tough questions in the Doctrine and Covenants, and you need to help your students find the answers to them.

Let us look at another example in Doctrine and Covenants 118. With our perspective of history, it is tempting to some to ask the Lord some questions about how he deals with his people. Again notice the date on this revelation—8 July 1838. What is going on in northern Missouri on 8 July? Only the first rumblings. So the Lord said:

"And next spring let them [the Twelve] depart to go over the great waters, and there promulgate my gospel, the fulness thereof, and bear record of my name.

"Let them take leave of my saints in the city of Far West, on the twenty-sixth day of April next" (vv. 4–5).

With the perspective of history, some might be tempted to say, "Lord, you know what is going to happen between 8 July 1838 and 26 April 1839. There will be names that go down in our history between now and then, names like Haun's Mill, Far West, Adam-ondi-Ahman, Crooked River. By the time April comes around, the Saints will be driven from Missouri. The Prophet will have spent the winter in jail. Mobs will still be prowling for any Mormons, especially the Twelve. Did you really mean it when you said they were to leave Far West in April?"

Joseph Fielding Smith in *Essentials in Church History* records simply: "On the 5th day of April, Samuel Bogart, the mobber, with John Whitmer and a few other apostates, came to the room occupied by the committee on removal and read this revelation [D&C 118] to Theodore Turley. With much laughter and assurance that it could not be fulfilled, they called on him to renounce Joseph Smith. . . . The apostates said: 'The twelve are now scattered all over creation; let them come here if they dare; if they do, they will be murdered.'"[12]

And do you remember what happened in April? A council was held in Illinois. Even Father Smith suggested that the Lord no longer required that of them—to go back in the face of mobsters who were after their lives. But Brigham Young must have picked up something from the Prophet, who said, "When the Lord commands, do it."[13] And so, as you know, they went back.

Let me read to you who was there, shortly after midnight, on April 26, at the temple site in Far West. The list includes Brigham Young, John Taylor, Orson Pratt, John E. Page, Heber C. Kimball, Wilford Woodruff, and George A. Smith. Three of the next Presidents of the Church were there to fulfill that revelation. Let me read to you who was not there, but should have been, because at one time they too were members of the Twelve—Thomas B. Marsh, William E. McLellin, Luke Johnson, William Smith, John Boynton, and Lyman Johnson. When the hammer struck the metal of those men, their steel apparently shattered. When it struck Brigham and Wilford and John Taylor, it made strong steel. Out of the forge comes the steel, and that is one of the great lessons for our students to learn.

In the Doctrine and Covenants, we are told simply that the Melchizedek Priesthood was restored. Do you remember the setting for that? Joseph had been up in the Colesville/Bainbridge area on trial—again!—and dragged into court. While in the act of being tried, his attorney asked if he could talk to Joseph Smith in a private room. They went into a back room and his attorney told him there was a mob outside waiting to kill him. He opened the window and let Joseph and Oliver escape. All that night they tried to make their way down to Harmony. Those of you who have driven along the Susquehanna River have seen the bogs and the marshes. This was June, and I'll bet the mosquitoes were big enough to carry them away.

In a letter written much later, we have a simple account of what followed. It says simply this: "They traveled all night, and just at the break of day, Oliver gave out entirely and exclaimed, 'O Lord! Brother Joseph, how long have we got to endure this thing?'" And Joseph said it was at that point that Peter, James, and John appeared and restored the Melchizedek Priesthood.[14]

I am not suggesting that if they had not been fleeing for their lives tired and exhausted, we would not have received the Melchizedek Priesthood. But it is interesting that it was at that very time, when the forge belched forth in red hot heat, that the great event took place.

The pioneers—not the Mormon pioneers but those on the Oregon Trail and in the California gold rush—coined a phrase for the trail. They wrote it in their journals over and over. It was simply, "I have seen the elephant."[15] That is how they viewed the tribulations of the trail, like some gigantic beast.

In a general conference, President Gordon B. Hinckley read from a diary of a thirteen-year-old girl whose family was converted in England. Let me just read some excerpts from that. Her family came across and joined two handcart companies that were, as you know, ill-fated. She said:

"We traveled from fifteen to twenty-five miles a day . . . till we got to the Platte River. . . . We caught up with the handcart companies that day. We watched them cross the river. There were great lumps of ice floating down the river. It was bitter cold. The next morning there were fourteen dead. . . . We went back to camp and had our prayers and . . . sang 'Come, Come Ye Saints, No Toil nor Labor Fear.' I wondered what made my mother cry [that night]. . . . The next morning my little sister was born. It was the 23rd of September. We named her Edith. She lived six weeks and died. . . . She was buried at the last crossing of the Sweetwater.

"[We ran into heavy snow. I became lost in the snow.] My feet and legs were frozen. . . . The men rubbed me with snow. They put my feet in a bucket of water. The pain was terrible. . . .

"When we arrived at Devils Gate it was bitter cold. We left many of our things there. . . . My brother James . . . was as well as he ever was when he went to bed [that night]. In the morning he was dead. . . .

"My feet were frozen; also my brother's and my sister's. It was nothing but snow. We could not drive the pegs in our tents. . . . We did not know what would become of us. . . .

"My mother had never got well. . . . She died between the Little and Big Mountains. . . . She was 43 years of age. . . .

"We arrived in Salt Lake City nine o'clock at night the 11th of December 1856. Three out of the four that were living were frozen. My mother was dead in the wagon. . . .

"Early next morning Brigham Young came. . . . When he saw our condition, our feet frozen and our mother dead, tears rolled down his cheeks. . . .

"The doctor amputated my toes . . . [while] the sisters were dressing mother for her grave. . . . When my feet were fixed they [carried] . . . us in to see our mother for the last time. Oh, how did we stand it? That afternoon she was buried."[16]

We sing, "Why should we mourn or think our lot is hard?"[17] I can give you a thousand reasons why they should have done so. But here are the concluding words of this young girl:

"I have thought often of my mother's words before we left England. 'Polly,

I want to go to Zion while my children are small, so they can be raised in the Gospel of Christ, for I know this is the true church.'"[18]

While we are talking about the forge making steel, Parley P. Pratt gives us another great example from his journal. Speaking about the Colesville Branch, he said:

"This Colesville branch was among the first organized by Joseph Smith, and constituted the first settlers of the members of the Church in Missouri. They had arrived late in the summer, and cut some hay for their cattle, sowed a little grain, and prepared some ground for cultivation, and were engaged during the fall and winter in building log cabins, etc. . . . Ten families lived in one log cabin, which was open and unfinished, while the frozen ground served for a floor. Our food consisted of beef and a little bread made of corn, which had been grated into coarse meal by rubbing the ears on a tin grater. [Then I love this understatement.] *This was rather an inconvenient way of living for a sick person; but it was for the gospel's sake, and all were very cheerful and happy.*

"We enjoyed many happy seasons in our prayer and other meetings, and *the Spirit of the Lord was poured out upon us, and even on the little children, insomuch that many of eight, ten or twelve years of age spake, and prayed, and prophesied.* . . . There was a spirit of peace and union, and love and good will manifested in this little Church in the wilderness, the memory of which will be ever dear to my heart."[19]

I say once again, out of the forge comes the steel.

In the inside back cover of the July 1989 *Ensign* is a painting, *Summer at the Heber C. Kimball Home,* by Al Rounds. It is a fine and lovely home in Nauvoo, with the temple in the background. The caption below the painting reads: "The Heber C. Kimball home in Nauvoo, shown with the Nauvoo Temple in the background, was erected in 1845. *The Kimball family lived there for only five months. Unable to sell the home before their departure from Nauvoo, they abandoned it* on 4 February 1846 to make the trek west" (emphasis added). This is what we mean by the Lord's forge, and greatness came of it.

Some time ago I ran across a poem that I have come to love. It does not even have a title. It is by Vilate Chamberlain Raile. Speaking of the pioneers she wrote:

They cut desire into short lengths
And fed it to the hungry fire of courage.
Long after—when the flames died—
Molten gold gleamed in the ashes.
They gathered it into bruised palms

And handed it to their children
And their children's children.[20]

What a beautiful description of the Lord's forge—"Molten gold gleamed in the ashes."

"Be Still and Know"

Let us go to the next lesson I hope my children learn from their teachers—"be still and know." It is an interesting beginning and ending message that the Lord gives—interesting if we tie it to what we know about the history of Jackson County, Missouri. Doctrine and Covenants 58 was given while the Prophet and others were in Zion on 1 August 1831. Now knowing what lay ahead of the Saints, with our perspective of history, these verses become very significant.

"Ye cannot behold with your natural eyes, for the present time, the design of your God concerning those things which shall come hereafter, and the glory which shall follow after much tribulation.

"For after much tribulation come the blessings. Wherefore the day cometh that ye shall be crowned with much glory; the hour is not yet, but is nigh at hand.

"Remember this, which I tell you before, that you may lay it to heart, and receive that which is to follow" (D&C 58:3–5).

That which was to follow included being mobbed, persecuted, and eventually driven out. That is the beginning message.

Keeping that in mind, let us look at Doctrine and Covenants 101, where the Lord gives another message as the Jackson County history has unfolded. The Lord said simply:

"And they that have been scattered shall be gathered. . . .

"And all they who have given their lives for my name shall be crowned.

"Therefore, let your hearts be comforted concerning Zion; for all flesh is in mine hands; *be still and know that I am God*" (D&C 101:13, 15–16; emphasis added).

What an interesting message to start and end with—one given as the Saints arrived in Zion, the other as they were driven out. If I could combine those, they would read something like this: "You cannot behold with your natural eyes the design of your God concerning you. Be still and know that I am God."

Brother Ross Cole used a phrase over and over that has really come to mean a lot to me. He calls some of the Lord's lessons "divine tutorials." There are dozens of examples of such tutorials from our Church's history. Asael Smith, grandfather of the Prophet, made a remarkable prediction. He said, "It has been borne in upon my soul that one of my descendants will promulgate a work to revolutionize the world of religious faith."[21]

Something that first hit me with sadness is an entry in the *History of the Church* by the Prophet about his grandfather. He said, "My grandfather, Asael Smith, long ago predicted that there would be a prophet raised up in his family, and my grand mother was fully satisfied that it was fulfilled in me." And then comes the statement: "My grandfather Asael died in East Stockholm, St Lawrence county, New York, after having received the Book of Mormon, and read it nearly through"; but he died before he could be baptized.[22] I do not know how others react to that, but something in me cried, "Oh, couldn't he have lived long enough to see the final fruition of his prophecy?"

But here is another perspective. Remember our two statements. We cannot behold with our natural eyes, so we should be still and come to know the Lord.

And the end result: from Asael Smith's loins come eighteen General Authorities, including eight Patriarchs to the Church, eight members of the Quorum of the Twelve, six Counselors in the First Presidency, two other General Authorities, and four Presidents of the Church. (On the following page is a chart of Asael Smith and his lineage.)

Perhaps he did not live to be baptized, but was Asael Smith cheated? Keeping those facts about his descendants in mind, note this statement by Brigham Young: "It was decreed in the counsels of eternity, long before the foundations of the earth were laid, that he [Joseph Smith] should be the man, in the last dispensation of this world, to bring forth the word of God to the people, and receive the fulness of the keys and power of the Priesthood of the Son of God. *The Lord had his eye upon him, and upon his father, and upon his father's father,* and upon their progenitors clear back to Abraham, and from Abraham to the flood, from the flood to Enoch, and from Enoch to Adam. *He has watched that family and that blood as it has circulated from its foundation to the birth of that man.*"[23]

When we talk about divine tutorials, consider Joseph Smith, Sr., who moved ten times in twenty years. He invested in the ginseng root, which looked for all purposes like an excellent investment; and his business partner absconded with the funds. He moved to another area, and they had the worst winter in many years and three successive crop failures. I am sure there were times when Joseph Smith, Sr., felt like crying out, "What am I doing wrong?" And the Lord's answer may well be summed up as "You cannot behold with your natural eyes. Be still and know that I need you in western New York so your son can be close to a hill called Cumorah."

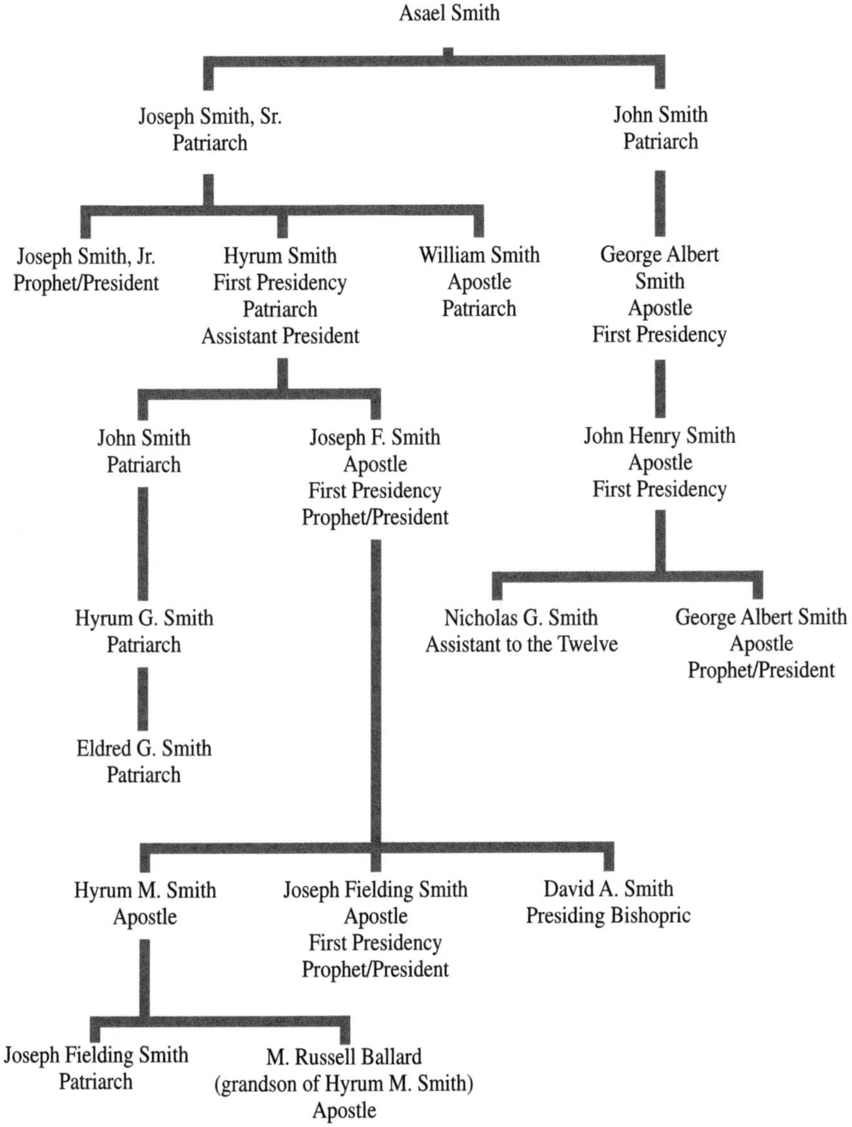

In recent years I have gained a greater appreciation for Emma Smith than I have ever had before. I would not want to whitewash Emma. I think she made some foolish choices, but then I think about the constant ridicule she had to endure, the constant terror of being mobbed. She saw her husband dragged out by angry men in the night, not knowing if he would come back alive. She saw her first three children die and one of the adopted twins die. She went through incredible challenges.

There is a family story about Joseph's arrival in Kirtland. He drove up to the Newel K. Whitney Store and said, "Newel K. Whitney! Thou art the man! . . . You've prayed me here, now what do you want of me?"[24] In one little line that I had missed before, he mentioned that they had traveled from New York by sleigh, and Emma was seven months pregnant with twins. That is over two hundred miles in the winter by sleigh when you are seven months pregnant with twins. Talk about divine tutorials. Did Emma pass the tests? I do not know, but I know this: I have a new and deeper appreciation for Emma.

Speaking of divine tutorials for Emma, remember what the Lord said to her in section 25. It is great counsel to an elect lady: "Murmur not because of the things which thou hast not seen, for they are withheld from thee and from the world, which is wisdom in me in a time to come" (v. 4).

I have tried to put myself in Emma's place and wonder if I could say, "Okay, I understand why I cannot see the pages. It is because you are not going to allow Joseph to show them to anyone." But then they move to David Whitmer's home in Fayette, and a few nights later Mary Whitmer comes back into the house to report that she has had the most incredible experience. Moroni appeared to her and told her that bringing three more adults into the home was quite a load. So to strengthen her, he showed Mary Whitmer the pages.[25]

How would you feel if you were Emma as Mary Whitmer came back into the cabin and told the story of seeing the plates? Talk about sacrifice. Did Emma not have a heavy load too—her parents angry, taking all the ridicule that came with marrying Joseph, acting as scribe, seeing her firstborn die shortly after birth? Talk about somebody who deserved to see the plates! But the Lord said, "You cannot behold with your natural eyes. Be still. Murmur not."

Well, a thousand such questions come out of Church history. Why Haun's Mill? Why is the way so hard? Why does the Lord let those things happen? And very often the only answer is that "you cannot behold with your natural eyes the design of your God concerning you. Be still and know that I am God and that I care for you and that my hand is in your life." If you can teach that kind of faith to my children, I will be eternally grateful.

The Stone Rolls On

The final lesson I hope you teach my children is that the stone continues to roll on. We are part of that great work. I used to love to travel. I now consider it a great privilege when I get out of a trip. And I was reading something the other day that I can really identify with, although we now travel by plane. Elder David O. McKay and Hugh J. Cannon, in December 1920, were asked by the First Presidency to take a tour of all the world missions. They were gone a little more than a year and traveled 62,500 miles. In President McKay's journal there is a choice entry that gently illustrates all we have said about the Lord's forge and divine tutorials and being still.

"It was storming when we went to bed, and the movement of the boat was keenly perceptible even when we went to sleep.

"The pitching of the vessel in the night awoke me. . . . Sleep from then until morning was only intermittent. Every nerve and muscle in my body responded to every movement of the boat. As this movement became more pronounced and intense, the contents of my digestive organs joined in unison with nerves and muscles. . . .

"[Brother Cannon awoke that morning and] invited me to breakfast, but I couldn't think of anything that this ship could put on a table that was worth eating. . . . However, before attempting to dress, I ate an apple Brother Hugh J. handed me.

"Without hurried exertion, I put on my clothes and started for the deck; but the swaying staircase and the madly moving world of water stirred my feelings with a yearning desire for solitude. Yielding, I hurried to my room, where in less time and seemingly with less effort than it takes to tell you, the apple and I parted company forever. I threw myself on the berth, and wondered what there was in common between a Jonathan apple and Jonah. . . . Though I arrived at no definite conclusions about the matter, one thing was most certain: My sympathy was wholly with the whale. . . .

"Hugh J. returned from breakfast looking as robust and rosy as an athlete, and smacking his lips in appreciation of an excellent meal. . . . Limp and dejected, I looked at him . . . and began, right then and there, to doubt the wisdom of the Revolutionary statesman who declared that 'all men are created equal.' . . .

"Feeling somewhat better [a little later], I started again for the deck. . . .

" . . . This time I reached only the top of the stairs, when that intense yearning to be alone drove me back to my cabin. Good-bye last night's dinner! Good-bye yesterday's Rotary luncheon! And during the next sixty hours, Good-bye everything I had ever eaten since I was a babe on Mother's knee. I am not sure I didn't even cross the threshold into the pre-existent state."[26]

He makes misery so delightful, but it was misery. It was sacrifice, and yet you know what comes out of that. The journal accounts of that worldwide tour are wonderful. Once, when they were in New Zealand, Elder McKay looked out over the

Maoris in a certain ranch and turned to his translator and said he would like to speak to the people without a translator. It was reported that as Elder McKay spoke the people wept, and he would see them nodding their heads. Even though Elder McKay spoke in English, the people had understood.[27]

It was on that same trip that Elder McKay had the beautiful vision in Apia harbor of the heavenly city and the Savior waiting to welcome the righteous.[28] The stone continues to roll. Not all of the great things happened with Joseph and Brigham.

I hope you let your students know that the story goes on today. Remember the story of the elders in World War II, in 1939, who were caught in Germany when the first Presidency asked all missionaries to get out. The mission president called on a football-playing elder from Idaho and said, "Elder, we have thirty-one missionaries lost somewhere between here and the Dutch border. It will be your mission to find them and see that they get out." And this young nineteen- or twenty-year-old Elder Kest talked about getting on a train and when they came to a station he would search inwardly, and if the Spirit said to get off, he would get off.

In Cologne there were thousands of soldiers and people in the station and he got off and began to whistle "Do what is right, let the consequence follow." One young missionary heard it and came, bringing a missionary couple. He then went in for six elders and found that they had been shipped back across the border into Germany. He bought ten train tickets and crossed into Germany without a visa. When he got to the first station, the Gestapo were waiting and they took him off the train and demanded to know what he was doing there without a visa. He said a thought popped into his mind to play dumb, so he would speak a few words of English and then throw in a word of Dutch and then a German word. He acted simpleminded. Finally they got disgusted and said, "Okay, you can go but first we have got to see what you have." So they started going through his pockets. And here he was with ten train tickets in his pocket. Let me read you one excerpt from this story:

"They confiscated binder, papers, passport, *all* the money on my person, and started going through each pocket in both coat and vest. I took the ten tickets out of my pocket and placed them on the table before me. No one seemed to *see* the tickets. The officer in charge gave me a receipt for the money, binder, papers and all my personal effects, and said, 'You have forty minutes to catch the return train to Holland. After that time we cannot guarantee your safety.'

"Taking the tickets from the table, I stuffed them in my pocket. *Not an eye flickered.* I had the strong impression that the action had been entirely unobserved. Hurriedly I left the station, my knees weak, my palms sweating."[29]

Does the stone cut out of the mountain without hands continue to roll? Of course it does. The great stories of faith go on. There are great things happening in Africa. There are great things happening in Russia and China. The stone rolls on—not with hands. It will fill the earth, and it will last forever. And we are a part of this great work.

From the early sections of the Doctrine and Covenants we get our call and our charge. A marvelous work is coming forth. Oh, we who embark in the service of God, let us serve him with all of our might—because the field is white (see D&C 4). You may not always believe that as you struggle to keep the attention of your class of LDS teenagers. But just think, thirty years from now, how great an increase in numbers we will see in Church membership. Think of the number of stake presidencies and bishoprics that have got to be found in the next thirty years.

For great will be our joy when we seek first the kingdom of God (see D&C 6:6; 18:16). That is my testimony and my prayer—that we can prepare our students for the coming years they will face. Hopefully, someday they will stand at a pulpit and talk about the "happy days" they knew when they were teenagers preparing for lifetimes of Church service and faithfulness.

Notes

From an address given at the Church Educational System symposium on the Doctrine and Covenants, August 1989, Brigham Young University, Provo, Utah.

1. Lorenzo Snow, *Deseret Evening News,* 15 June 1901, 1; emphasis added.
2. Benjamin Franklin, "Franklin's Formula for Successful Living, Number Three," in George L. Rogers, ed., *Benjamin Franklin's The Art of Virtue: His Formula for Successful Living* (Eden Prairie, Minn.: Acorn Publishing, 1986), 88–90.
3. Mary Nichols, *Alvin Nichols—Utah Pioneer, 1819–1899* (n.p., 1958), 60; emphasis added.
4. "Mary Elizabeth Rollins Lightner," *Utah Genealogical and Historical Magazine,* July 1926, 194.
5. Ibid., 197.
6. Parley P. Pratt, ed., *Autobiography of Parley P. Pratt,* Classics in Mormon Literature series (Salt Lake City: Deseret Book Co., 1985), 118.
7. In Susan W. Easton, "Suffering and Death on the Plains of Iowa," *Brigham Young University Studies,* Fall 1981, 436–37.
8. Ibid., 438.
9. Boyd Gibbons, "The Itch to Move West," *National Geographic,* August 1986, 165.
10. Ibid., 174.
11. Joseph Smith, *History of The Church of Jesus Christ of Latter-day Saints,* 7 vols., 2d ed. rev., ed. B. H. Roberts (Salt Lake City: The Church of Jesus Christ of Latter-day Saints, 1932–51), 3:250, 254.
12. Joseph Fielding Smith, *Essentials in Church History,* Classics in Mormon Literature series (Salt Lake City: Deseret Book Co., 1979), 216.
13. Smith, *History of the Church,* 2:170.
14. Letter from Addison Everett to Oliver B. Huntington, as quoted in Stanley R. Gunn, *Oliver Cowdery—Second Elder and Scribe* (Salt Lake City: Bookcraft, 1962), 48.
15. See Gibbons, "Itch to Move West," 175.

16. "Life of Mary Ann Goble Pay," as quoted by Gordon B. Hinckley, in Conference Report, April 1970, 22–23.
17. *Hymns of The Church of Jesus Christ of Latter-day Saints* (Salt Lake City: The Church of Jesus Christ of Latter-day Saints, 1985), no. 30.
18. "Life of Mary Ann Goble Pay," in Conference Report, April 1970, 23.
19. Pratt, *Autobiography of Parley P. Pratt,* 56; emphasis added.
20. In Asahel D. Woodruff, *Parent and Youth* (Salt Lake City: Deseret Sunday School Union Board, 1952), 124.
21. Joseph Fielding Smith, *Church History and Modern Revelation,* 2 vols. (Salt Lake City: Deseret Book Co, 1953), 1:4.
22. Smith, *History of the Church,* 2:443.
23. Brigham Young, in *Journal of Discourses,* 26 vols. (London: Latter-day Saints' Book Depot, 1854–56), 7:289–90; emphasis added.
24. Smith, *History of the Church,* 1:146.
25. See Andrew Jenson, *Historical Record,* October 1888, 621.
26. David O. McKay, *Home Memories of President David O. McKay,* comp. Llewelyn R. McKay (Salt Lake City: Deseret Book Co., 1956), 39–41.
27. See *Cherished Experiences,* comp. Clare Middlemiss (Salt Lake City: Deseret Book Co., 1955), 77.
28. Ibid., 102.
29. M. Douglas Wood, "The Lord Stood at Our Side," in Margie Calhoun Jensen, comp., *Stories of Insight and Inspiration* (Salt Lake City: Bookcraft, 1976), 178–82.

Scripture Index

OLD TESTAMENT

NEW TESTAMENT

MATTHEW

MARK

LUKE

JOHN

BOOK OF MORMON

PEARL OF GREAT PRICE

MOSES

ABRAHAM

JOSEPH SMITH—MATTHEW

JOSEPH SMITH—HISTORY

ARTICLES OF FAITH

Subject Index